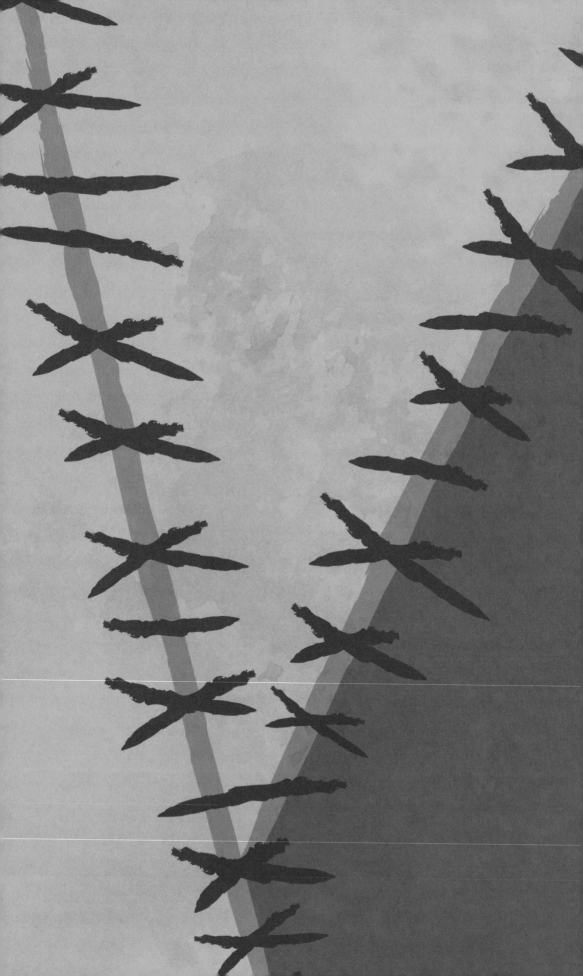

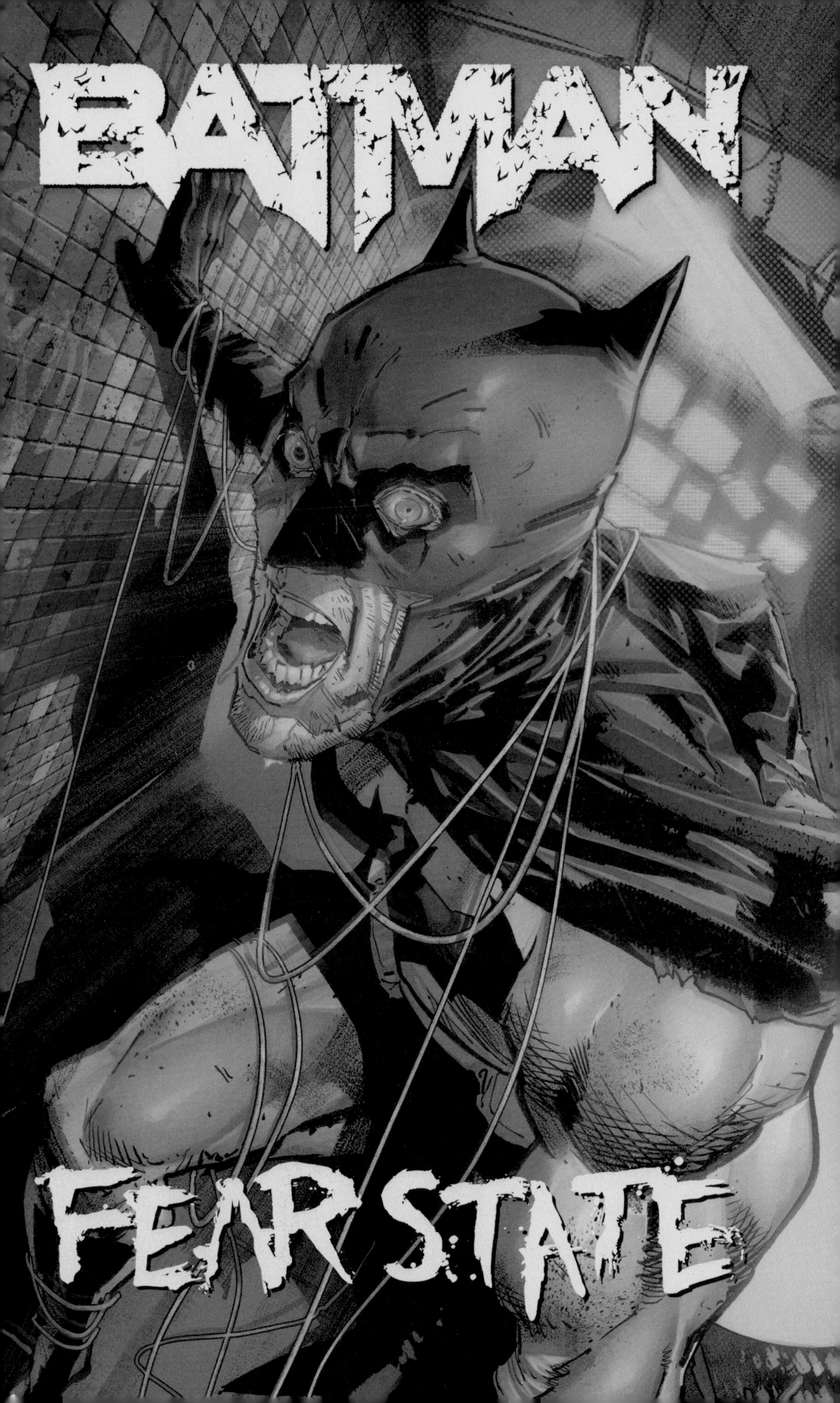
BATMAN
FEAR STATE

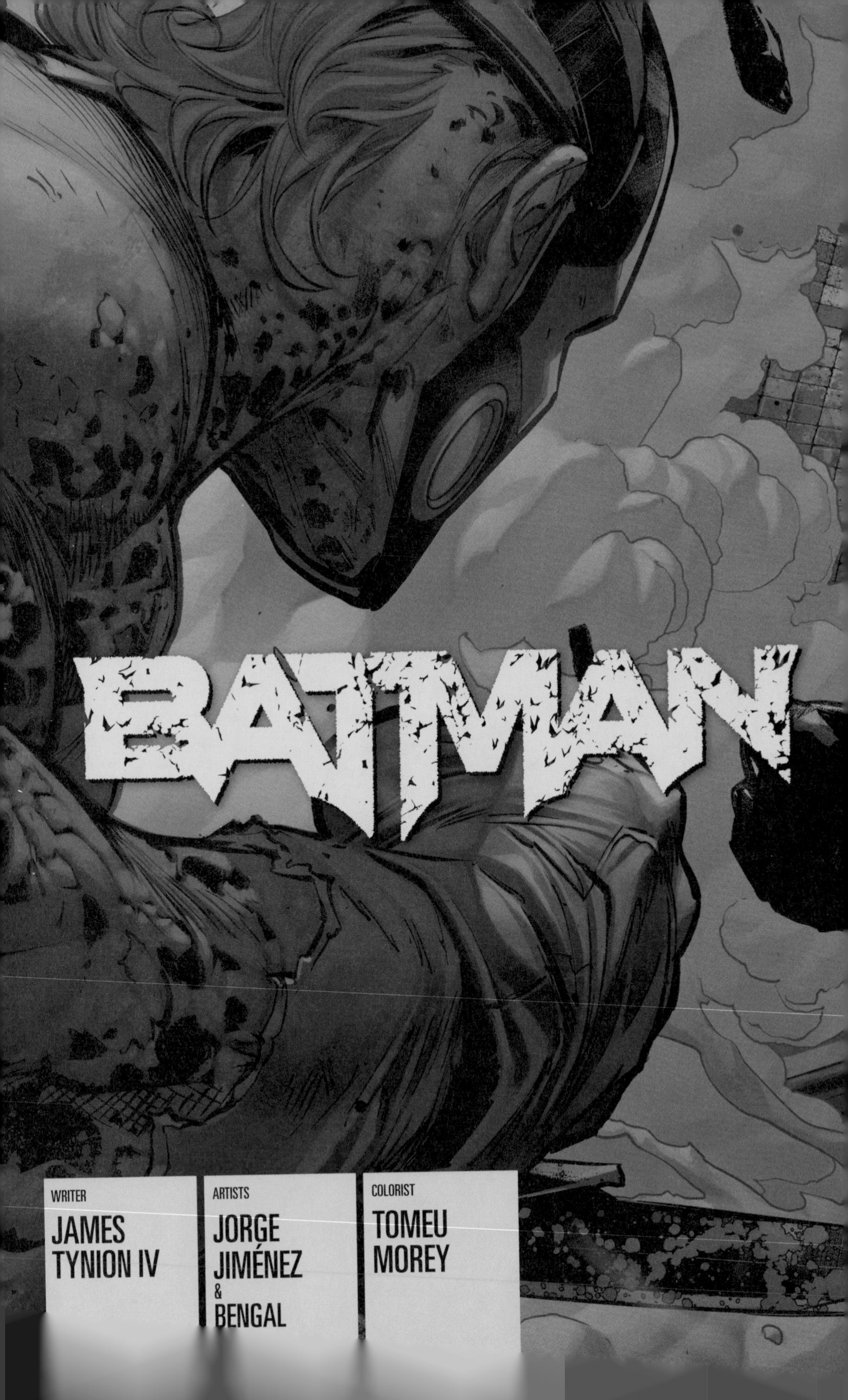

BATMAN

WRITER
JAMES TYNION IV

ARTISTS
JORGE JIMÉNEZ & BENGAL

COLORIST
TOMEU MOREY

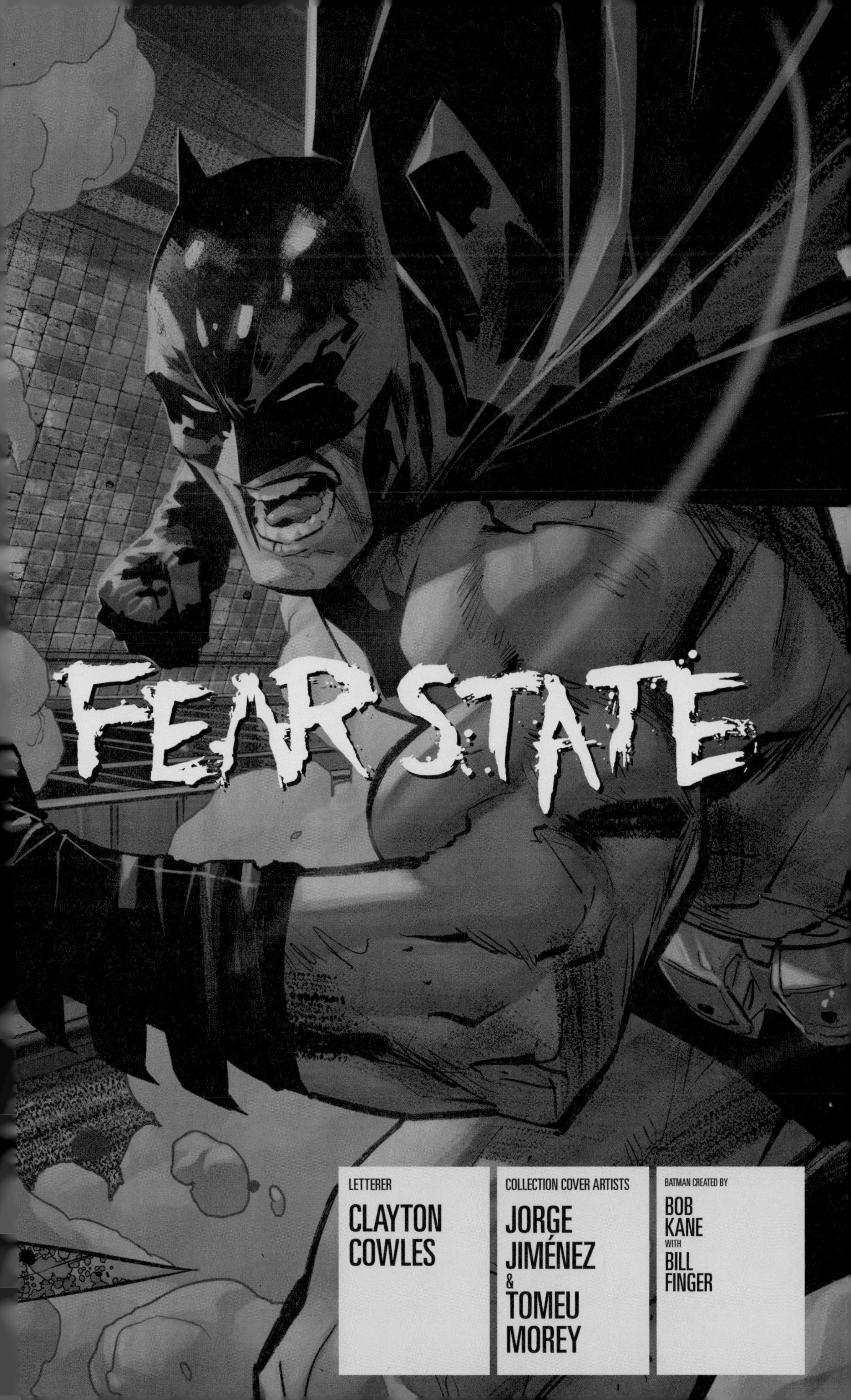

FEAR STATE

LETTERER
CLAYTON COWLES

COLLECTION COVER ARTISTS
JORGE JIMÉNEZ & TOMEU MOREY

BATMAN CREATED BY
BOB KANE WITH BILL FINGER

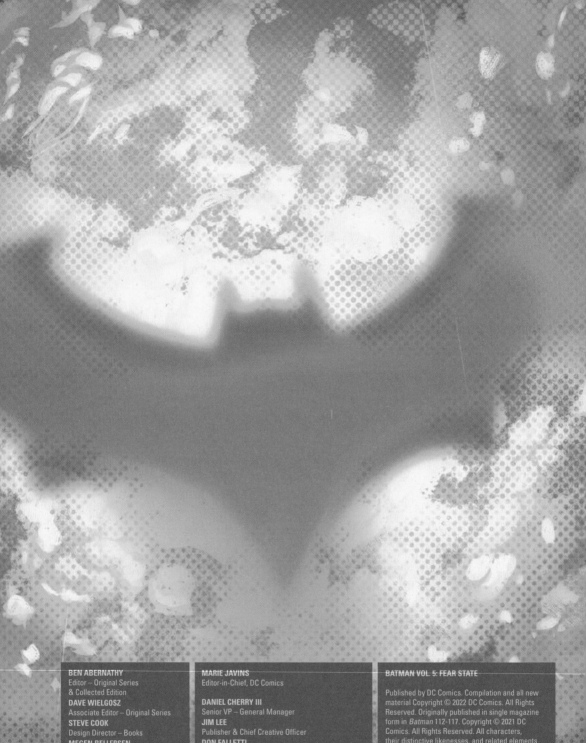

BEN ABERNATHY
Editor – Original Series
& Collected Edition
DAVE WIELGOSZ
Associate Editor – Original Series
STEVE COOK
Design Director – Books
MEGEN BELLERSEN
Publication Design
CHRISTY SAWYER
Publication Production

MARIE JAVINS
Editor-in-Chief, DC Comics

DANIEL CHERRY III
Senior VP – General Manager
JIM LEE
Publisher & Chief Creative Officer
DON FALLETTI
VP – Manufacturing Operations
& Workflow Management
LAWRENCE GANEM
VP – Talent Services
ALISON GILL
Senior VP – Manufacturing & Operations
JEFFREY KAUFMAN
VP – Editorial Strategy & Programming
NICK J. NAPOLITANO
VP – Manufacturing Administration & Design
NANCY SPEARS
VP – Revenue

BATMAN VOL. 5: FEAR STATE

Published by DC Comics. Compilation and all new
material Copyright © 2022 DC Comics. All Rights
Reserved. Originally published in single magazine
form in *Batman* 112-117. Copyright © 2021 DC
Comics. All Rights Reserved. All characters,
their distinctive likenesses, and related elements
featured in this publication are trademarks of DC
Comics. The stories, characters, and incidents
featured in this publication are entirely fictional.
DC Comics does not read or accept unsolicited
submissions of ideas, stories, or artwork.
DC – a WarnerMedia Company.

DC Comics,
2900 West Alameda Ave.,
Burbank, CA 91505
Printed by Transcontinental Interglobe,
Beauceville, QC, Canada. 2/4/22. First Printing.
ISBN: 978-1-77951-430-1

Library of Congress Cataloging-in-Publication
Data is available.

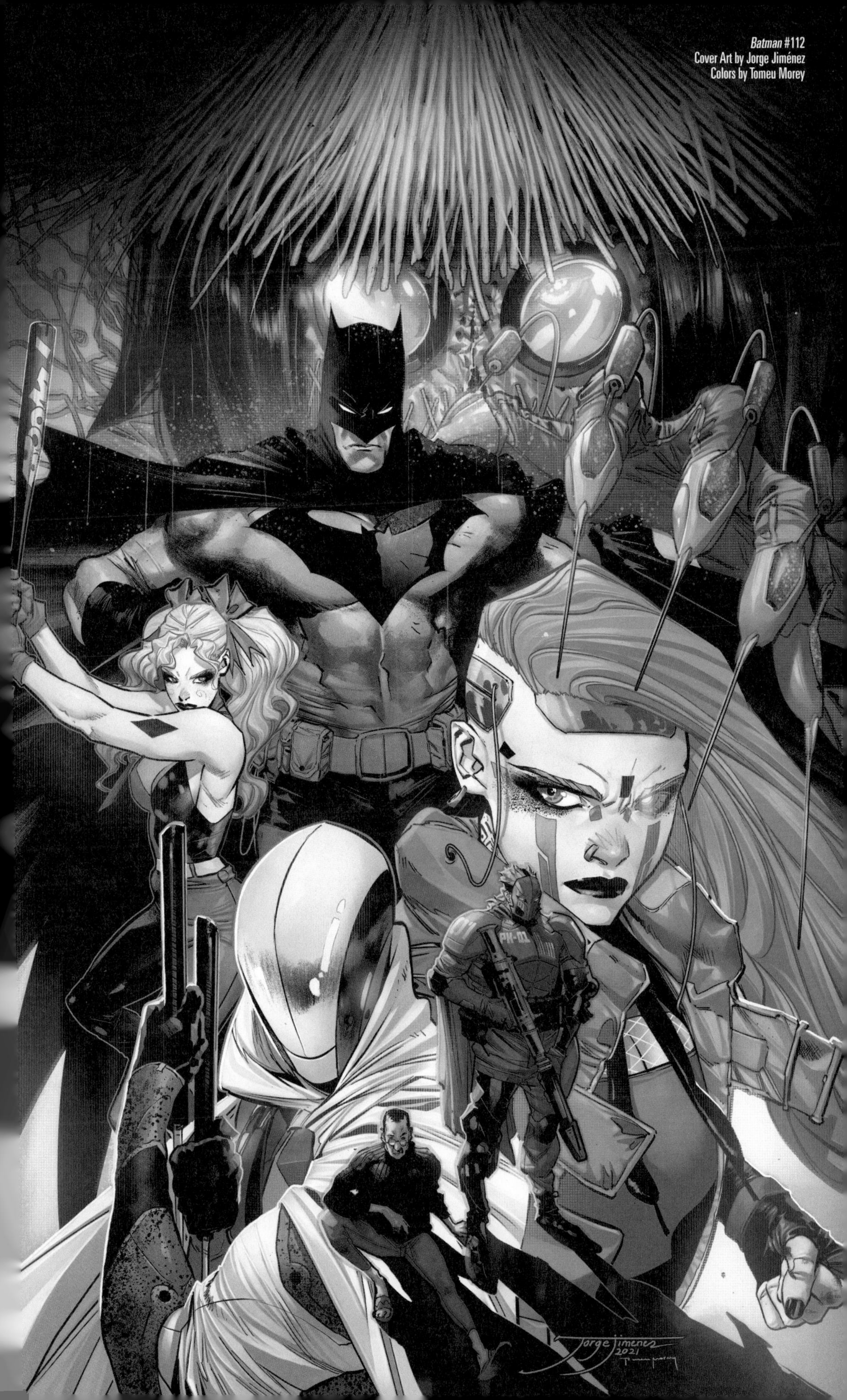

Batman #112
Cover Art by Jorge Jiménez
Colors by Tomeu Morey

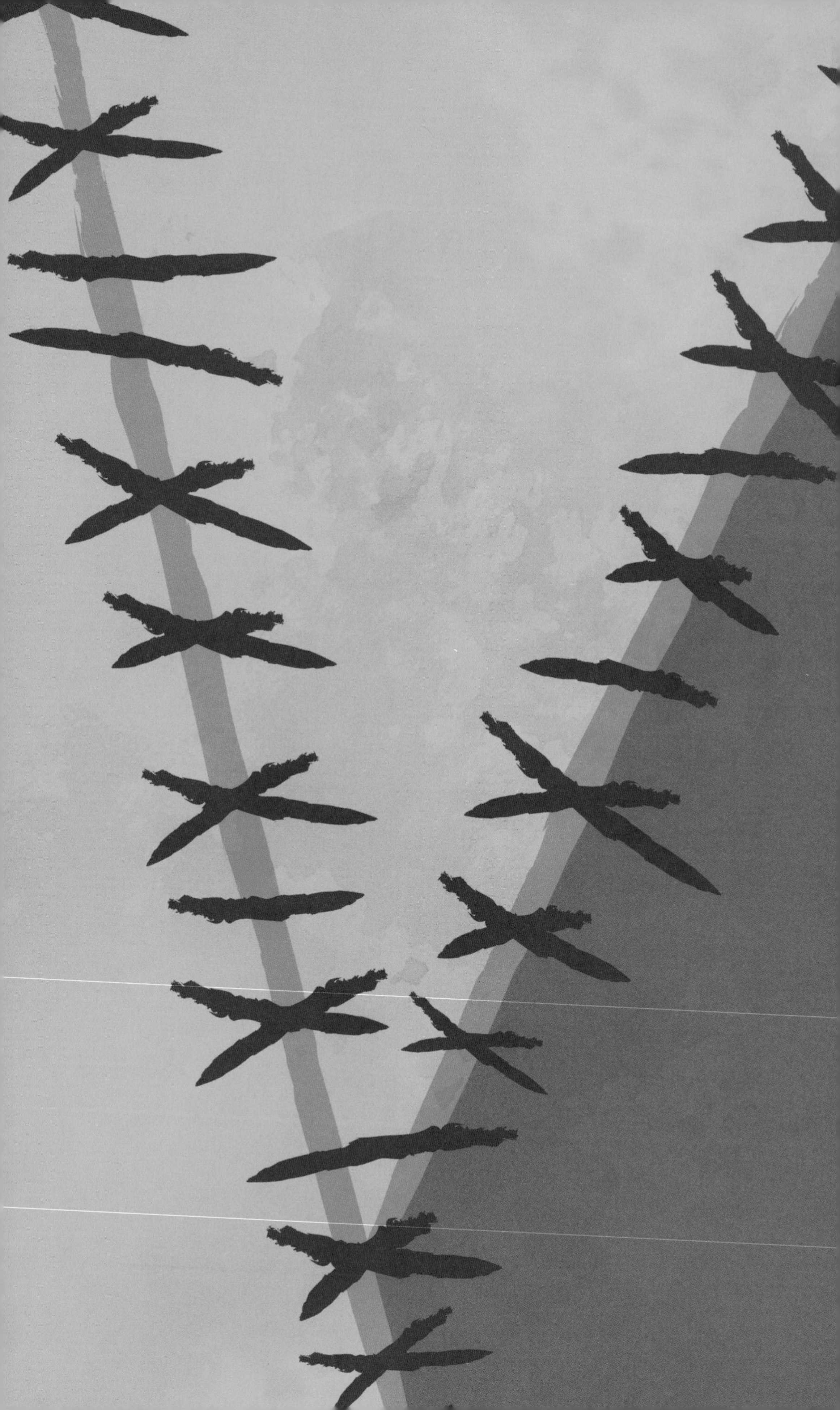

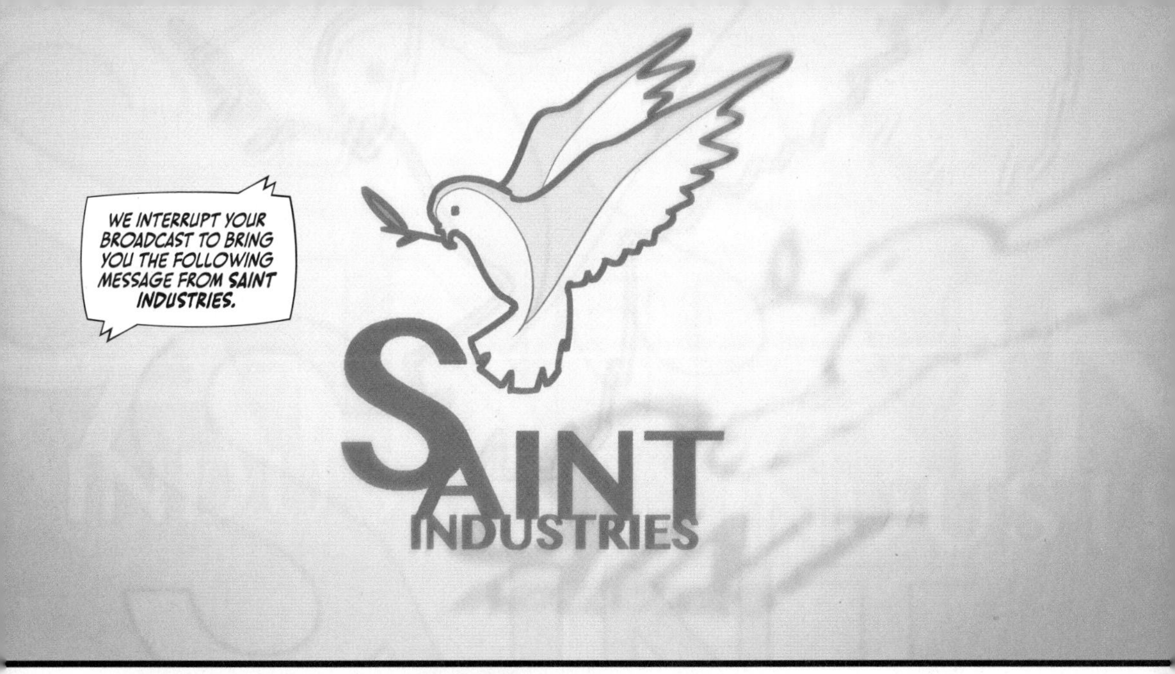

WE INTERRUPT YOUR BROADCAST TO BRING YOU THE FOLLOWING MESSAGE FROM SAINT INDUSTRIES.
SAINT INDUSTRIES

JAMES TYNION IV WRITER
JORGE JIMENEZ ARTIST

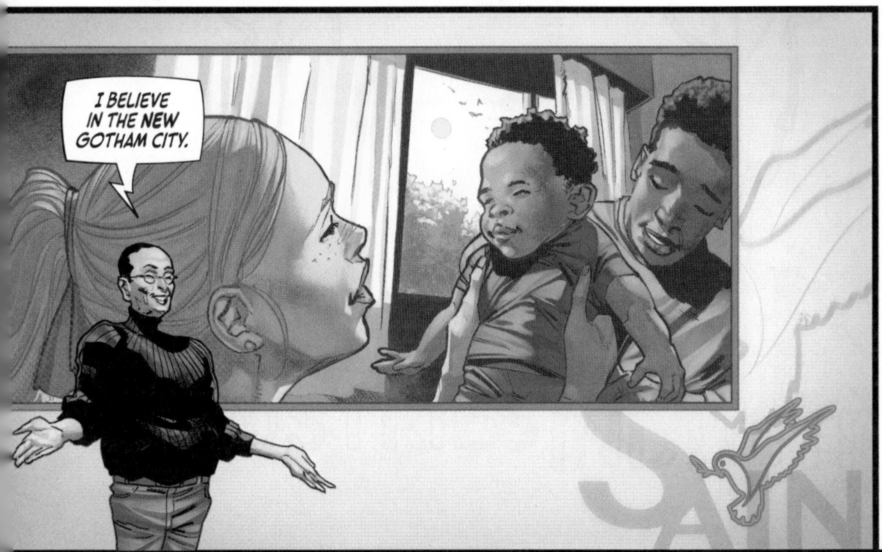

I BELIEVE IN THE NEW GOTHAM CITY.

TOMEU MOREY COLORS
CLAYTON COWLES LETTERS
JIMENEZ & MOREY COVER
JORGE MOLINA, KAEL NGU & LUCIO PARRILLO VARIANT COVERS

DAVE WIELGOSZ ASSOC. EDITOR
BEN ABERNATHY EDITOR
BATMAN CREATED BY BOB KANE WITH BILL FINGER

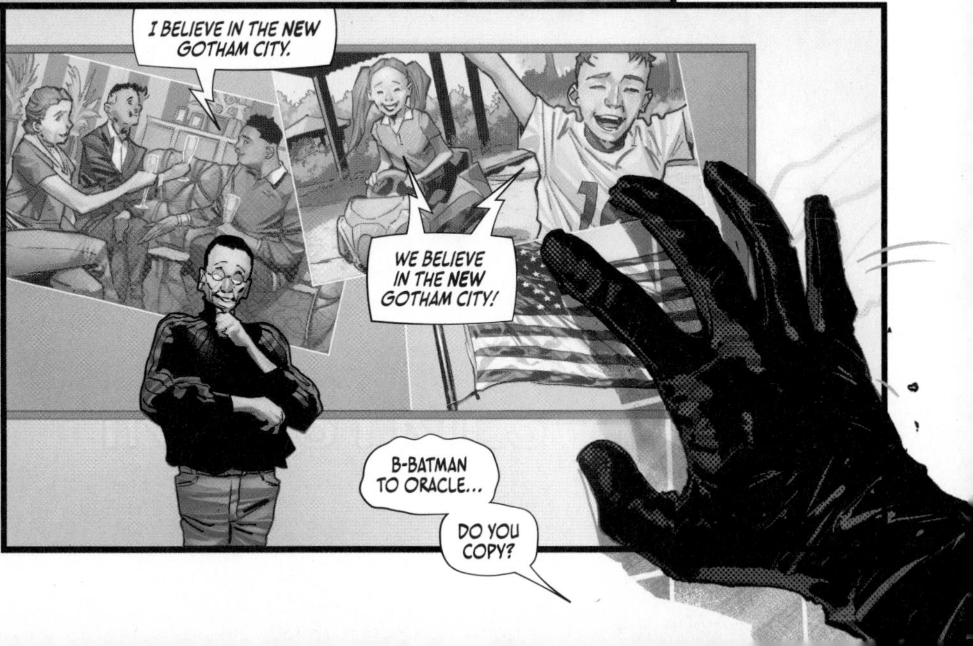

I BELIEVE IN THE NEW GOTHAM CITY.
WE BELIEVE IN THE NEW GOTHAM CITY!
B-BATMAN TO ORACLE...
DO YOU COPY?

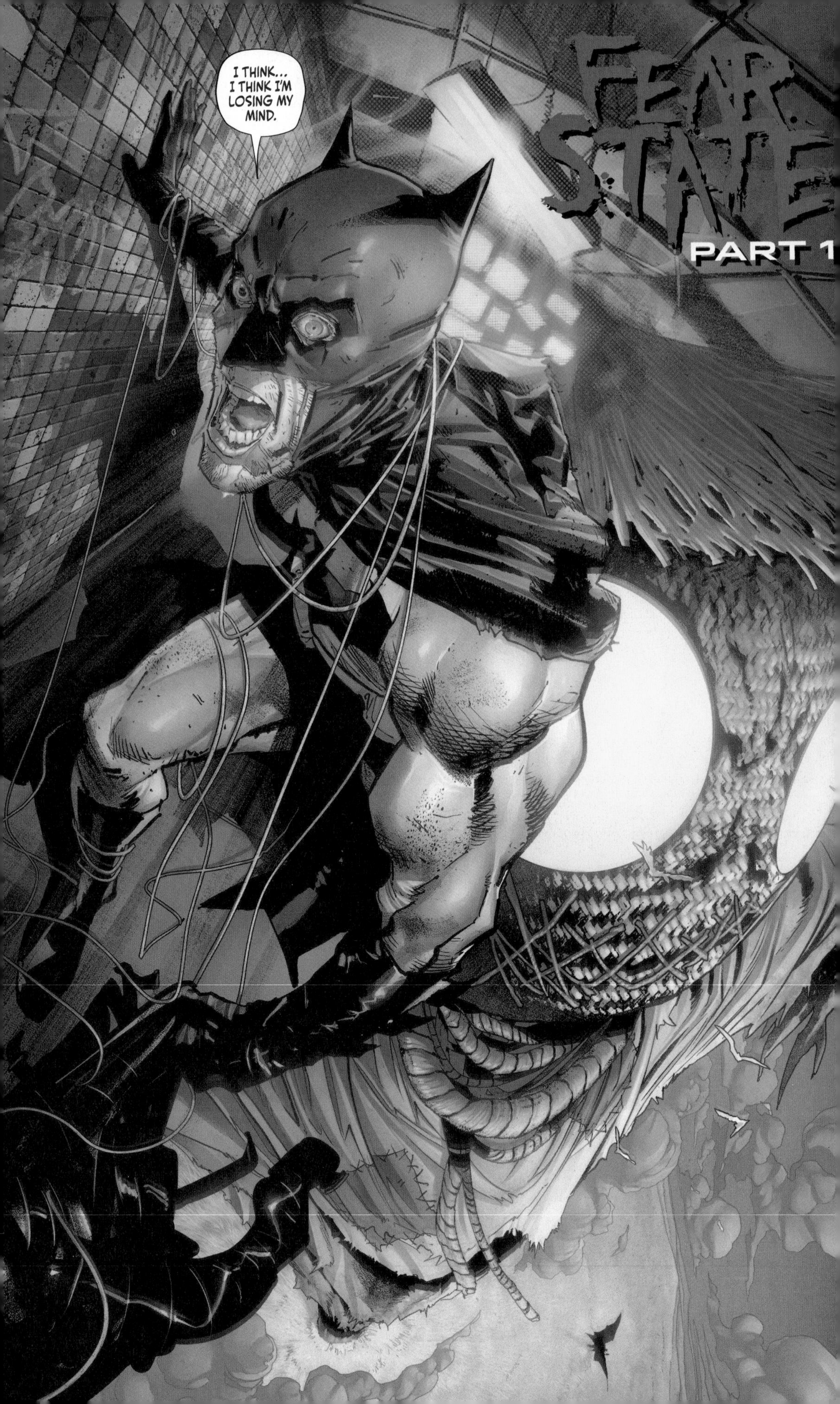
I THINK... I THINK I'M LOSING MY MIND.
FEAR STATE
PART 1

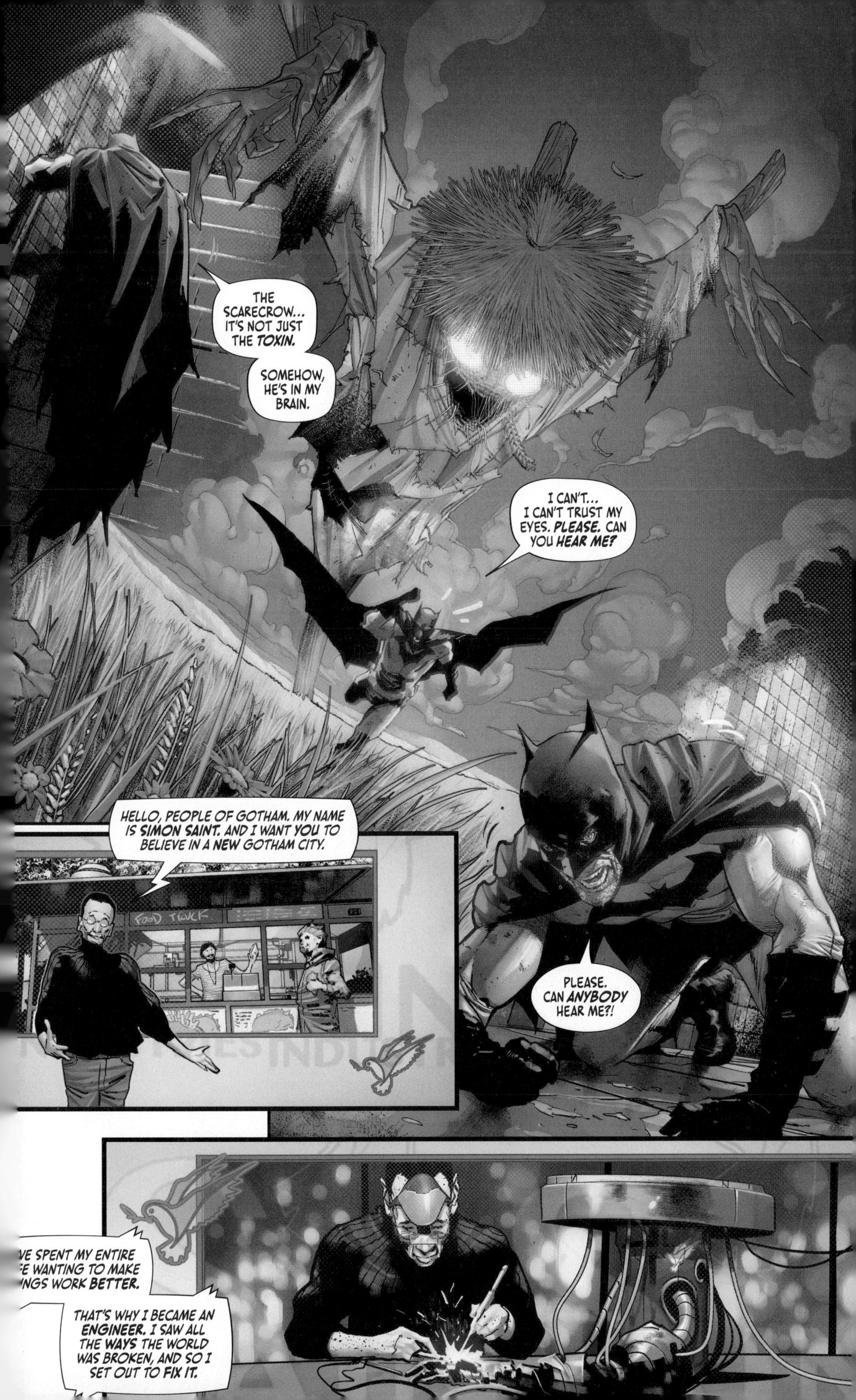

THE SCARECROW... IT'S NOT JUST THE *TOXIN.*
SOMEHOW, HE'S IN MY BRAIN.
I CAN'T... I CAN'T TRUST MY EYES. ***PLEASE.*** CAN YOU ***HEAR ME?***
HELLO, PEOPLE OF GOTHAM. MY NAME IS **SIMON SAINT.** *AND I WANT* **YOU** *TO BELIEVE IN A* **NEW** *GOTHAM CITY.*
FOOD TRUCK
PLEASE. CAN ***ANYBODY*** HEAR ME?!
'VE SPENT MY ENTIRE FE WANTING TO MAKE INGS WORK **BETTER.**
THAT'S WHY I BECAME AN **ENGINEER.** *I SAW ALL THE* **WAYS** *THE WORLD WAS BROKEN, AND SO I SET OUT TO* **FIX IT.**

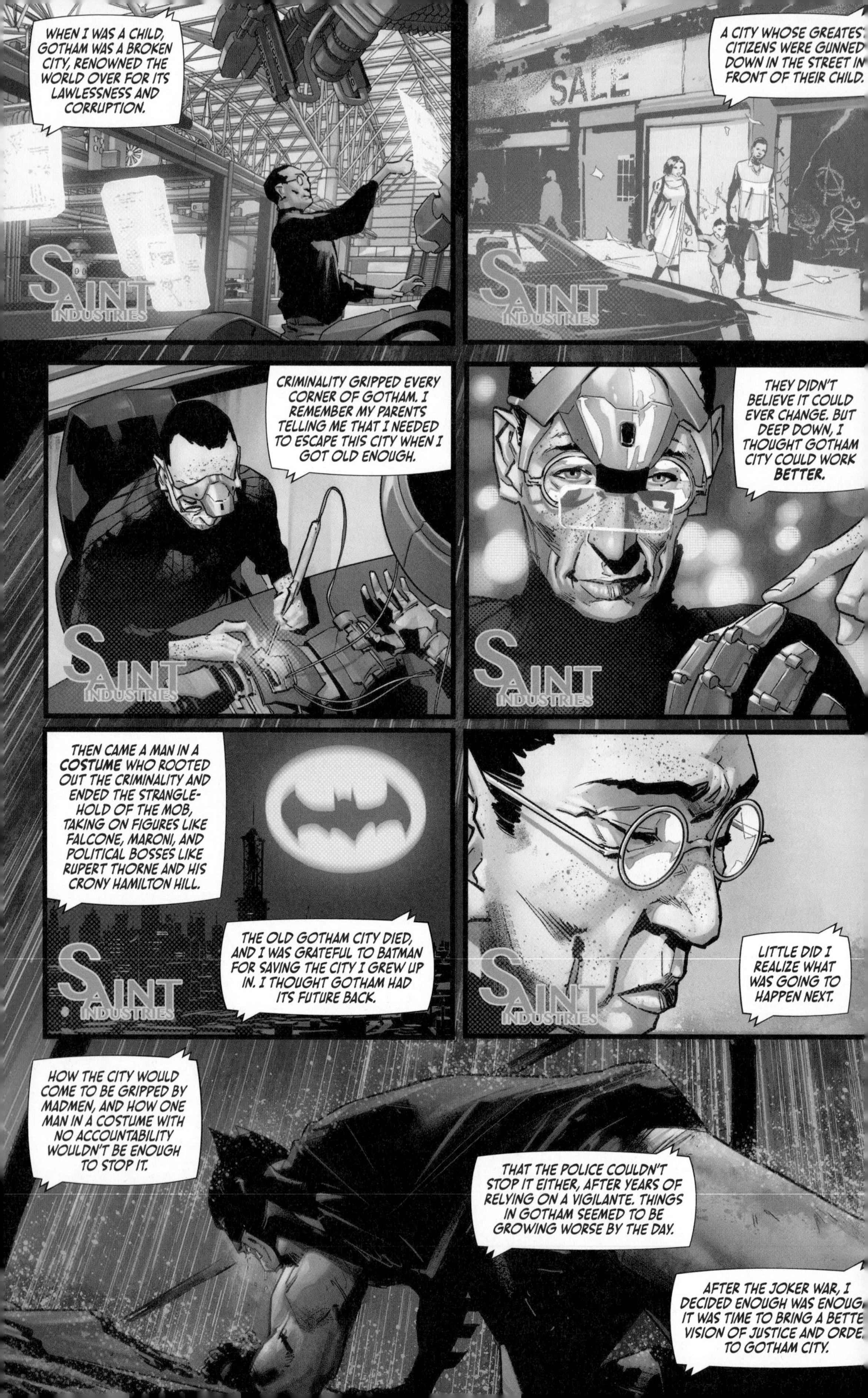
WHEN I WAS A CHILD, GOTHAM WAS A BROKEN CITY, RENOWNED THE WORLD OVER FOR ITS LAWLESSNESS AND CORRUPTION.
SAINT INDUSTRIES
A CITY WHOSE GREATES CITIZENS WERE GUNNED DOWN IN THE STREET IN FRONT OF THEIR CHILD.
SALE
SAINT INDUSTRIES
CRIMINALITY GRIPPED EVERY CORNER OF GOTHAM. I REMEMBER MY PARENTS TELLING ME THAT I NEEDED TO ESCAPE THIS CITY WHEN I GOT OLD ENOUGH.
SAINT INDUSTRIES
THEY DIDN'T BELIEVE IT COULD EVER CHANGE. BUT DEEP DOWN, I THOUGHT GOTHAM CITY COULD WORK BETTER.
SAINT INDUSTRIES
THEN CAME A MAN IN A COSTUME WHO ROOTED OUT THE CRIMINALITY AND ENDED THE STRANGLE-HOLD OF THE MOB, TAKING ON FIGURES LIKE FALCONE, MARONI, AND POLITICAL BOSSES LIKE RUPERT THORNE AND HIS CRONY HAMILTON HILL.
THE OLD GOTHAM CITY DIED, AND I WAS GRATEFUL TO BATMAN FOR SAVING THE CITY I GREW UP IN. I THOUGHT GOTHAM HAD ITS FUTURE BACK.
SAINT INDUSTRIES
LITTLE DID I REALIZE WHAT WAS GOING TO HAPPEN NEXT.
SAINT INDUSTRIES
HOW THE CITY WOULD COME TO BE GRIPPED BY MADMEN, AND HOW ONE MAN IN A COSTUME WITH NO ACCOUNTABILITY WOULDN'T BE ENOUGH TO STOP IT.
THAT THE POLICE COULDN'T STOP IT EITHER, AFTER YEARS OF RELYING ON A VIGILANTE. THINGS IN GOTHAM SEEMED TO BE GROWING WORSE BY THE DAY.
AFTER THE JOKER WAR, I DECIDED ENOUGH WAS ENOUG IT WAS TIME TO BRING A BETTE VISION OF JUSTICE AND ORDE TO GOTHAM CITY.

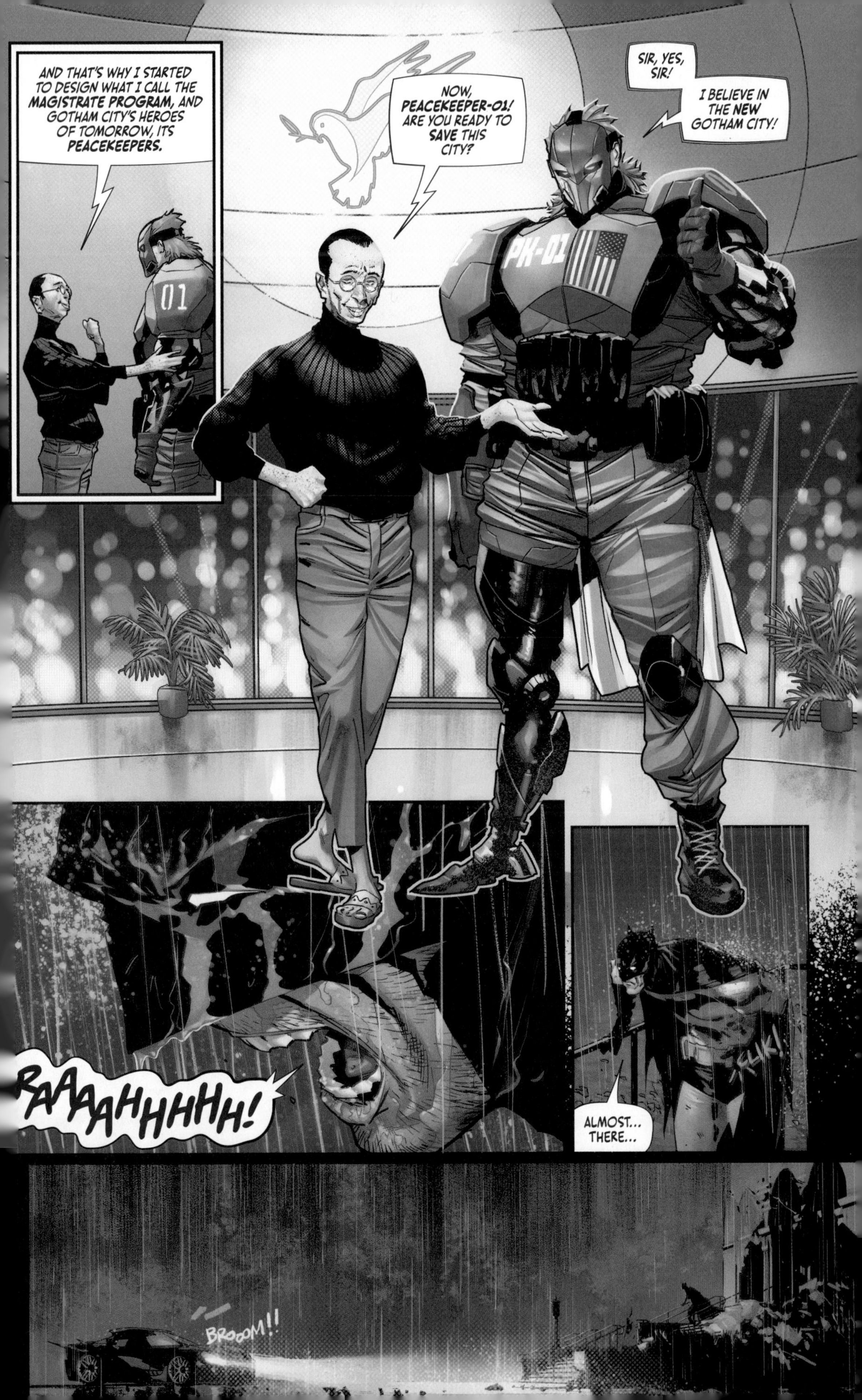
AND THAT'S WHY I STARTED TO DESIGN WHAT I CALL THE MAGISTRATE PROGRAM, AND GOTHAM CITY'S HEROES OF TOMORROW, ITS PEACEKEEPERS.
01
NOW, PEACEKEEPER-01! ARE YOU READY TO SAVE THIS CITY?
SIR, YES, SIR!
I BELIEVE IN THE NEW GOTHAM CITY!
PK-01
RAAAAHHHHH!
CLIK!
ALMOST... THERE...
BROOOM!!

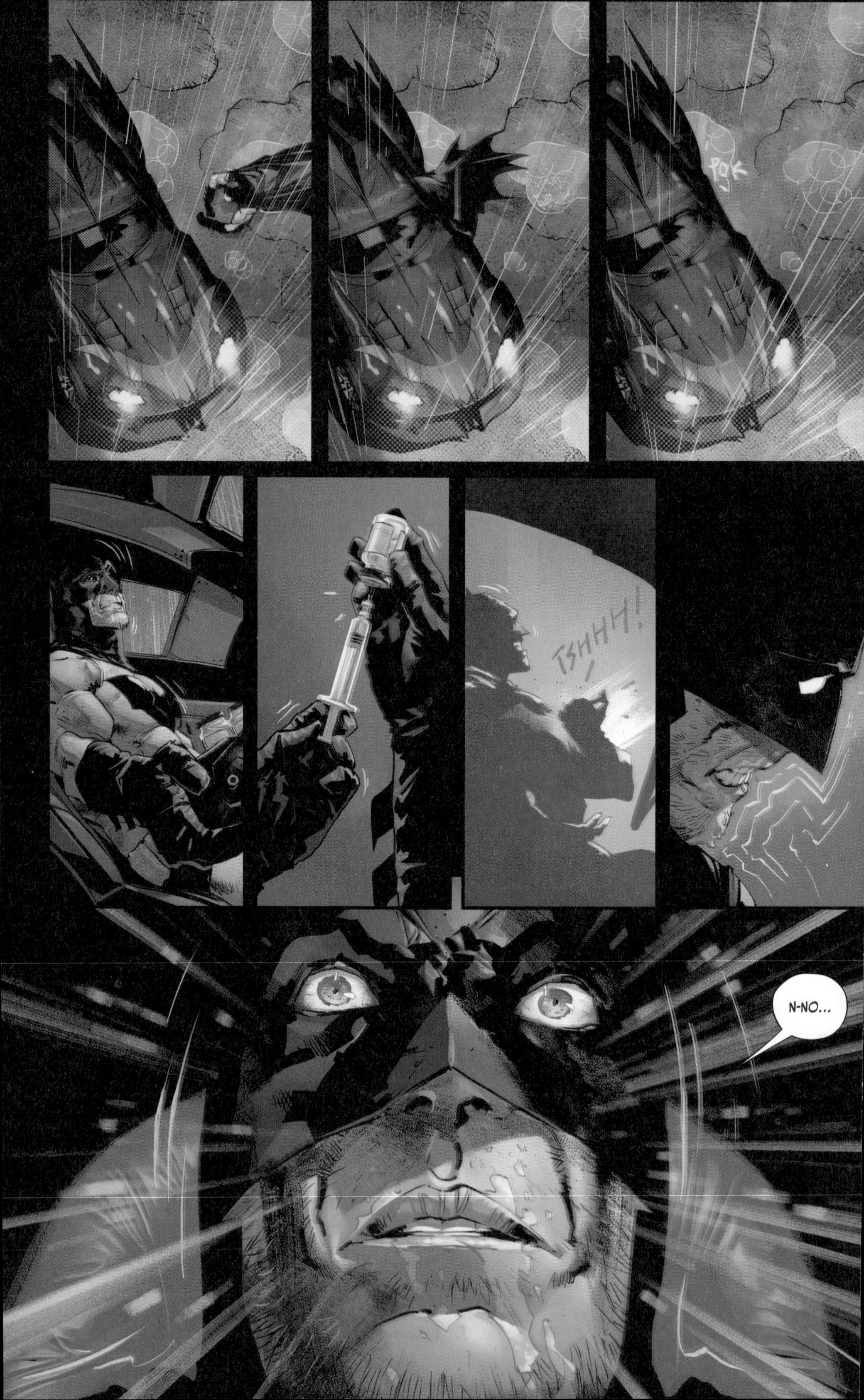
POK
TSHHH!
N-NO...

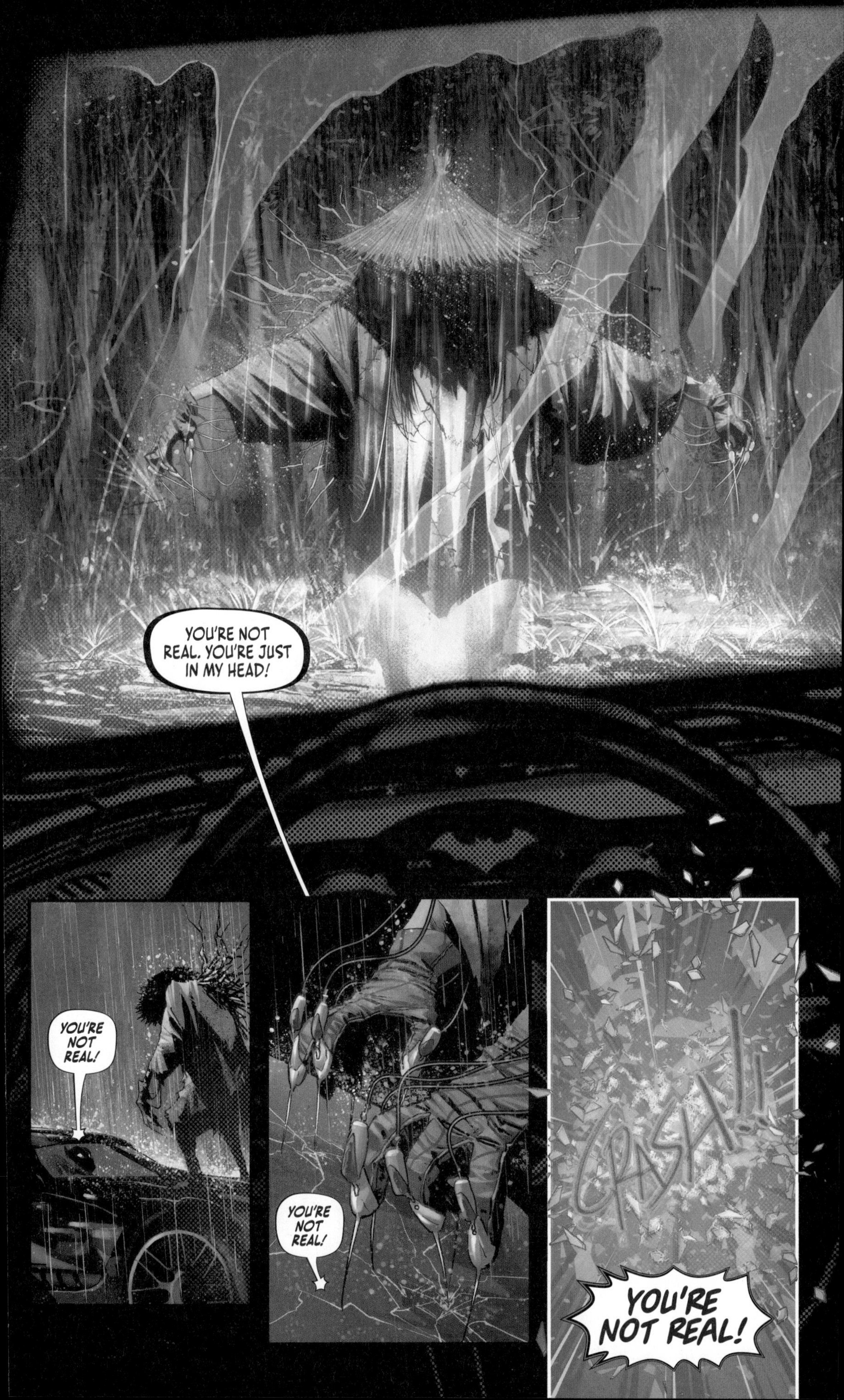
YOU'RE NOT REAL. YOU'RE JUST IN MY HEAD!
YOU'RE NOT REAL!
YOU'RE NOT REAL!
CRASH!!
YOU'RE NOT REAL!

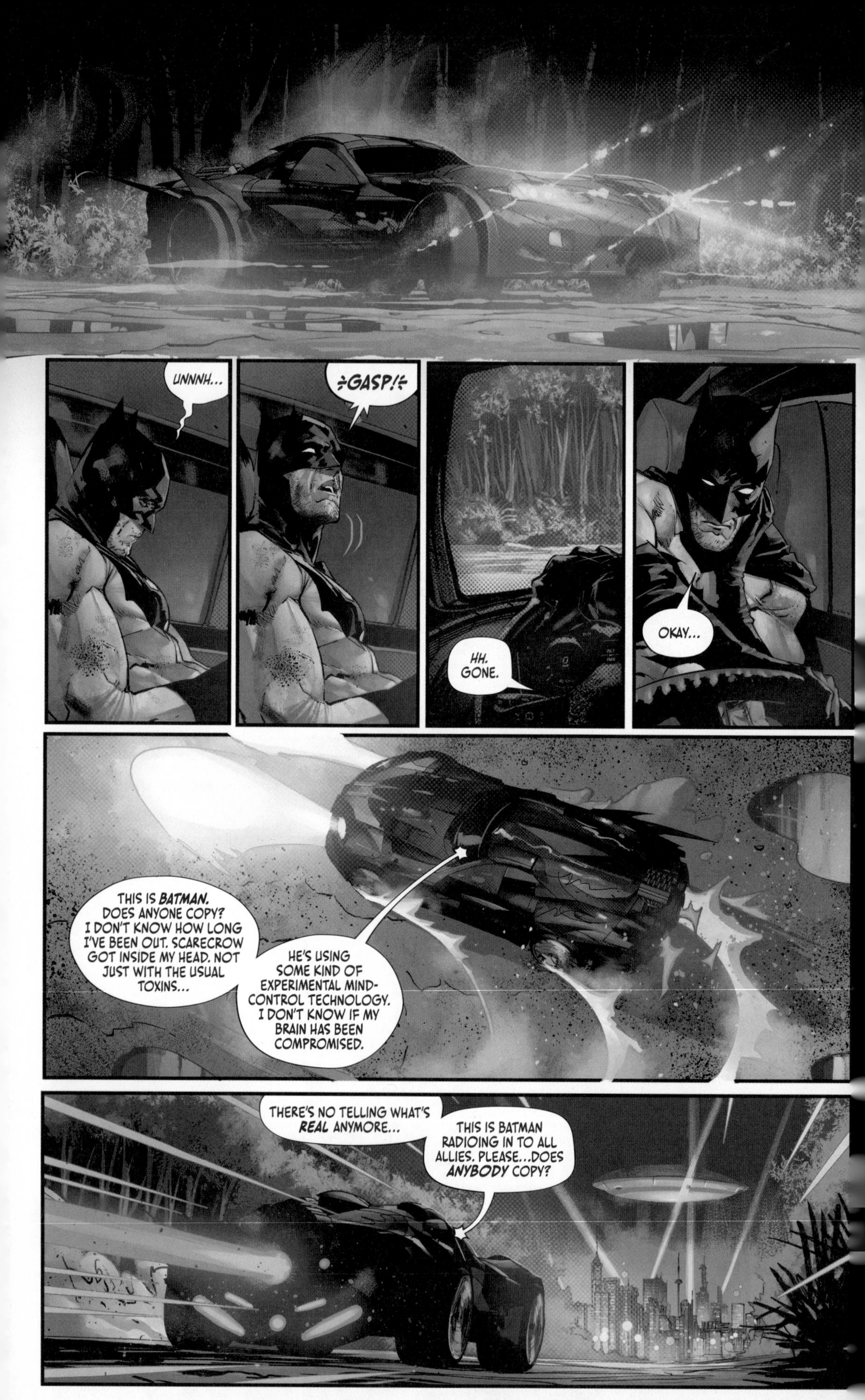
UNNNH...
GASP!
HH. GONE.
OKAY...
THIS IS BATMAN. DOES ANYONE COPY? I DON'T KNOW HOW LONG I'VE BEEN OUT. SCARECROW GOT INSIDE MY HEAD. NOT JUST WITH THE USUAL TOXINS...
HE'S USING SOME KIND OF EXPERIMENTAL MIND-CONTROL TECHNOLOGY. I DON'T KNOW IF MY BRAIN HAS BEEN COMPROMISED.
THERE'S NO TELLING WHAT'S REAL ANYMORE...
THIS IS BATMAN RADIOING IN TO ALL ALLIES. PLEASE...DOES ANYBODY COPY?

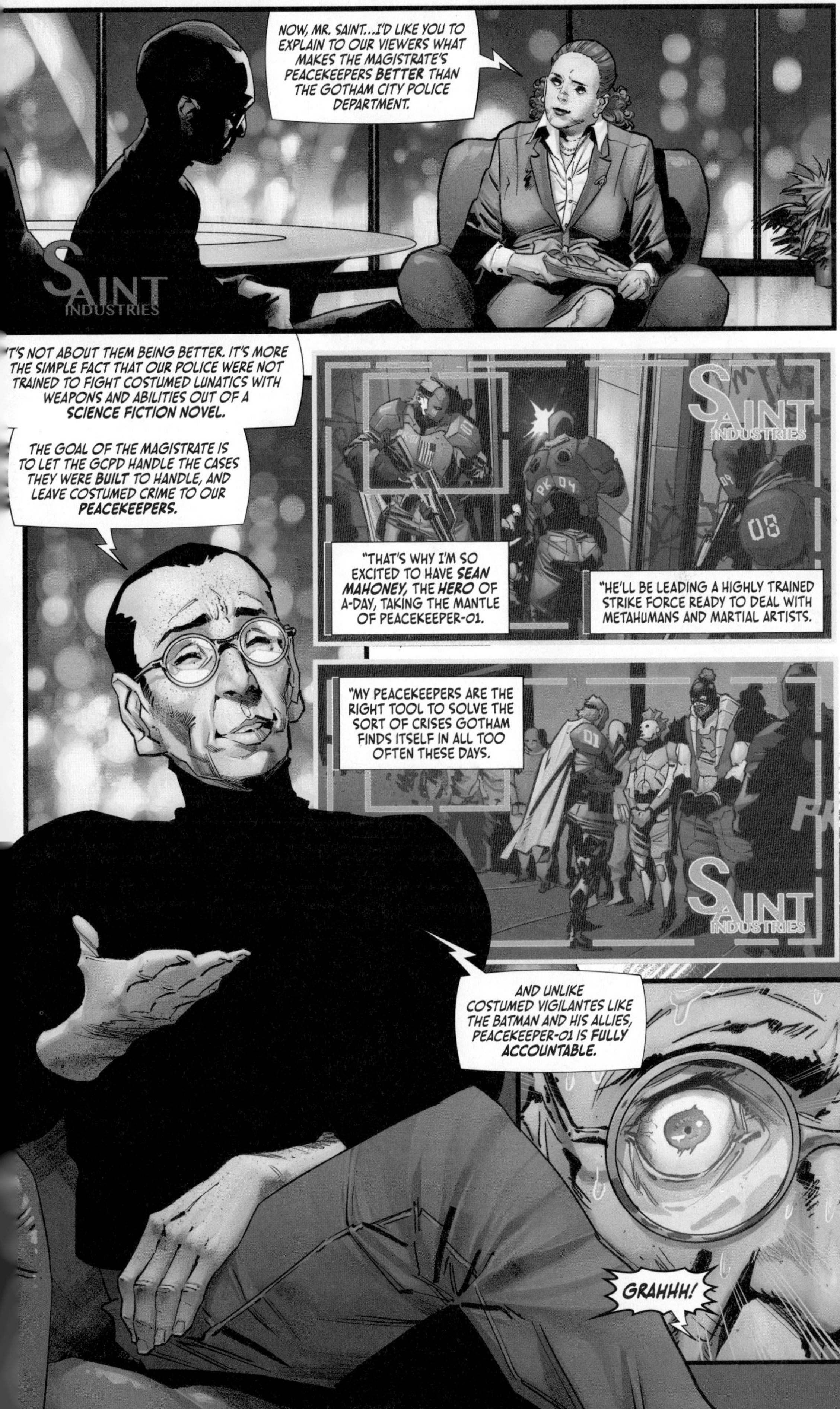

NOW, MR. SAINT...I'D LIKE YOU TO EXPLAIN TO OUR VIEWERS WHAT MAKES THE MAGISTRATE'S PEACEKEEPERS BETTER THAN THE GOTHAM CITY POLICE DEPARTMENT.
SAINT INDUSTRIES
IT'S NOT ABOUT THEM BEING BETTER. IT'S MORE THE SIMPLE FACT THAT OUR POLICE WERE NOT TRAINED TO FIGHT COSTUMED LUNATICS WITH WEAPONS AND ABILITIES OUT OF A SCIENCE FICTION NOVEL.
THE GOAL OF THE MAGISTRATE IS TO LET THE GCPD HANDLE THE CASES THEY WERE BUILT TO HANDLE, AND LEAVE COSTUMED CRIME TO OUR PEACEKEEPERS.
SAINT INDUSTRIES
"THAT'S WHY I'M SO EXCITED TO HAVE SEAN MAHONEY, THE HERO OF A-DAY, TAKING THE MANTLE OF PEACEKEEPER-01.
"HE'LL BE LEADING A HIGHLY TRAINED STRIKE FORCE READY TO DEAL WITH METAHUMANS AND MARTIAL ARTISTS.
"MY PEACEKEEPERS ARE THE RIGHT TOOL TO SOLVE THE SORT OF CRISES GOTHAM FINDS ITSELF IN ALL TOO OFTEN THESE DAYS.
SAINT INDUSTRIES
AND UNLIKE COSTUMED VIGILANTES LIKE THE BATMAN AND HIS ALLIES, PEACEKEEPER-01 IS FULLY ACCOUNTABLE.
GRAHHH!

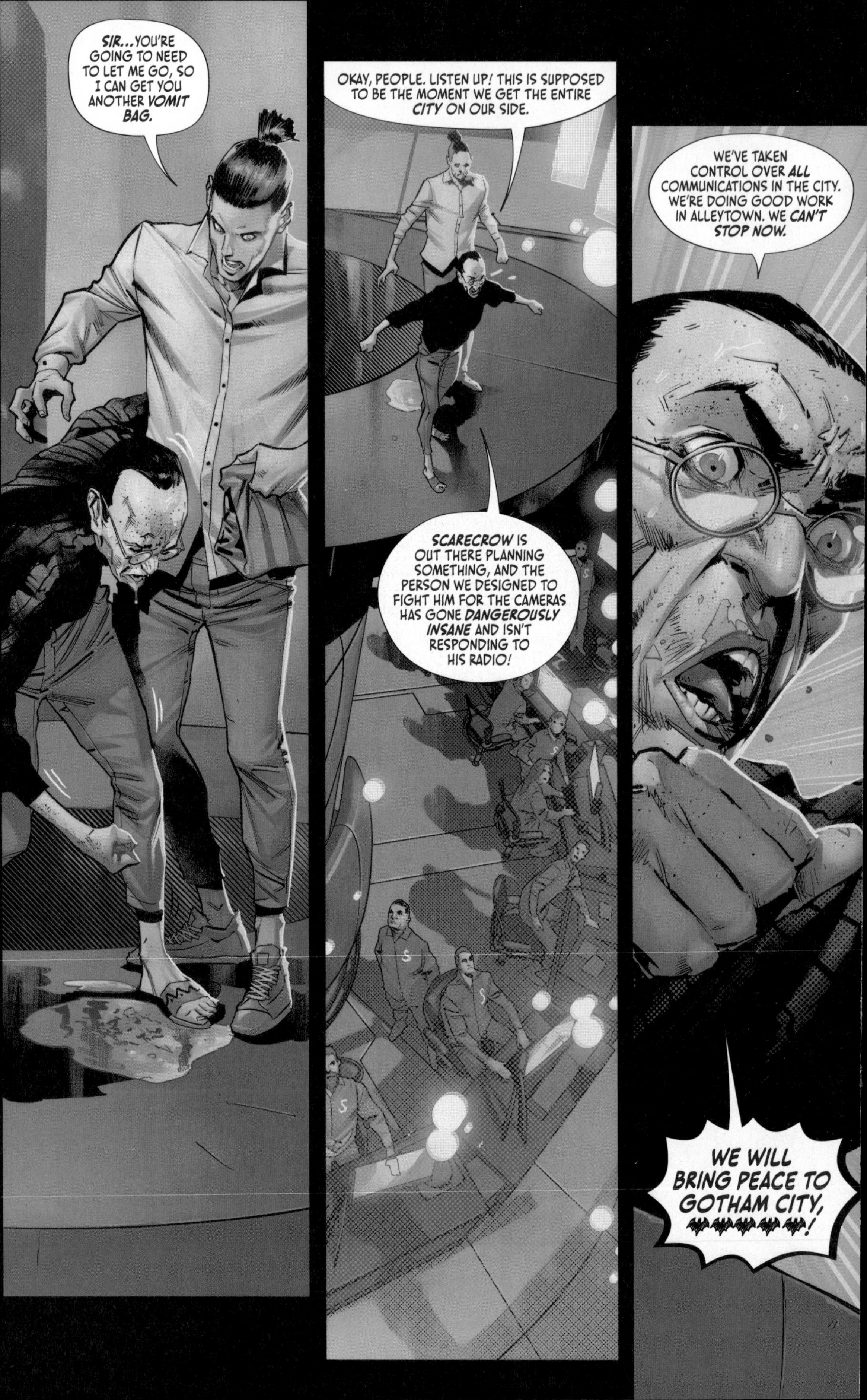
SIR...YOU'RE GOING TO NEED TO LET ME GO, SO I CAN GET YOU ANOTHER VOMIT BAG.
OKAY, PEOPLE. LISTEN UP! THIS IS SUPPOSED TO BE THE MOMENT WE GET THE ENTIRE CITY ON OUR SIDE.
SCARECROW IS OUT THERE PLANNING SOMETHING, AND THE PERSON WE DESIGNED TO FIGHT HIM FOR THE CAMERAS HAS GONE DANGEROUSLY INSANE AND ISN'T RESPONDING TO HIS RADIO!
WE'VE TAKEN CONTROL OVER ALL COMMUNICATIONS IN THE CITY. WE'RE DOING GOOD WORK IN ALLEYTOWN. WE CAN'T STOP NOW.
WE WILL BRING PEACE TO GOTHAM CITY,

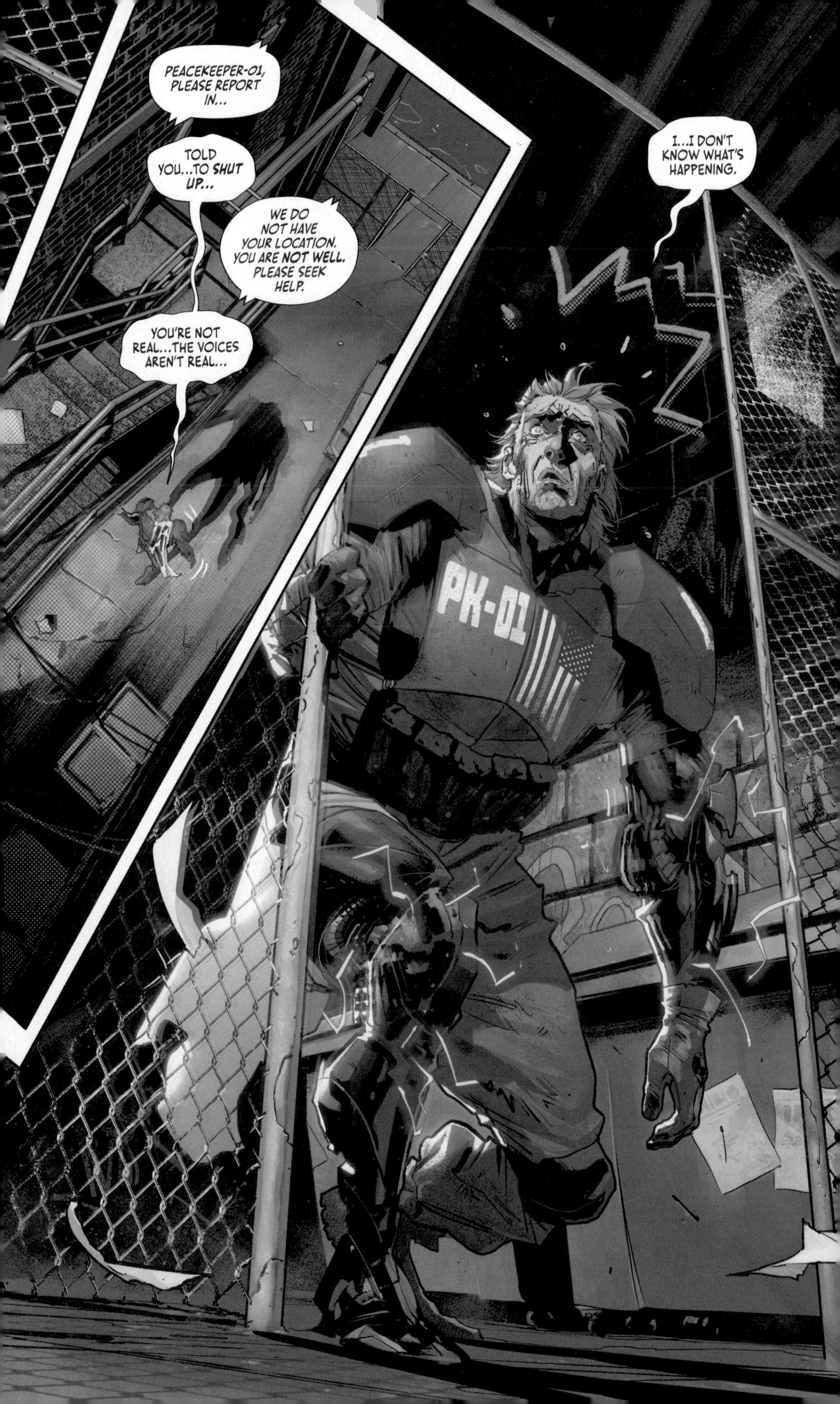
PEACEKEEPER-01, PLEASE REPORT IN...
TOLD YOU...TO SHUT UP...
WE DO NOT HAVE YOUR LOCATION. YOU ARE NOT WELL. PLEASE SEEK HELP.
YOU'RE NOT REAL...THE VOICES AREN'T REAL...
I...I DON'T KNOW WHAT'S HAPPENING.
PK-01

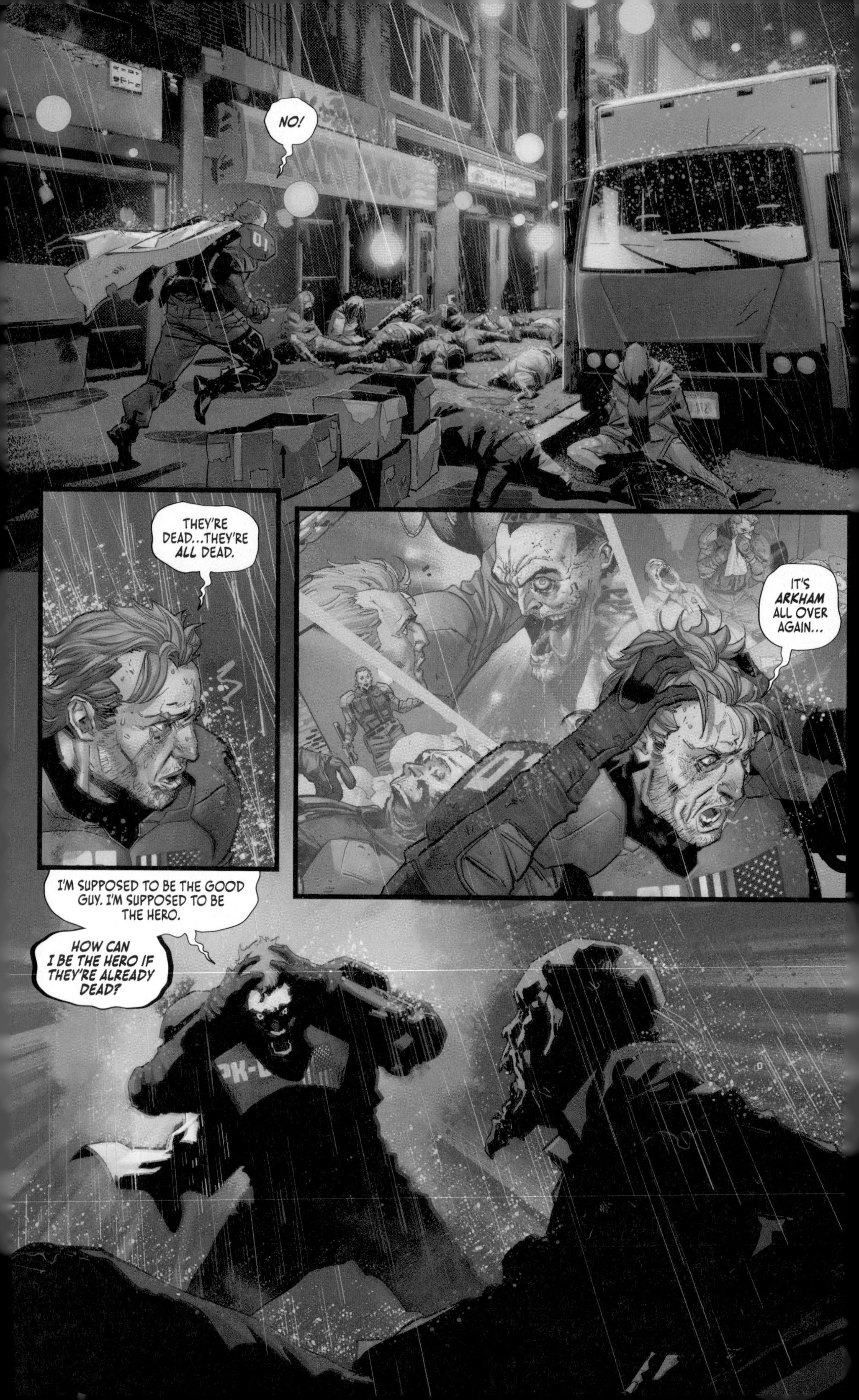
NO!
THEY'RE DEAD...THEY'RE ALL DEAD.
IT'S ARKHAM ALL OVER AGAIN...
I'M SUPPOSED TO BE THE GOOD GUY. I'M SUPPOSED TO BE THE HERO.
HOW CAN I BE THE HERO IF THEY'RE ALREADY DEAD?

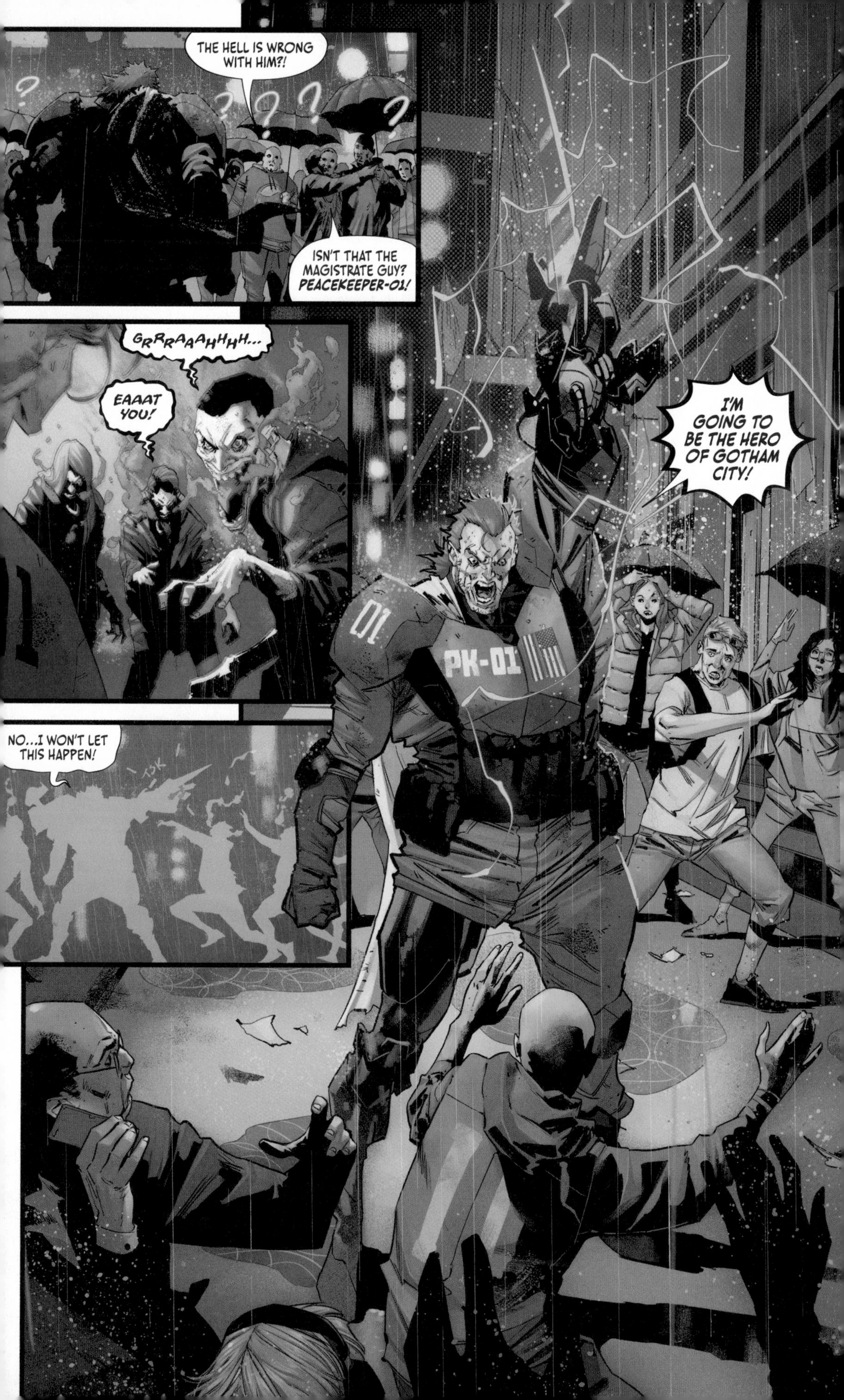
THE HELL IS WRONG WITH HIM?!
ISN'T THAT THE MAGISTRATE GUY? *PEACEKEEPER-01!*
GRRRAAAHHHH...
EAAAT YOU!
NO...I WON'T LET THIS HAPPEN!
I'M GOING TO BE THE HERO OF GOTHAM CITY!
01
PK-01

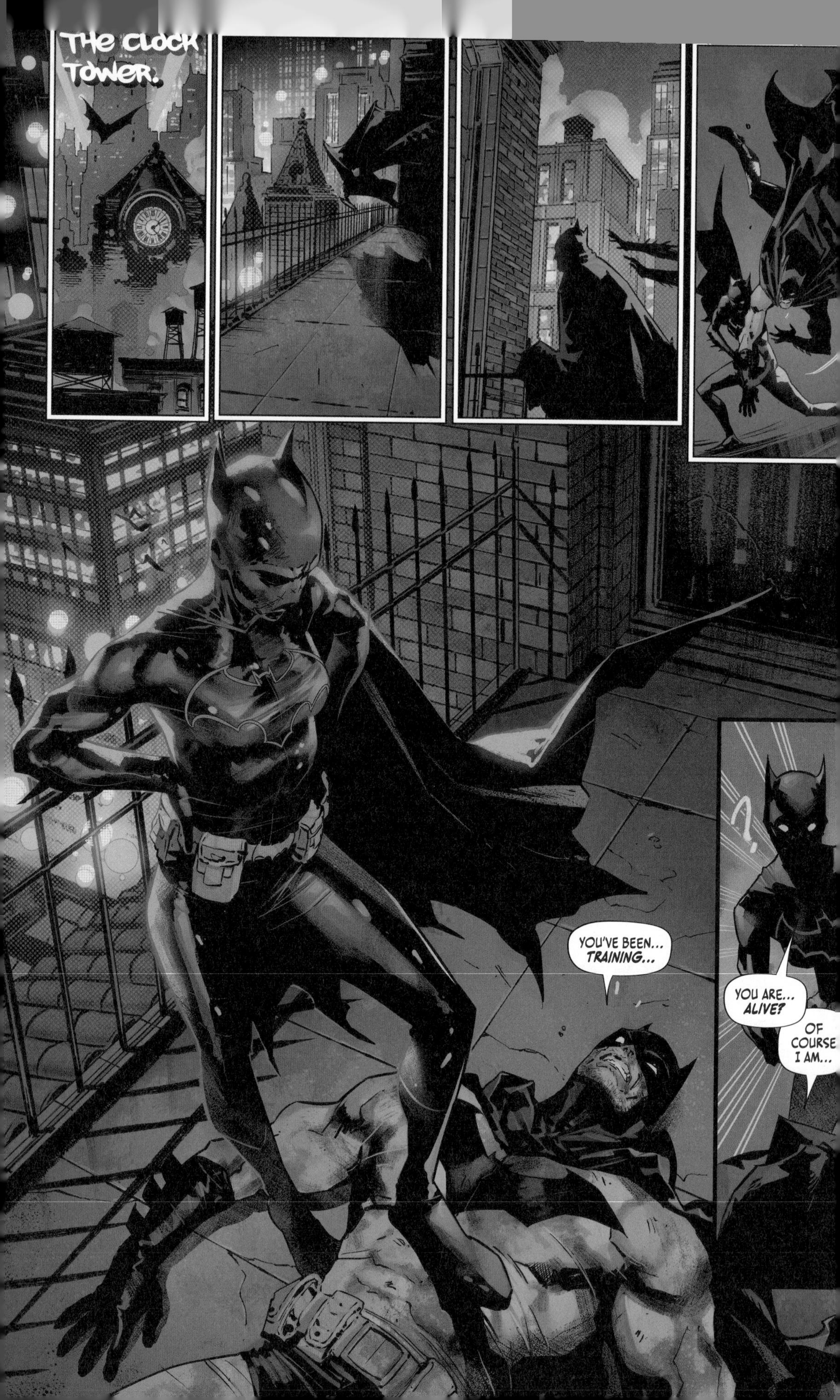
THE CLOCK TOWER.
YOU'VE BEEN... TRAINING...
?
YOU ARE... ALIVE?
OF COURSE I AM...

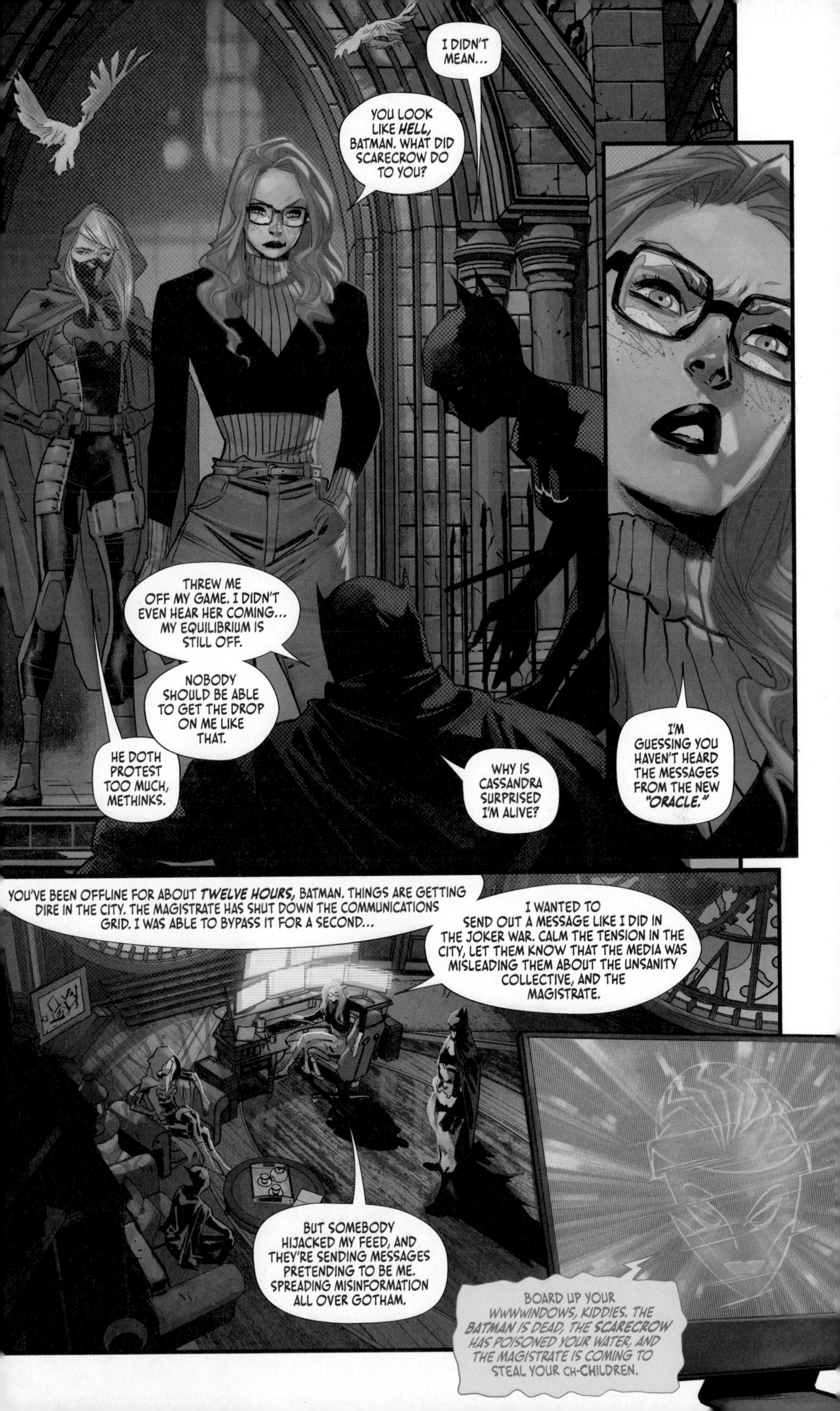
I DIDN'T MEAN...
YOU LOOK LIKE HELL, BATMAN. WHAT DID SCARECROW DO TO YOU?
THREW ME OFF MY GAME. I DIDN'T EVEN HEAR HER COMING... MY EQUILIBRIUM IS STILL OFF.
NOBODY SHOULD BE ABLE TO GET THE DROP ON ME LIKE THAT.
HE DOTH PROTEST TOO MUCH, METHINKS.
WHY IS CASSANDRA SURPRISED I'M ALIVE?
I'M GUESSING YOU HAVEN'T HEARD THE MESSAGES FROM THE NEW "ORACLE."
YOU'VE BEEN OFFLINE FOR ABOUT TWELVE HOURS, BATMAN. THINGS ARE GETTING DIRE IN THE CITY. THE MAGISTRATE HAS SHUT DOWN THE COMMUNICATIONS GRID. I WAS ABLE TO BYPASS IT FOR A SECOND...
I WANTED TO SEND OUT A MESSAGE LIKE I DID IN THE JOKER WAR. CALM THE TENSION IN THE CITY, LET THEM KNOW THAT THE MEDIA WAS MISLEADING THEM ABOUT THE UNSANITY COLLECTIVE, AND THE MAGISTRATE.
BUT SOMEBODY HIJACKED MY FEED, AND THEY'RE SENDING MESSAGES PRETENDING TO BE ME. SPREADING MISINFORMATION ALL OVER GOTHAM.
BOARD UP YOUR WWWWINDOWS, KIDDIES. THE BATMAN IS DEAD, THE SCARECROW HAS POISONED YOUR WATER, AND THE MAGISTRATE IS COMING TO STEAL YOUR CH-CHILDREN.

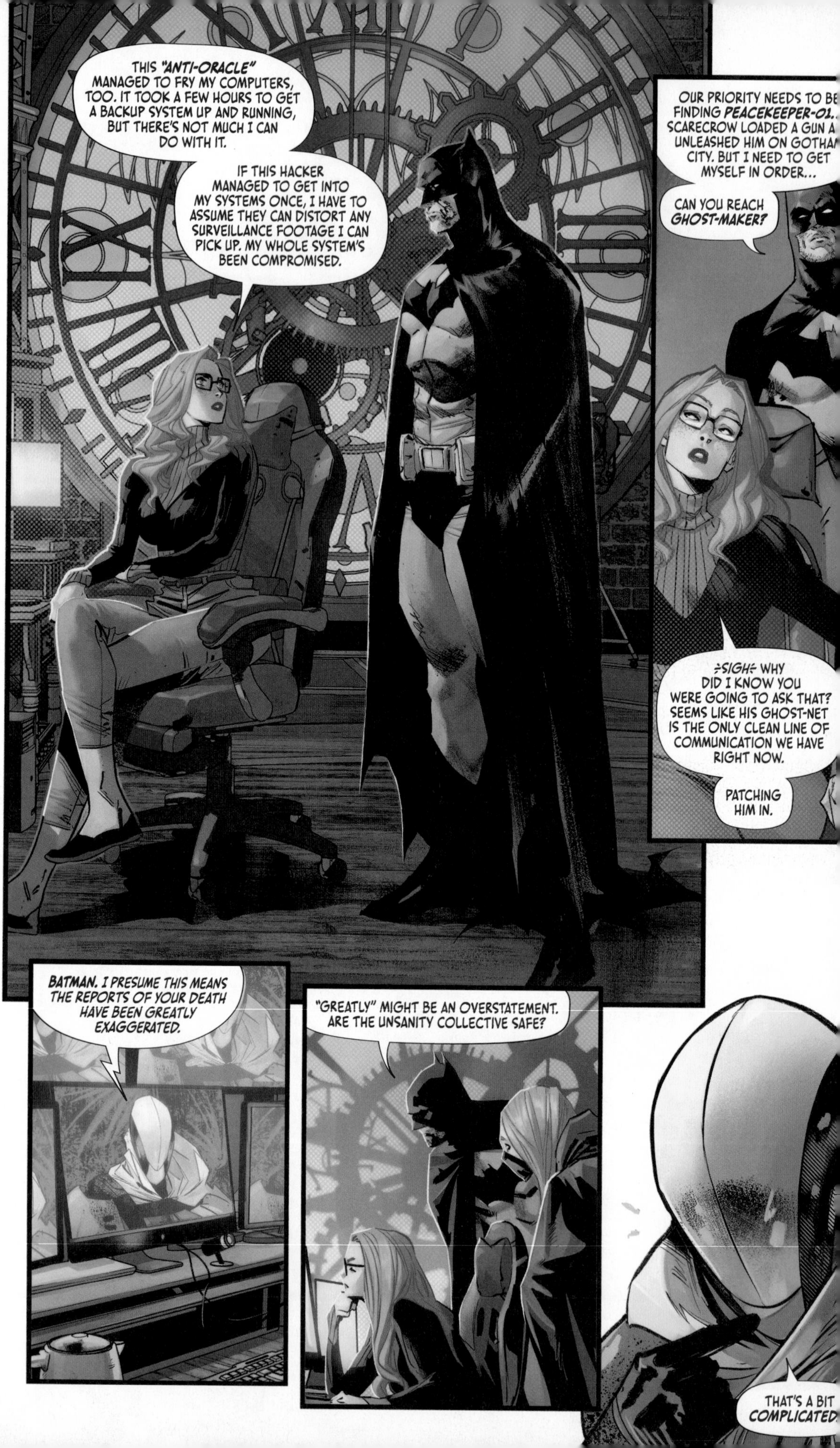
THIS "ANTI-ORACLE" MANAGED TO FRY MY COMPUTERS, TOO. IT TOOK A FEW HOURS TO GET A BACKUP SYSTEM UP AND RUNNING, BUT THERE'S NOT MUCH I CAN DO WITH IT.
IF THIS HACKER MANAGED TO GET INTO MY SYSTEMS ONCE, I HAVE TO ASSUME THEY CAN DISTORT ANY SURVEILLANCE FOOTAGE I CAN PICK UP. MY WHOLE SYSTEM'S BEEN COMPROMISED.
OUR PRIORITY NEEDS TO BE FINDING PEACEKEEPER-01.. SCARECROW LOADED A GUN A UNLEASHED HIM ON GOTHA CITY. BUT I NEED TO GET MYSELF IN ORDER...
CAN YOU REACH GHOST-MAKER?
≑SIGH≑ WHY DID I KNOW YOU WERE GOING TO ASK THAT? SEEMS LIKE HIS GHOST-NET IS THE ONLY CLEAN LINE OF COMMUNICATION WE HAVE RIGHT NOW.
PATCHING HIM IN.
BATMAN. I PRESUME THIS MEANS THE REPORTS OF YOUR DEATH HAVE BEEN GREATLY EXAGGERATED.
"GREATLY" MIGHT BE AN OVERSTATEMENT. ARE THE UNSANITY COLLECTIVE SAFE?
THAT'S A BIT COMPLICATED

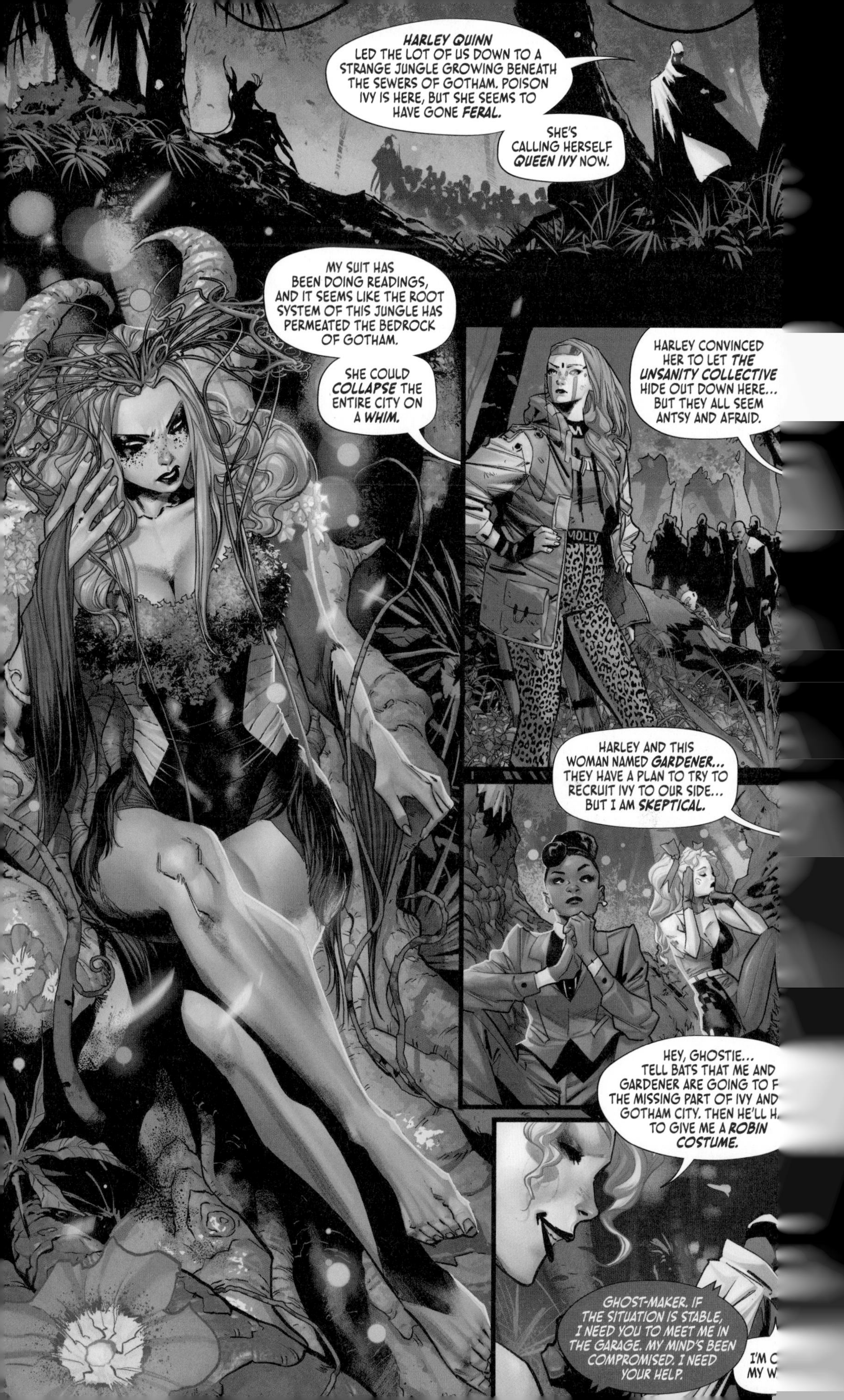
HARLEY QUINN LED THE LOT OF US DOWN TO A STRANGE JUNGLE GROWING BENEATH THE SEWERS OF GOTHAM. POISON IVY IS HERE, BUT SHE SEEMS TO HAVE GONE FERAL.
SHE'S CALLING HERSELF QUEEN IVY NOW.
MY SUIT HAS BEEN DOING READINGS, AND IT SEEMS LIKE THE ROOT SYSTEM OF THIS JUNGLE HAS PERMEATED THE BEDROCK OF GOTHAM.
SHE COULD COLLAPSE THE ENTIRE CITY ON A WHIM.
HARLEY CONVINCED HER TO LET THE UNSANITY COLLECTIVE HIDE OUT DOWN HERE... BUT THEY ALL SEEM ANTSY AND AFRAID.
MOLLY
HARLEY AND THIS WOMAN NAMED GARDENER... THEY HAVE A PLAN TO TRY TO RECRUIT IVY TO OUR SIDE... BUT I AM SKEPTICAL.
HEY, GHOSTIE... TELL BATS THAT ME AND GARDENER ARE GOING TO F THE MISSING PART OF IVY AND GOTHAM CITY. THEN HE'LL H TO GIVE ME A ROBIN COSTUME.
GHOST-MAKER. IF THE SITUATION IS STABLE, I NEED YOU TO MEET ME IN THE GARAGE. MY MIND'S BEEN COMPROMISED. I NEED YOUR HELP.
I'M C MY W

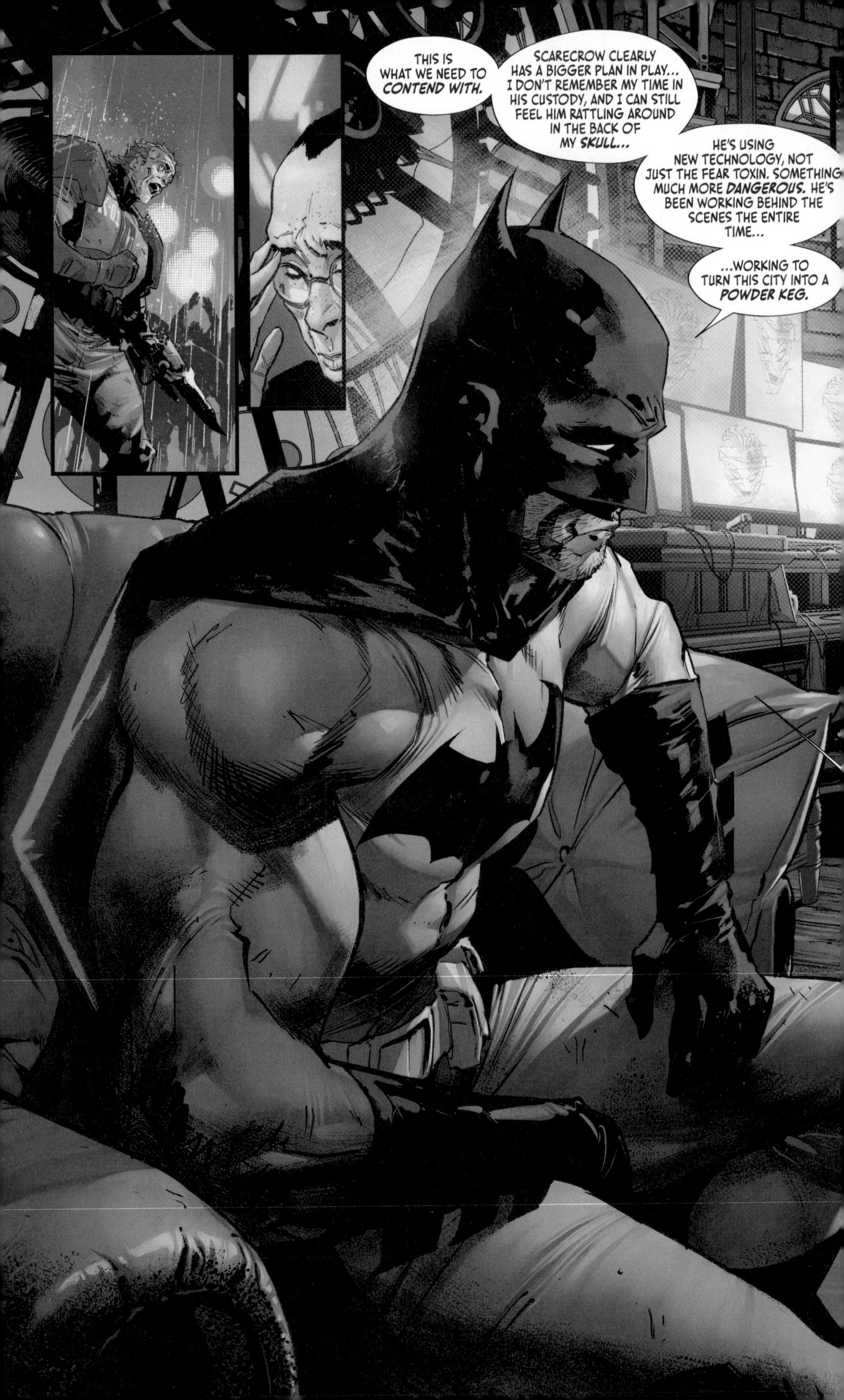
THIS IS WHAT WE NEED TO CONTEND WITH.
SCARECROW CLEARLY HAS A BIGGER PLAN IN PLAY... I DON'T REMEMBER MY TIME IN HIS CUSTODY, AND I CAN STILL FEEL HIM RATTLING AROUND IN THE BACK OF MY SKULL...
HE'S USING NEW TECHNOLOGY, NOT JUST THE FEAR TOXIN. SOMETHING MUCH MORE DANGEROUS. HE'S BEEN WORKING BEHIND THE SCENES THE ENTIRE TIME...
...WORKING TO TURN THIS CITY INTO A POWDER KEG.

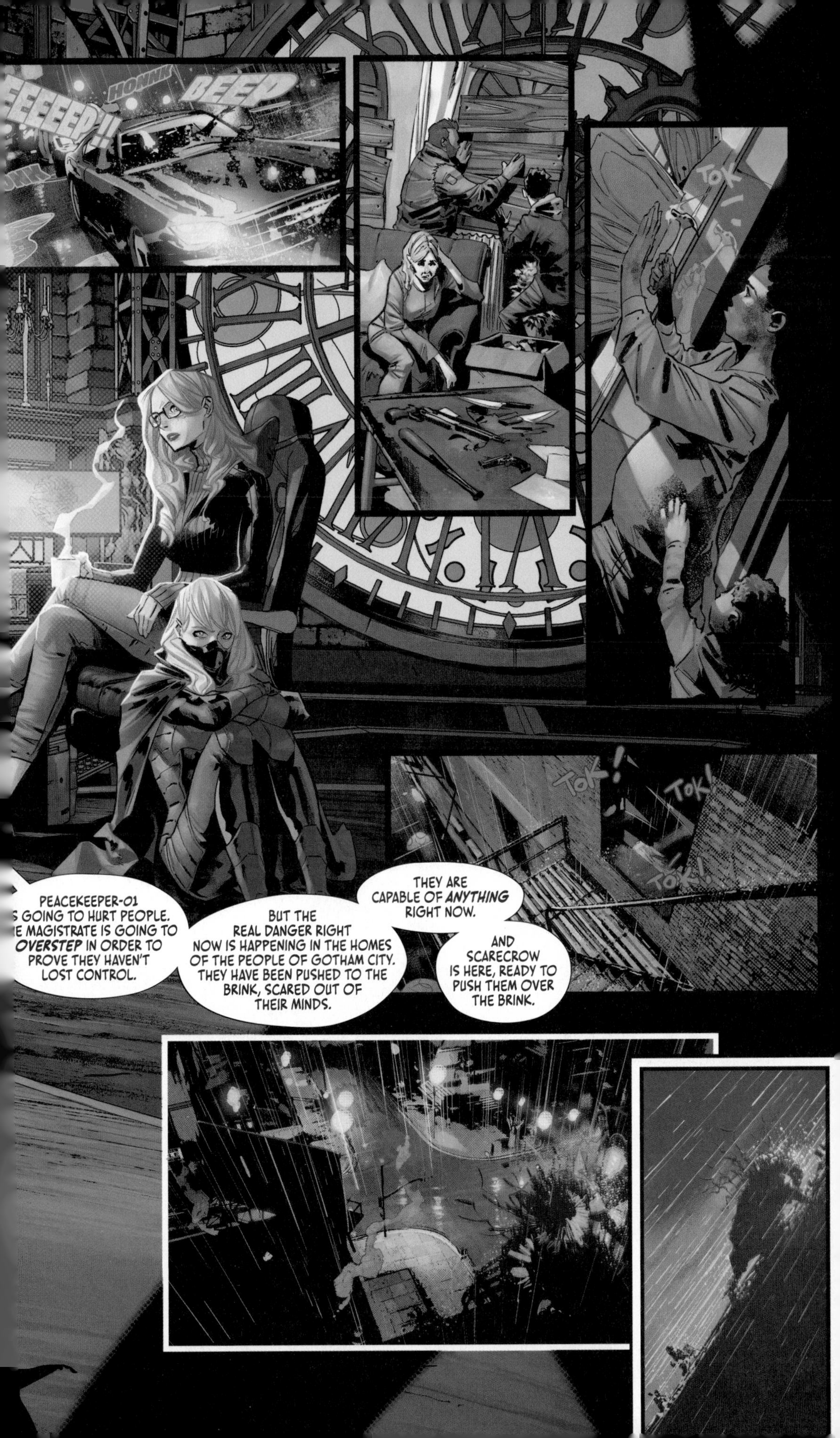
EEEEEEP!!
HONNK
BEEP
TOK!
PEACEKEEPER-01 S GOING TO HURT PEOPLE. E MAGISTRATE IS GOING TO *OVERSTEP* IN ORDER TO PROVE THEY HAVEN'T LOST CONTROL.
BUT THE REAL DANGER RIGHT NOW IS HAPPENING IN THE HOMES OF THE PEOPLE OF GOTHAM CITY. THEY HAVE BEEN PUSHED TO THE BRINK, SCARED OUT OF THEIR MINDS.
THEY ARE CAPABLE OF *ANYTHING* RIGHT NOW.
AND SCARECROW IS HERE, READY TO PUSH THEM OVER THE BRINK.
TOK!
TOK!
TOK!

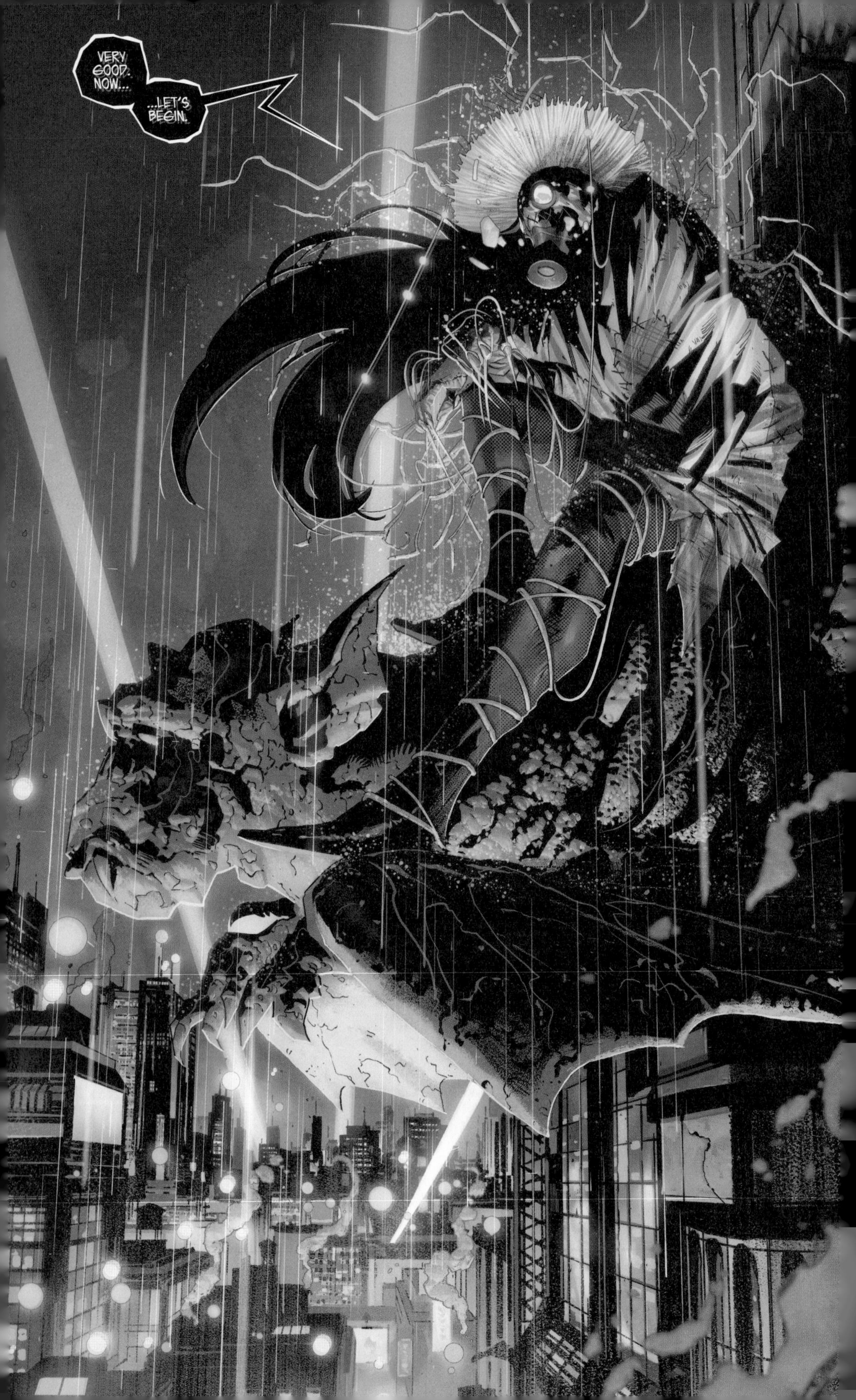
VERY GOOD. NOW...
...LET'S BEGIN.

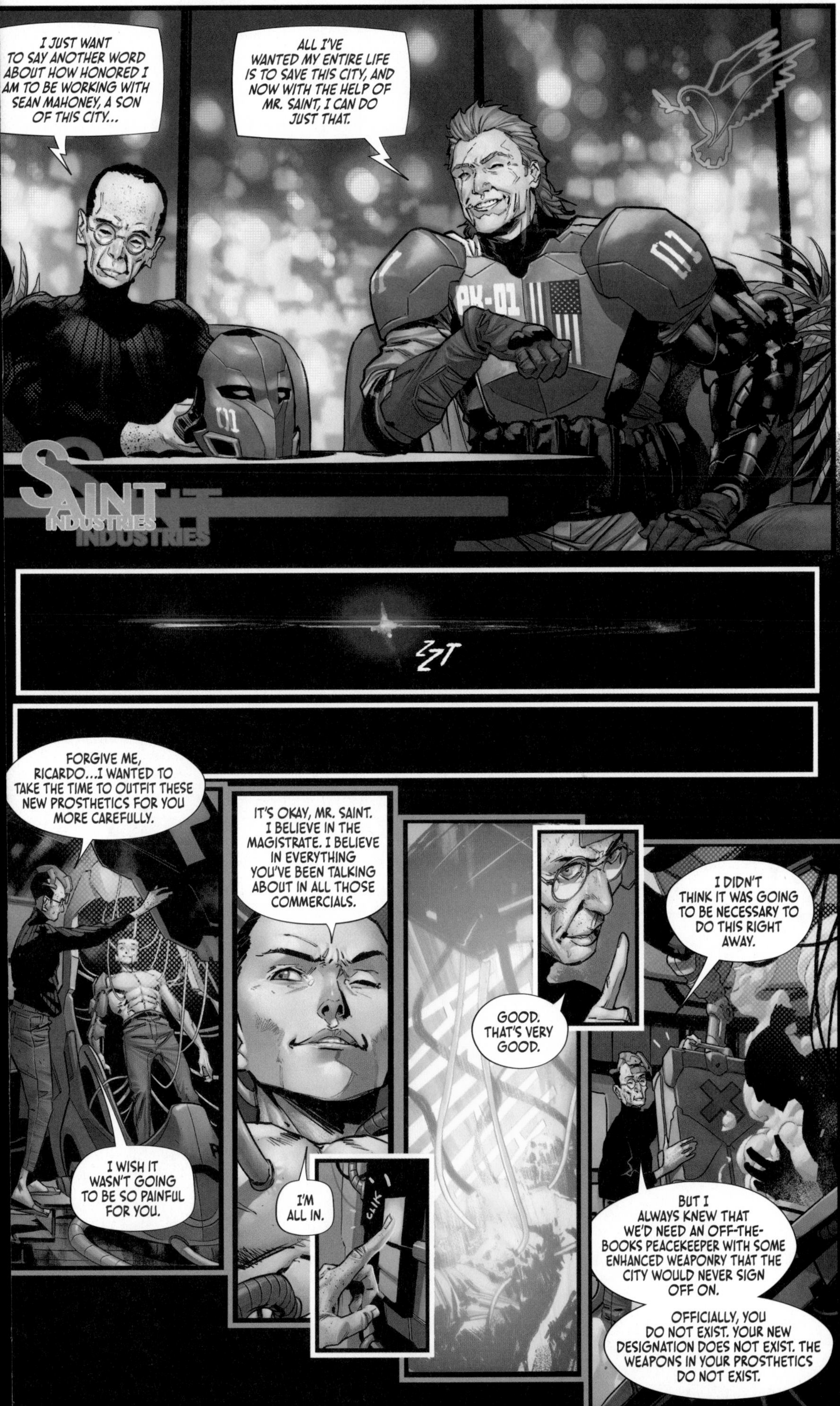
I JUST WANT TO SAY ANOTHER WORD ABOUT HOW HONORED I AM TO BE WORKING WITH SEAN MAHONEY, A SON OF THIS CITY...
ALL I'VE WANTED MY ENTIRE LIFE IS TO SAVE THIS CITY, AND NOW WITH THE HELP OF MR. SAINT, I CAN DO JUST THAT.
PK-01
SAINT INDUSTRIES
ZZT
FORGIVE ME, RICARDO...I WANTED TO TAKE THE TIME TO OUTFIT THESE NEW PROSTHETICS FOR YOU MORE CAREFULLY.
I WISH IT WASN'T GOING TO BE SO PAINFUL FOR YOU.
IT'S OKAY, MR. SAINT. I BELIEVE IN THE MAGISTRATE. I BELIEVE IN EVERYTHING YOU'VE BEEN TALKING ABOUT IN ALL THOSE COMMERCIALS.
I'M ALL IN.
CLIK
GOOD. THAT'S VERY GOOD.
I DIDN'T THINK IT WAS GOING TO BE NECESSARY TO DO THIS RIGHT AWAY.
BUT I ALWAYS KNEW THAT WE'D NEED AN OFF-THE-BOOKS PEACEKEEPER WITH SOME ENHANCED WEAPONRY THAT THE CITY WOULD NEVER SIGN OFF ON.
OFFICIALLY, YOU DO NOT EXIST. YOUR NEW DESIGNATION DOES NOT EXIST. THE WEAPONS IN YOUR PROSTHETICS DO NOT EXIST.

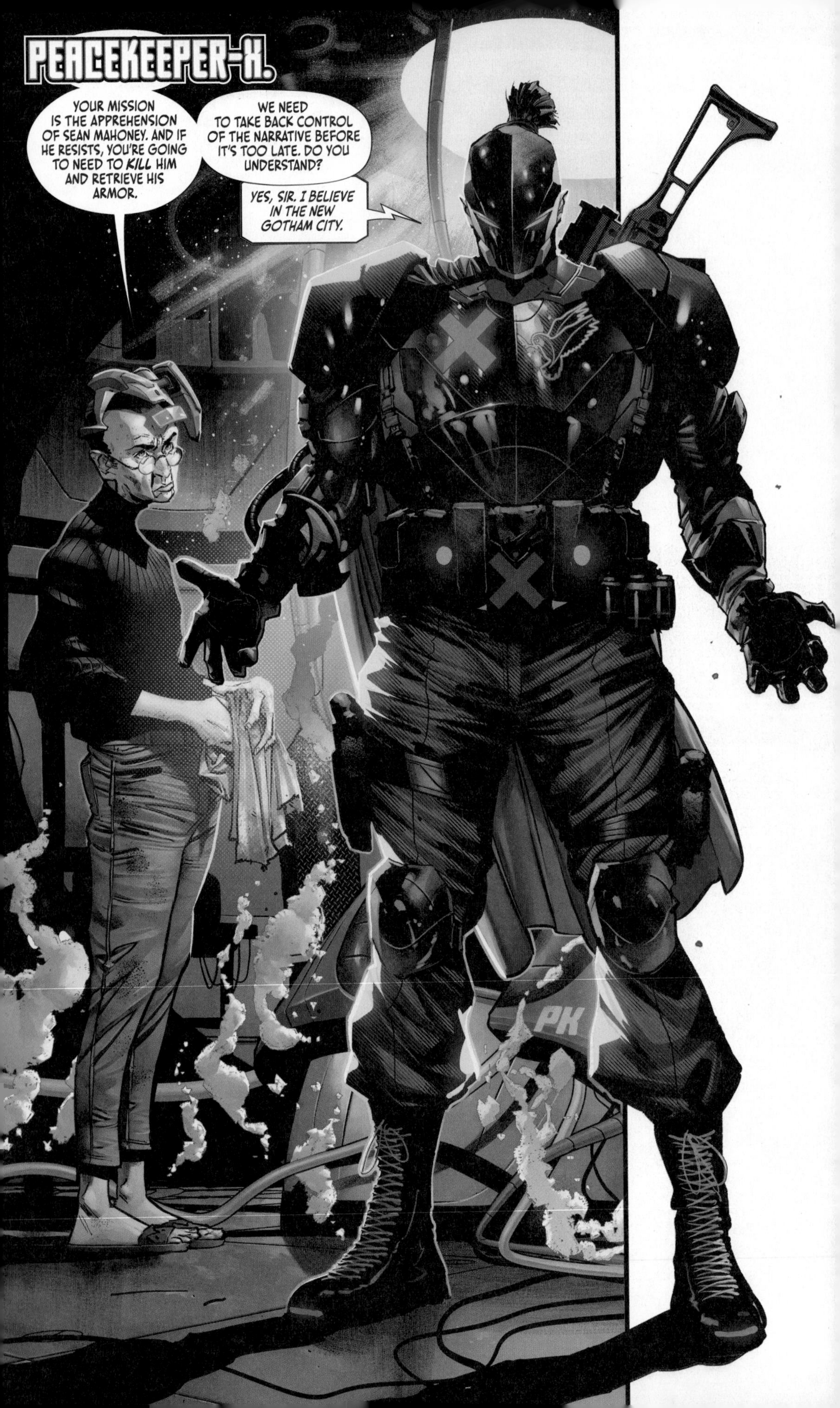
PEACEKEEPER-X.
YOUR MISSION IS THE APPREHENSION OF SEAN MAHONEY. AND IF HE RESISTS, YOU'RE GOING TO NEED TO *KILL* HIM AND RETRIEVE HIS ARMOR.
WE NEED TO TAKE BACK CONTROL OF THE NARRATIVE BEFORE IT'S TOO LATE. DO YOU UNDERSTAND?
YES, SIR. I BELIEVE IN THE NEW GOTHAM CITY.
PK

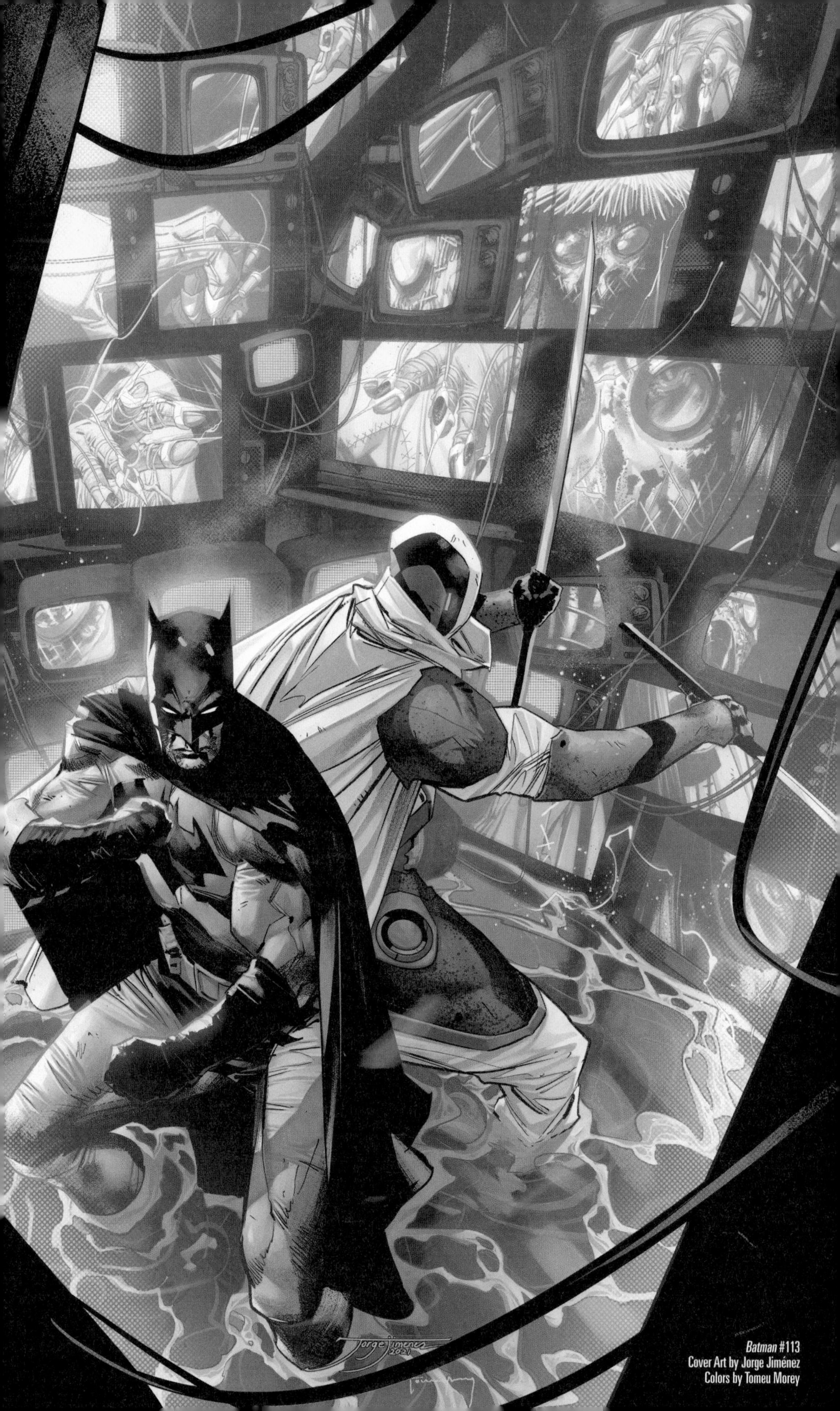

Batman #113
Cover Art by Jorge Jiménez
Colors by Tomeu Morey

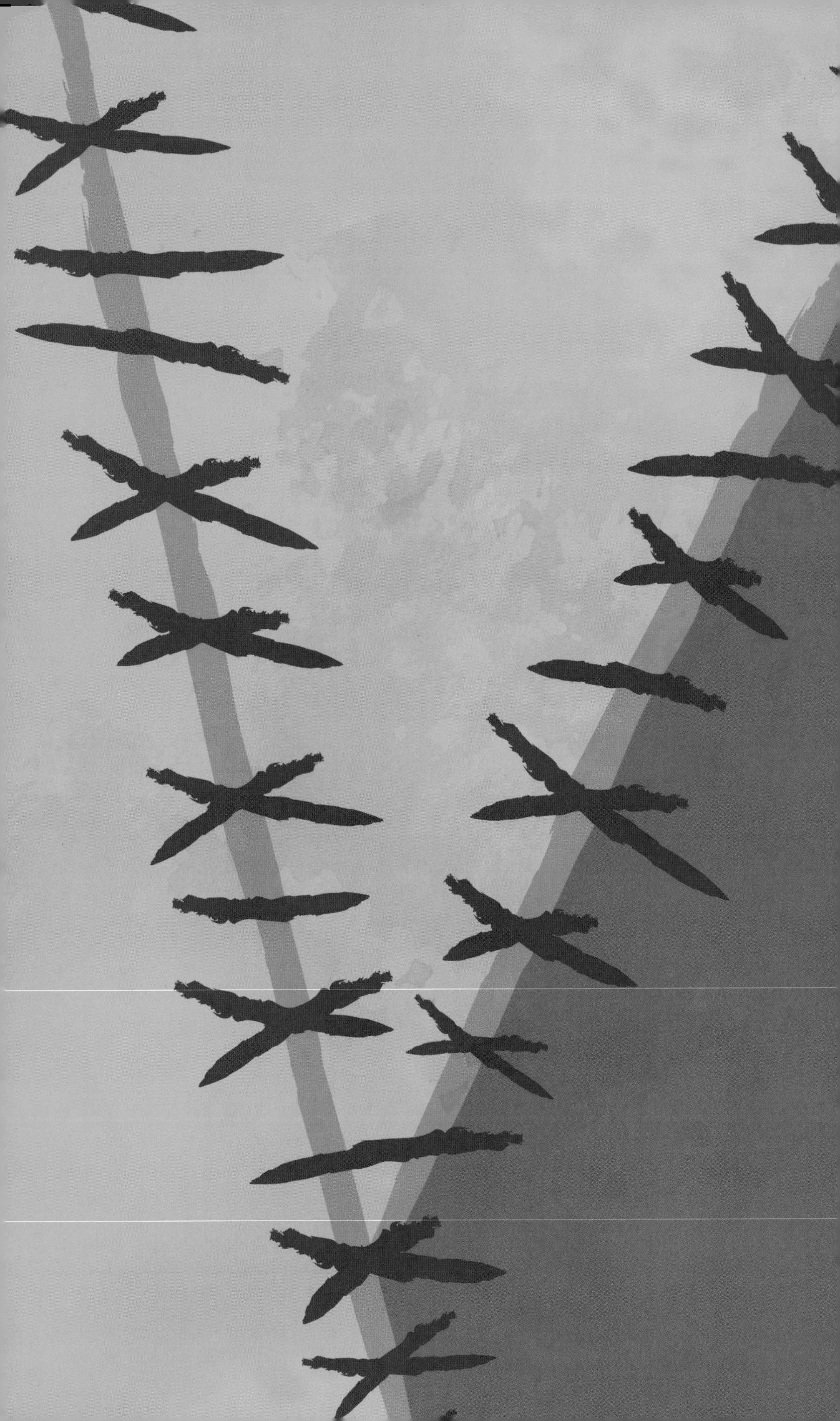

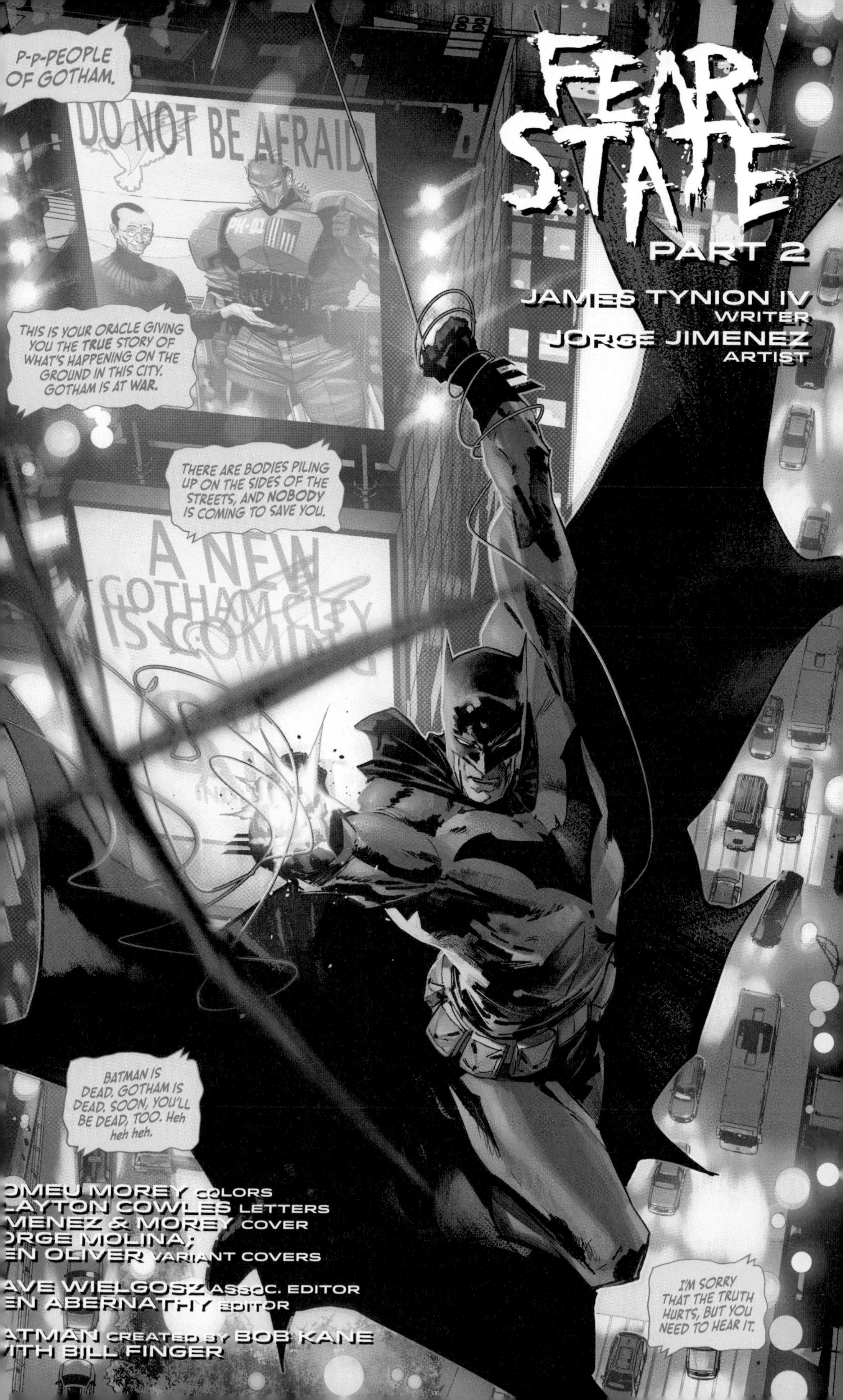
P-p-PEOPLE OF GOTHAM.
DO NOT BE AFRAID
THIS IS YOUR ORACLE GIVING YOU THE TRUE STORY OF WHAT'S HAPPENING ON THE GROUND IN THIS CITY. GOTHAM IS AT WAR.
PK-01
FEAR STATE
PART 2
JAMES TYNION IV WRITER
JORGE JIMENEZ ARTIST
THERE ARE BODIES PILING UP ON THE SIDES OF THE STREETS, AND NOBODY IS COMING TO SAVE YOU.
A NEW GOTHAM CITY IS COMING
BATMAN IS DEAD. GOTHAM IS DEAD. SOON, YOU'LL BE DEAD, TOO. Heh heh heh.
OMEU MOREY COLORS
LAYTON COWLES LETTERS
IMENEZ & MOREY COVER
ORGE MOLINA;
EN OLIVER VARIANT COVERS
AVE WIELGOSZ ASSOC. EDITOR
EN ABERNATHY EDITOR
ATMAN CREATED BY BOB KANE
VITH BILL FINGER
I'M SORRY THAT THE TRUTH HURTS, BUT YOU NEED TO HEAR IT.

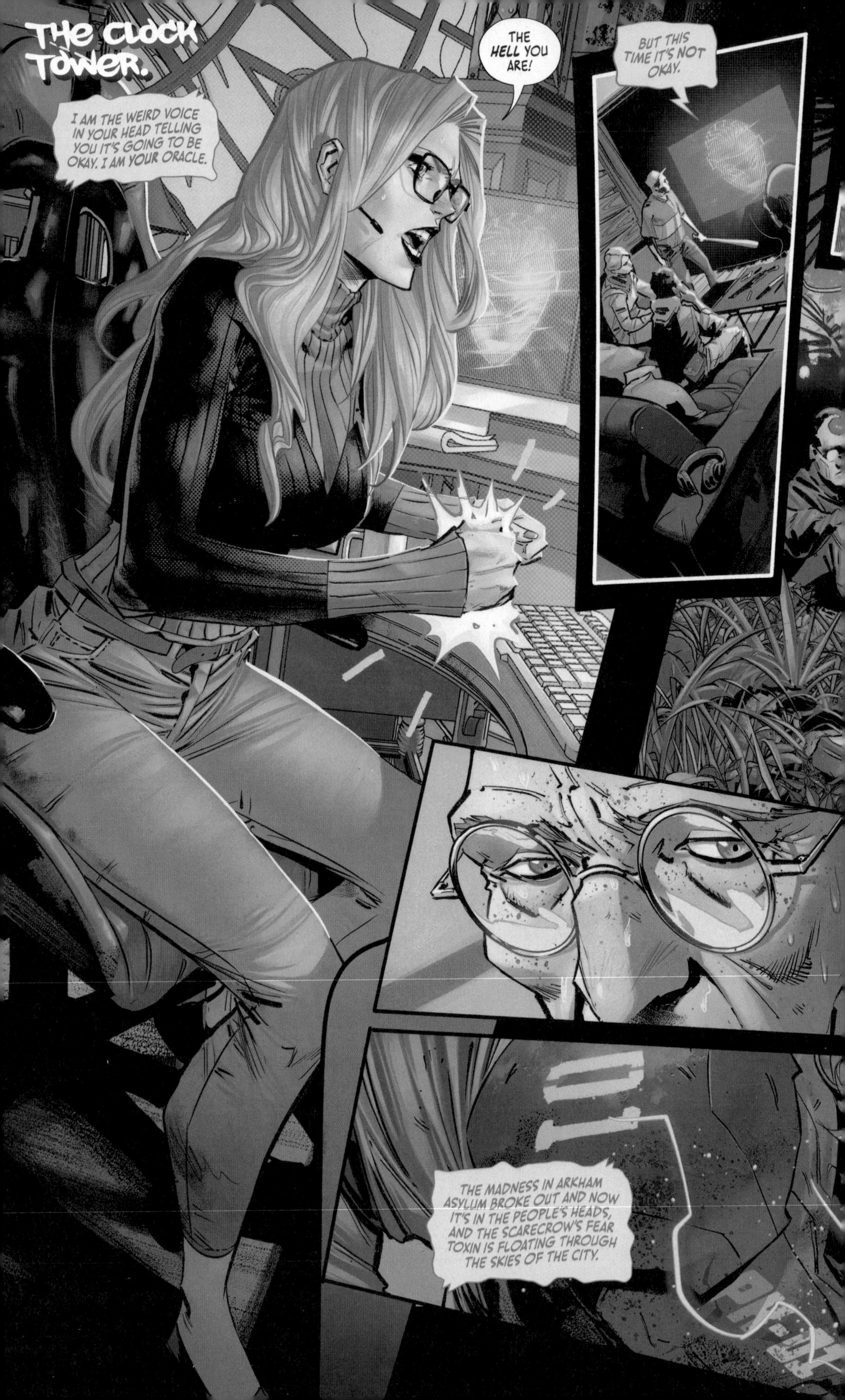
THE CLOCK TOWER.
I AM THE WEIRD VOICE IN YOUR HEAD TELLING YOU IT'S GOING TO BE OKAY. I AM YOUR ORACLE.
THE HELL YOU ARE!
BUT THIS TIME IT'S NOT OKAY.
THE MADNESS IN ARKHAM ASYLUM BROKE OUT AND NOW IT'S IN THE PEOPLE'S HEADS, AND THE SCARECROW'S FEAR TOXIN IS FLOATING THROUGH THE SKIES OF THE CITY.

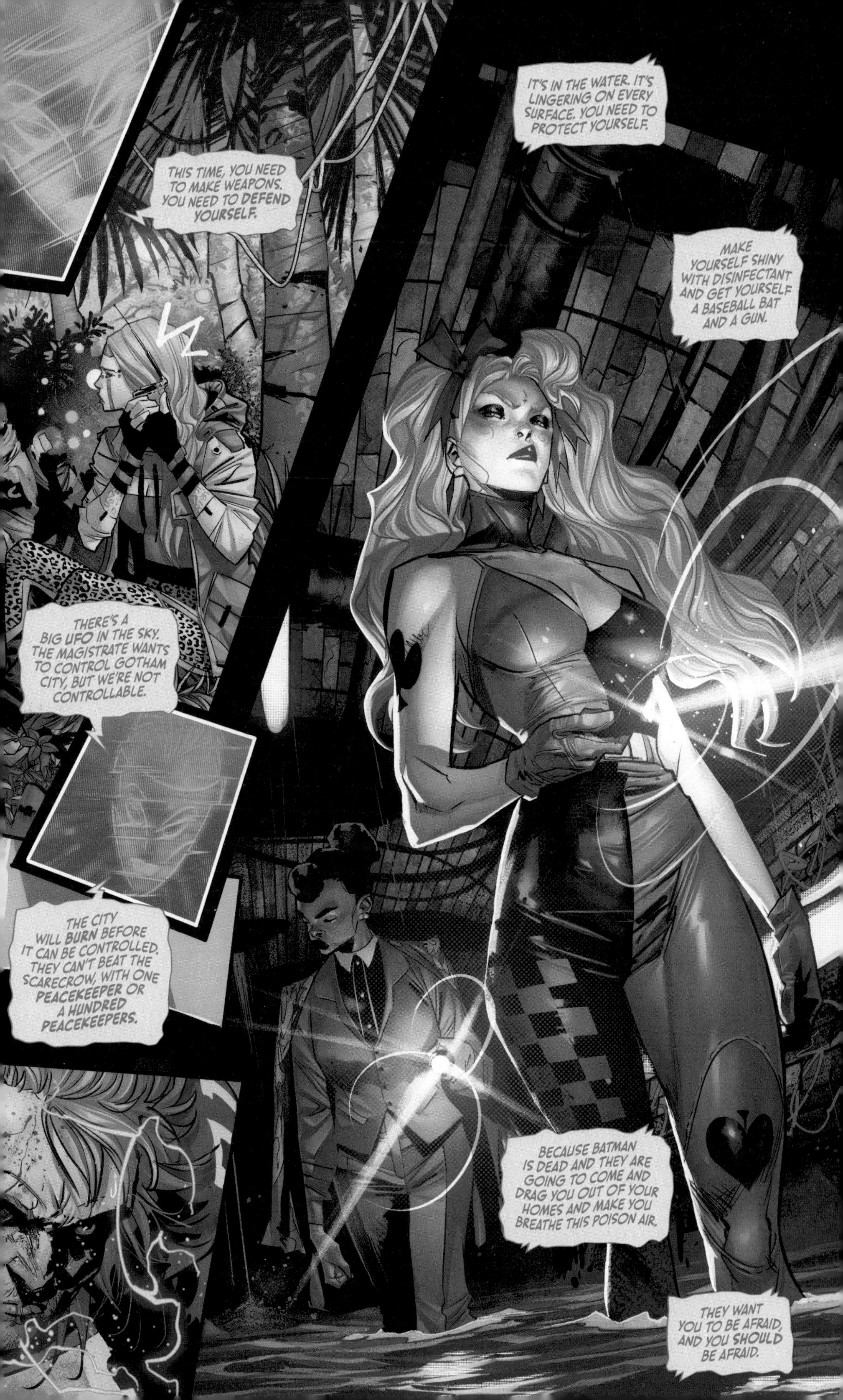

THIS TIME, YOU NEED TO MAKE WEAPONS. YOU NEED TO DEFEND YOURSELF.
IT'S IN THE WATER. IT'S LINGERING ON EVERY SURFACE. YOU NEED TO PROTECT YOURSELF.
MAKE YOURSELF SHINY WITH DISINFECTANT AND GET YOURSELF A BASEBALL BAT AND A GUN.
THERE'S A BIG UFO IN THE SKY. THE MAGISTRATE WANTS TO CONTROL GOTHAM CITY, BUT WE'RE NOT CONTROLLABLE.
THE CITY WILL BURN BEFORE IT CAN BE CONTROLLED. THEY CAN'T BEAT THE SCARECROW, WITH ONE PEACEKEEPER OR A HUNDRED PEACEKEEPERS.
BECAUSE BATMAN IS DEAD AND THEY ARE GOING TO COME AND DRAG YOU OUT OF YOUR HOMES AND MAKE YOU BREATHE THIS POISON AIR.
THEY WANT YOU TO BE AFRAID, AND YOU SHOULD BE AFRAID.

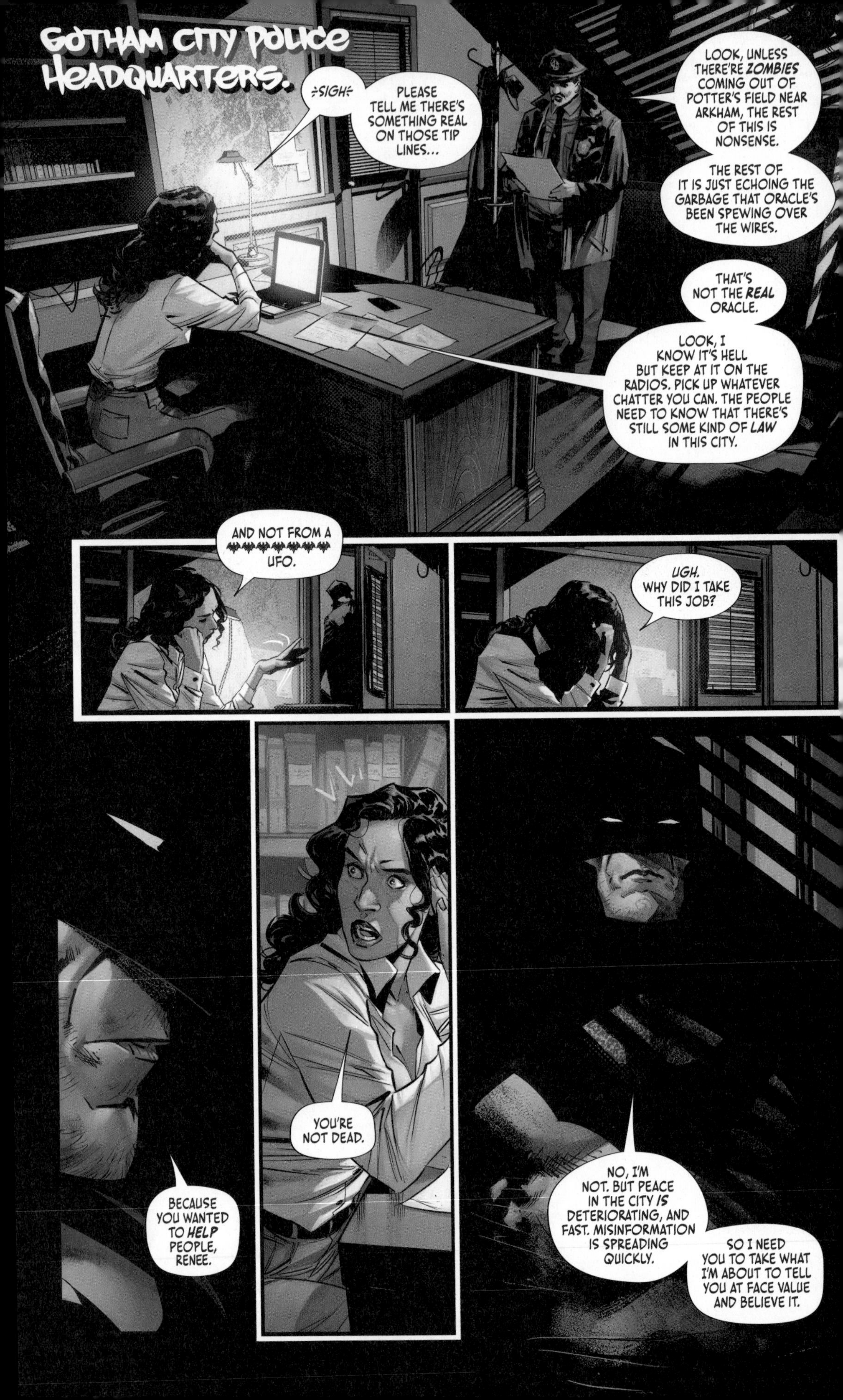
GOTHAM CITY POLICE HEADQUARTERS.
⸗SIGH⸗
PLEASE TELL ME THERE'S SOMETHING REAL ON THOSE TIP LINES...
LOOK, UNLESS THERE'RE *ZOMBIES* COMING OUT OF POTTER'S FIELD NEAR ARKHAM, THE REST OF THIS IS NONSENSE.
THE REST OF IT IS JUST ECHOING THE GARBAGE THAT ORACLE'S BEEN SPEWING OVER THE WIRES.
THAT'S NOT THE *REAL* ORACLE.
LOOK, I KNOW IT'S HELL BUT KEEP AT IT ON THE RADIOS. PICK UP WHATEVER CHATTER YOU CAN. THE PEOPLE NEED TO KNOW THAT THERE'S STILL SOME KIND OF *LAW* IN THIS CITY.
AND NOT FROM A UFO.
UGH. WHY DID I TAKE THIS JOB?
BECAUSE YOU WANTED TO *HELP* PEOPLE, RENEE.
YOU'RE NOT DEAD.
NO, I'M NOT. BUT PEACE IN THE CITY *IS* DETERIORATING, AND FAST. MISINFORMATION IS SPREADING QUICKLY.
SO I NEED YOU TO TAKE WHAT I'M ABOUT TO TELL YOU AT FACE VALUE AND BELIEVE IT.

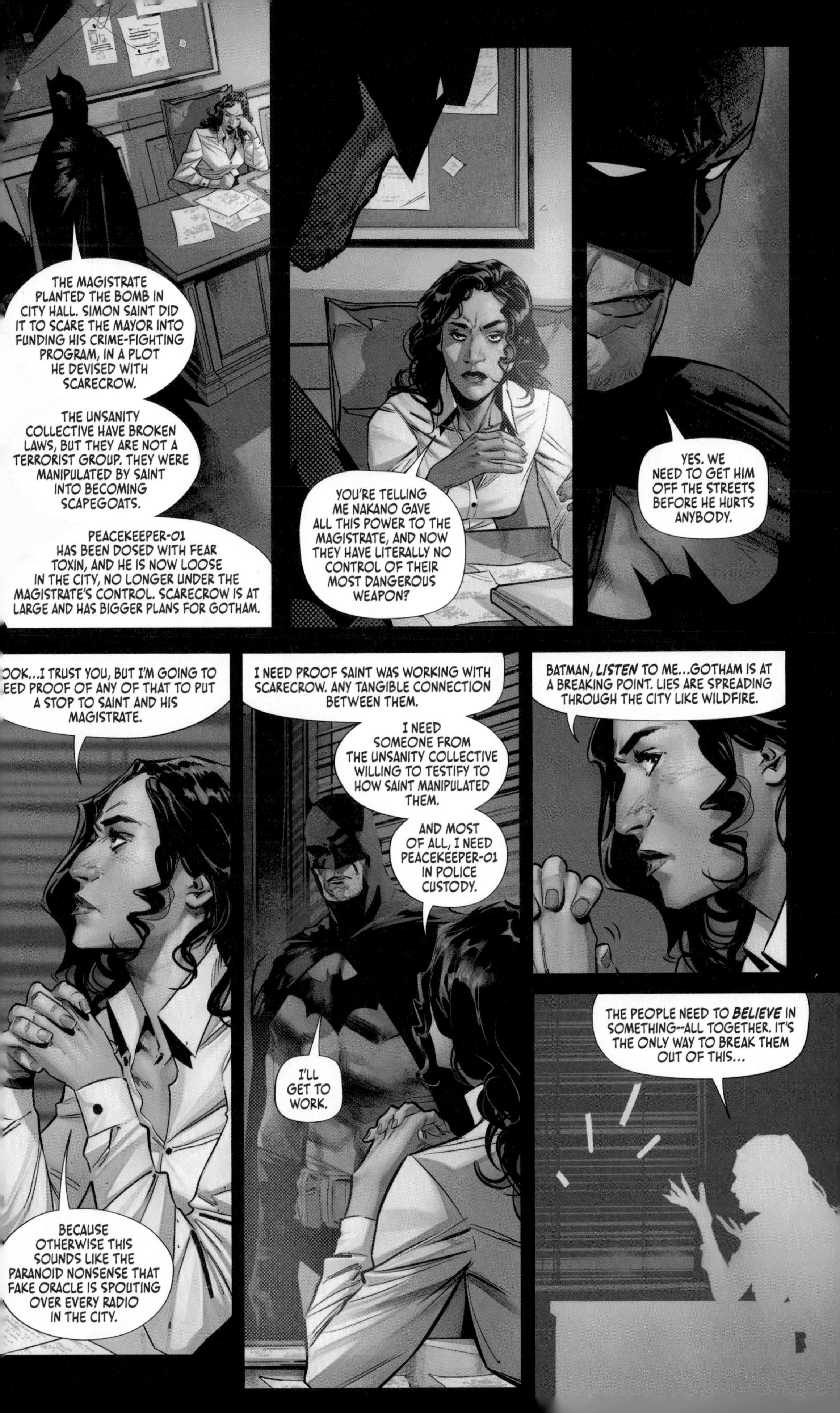
THE MAGISTRATE PLANTED THE BOMB IN CITY HALL. SIMON SAINT DID IT TO SCARE THE MAYOR INTO FUNDING HIS CRIME-FIGHTING PROGRAM, IN A PLOT HE DEVISED WITH SCARECROW.
THE UNSANITY COLLECTIVE HAVE BROKEN LAWS, BUT THEY ARE NOT A TERRORIST GROUP. THEY WERE MANIPULATED BY SAINT INTO BECOMING SCAPEGOATS.
PEACEKEEPER-01 HAS BEEN DOSED WITH FEAR TOXIN, AND HE IS NOW LOOSE IN THE CITY, NO LONGER UNDER THE MAGISTRATE'S CONTROL. SCARECROW IS AT LARGE AND HAS BIGGER PLANS FOR GOTHAM.
YOU'RE TELLING ME NAKANO GAVE ALL THIS POWER TO THE MAGISTRATE, AND NOW THEY HAVE LITERALLY NO CONTROL OF THEIR MOST DANGEROUS WEAPON?
YES. WE NEED TO GET HIM OFF THE STREETS BEFORE HE HURTS ANYBODY.
OOK...I TRUST YOU, BUT I'M GOING TO EED PROOF OF ANY OF THAT TO PUT A STOP TO SAINT AND HIS MAGISTRATE.
BECAUSE OTHERWISE THIS SOUNDS LIKE THE PARANOID NONSENSE THAT FAKE ORACLE IS SPOUTING OVER EVERY RADIO IN THE CITY.
I NEED PROOF SAINT WAS WORKING WITH SCARECROW. ANY TANGIBLE CONNECTION BETWEEN THEM.
I NEED SOMEONE FROM THE UNSANITY COLLECTIVE WILLING TO TESTIFY TO HOW SAINT MANIPULATED THEM.
AND MOST OF ALL, I NEED PEACEKEEPER-01 IN POLICE CUSTODY.
I'LL GET TO WORK.
BATMAN, LISTEN TO ME...GOTHAM IS AT A BREAKING POINT. LIES ARE SPREADING THROUGH THE CITY LIKE WILDFIRE.
THE PEOPLE NEED TO BELIEVE IN SOMETHING--ALL TOGETHER. IT'S THE ONLY WAY TO BREAK THEM OUT OF THIS...

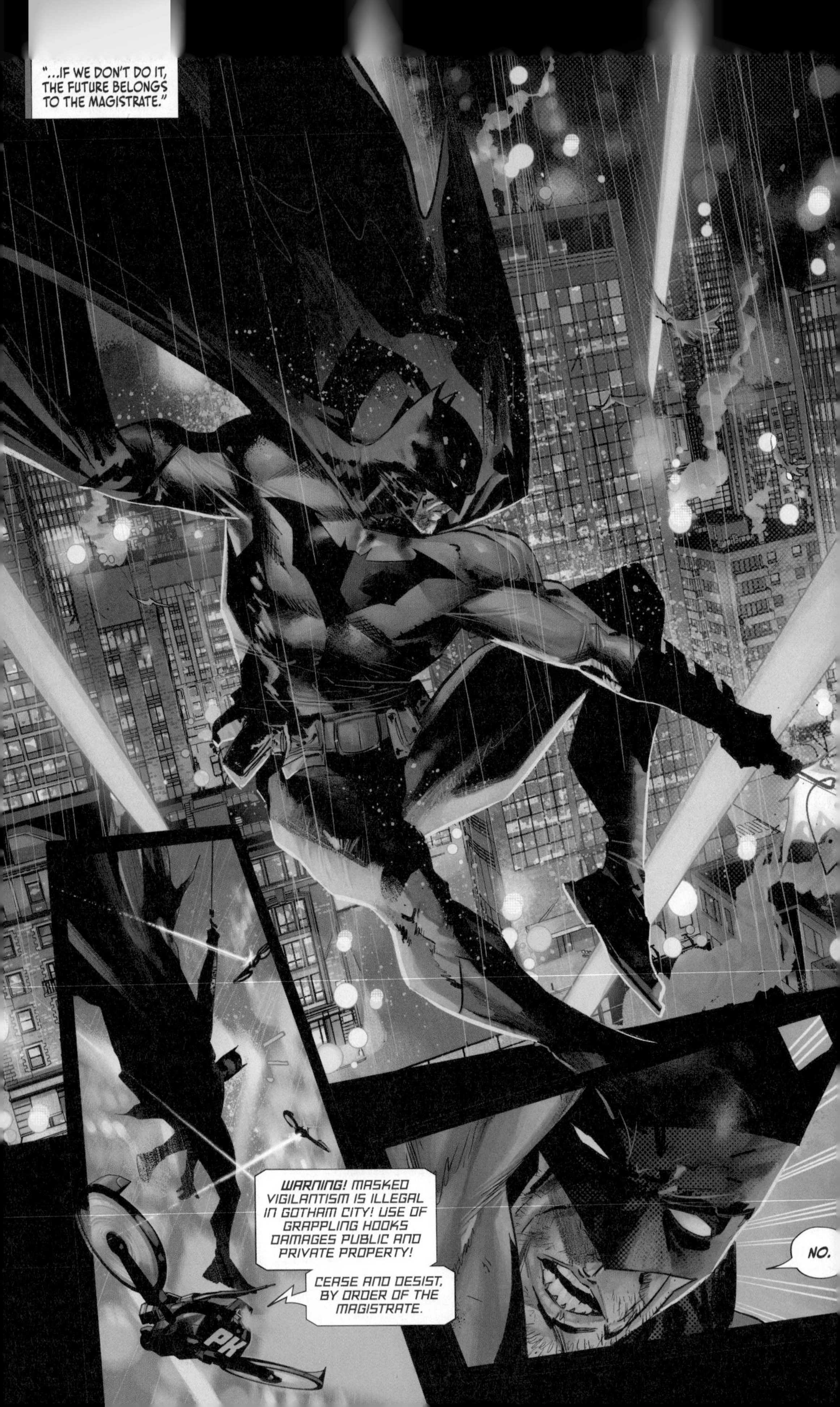
"...IF WE DON'T DO IT, THE FUTURE BELONGS TO THE MAGISTRATE."
WARNING! MASKED VIGILANTISM IS ILLEGAL IN GOTHAM CITY! USE OF GRAPPLING HOOKS DAMAGES PUBLIC AND PRIVATE PROPERTY!
CEASE AND DESIST, BY ORDER OF THE MAGISTRATE.
NO.
PK

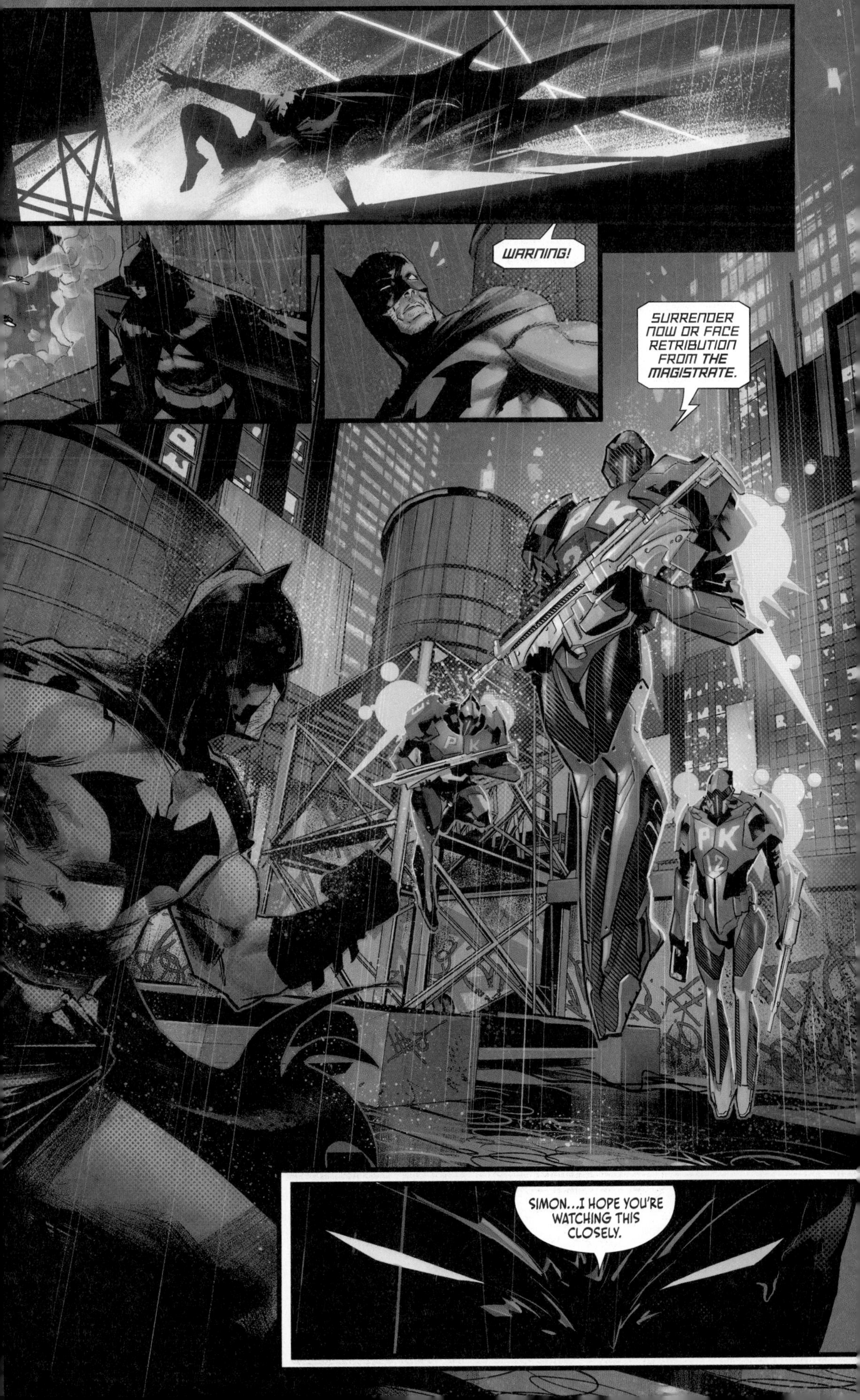
WARNING!
SURRENDER NOW OR FACE RETRIBUTION FROM THE MAGISTRATE.
SIMON...I HOPE YOU'RE WATCHING THIS CLOSELY.

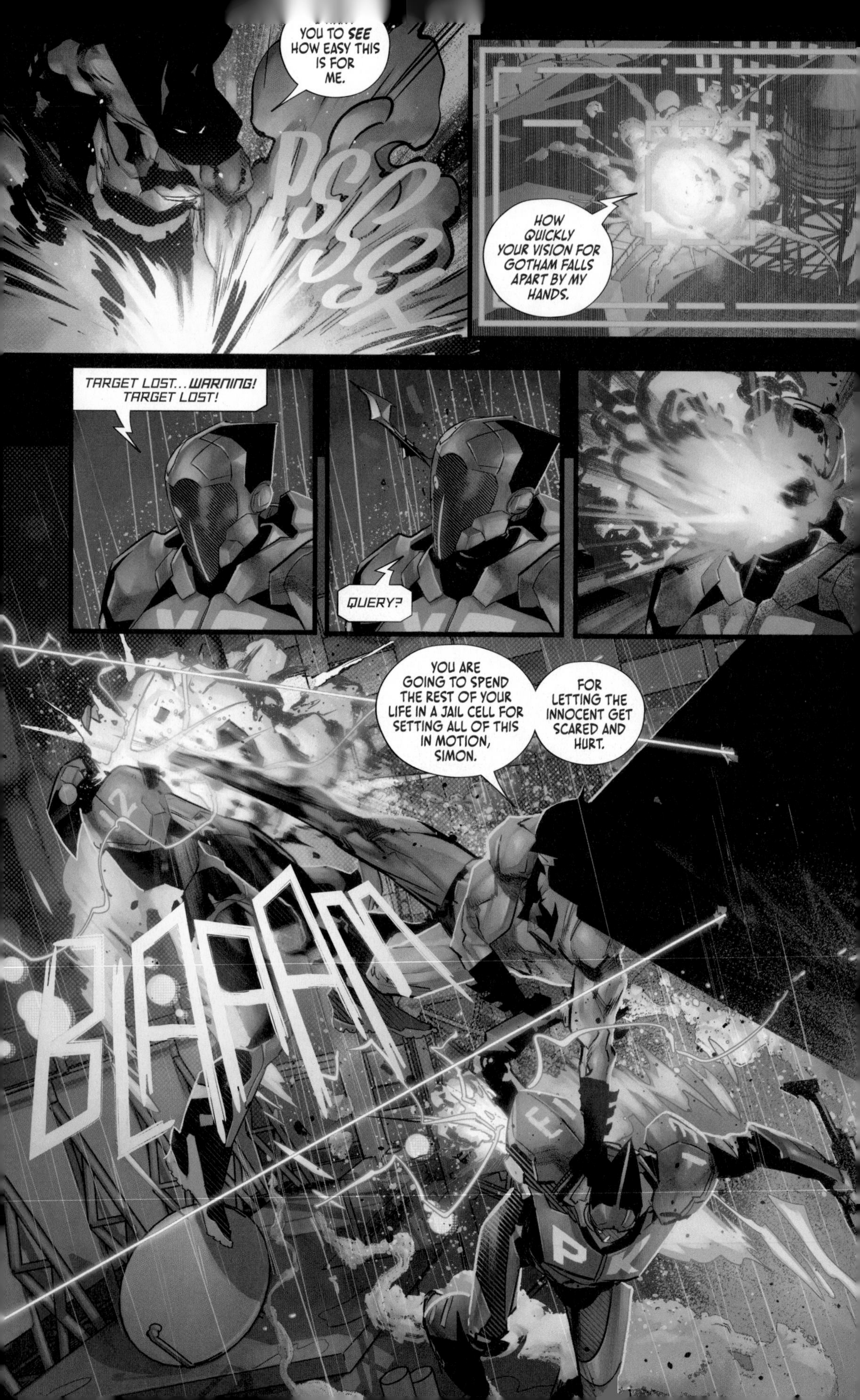
YOU TO SEE HOW EASY THIS IS FOR ME.
PSSSK
HOW QUICKLY YOUR VISION FOR GOTHAM FALLS APART BY MY HANDS.
TARGET LOST...WARNING! TARGET LOST!
QUERY?
YOU ARE GOING TO SPEND THE REST OF YOUR LIFE IN A JAIL CELL FOR SETTING ALL OF THIS IN MOTION, SIMON.
FOR LETTING THE INNOCENT GET SCARED AND HURT.
BLAAAM

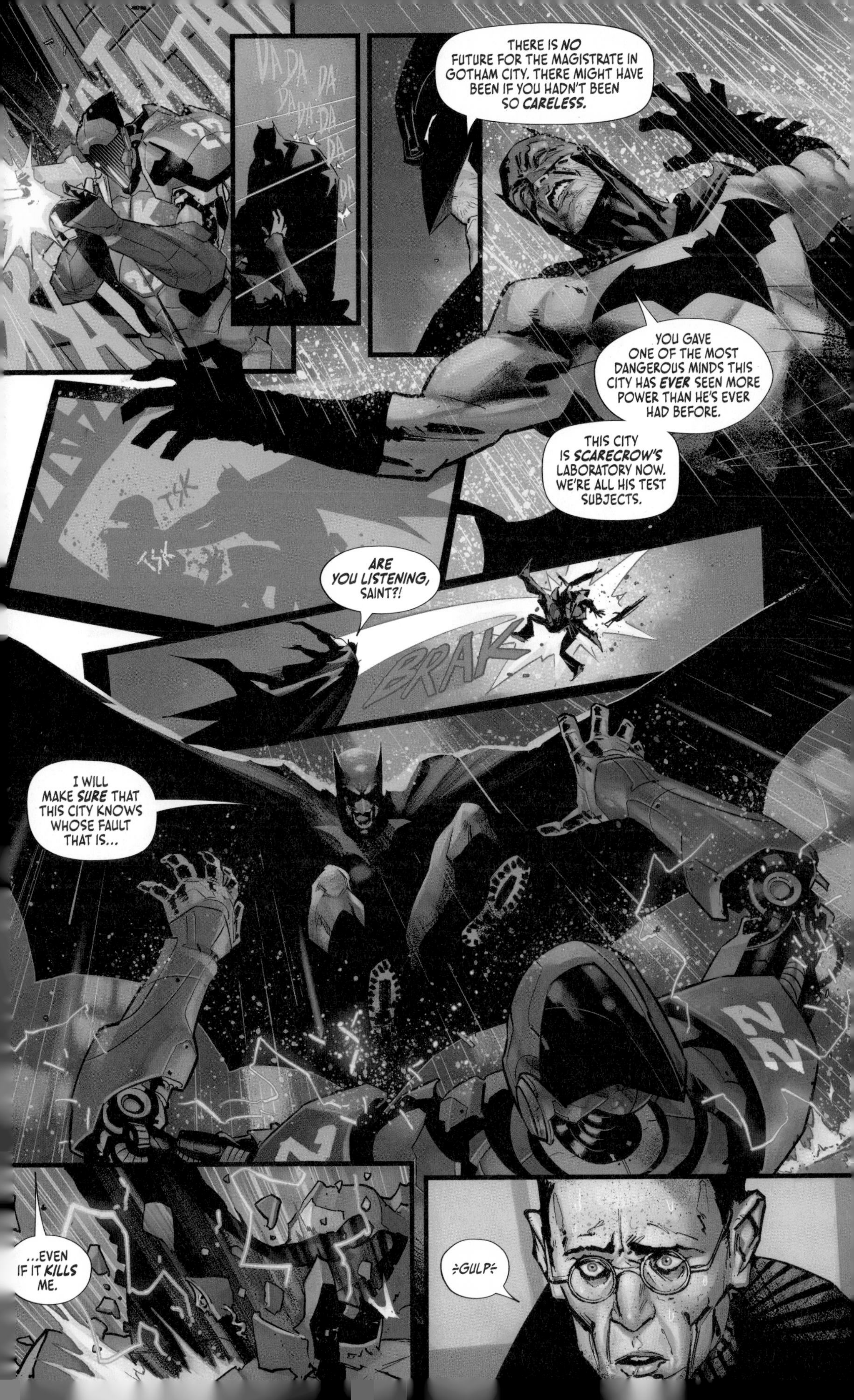

VA DA DA DA DA DA DA
THERE IS NO FUTURE FOR THE MAGISTRATE IN GOTHAM CITY. THERE MIGHT HAVE BEEN IF YOU HADN'T BEEN SO CARELESS.
YOU GAVE ONE OF THE MOST DANGEROUS MINDS THIS CITY HAS EVER SEEN MORE POWER THAN HE'S EVER HAD BEFORE.
THIS CITY IS SCARECROW'S LABORATORY NOW. WE'RE ALL HIS TEST SUBJECTS.
TSK
TSK
ARE YOU LISTENING, SAINT?!
BRAK
I WILL MAKE SURE THAT THIS CITY KNOWS WHOSE FAULT THAT IS...
...EVEN IF IT KILLS ME.
≑GULP≑

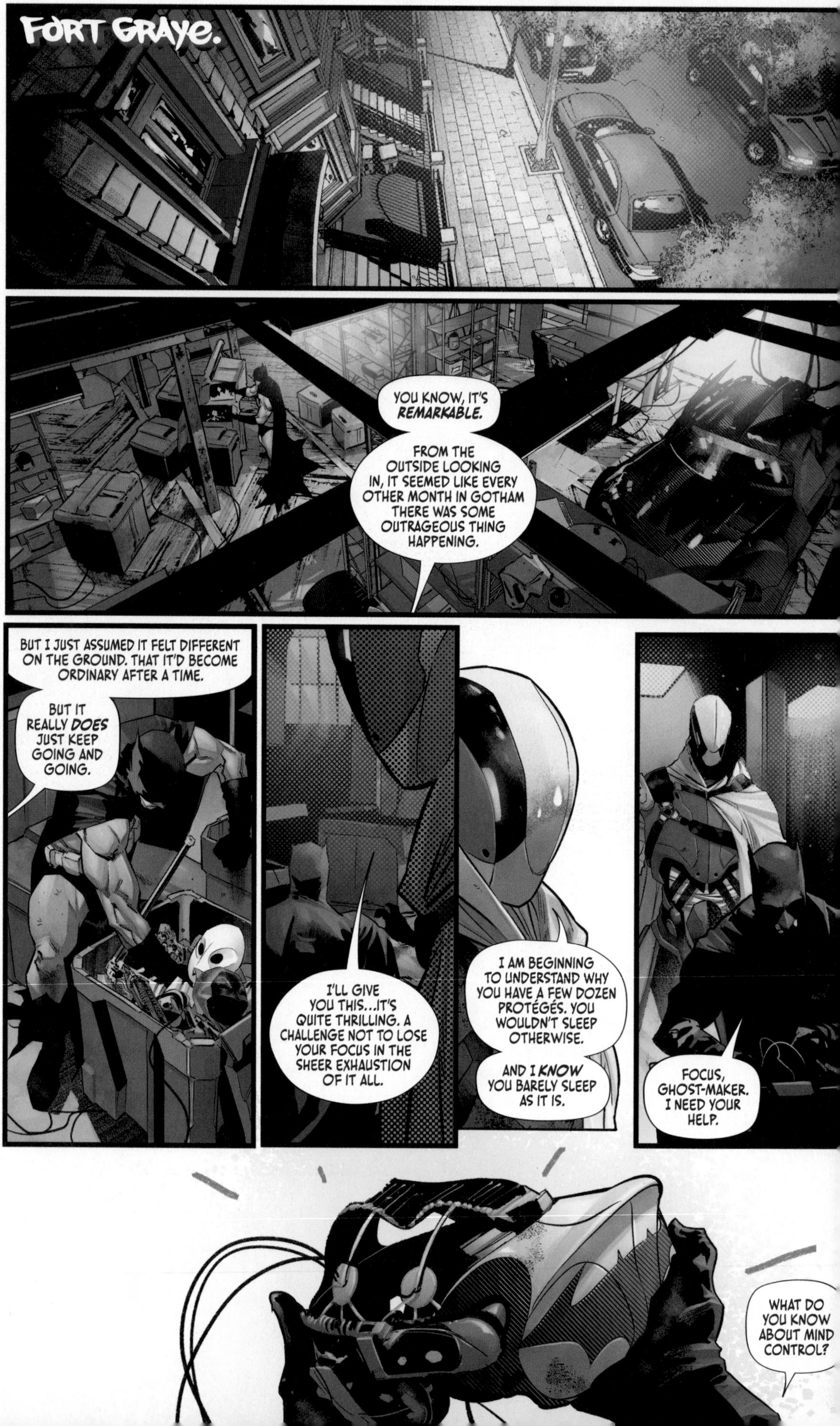
FORT GRAYE.
YOU KNOW, IT'S REMARKABLE.
FROM THE OUTSIDE LOOKING IN, IT SEEMED LIKE EVERY OTHER MONTH IN GOTHAM THERE WAS SOME OUTRAGEOUS THING HAPPENING.
BUT I JUST ASSUMED IT FELT DIFFERENT ON THE GROUND. THAT IT'D BECOME ORDINARY AFTER A TIME.
BUT IT REALLY DOES JUST KEEP GOING AND GOING.
I'LL GIVE YOU THIS...IT'S QUITE THRILLING. A CHALLENGE NOT TO LOSE YOUR FOCUS IN THE SHEER EXHAUSTION OF IT ALL.
I AM BEGINNING TO UNDERSTAND WHY YOU HAVE A FEW DOZEN PROTÉGÉS. YOU WOULDN'T SLEEP OTHERWISE.
AND I KNOW YOU BARELY SLEEP AS IT IS.
FOCUS, GHOST-MAKER. I NEED YOUR HELP.
WHAT DO YOU KNOW ABOUT MIND CONTROL?

NOW THERE'S A TRULY MAGNIFICENT QUESTION. BRAVA TO YOU.

WHEN I WAS IN ARKHAM, CRANE GOT INSIDE OF MY HEAD. IT WASN'T LIKE THE USUAL EXPERIENCE ON FEAR TOXIN.

IT WAS AS IF SOMEONE WAS PRESSING A FINGER ON THE FEAR CENTER OF MY BRAIN. I NEED TO KNOW IF THERE'S BEEN ANYTHING PLANTED IN MY MIND.

I'M TOO DANGEROUS TO BE IN THE FIELD IF I'VE BEEN COMPROMISED.

YOU REALLY DO HAVE A HIGH OPINION OF YOURSELF, DON'T YOU? AND PLEASE, WHAT ON EARTH ARE YOU WEARING?

I STARTED DEVELOPING THIS WITH CYBORG WORKING ON THE LEAGUE. A TECHNOLOGICAL APPROXIMATION OF SHORT-RANGE TELEPATHY BASED ON MOTHER BOX TECH.

YOU HAVE A BAT-MIND-CONTROL HELMET.

IF YOU THINK THAT'S OUT THERE, YOU SHOULD GO THROUGH THE REST OF THESE BOXES WITH ME SOMETIME.

IT'S VERY RUDIMENTARY. I WOULD CALL MARTIAN MANHUNTER IF I THOUGHT WE HAD THE TIME.

WHY ARE YOU ASKING ME?

THERE'S A RISK OF BURNING OUT THE MORAL CENTER OF THE USER'S BRAIN. ONLY A SMALL ONE. BUT ENOUGH.

AH, SO ONLY A PSYCHOPATH WILL DO.

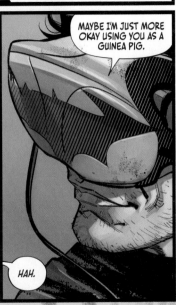

MAYBE I'M JUST MORE OKAY USING YOU AS A GUINEA PIG.

HAH.

JUST TO WARN YOU--I'M LIKELY TO PLANT A DEEP, SUBCONSCIOUS INFERIORITY COMPLEX OF MYSELF IN YOUR MIND.

NO, YOU WON'T.

WHY NOT?

YOU'D NEVER KNOW WHEN YOU BEAT ME HONESTLY, OR IF YOU ONLY BEAT ME WHEN CHEATING. NOW HURRY UP.

TESTING, ONE, TWO...

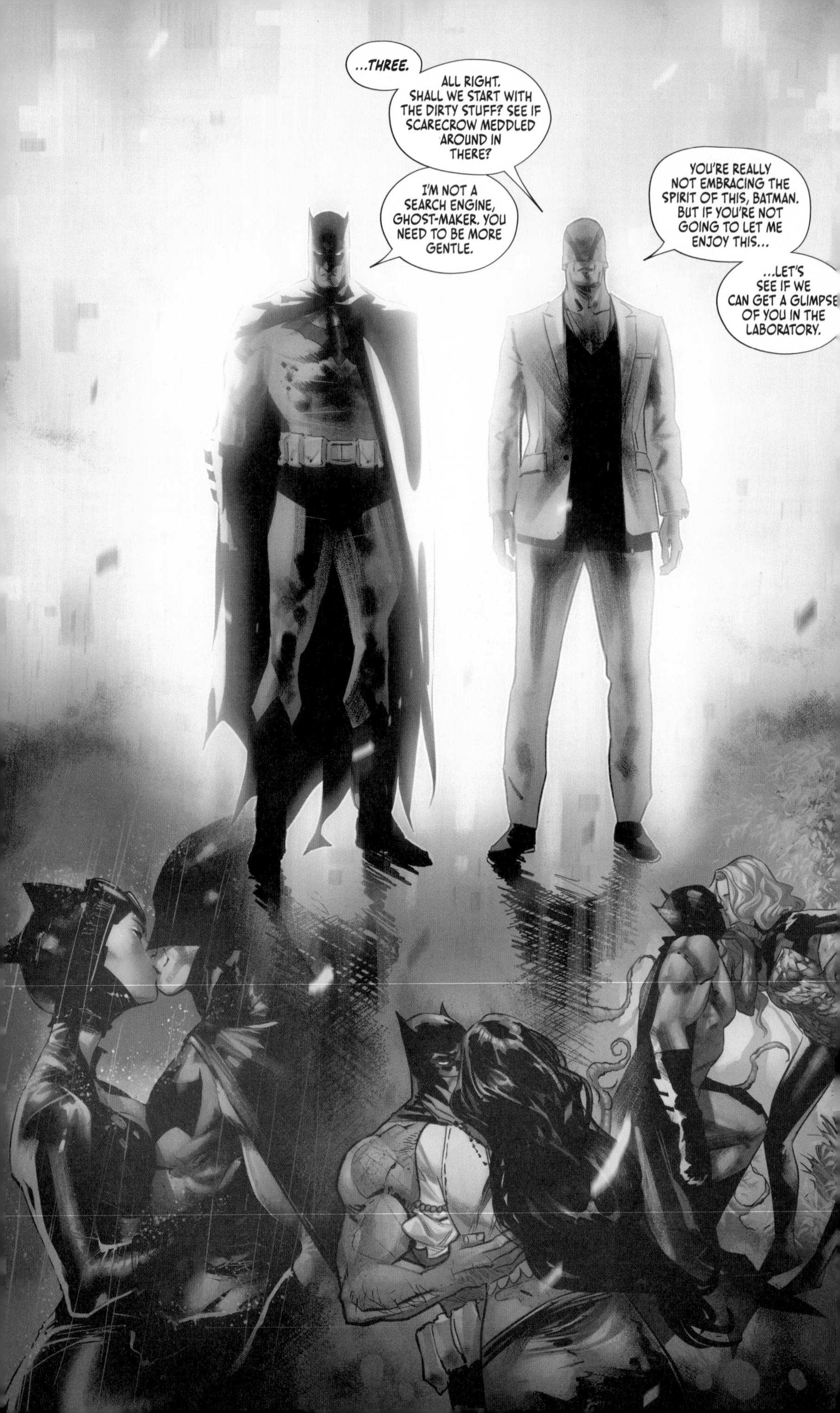
...THREE.
ALL RIGHT. SHALL WE START WITH THE DIRTY STUFF? SEE IF SCARECROW MEDDLED AROUND IN THERE?
I'M NOT A SEARCH ENGINE, GHOST-MAKER. YOU NEED TO BE MORE GENTLE.
YOU'RE REALLY NOT EMBRACING THE SPIRIT OF THIS, BATMAN. BUT IF YOU'RE NOT GOING TO LET ME ENJOY THIS...
...LET'S SEE IF WE CAN GET A GLIMPSE OF YOU IN THE LABORATORY.

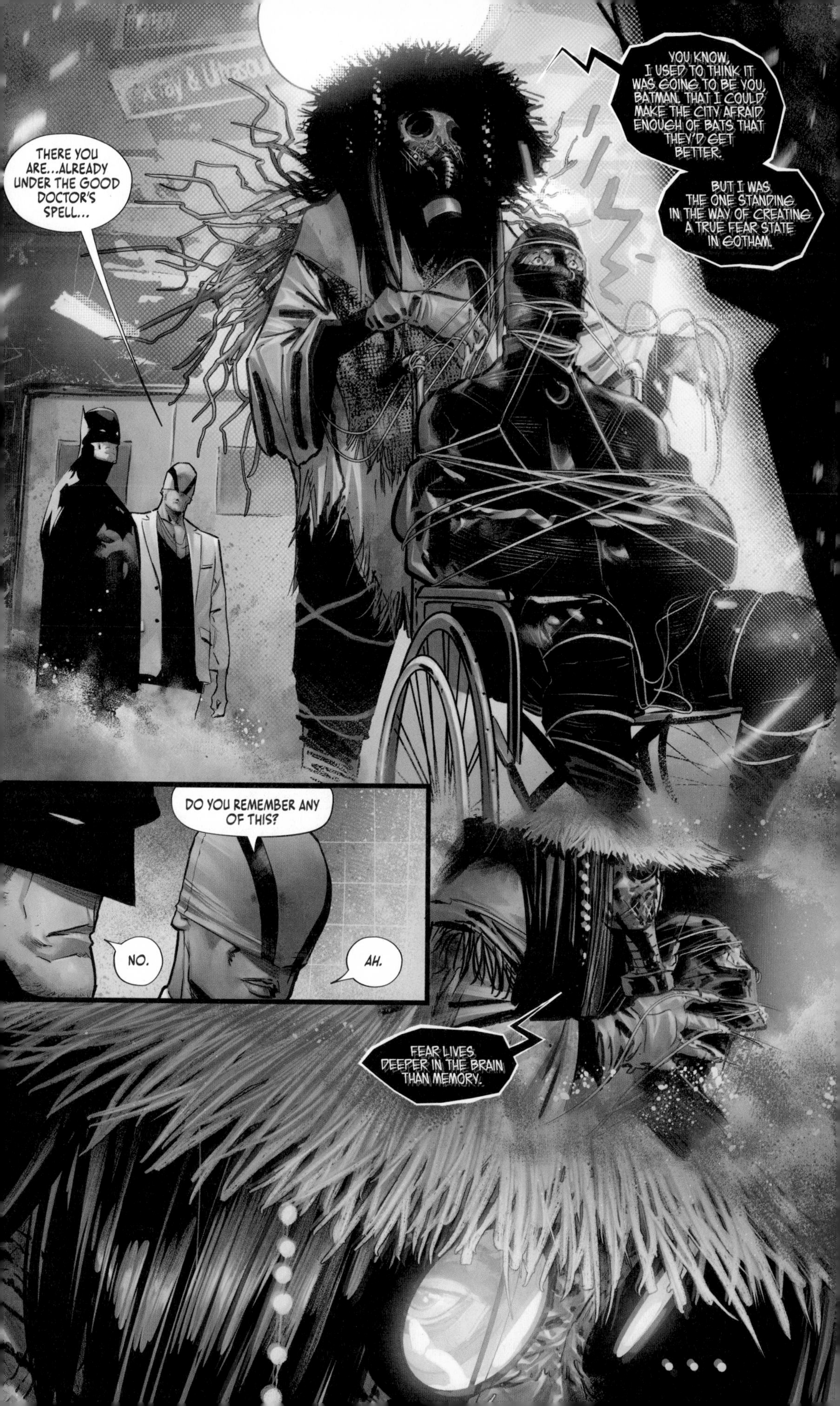
THERE YOU ARE...ALREADY UNDER THE GOOD DOCTOR'S SPELL...
YOU KNOW, I USED TO THINK IT WAS GOING TO BE YOU, BATMAN. THAT I COULD MAKE THE CITY AFRAID ENOUGH OF BATS THAT THEY'D GET BETTER.
BUT I WAS THE ONE STANDING IN THE WAY OF CREATING A TRUE FEAR STATE IN GOTHAM.
DO YOU REMEMBER ANY OF THIS?
NO.
AH.
FEAR LIVES DEEPER IN THE BRAIN THAN MEMORY.

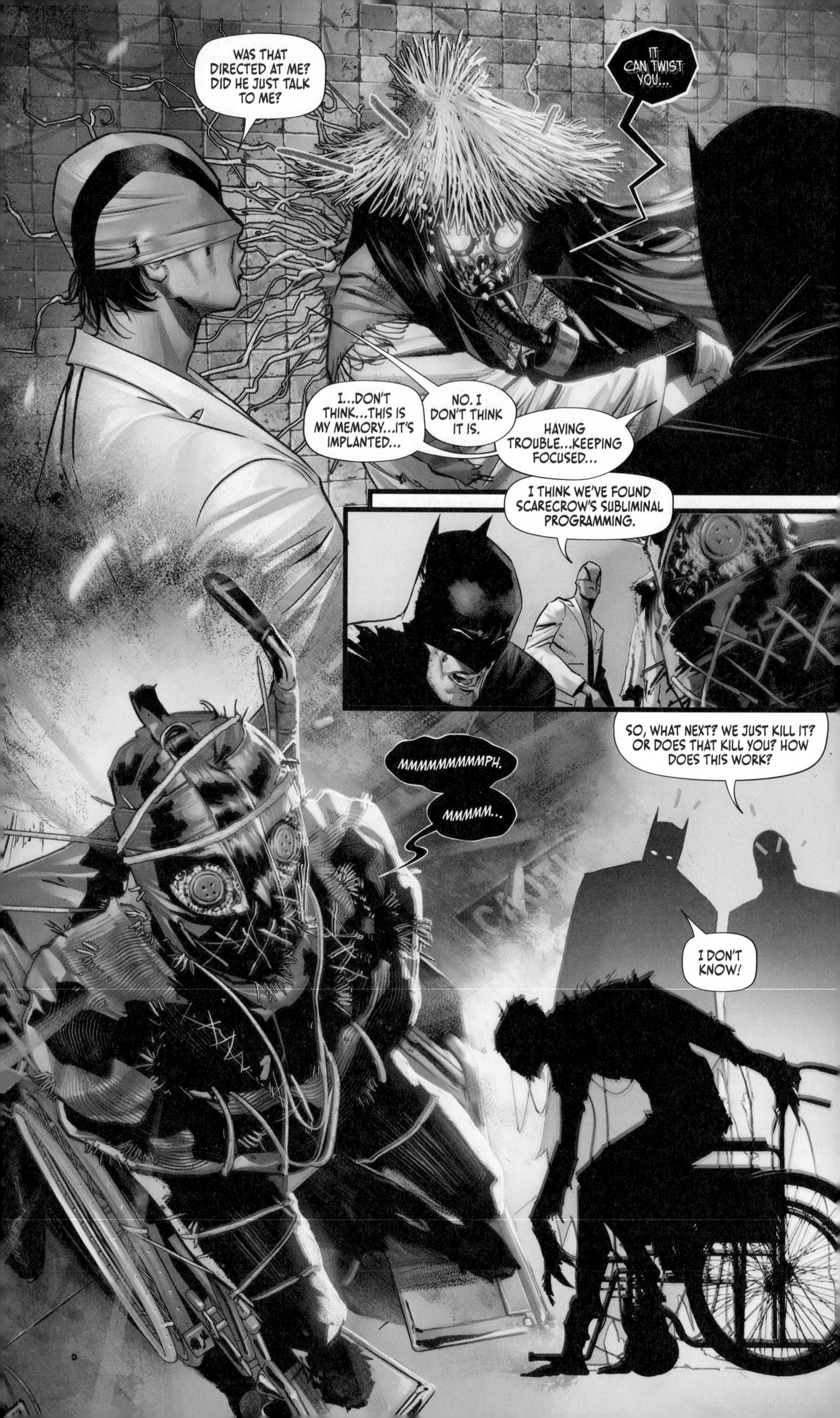
WAS THAT DIRECTED AT ME? DID HE JUST TALK TO ME?
IT CAN TWIST YOU...
I...DON'T THINK...THIS IS MY MEMORY...IT'S IMPLANTED...
NO. I DON'T THINK IT IS.
HAVING TROUBLE...KEEPING FOCUSED...
I THINK WE'VE FOUND SCARECROW'S SUBLIMINAL PROGRAMMING.
SO, WHAT NEXT? WE JUST KILL IT? OR DOES THAT KILL YOU? HOW DOES THIS WORK?
MMMMMMMMMPH.
MMMMM...
I DON'T KNOW!

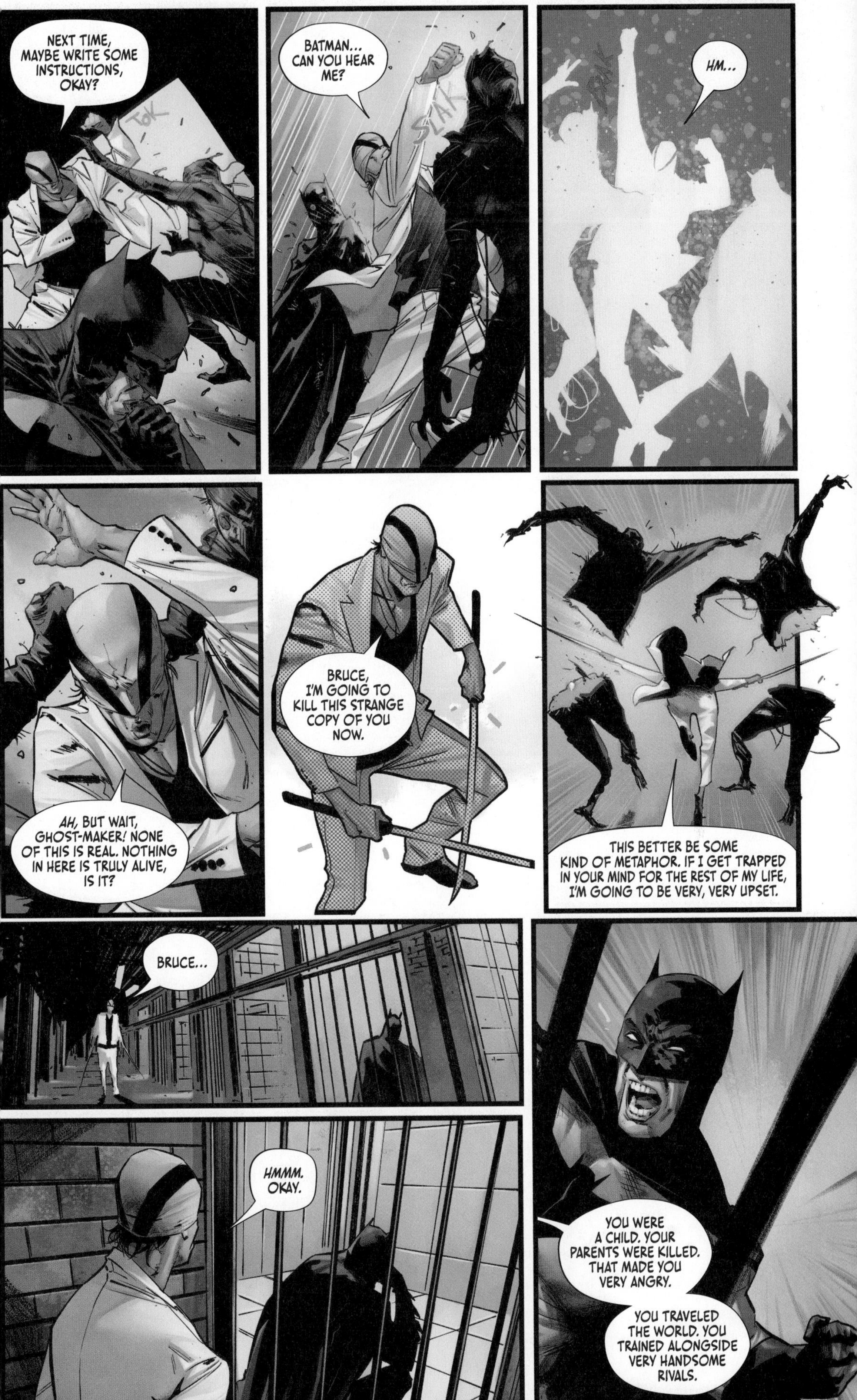
NEXT TIME, MAYBE WRITE SOME INSTRUCTIONS, OKAY?
TOK
BATMAN... CAN YOU HEAR ME?
SLAK
HM...
AH, BUT WAIT, GHOST-MAKER! NONE OF THIS IS REAL. NOTHING IN HERE IS TRULY ALIVE, IS IT?
BRUCE, I'M GOING TO KILL THIS STRANGE COPY OF YOU NOW.
THIS BETTER BE SOME KIND OF METAPHOR. IF I GET TRAPPED IN YOUR MIND FOR THE REST OF MY LIFE, I'M GOING TO BE VERY, VERY UPSET.
BRUCE...
HMMM. OKAY.
YOU WERE A CHILD. YOUR PARENTS WERE KILLED. THAT MADE YOU VERY ANGRY.
YOU TRAVELED THE WORLD. YOU TRAINED ALONGSIDE VERY HANDSOME RIVALS.

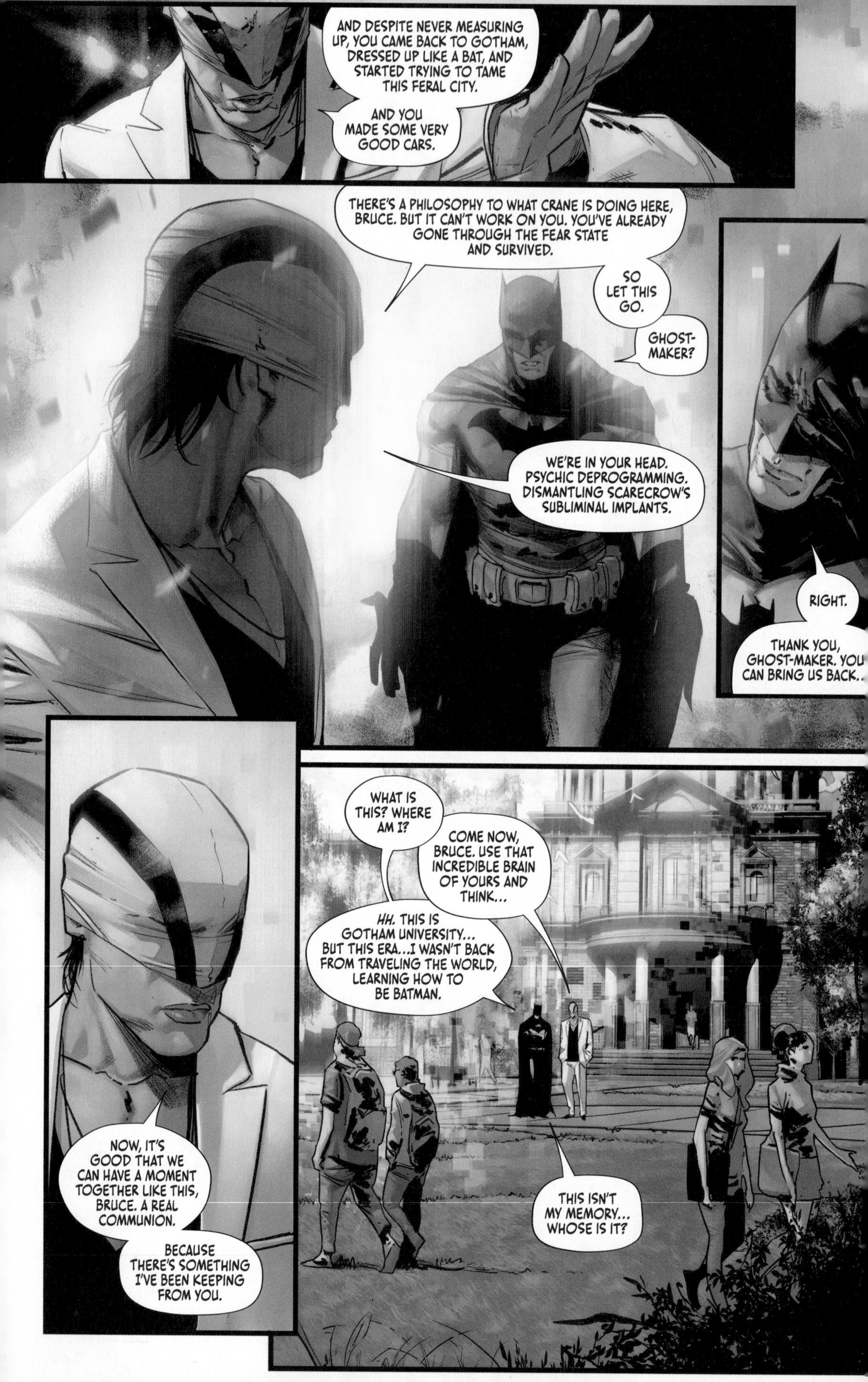
AND DESPITE NEVER MEASURING UP, YOU CAME BACK TO GOTHAM, DRESSED UP LIKE A BAT, AND STARTED TRYING TO TAME THIS FERAL CITY.
AND YOU MADE SOME VERY GOOD CARS.
THERE'S A PHILOSOPHY TO WHAT CRANE IS DOING HERE, BRUCE. BUT IT CAN'T WORK ON YOU. YOU'VE ALREADY GONE THROUGH THE FEAR STATE AND SURVIVED.
SO LET THIS GO.
GHOST-MAKER?
WE'RE IN YOUR HEAD. PSYCHIC DEPROGRAMMING. DISMANTLING SCARECROW'S SUBLIMINAL IMPLANTS.
RIGHT.
THANK YOU, GHOST-MAKER. YOU CAN BRING US BACK...
NOW, IT'S GOOD THAT WE CAN HAVE A MOMENT TOGETHER LIKE THIS, BRUCE. A REAL COMMUNION.
BECAUSE THERE'S SOMETHING I'VE BEEN KEEPING FROM YOU.
WHAT IS THIS? WHERE AM I?
COME NOW, BRUCE. USE THAT INCREDIBLE BRAIN OF YOURS AND THINK...
HH. THIS IS GOTHAM UNIVERSITY... BUT THIS ERA...I WASN'T BACK FROM TRAVELING THE WORLD, LEARNING HOW TO BE BATMAN.
THIS ISN'T MY MEMORY... WHOSE IS IT?

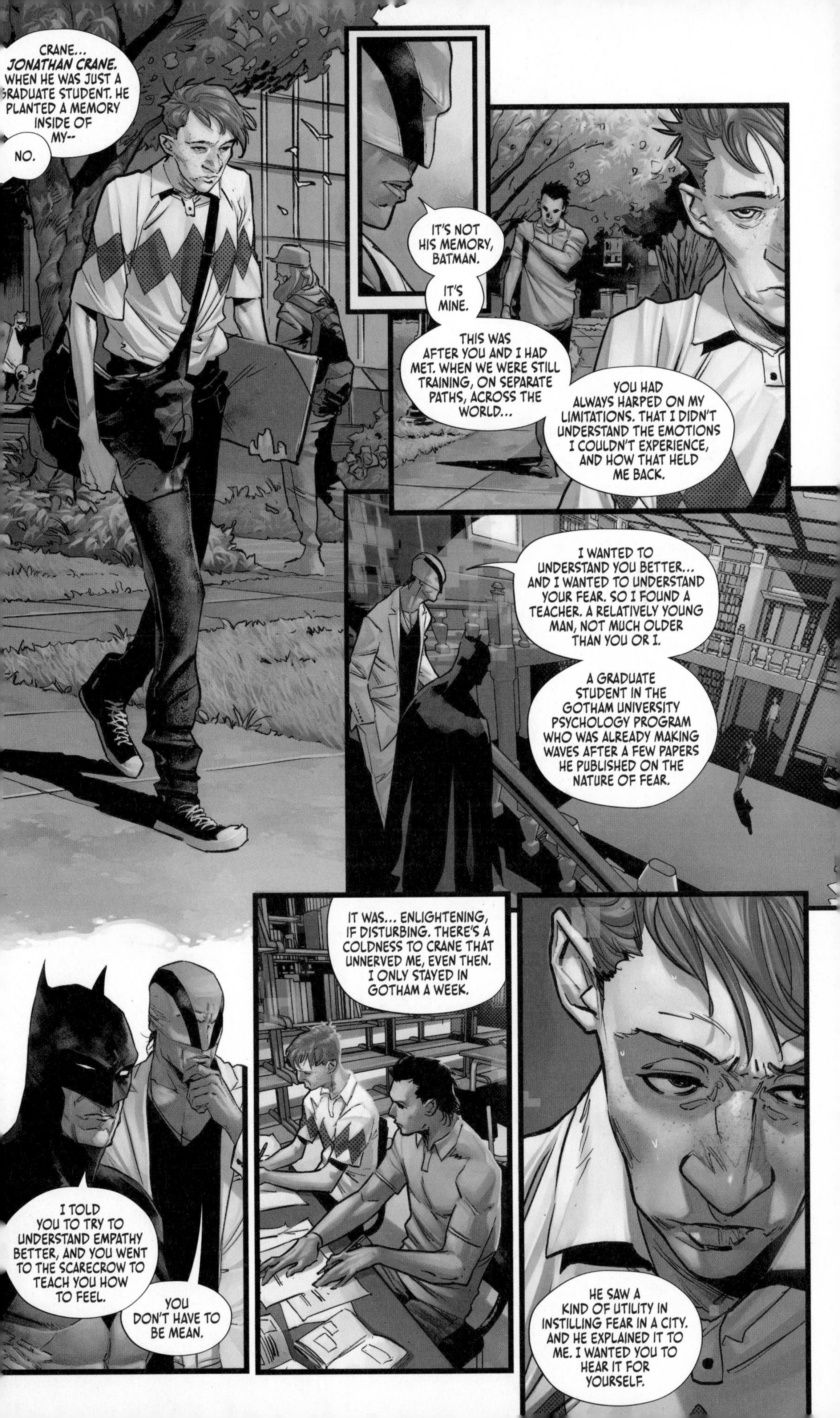
CRANE... *JONATHAN CRANE.* WHEN HE WAS JUST A GRADUATE STUDENT. HE PLANTED A MEMORY INSIDE OF MY--
NO.
IT'S NOT HIS MEMORY, BATMAN.
IT'S MINE.
THIS WAS AFTER YOU AND I HAD MET. WHEN WE WERE STILL TRAINING, ON SEPARATE PATHS, ACROSS THE WORLD...
YOU HAD ALWAYS HARPED ON MY LIMITATIONS. THAT I DIDN'T UNDERSTAND THE EMOTIONS I COULDN'T EXPERIENCE, AND HOW THAT HELD ME BACK.
I WANTED TO UNDERSTAND YOU BETTER... AND I WANTED TO UNDERSTAND YOUR FEAR. SO I FOUND A TEACHER. A RELATIVELY YOUNG MAN, NOT MUCH OLDER THAN YOU OR I.
A GRADUATE STUDENT IN THE GOTHAM UNIVERSITY PSYCHOLOGY PROGRAM WHO WAS ALREADY MAKING WAVES AFTER A FEW PAPERS HE PUBLISHED ON THE NATURE OF FEAR.
I TOLD YOU TO TRY TO UNDERSTAND EMPATHY BETTER, AND YOU WENT TO THE SCARECROW TO TEACH YOU HOW TO FEEL.
YOU DON'T HAVE TO BE MEAN.
IT WAS... ENLIGHTENING, IF DISTURBING. THERE'S A COLDNESS TO CRANE THAT UNNERVED ME, EVEN THEN. I ONLY STAYED IN GOTHAM A WEEK.
HE SAW A KIND OF UTILITY IN INSTILLING FEAR IN A CITY. AND HE EXPLAINED IT TO ME. I WANTED YOU TO HEAR IT FOR YOURSELF.

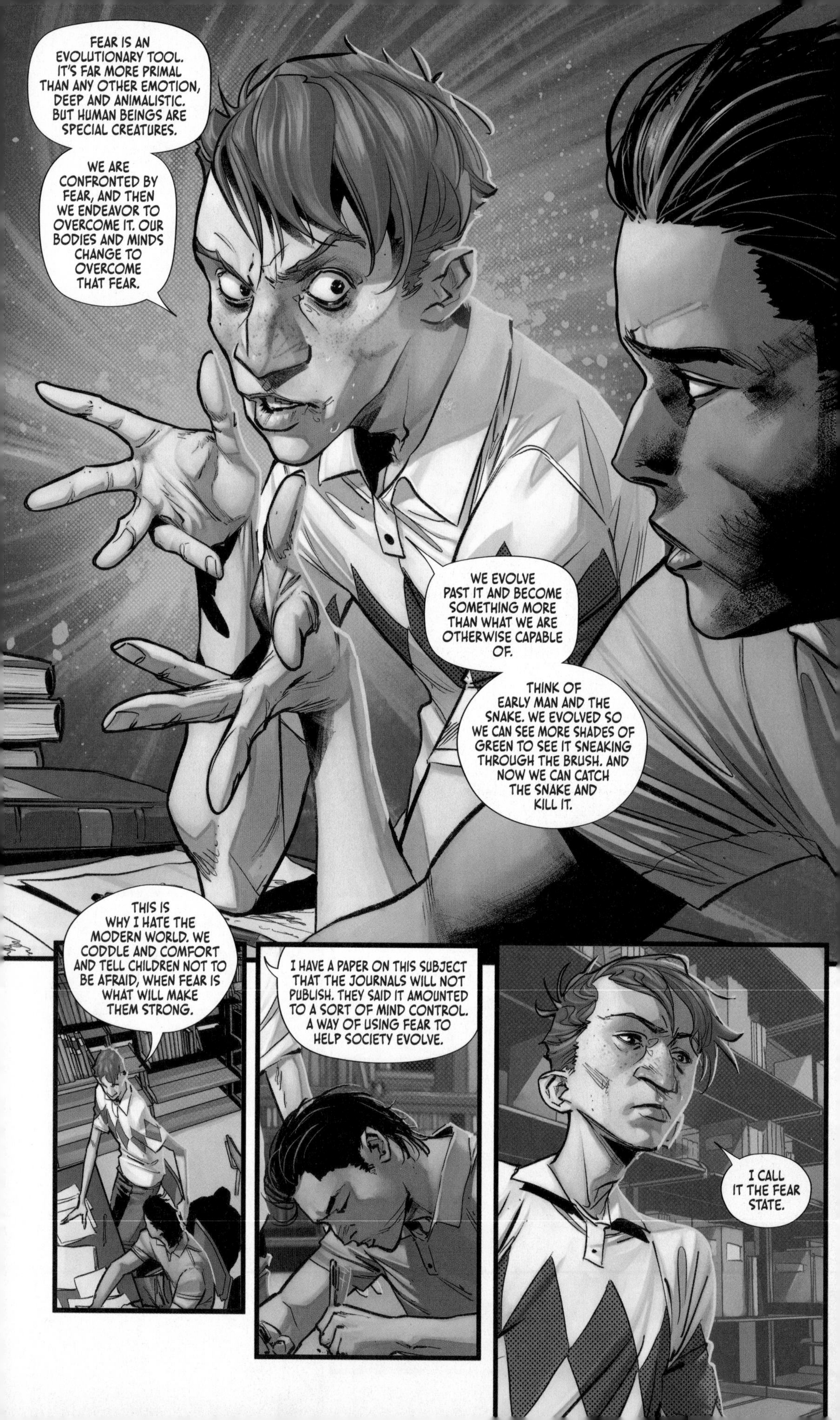

FEAR IS AN EVOLUTIONARY TOOL. IT'S FAR MORE PRIMAL THAN ANY OTHER EMOTION, DEEP AND ANIMALISTIC. BUT HUMAN BEINGS ARE SPECIAL CREATURES.
WE ARE CONFRONTED BY FEAR, AND THEN WE ENDEAVOR TO OVERCOME IT. OUR BODIES AND MINDS CHANGE TO OVERCOME THAT FEAR.
WE EVOLVE PAST IT AND BECOME SOMETHING MORE THAN WHAT WE ARE OTHERWISE CAPABLE OF.
THINK OF EARLY MAN AND THE SNAKE. WE EVOLVED SO WE CAN SEE MORE SHADES OF GREEN TO SEE IT SNEAKING THROUGH THE BRUSH. AND NOW WE CAN CATCH THE SNAKE AND KILL IT.
THIS IS WHY I HATE THE MODERN WORLD. WE CODDLE AND COMFORT AND TELL CHILDREN NOT TO BE AFRAID, WHEN FEAR IS WHAT WILL MAKE THEM STRONG.
I HAVE A PAPER ON THIS SUBJECT THAT THE JOURNALS WILL NOT PUBLISH. THEY SAID IT AMOUNTED TO A SORT OF MIND CONTROL. A WAY OF USING FEAR TO HELP SOCIETY EVOLVE.
I CALL IT THE FEAR STATE.

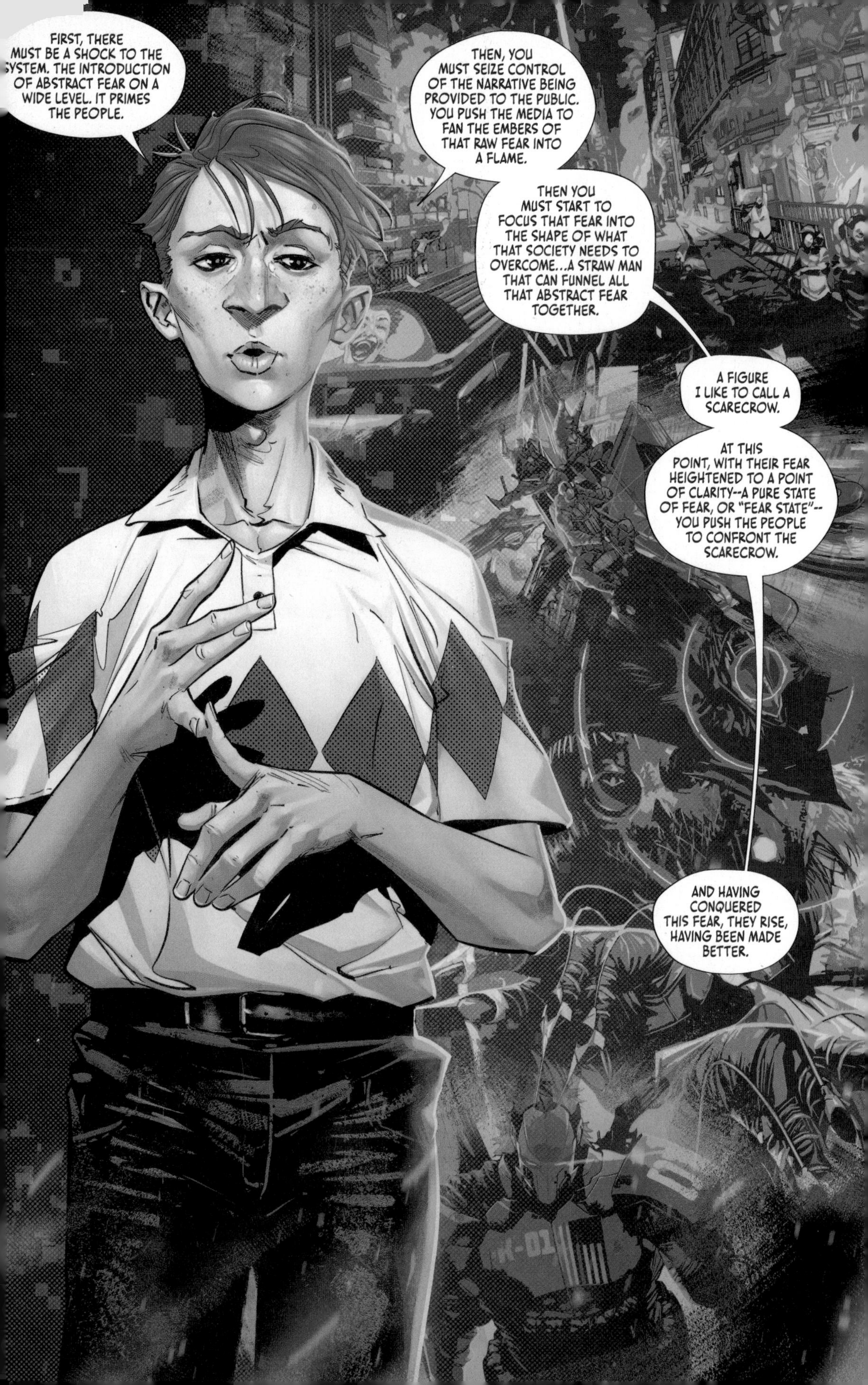
FIRST, THERE MUST BE A SHOCK TO THE SYSTEM. THE INTRODUCTION OF ABSTRACT FEAR ON A WIDE LEVEL. IT PRIMES THE PEOPLE.
THEN, YOU MUST SEIZE CONTROL OF THE NARRATIVE BEING PROVIDED TO THE PUBLIC. YOU PUSH THE MEDIA TO FAN THE EMBERS OF THAT RAW FEAR INTO A FLAME.
THEN YOU MUST START TO FOCUS THAT FEAR INTO THE SHAPE OF WHAT THAT SOCIETY NEEDS TO OVERCOME...A STRAW MAN THAT CAN FUNNEL ALL THAT ABSTRACT FEAR TOGETHER.
A FIGURE I LIKE TO CALL A SCARECROW.
AT THIS POINT, WITH THEIR FEAR HEIGHTENED TO A POINT OF CLARITY--A PURE STATE OF FEAR, OR "FEAR STATE"--YOU PUSH THE PEOPLE TO CONFRONT THE SCARECROW.
AND HAVING CONQUERED THIS FEAR, THEY RISE, HAVING BEEN MADE BETTER.

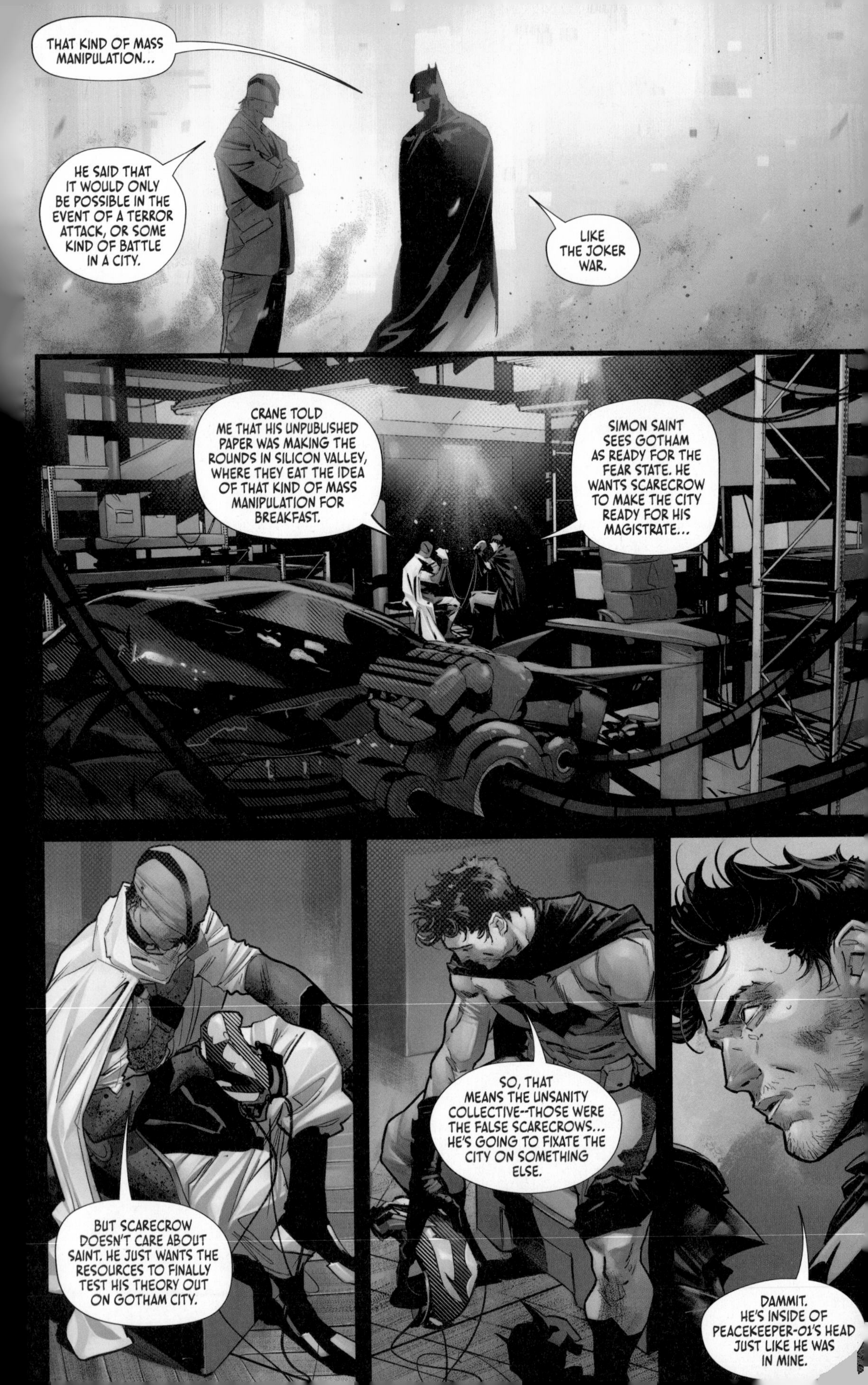
THAT KIND OF MASS MANIPULATION...
HE SAID THAT IT WOULD ONLY BE POSSIBLE IN THE EVENT OF A TERROR ATTACK, OR SOME KIND OF BATTLE IN A CITY.
LIKE THE JOKER WAR.
CRANE TOLD ME THAT HIS UNPUBLISHED PAPER WAS MAKING THE ROUNDS IN SILICON VALLEY, WHERE THEY EAT THE IDEA OF THAT KIND OF MASS MANIPULATION FOR BREAKFAST.
SIMON SAINT SEES GOTHAM AS READY FOR THE FEAR STATE. HE WANTS SCARECROW TO MAKE THE CITY READY FOR HIS MAGISTRATE...
BUT SCARECROW DOESN'T CARE ABOUT SAINT. HE JUST WANTS THE RESOURCES TO FINALLY TEST HIS THEORY OUT ON GOTHAM CITY.
SO, THAT MEANS THE UNSANITY COLLECTIVE--THOSE WERE THE FALSE SCARECROWS... HE'S GOING TO FIXATE THE CITY ON SOMETHING ELSE.
DAMMIT. HE'S INSIDE OF PEACEKEEPER-01'S HEAD JUST LIKE HE WAS IN MINE.

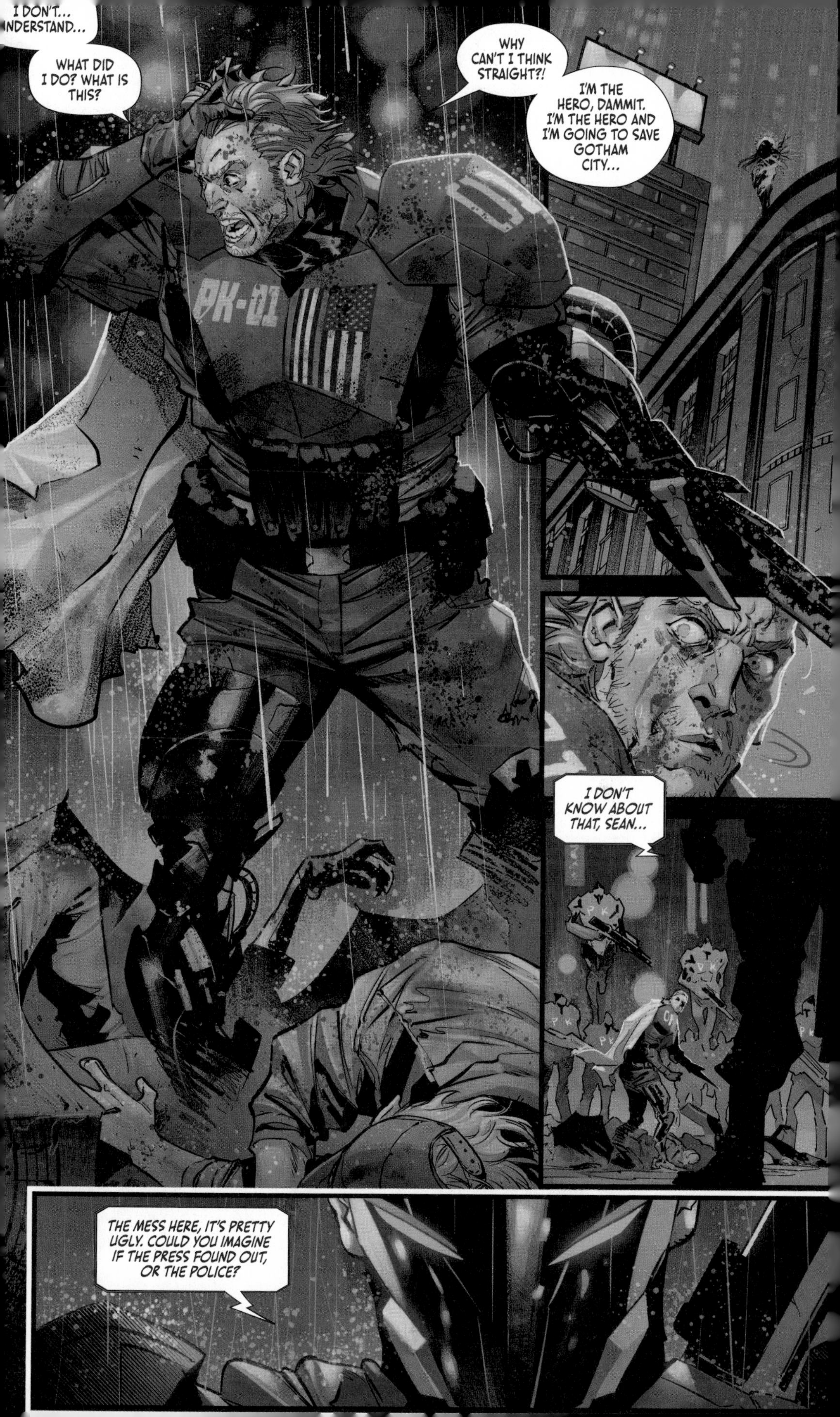
I DON'T... UNDERSTAND...
WHAT DID I DO? WHAT IS THIS?
WHY CAN'T I THINK STRAIGHT?!
I'M THE HERO, DAMMIT. I'M THE HERO AND I'M GOING TO SAVE GOTHAM CITY...
PK-01
I DON'T KNOW ABOUT THAT, SEAN...
THE MESS HERE, IT'S PRETTY UGLY. COULD YOU IMAGINE IF THE PRESS FOUND OUT, OR THE POLICE?

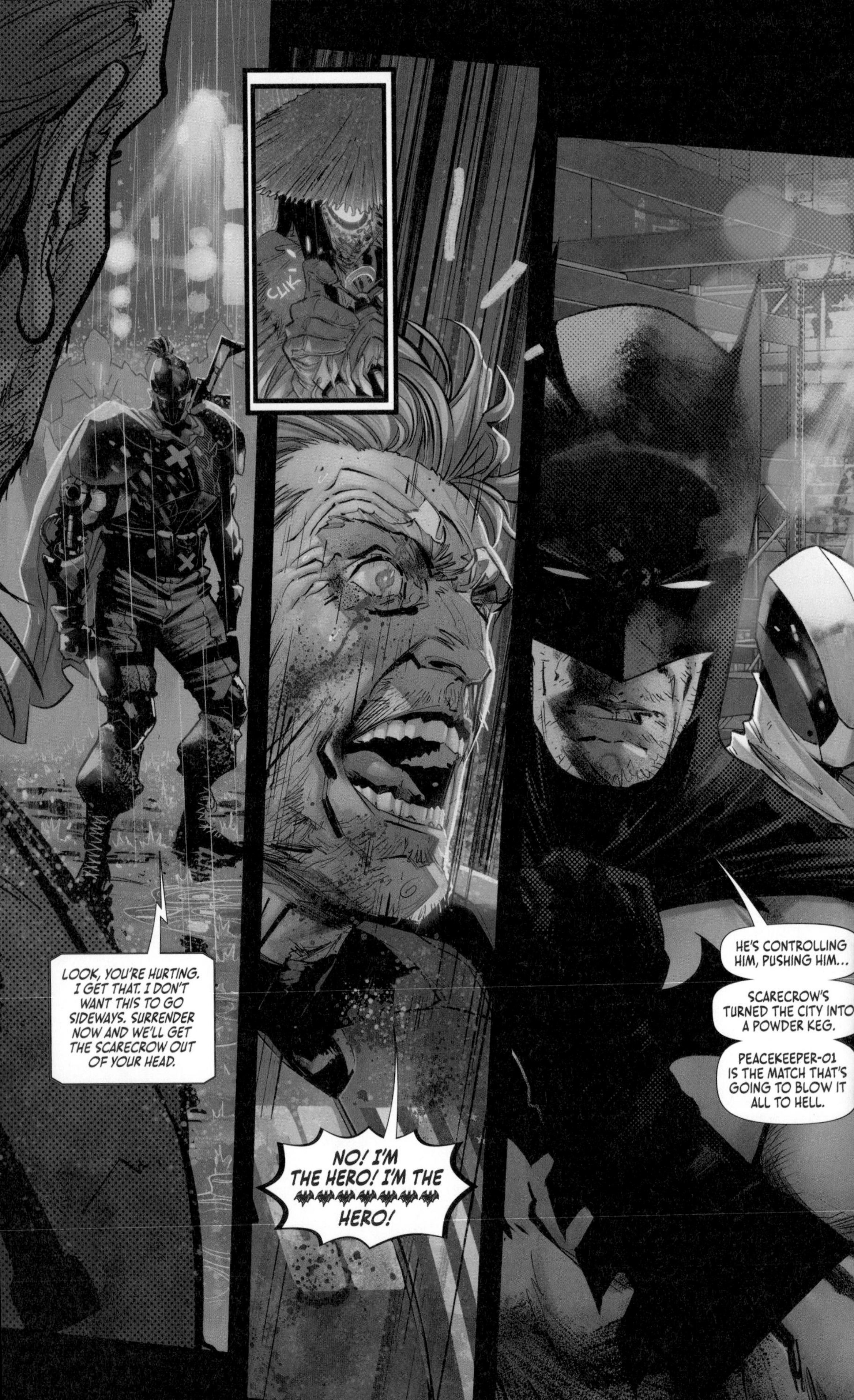
CLIK
LOOK, YOU'RE HURTING. I GET THAT. I DON'T WANT THIS TO GO SIDEWAYS. SURRENDER NOW AND WE'LL GET THE SCARECROW OUT OF YOUR HEAD.
NO! I'M THE HERO! I'M THE [symbols] HERO!
HE'S CONTROLLING HIM, PUSHING HIM...
SCARECROW'S TURNED THE CITY INTO A POWDER KEG.
PEACEKEEPER-01 IS THE MATCH THAT'S GOING TO BLOW IT ALL TO HELL.

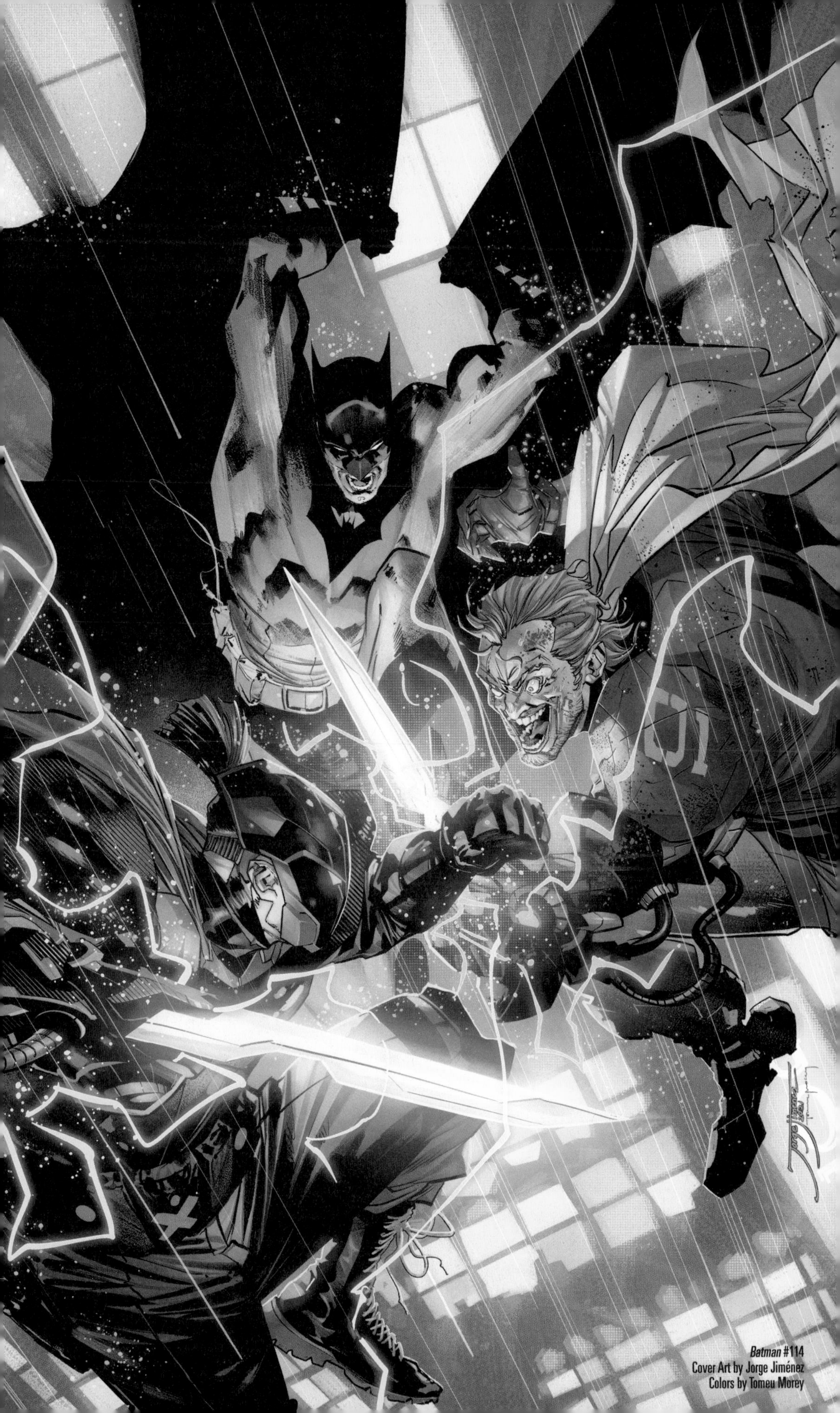

Batman #114
Cover Art by Jorge Jiménez
Colors by Tomeu Morey

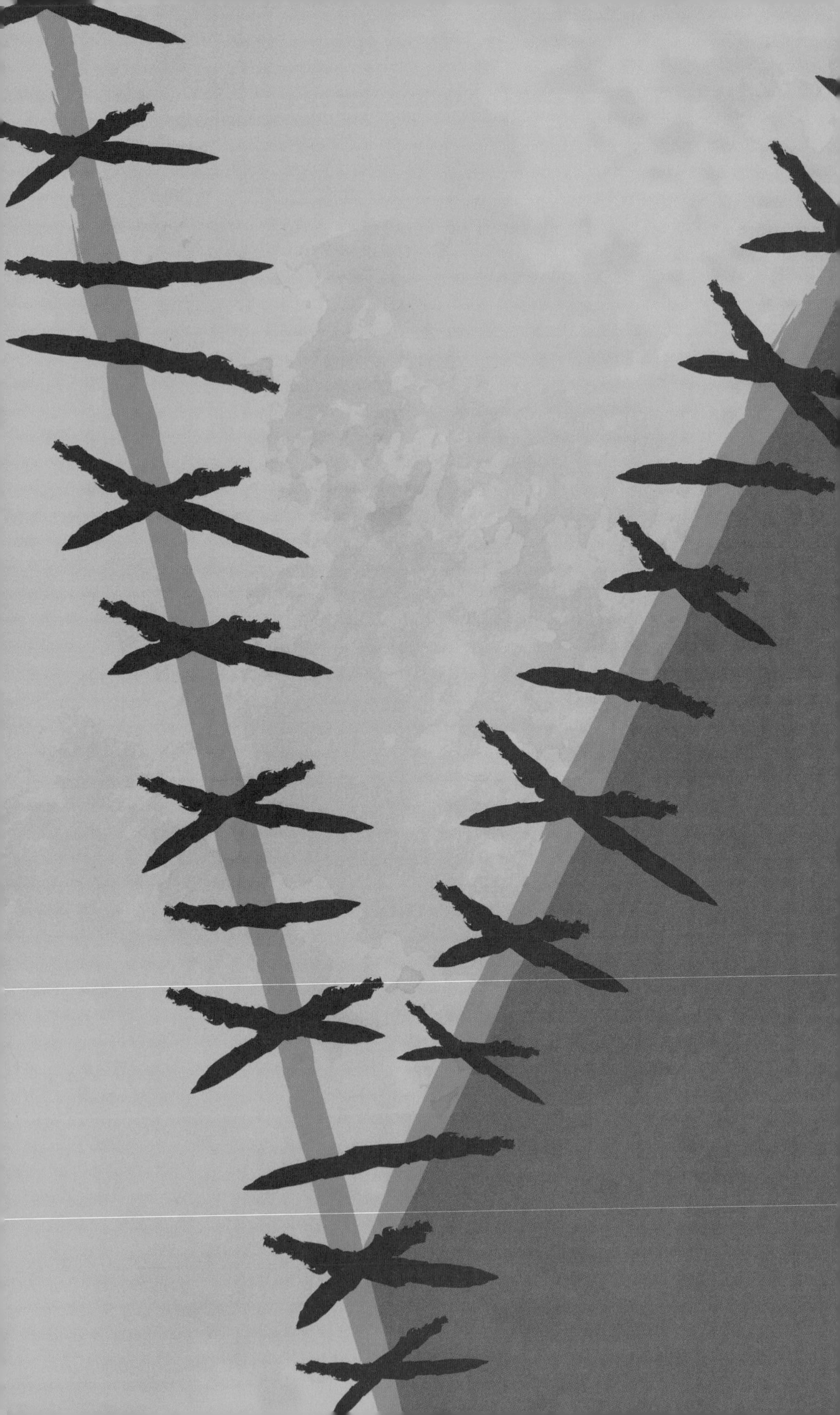

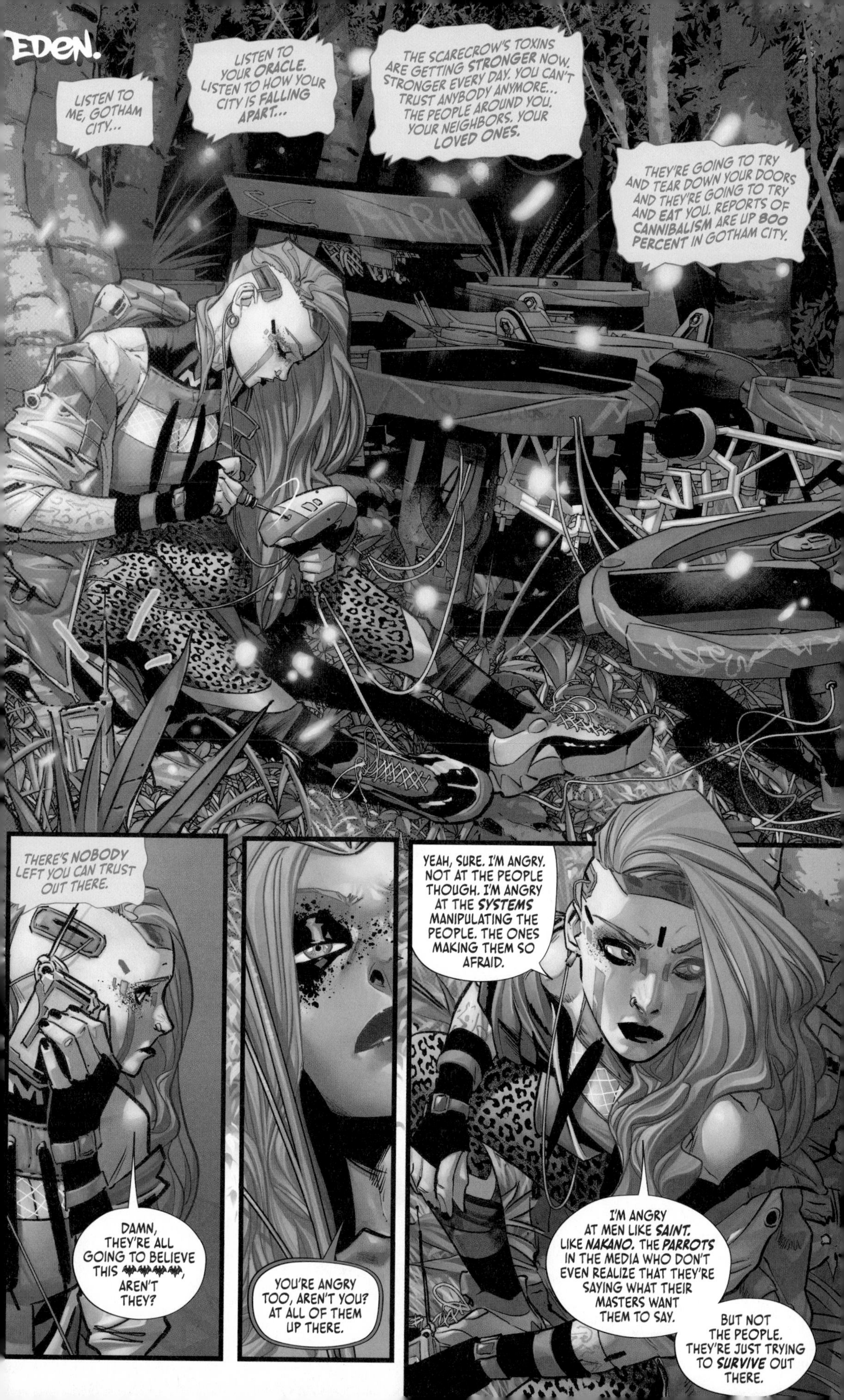
EDEN.
LISTEN TO ME, GOTHAM CITY...
LISTEN TO YOUR ORACLE. LISTEN TO HOW YOUR CITY IS FALLING APART...
THE SCARECROW'S TOXINS ARE GETTING STRONGER NOW. STRONGER EVERY DAY. YOU CAN'T TRUST ANYBODY ANYMORE... THE PEOPLE AROUND YOU. YOUR NEIGHBORS. YOUR LOVED ONES.
THEY'RE GOING TO TRY AND TEAR DOWN YOUR DOORS AND THEY'RE GOING TO TRY AND EAT YOU. REPORTS OF CANNIBALISM ARE UP 800 PERCENT IN GOTHAM CITY.
THERE'S NOBODY LEFT YOU CAN TRUST OUT THERE.
DAMN, THEY'RE ALL GOING TO BELIEVE THIS [symbols], AREN'T THEY?
YOU'RE ANGRY TOO, AREN'T YOU? AT ALL OF THEM UP THERE.
YEAH, SURE. I'M ANGRY. NOT AT THE PEOPLE THOUGH. I'M ANGRY AT THE SYSTEMS MANIPULATING THE PEOPLE. THE ONES MAKING THEM SO AFRAID.
I'M ANGRY AT MEN LIKE SAINT. LIKE NAKANO. THE PARROTS IN THE MEDIA WHO DON'T EVEN REALIZE THAT THEY'RE SAYING WHAT THEIR MASTERS WANT THEM TO SAY.
BUT NOT THE PEOPLE. THEY'RE JUST TRYING TO SURVIVE OUT THERE.

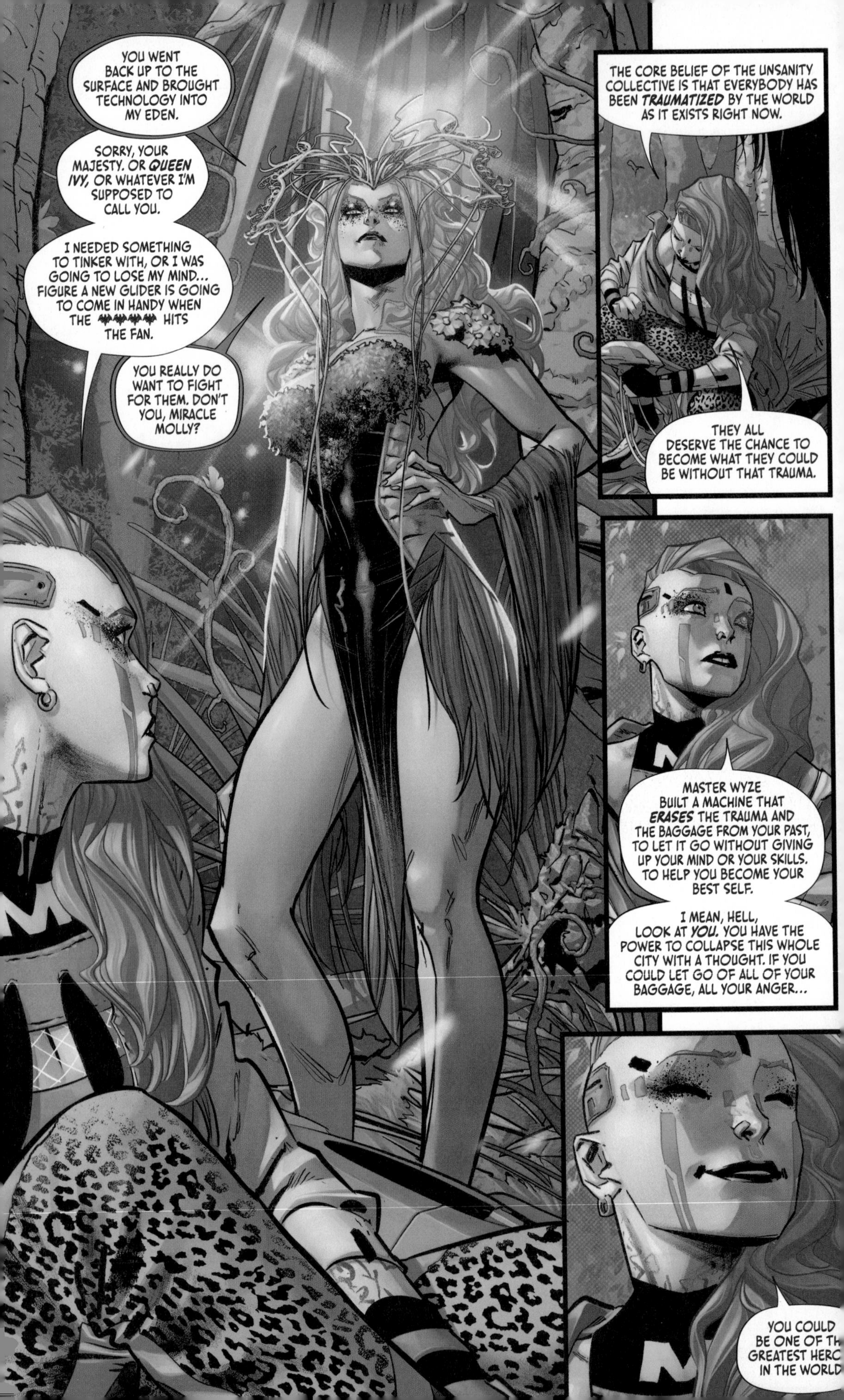
YOU WENT BACK UP TO THE SURFACE AND BROUGHT TECHNOLOGY INTO MY EDEN.
SORRY, YOUR MAJESTY. OR QUEEN IVY, OR WHATEVER I'M SUPPOSED TO CALL YOU.
I NEEDED SOMETHING TO TINKER WITH, OR I WAS GOING TO LOSE MY MIND... FIGURE A NEW GLIDER IS GOING TO COME IN HANDY WHEN THE HITS THE FAN.
YOU REALLY DO WANT TO FIGHT FOR THEM. DON'T YOU, MIRACLE MOLLY?
THE CORE BELIEF OF THE UNSANITY COLLECTIVE IS THAT EVERYBODY HAS BEEN TRAUMATIZED BY THE WORLD AS IT EXISTS RIGHT NOW.
THEY ALL DESERVE THE CHANCE TO BECOME WHAT THEY COULD BE WITHOUT THAT TRAUMA.
MASTER WYZE BUILT A MACHINE THAT ERASES THE TRAUMA AND THE BAGGAGE FROM YOUR PAST, TO LET IT GO WITHOUT GIVING UP YOUR MIND OR YOUR SKILLS. TO HELP YOU BECOME YOUR BEST SELF.
I MEAN, HELL, LOOK AT YOU. YOU HAVE THE POWER TO COLLAPSE THIS WHOLE CITY WITH A THOUGHT. IF YOU COULD LET GO OF ALL OF YOUR BAGGAGE, ALL YOUR ANGER...
YOU COULD BE ONE OF TH GREATEST HERC IN THE WORLD

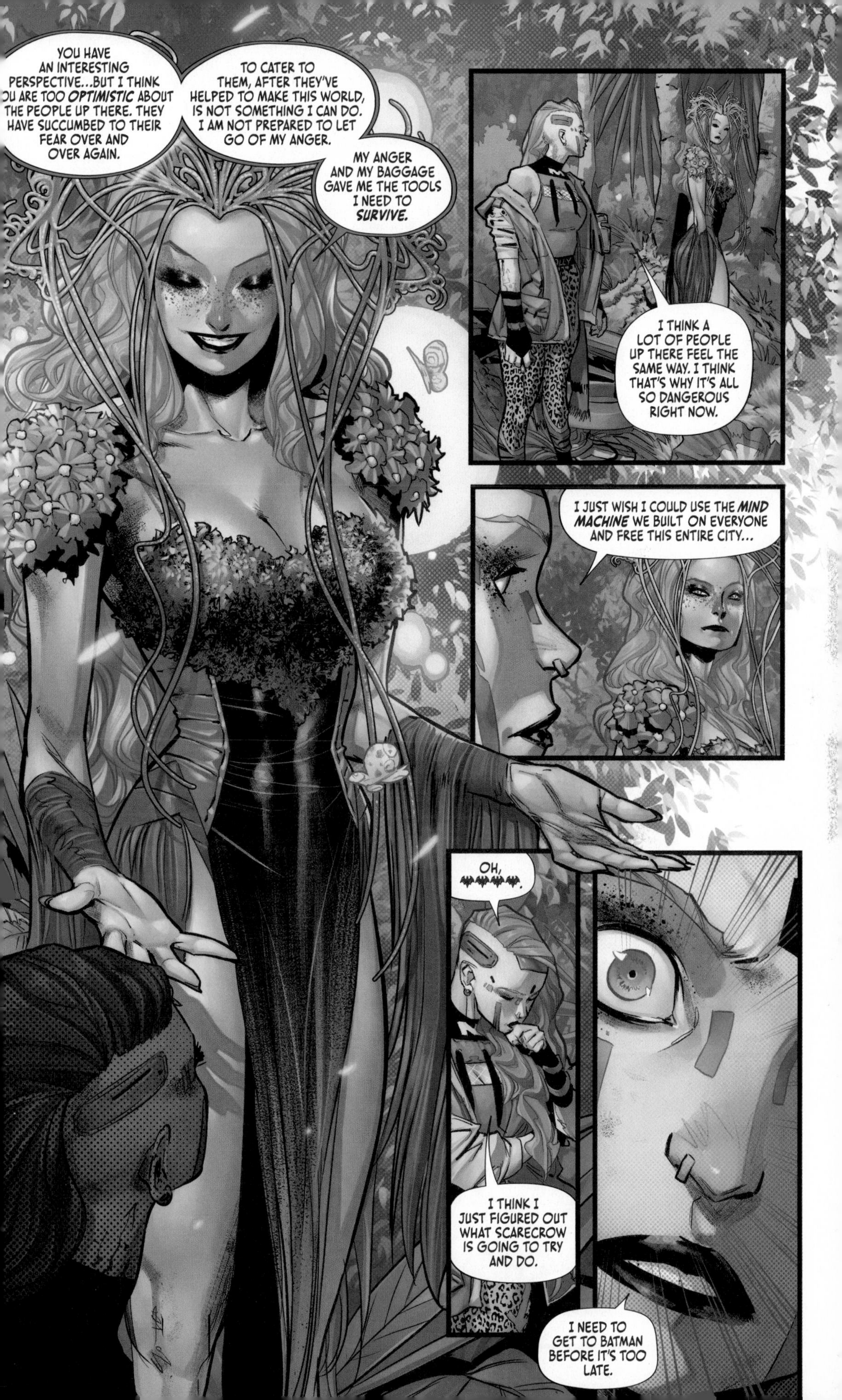

YOU HAVE AN INTERESTING PERSPECTIVE...BUT I THINK YOU ARE TOO *OPTIMISTIC* ABOUT THE PEOPLE UP THERE. THEY HAVE SUCCUMBED TO THEIR FEAR OVER AND OVER AGAIN.
TO CATER TO THEM, AFTER THEY'VE HELPED TO MAKE THIS WORLD, IS NOT SOMETHING I CAN DO. I AM NOT PREPARED TO LET GO OF MY ANGER.
MY ANGER AND MY BAGGAGE GAVE ME THE TOOLS I NEED TO ***SURVIVE.***
I THINK A LOT OF PEOPLE UP THERE FEEL THE SAME WAY. I THINK THAT'S WHY IT'S ALL SO DANGEROUS RIGHT NOW.
I JUST WISH I COULD USE THE ***MIND MACHINE*** WE BUILT ON EVERYONE AND FREE THIS ENTIRE CITY...
OH,
I THINK I JUST FIGURED OUT WHAT SCARECROW IS GOING TO TRY AND DO.
I NEED TO GET TO BATMAN BEFORE IT'S TOO LATE.

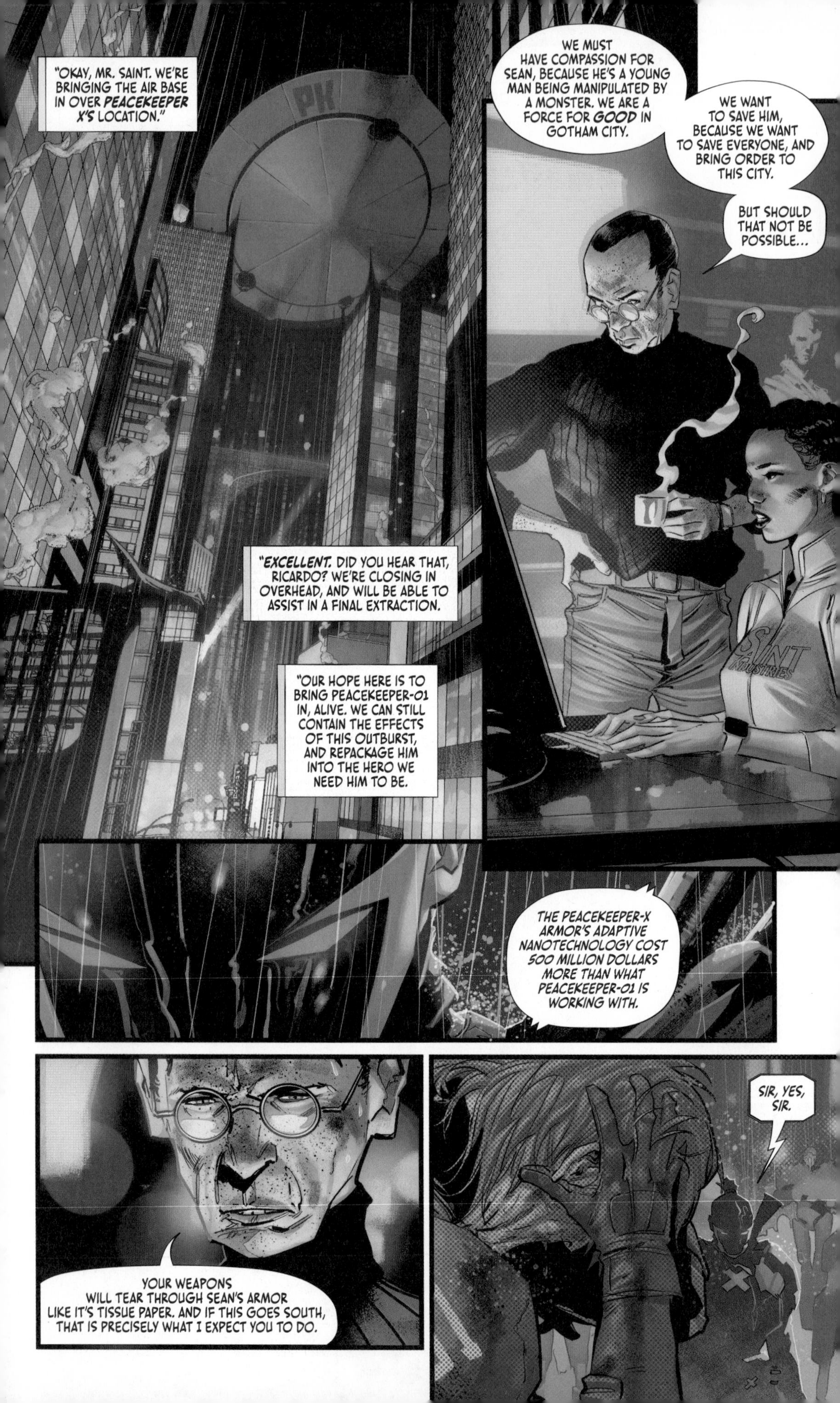
"OKAY, MR. SAINT. WE'RE BRINGING THE AIR BASE IN OVER *PEACEKEEPER X'S* LOCATION."
WE MUST HAVE COMPASSION FOR SEAN, BECAUSE HE'S A YOUNG MAN BEING MANIPULATED BY A MONSTER. WE ARE A FORCE FOR *GOOD* IN GOTHAM CITY.
WE WANT TO SAVE HIM, BECAUSE WE WANT TO SAVE EVERYONE, AND BRING ORDER TO THIS CITY.
BUT SHOULD THAT NOT BE POSSIBLE...
PK
SAINT INDUSTRIES
"*EXCELLENT.* DID YOU HEAR THAT, RICARDO? WE'RE CLOSING IN OVERHEAD, AND WILL BE ABLE TO ASSIST IN A FINAL EXTRACTION.
"OUR HOPE HERE IS TO BRING PEACEKEEPER-01 IN, ALIVE. WE CAN STILL CONTAIN THE EFFECTS OF THIS OUTBURST, AND REPACKAGE HIM INTO THE HERO WE NEED HIM TO BE.
THE PEACEKEEPER-X ARMOR'S ADAPTIVE NANOTECHNOLOGY COST 500 MILLION DOLLARS MORE THAN WHAT PEACEKEEPER-01 IS WORKING WITH.
YOUR WEAPONS WILL TEAR THROUGH SEAN'S ARMOR LIKE IT'S TISSUE PAPER. AND IF THIS GOES SOUTH, THAT IS PRECISELY WHAT I EXPECT YOU TO DO.
SIR, YES, SIR.

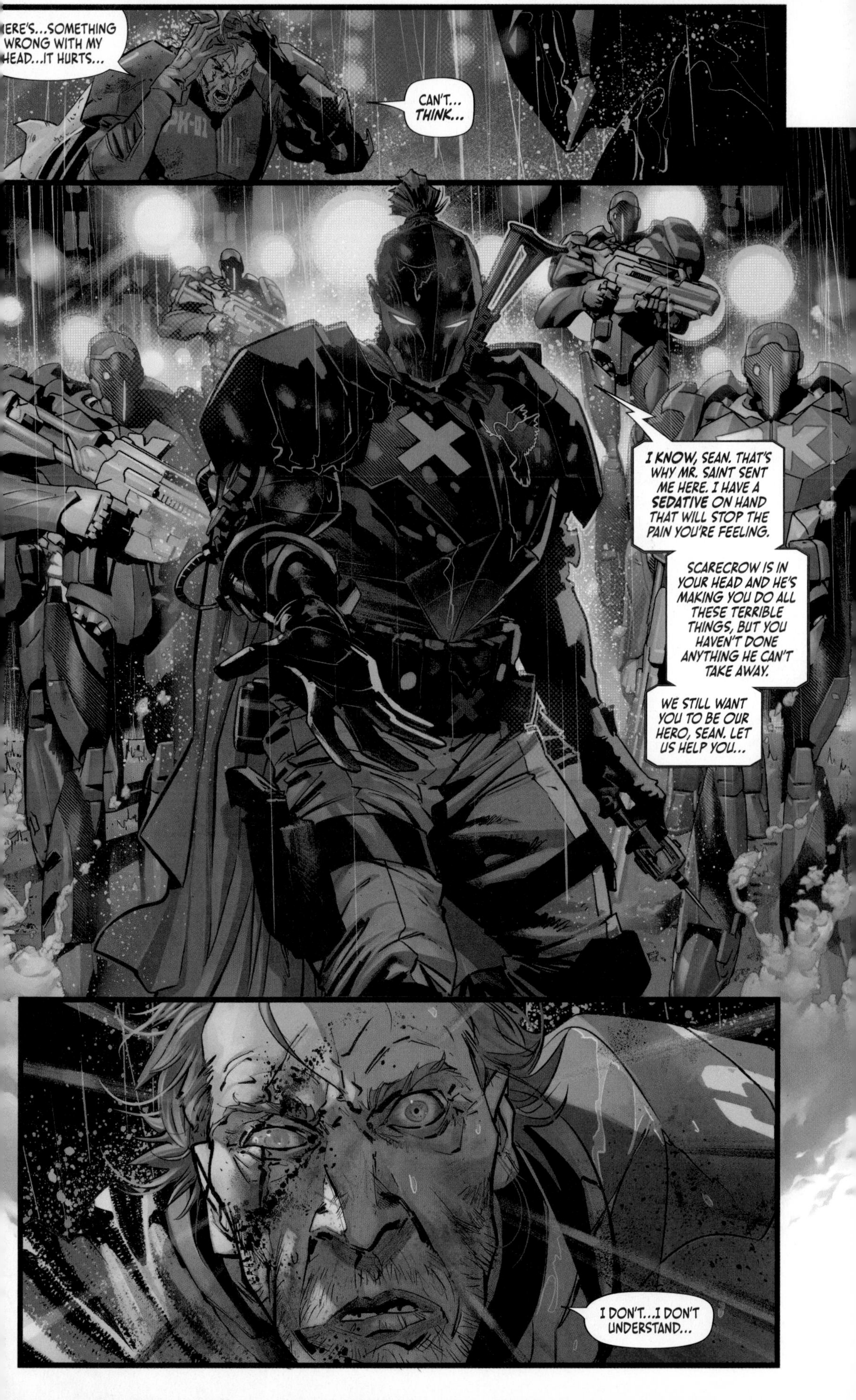
ERE'S...SOMETHING WRONG WITH MY HEAD...IT HURTS...
CAN'T... THINK...
I KNOW, SEAN. THAT'S WHY MR. SAINT SENT ME HERE. I HAVE A SEDATIVE ON HAND THAT WILL STOP THE PAIN YOU'RE FEELING.
SCARECROW IS IN YOUR HEAD AND HE'S MAKING YOU DO ALL THESE TERRIBLE THINGS, BUT YOU HAVEN'T DONE ANYTHING HE CAN'T TAKE AWAY.
WE STILL WANT YOU TO BE OUR HERO, SEAN. LET US HELP YOU...
I DON'T...I DON'T UNDERSTAND...

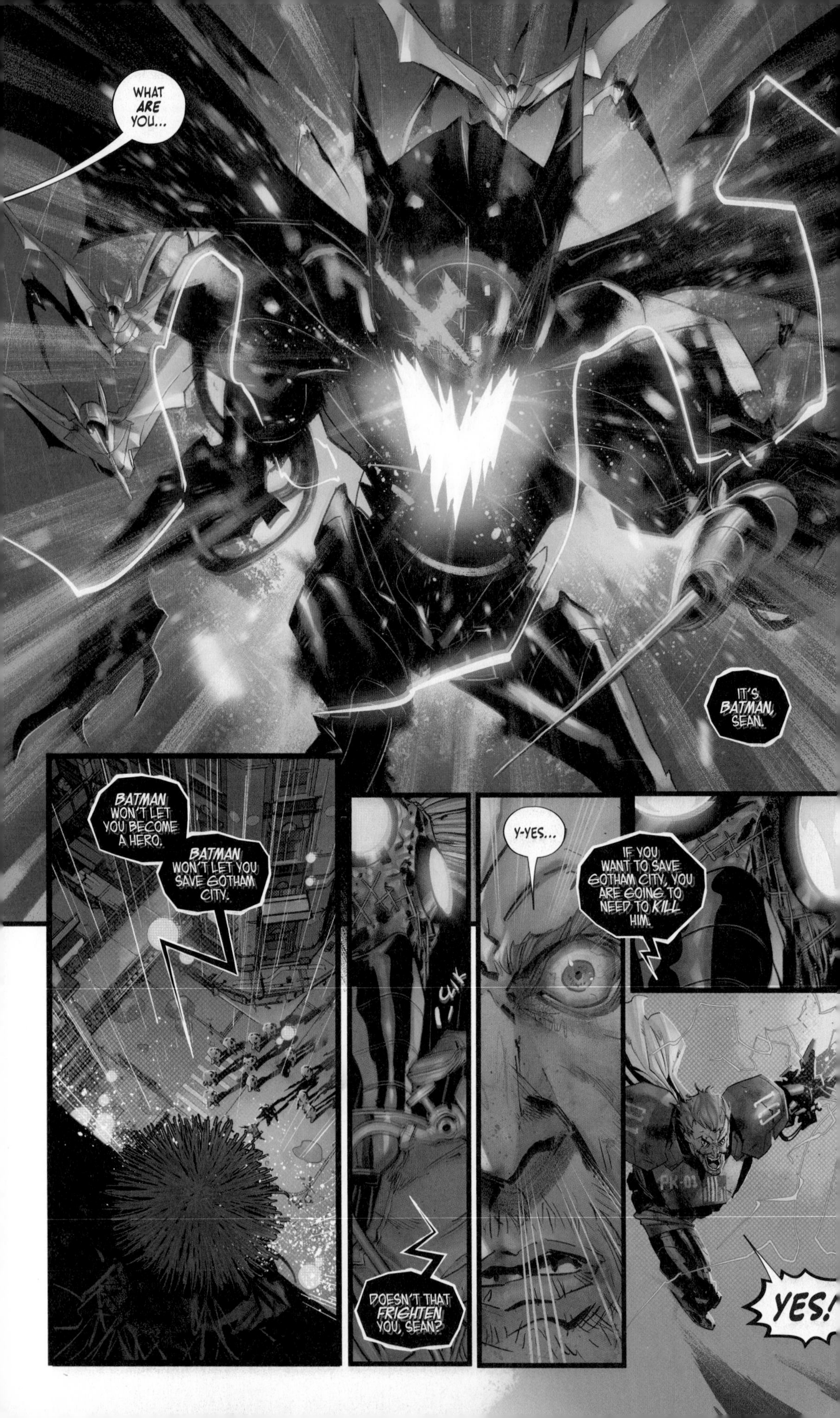
WHAT ARE YOU...
IT'S BATMAN, SEAN.
BATMAN WON'T LET YOU BECOME A HERO.
BATMAN WON'T LET YOU SAVE GOTHAM CITY.
DOESN'T THAT FRIGHTEN YOU, SEAN?
Y-YES...
IF YOU WANT TO SAVE GOTHAM CITY, YOU ARE GOING TO NEED TO KILL HIM.
YES!

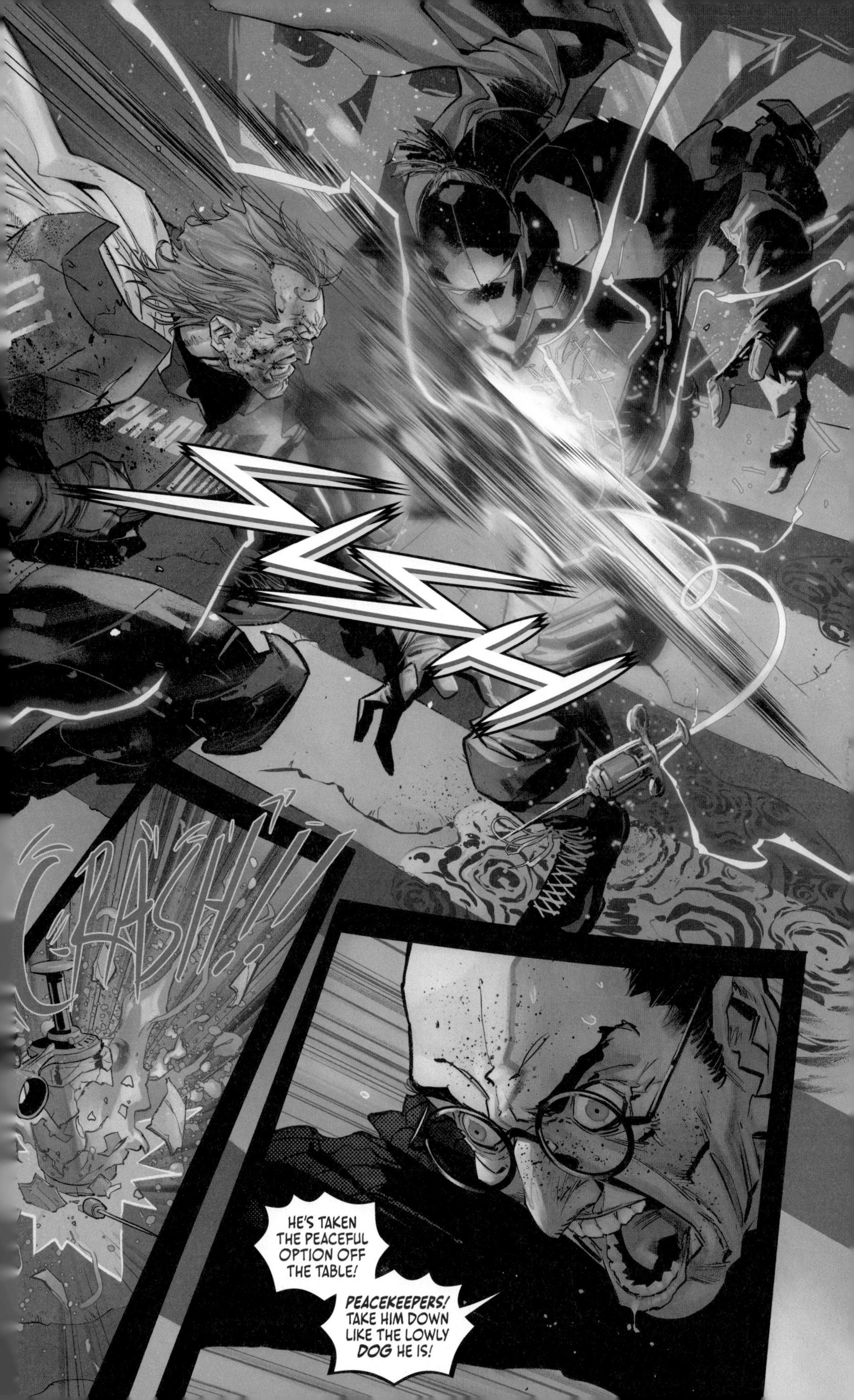
CRASH!!
HE'S TAKEN THE PEACEFUL OPTION OFF THE TABLE!
PEACEKEEPERS! TAKE HIM DOWN LIKE THE LOWLY DOG HE IS!

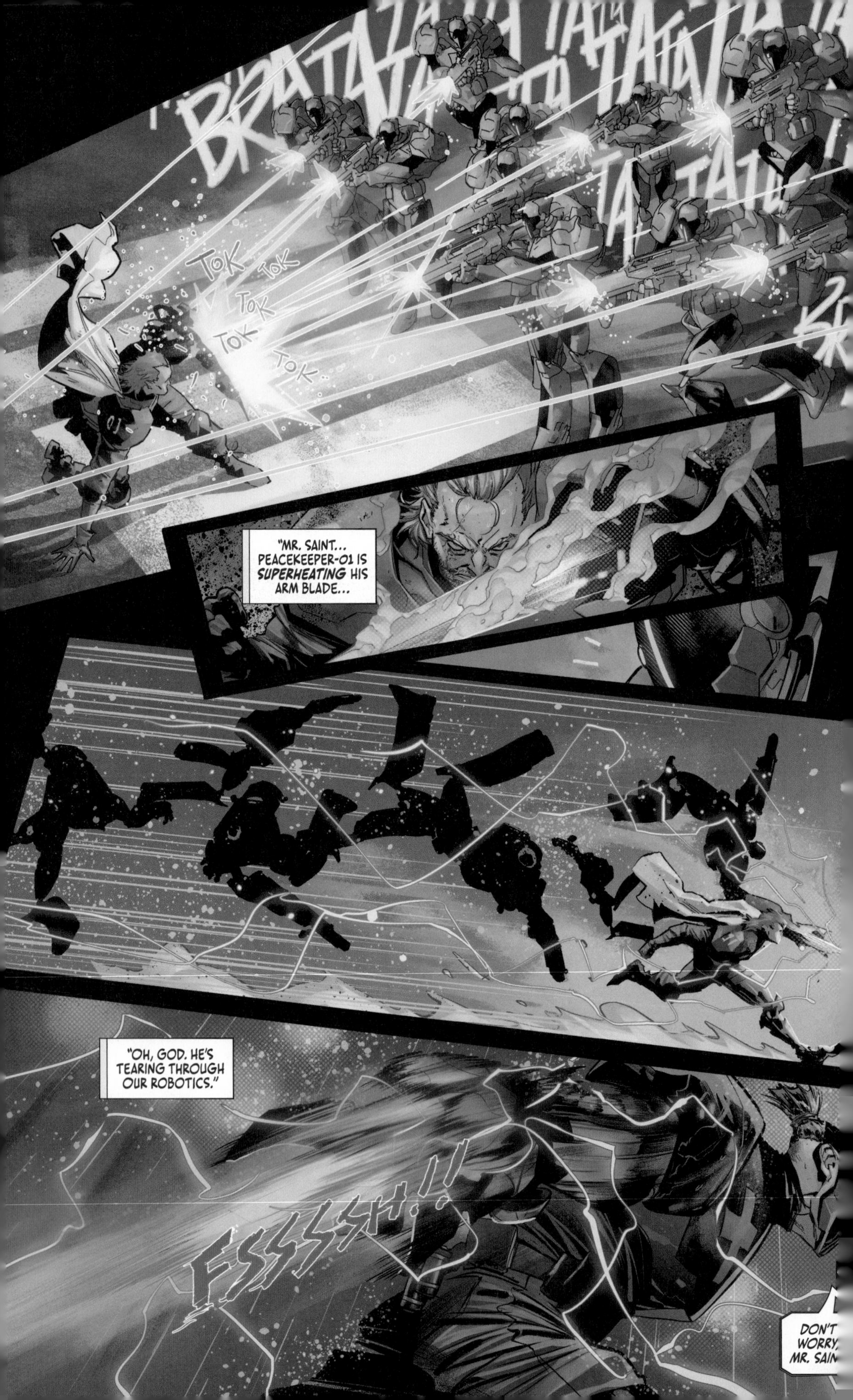
BRATATATATATATATATA
TOK
TOK
TOK
TOK
TOK
"MR. SAINT... PEACEKEEPER-01 IS SUPERHEATING HIS ARM BLADE...
"OH, GOD. HE'S TEARING THROUGH OUR ROBOTICS."
FSSSSH!!
DON'T WORRY, MR. SAIN

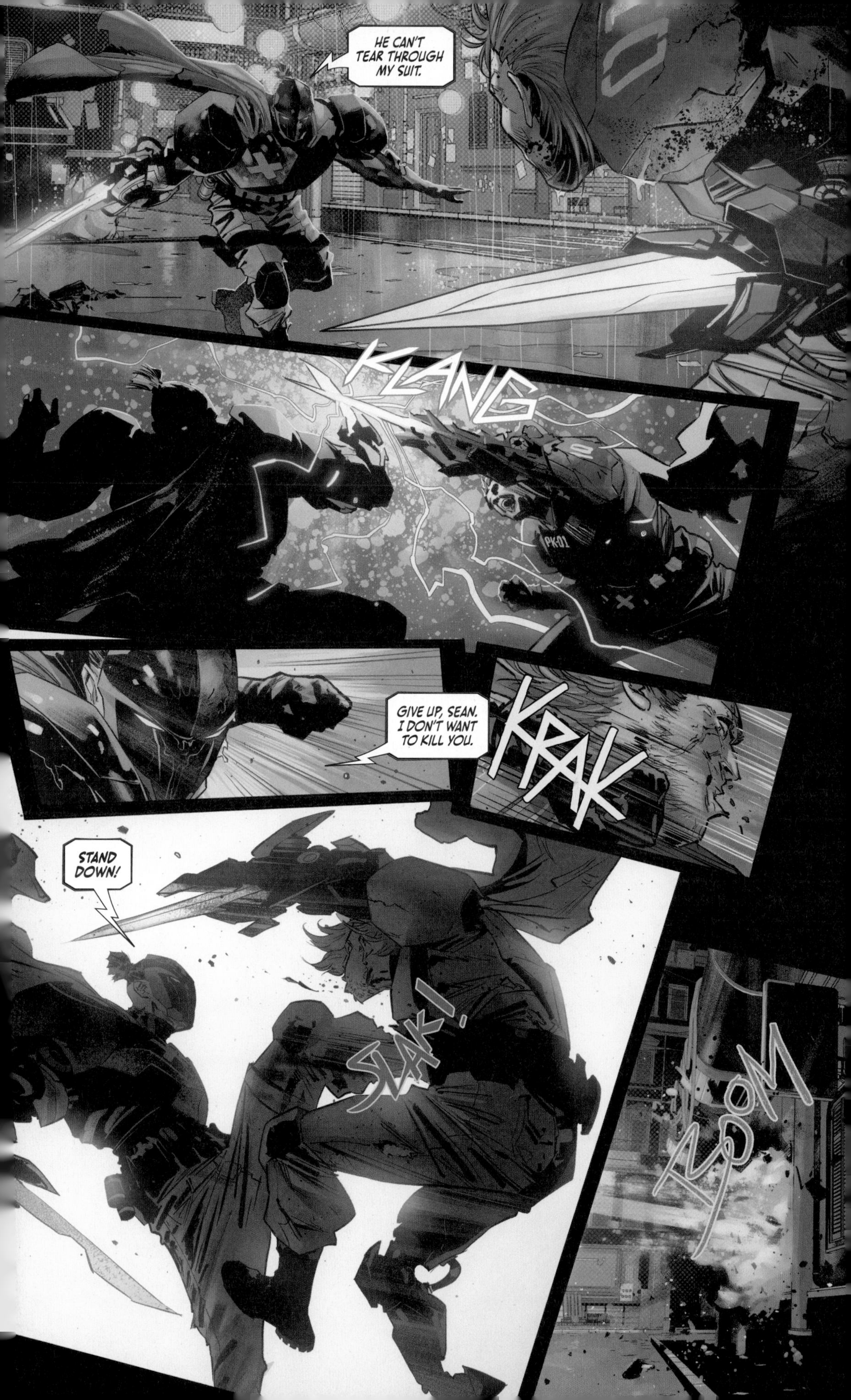
HE CAN'T TEAR THROUGH MY SUIT.
KLANG
PK-01
GIVE UP, SEAN. I DON'T WANT TO KILL YOU.
KRAK
STAND DOWN!
SLAK!
FOOM

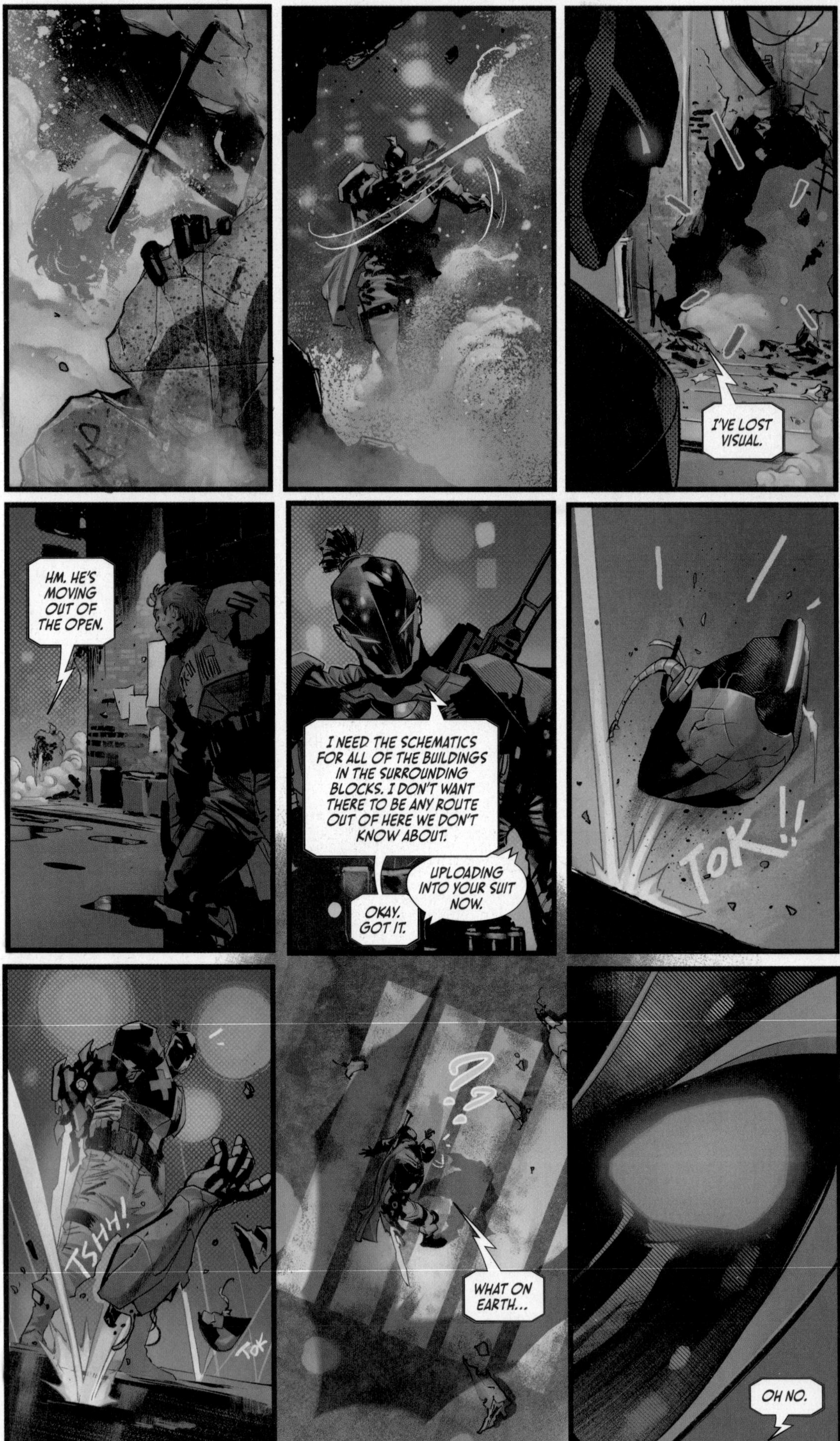

I'VE LOST VISUAL.
HM. HE'S MOVING OUT OF THE OPEN.
I NEED THE SCHEMATICS FOR ALL OF THE BUILDINGS IN THE SURROUNDING BLOCKS. I DON'T WANT THERE TO BE ANY ROUTE OUT OF HERE WE DON'T KNOW ABOUT.
OKAY. GOT IT.
UPLOADING INTO YOUR SUIT NOW.
TOK!!
TSHH!
TOK
??
WHAT ON EARTH...
OH NO.

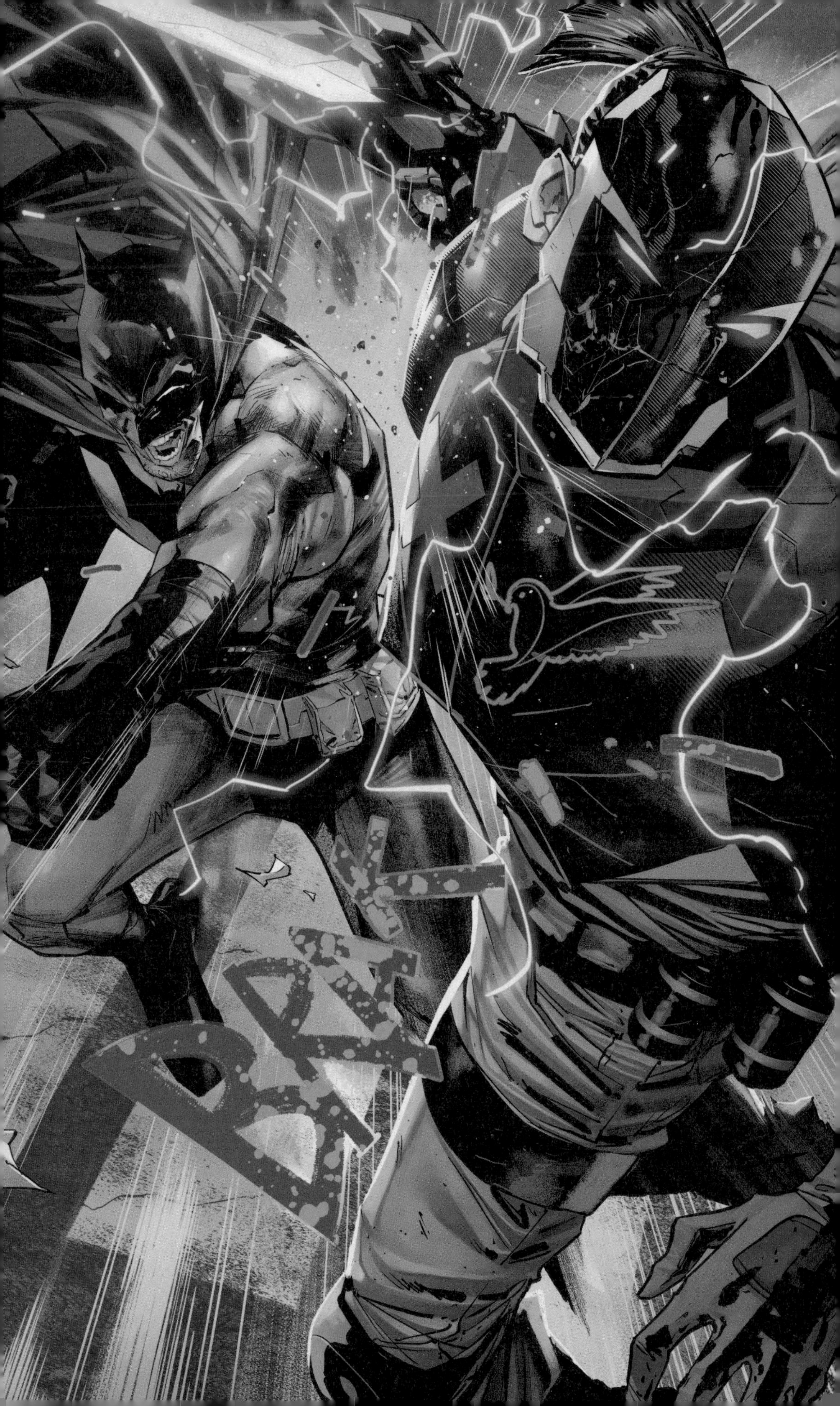

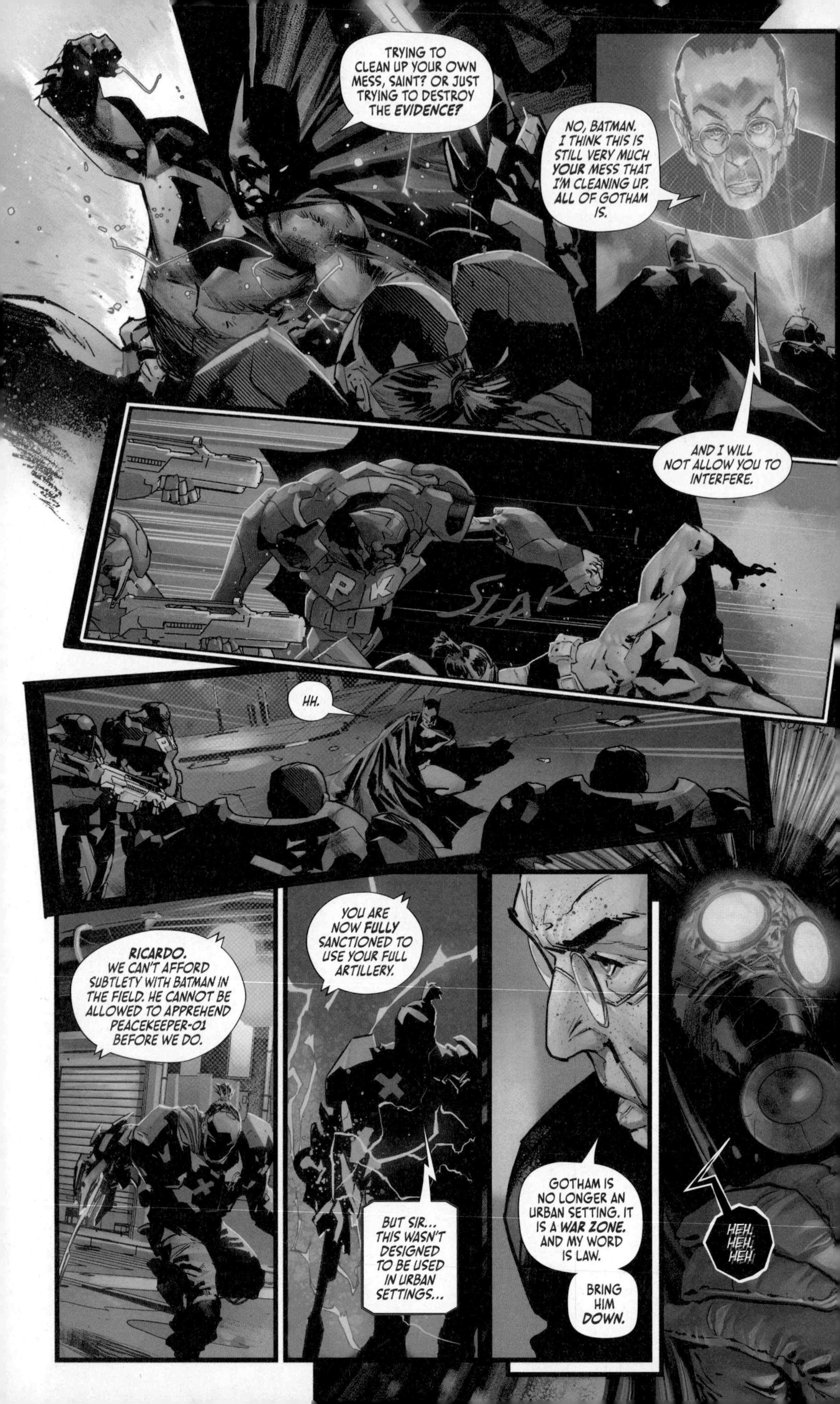

TRYING TO CLEAN UP YOUR OWN MESS, SAINT? OR JUST TRYING TO DESTROY THE EVIDENCE?
NO, BATMAN. I THINK THIS IS STILL VERY MUCH YOUR MESS THAT I'M CLEANING UP. ALL OF GOTHAM IS.
AND I WILL NOT ALLOW YOU TO INTERFERE.
PK
SLAK
HH.
RICARDO. WE CAN'T AFFORD SUBTLETY WITH BATMAN IN THE FIELD. HE CANNOT BE ALLOWED TO APPREHEND PEACEKEEPER-01 BEFORE WE DO.
YOU ARE NOW FULLY SANCTIONED TO USE YOUR FULL ARTILLERY.
BUT SIR... THIS WASN'T DESIGNED TO BE USED IN URBAN SETTINGS...
GOTHAM IS NO LONGER AN URBAN SETTING. IT IS A WAR ZONE. AND MY WORD IS LAW.
BRING HIM DOWN.
HEH. HEH. HEH

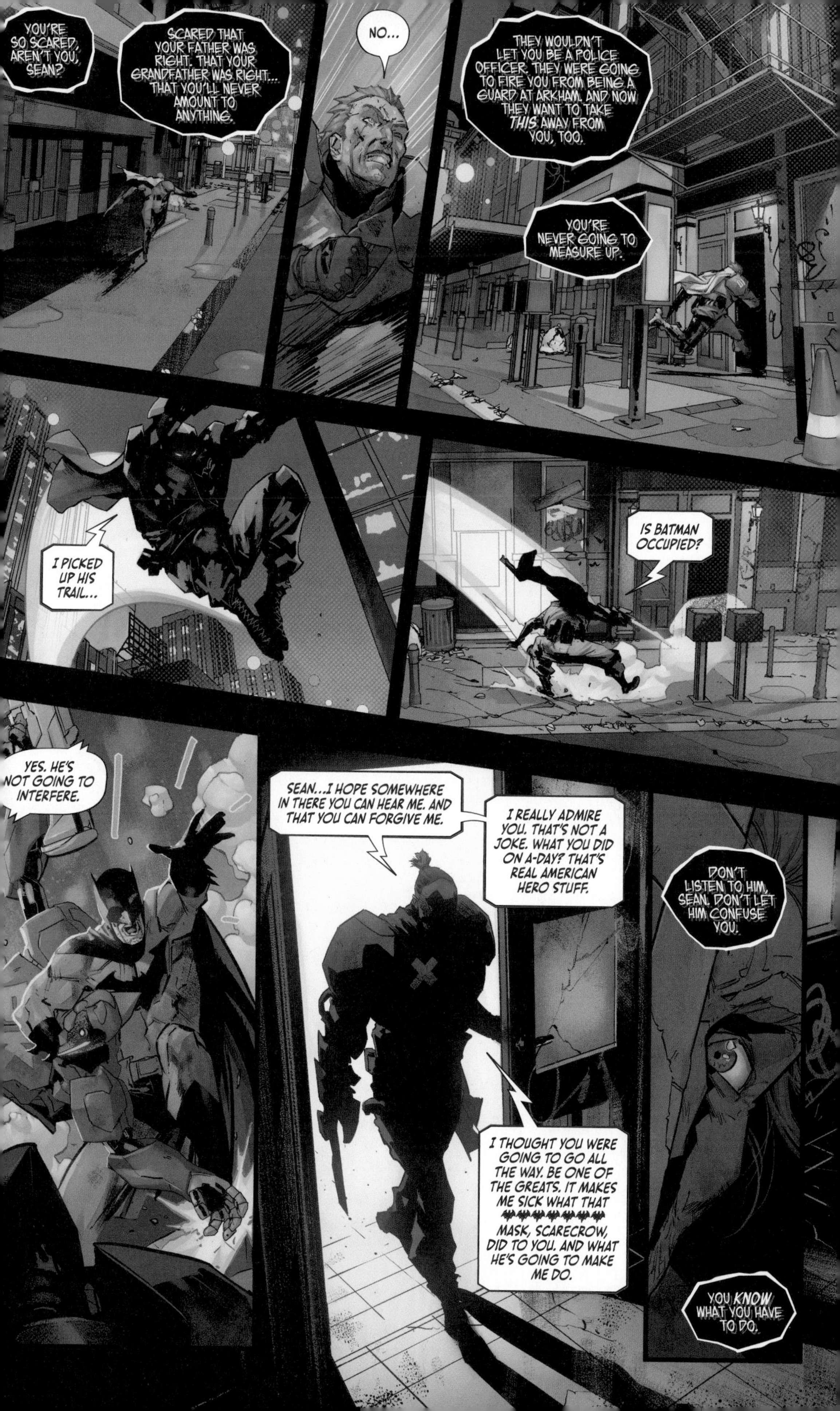
YOU'RE SO SCARED, AREN'T YOU, SEAN?
SCARED THAT YOUR FATHER WAS RIGHT. THAT YOUR GRANDFATHER WAS RIGHT... THAT YOU'LL NEVER AMOUNT TO ANYTHING.
NO...
THEY WOULDN'T LET YOU BE A POLICE OFFICER. THEY WERE GOING TO FIRE YOU FROM BEING A GUARD AT ARKHAM. AND NOW THEY WANT TO TAKE THIS AWAY FROM YOU, TOO.
YOU'RE NEVER GOING TO MEASURE UP.
I PICKED UP HIS TRAIL...
IS BATMAN OCCUPIED?
YES. HE'S NOT GOING TO INTERFERE.
SEAN...I HOPE SOMEWHERE IN THERE YOU CAN HEAR ME. AND THAT YOU CAN FORGIVE ME.
I REALLY ADMIRE YOU. THAT'S NOT A JOKE. WHAT YOU DID ON A-DAY? THAT'S REAL AMERICAN HERO STUFF.
I THOUGHT YOU WERE GOING TO GO ALL THE WAY. BE ONE OF THE GREATS. IT MAKES ME SICK WHAT THAT MASK, SCARECROW, DID TO YOU. AND WHAT HE'S GOING TO MAKE ME DO.
DON'T LISTEN TO HIM, SEAN. DON'T LET HIM CONFUSE YOU.
YOU KNOW WHAT YOU HAVE TO DO.

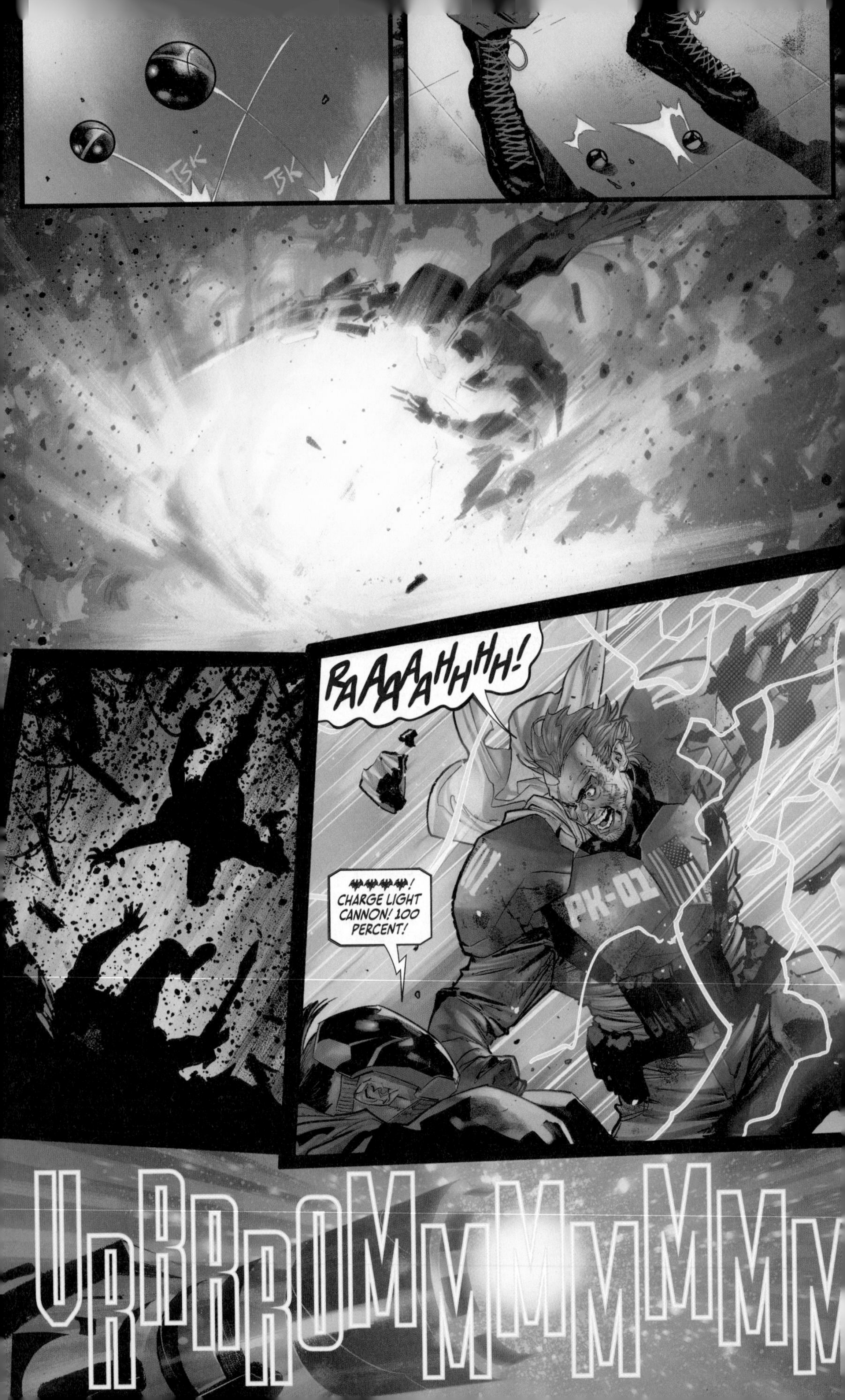
TSK
TSK
RAAAAAHHHH!
CHARGE LIGHT CANNON! 100 PERCENT!
URRROMMMMMMMMM

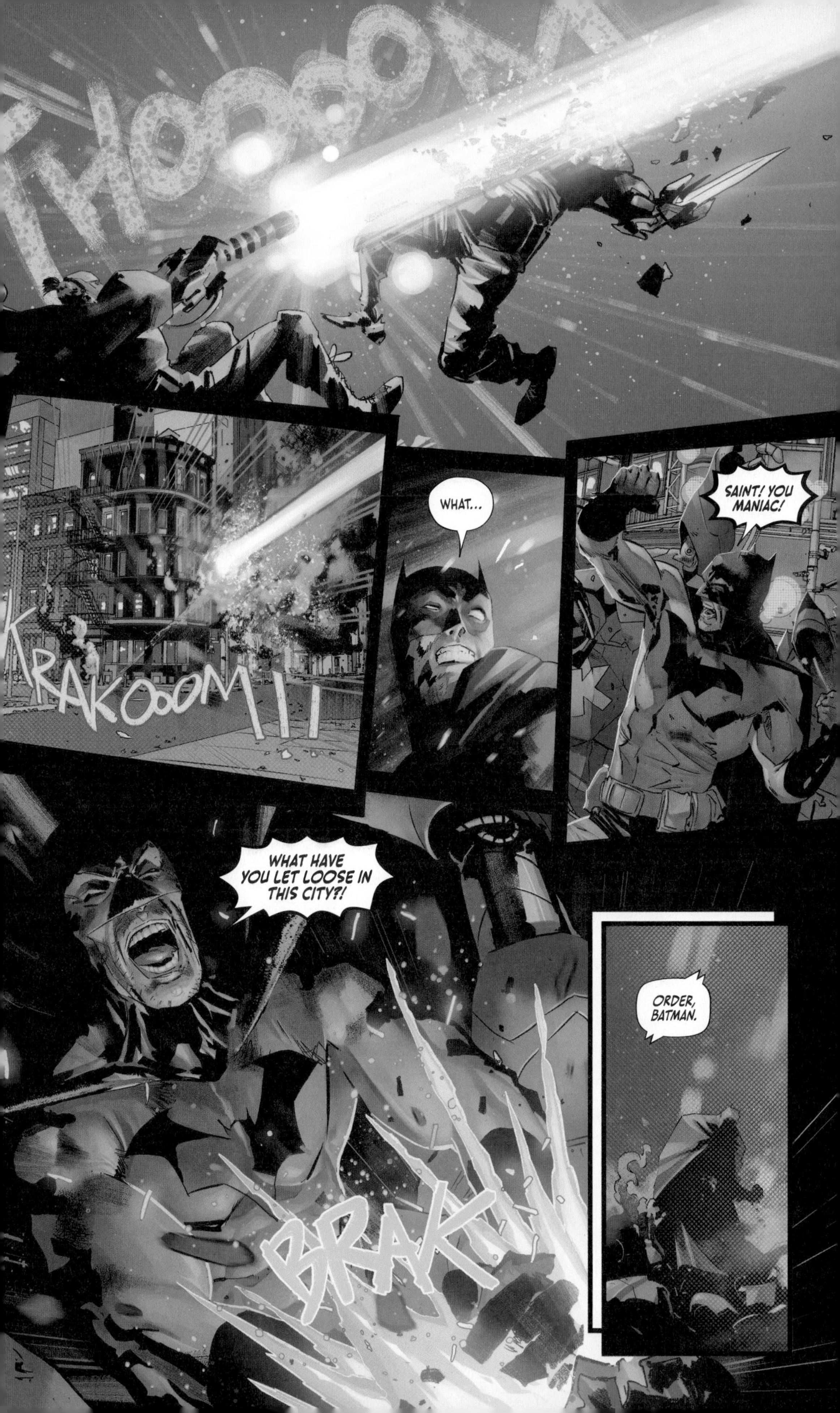
THOOOOOM
KRAKOOOM!!
WHAT...
SAINT! YOU MANIAC!
WHAT HAVE YOU LET LOOSE IN THIS CITY?!
BRAK
ORDER, BATMAN.

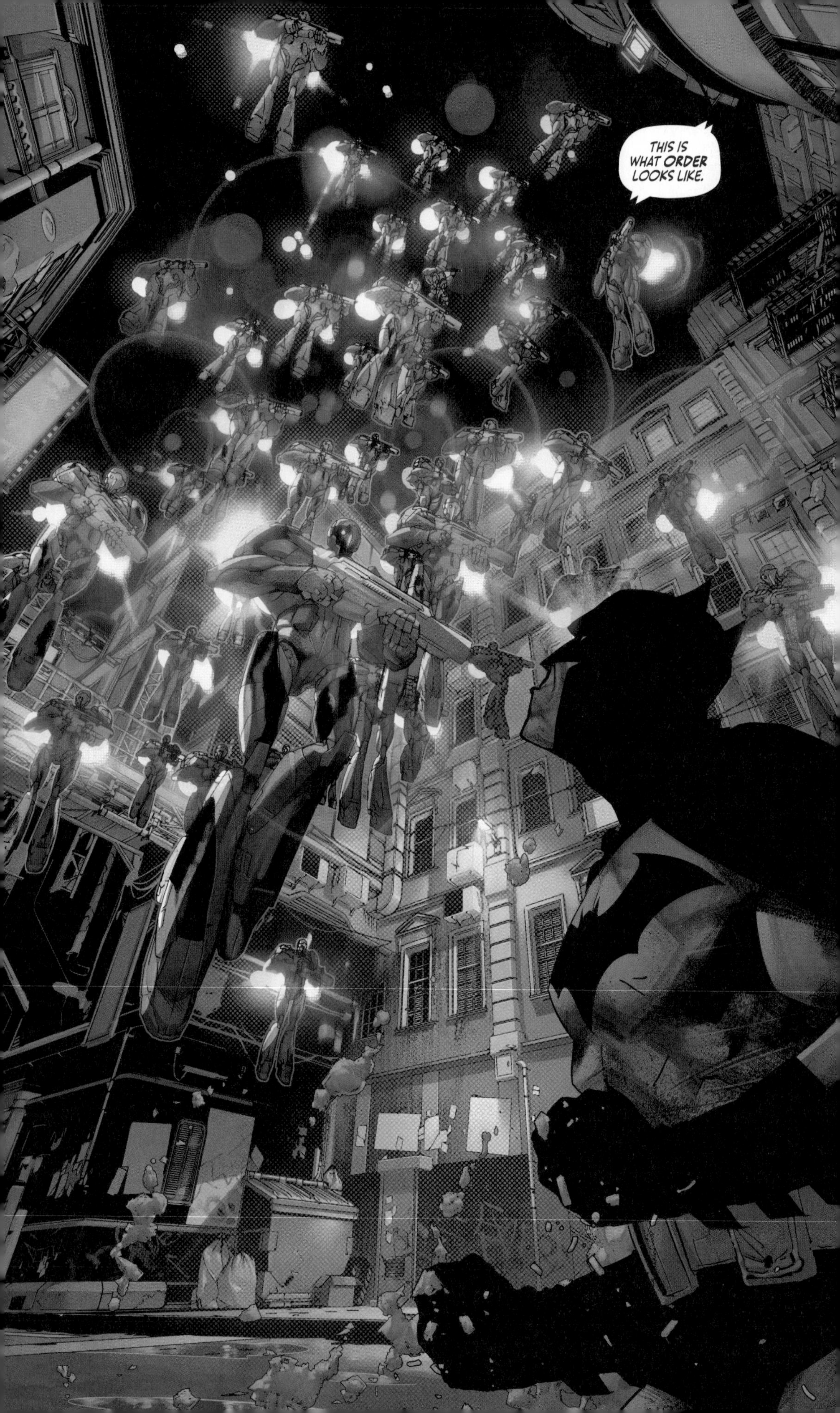
THIS IS WHAT ORDER LOOKS LIKE.

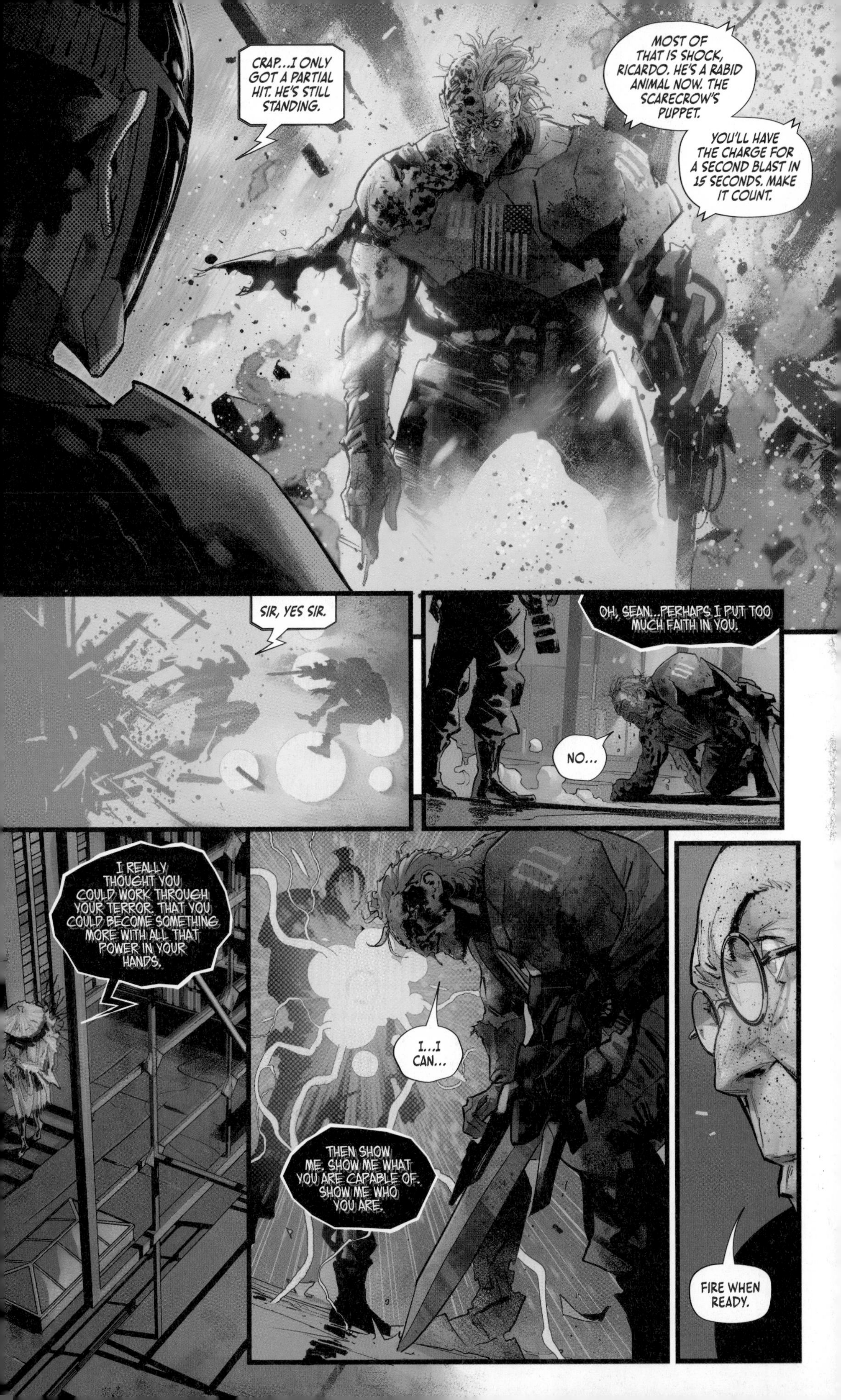
CRAP...I ONLY GOT A PARTIAL HIT. HE'S STILL STANDING.
MOST OF THAT IS SHOCK, RICARDO. HE'S A RABID ANIMAL NOW. THE SCARECROW'S PUPPET.
YOU'LL HAVE THE CHARGE FOR A SECOND BLAST IN 15 SECONDS. MAKE IT COUNT.
SIR, YES SIR.
OH, SEAN...PERHAPS I PUT TOO MUCH FAITH IN YOU.
NO...
I REALLY THOUGHT YOU COULD WORK THROUGH YOUR TERROR. THAT YOU COULD BECOME SOMETHING MORE WITH ALL THAT POWER IN YOUR HANDS.
I...I CAN...
THEN SHOW ME. SHOW ME WHAT YOU ARE CAPABLE OF. SHOW ME WHO YOU ARE.
FIRE WHEN READY.

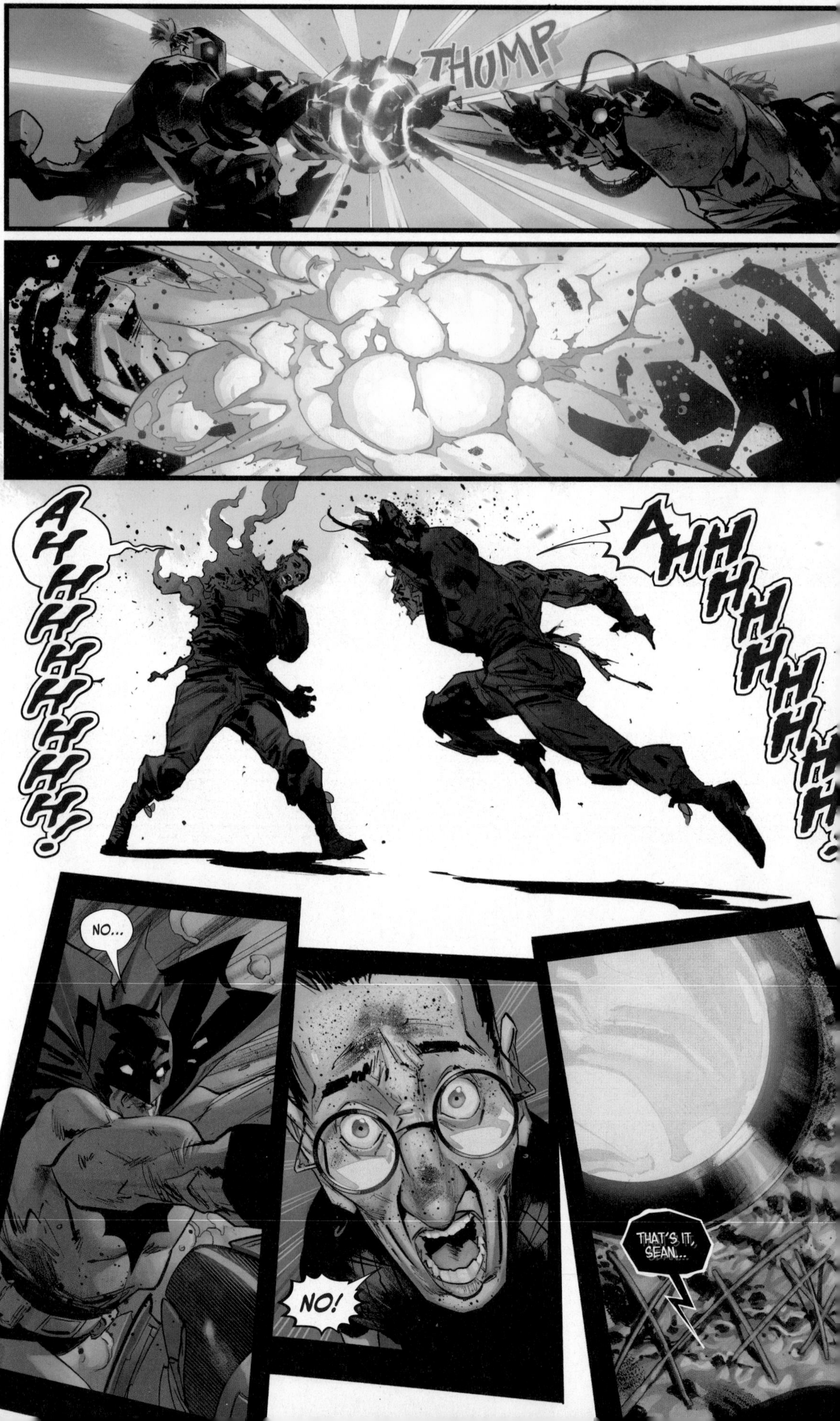
THUMP!
AHHHHHHHHH!
AHHHHHHHH
NO...
NO!
THAT'S IT, SEAN...

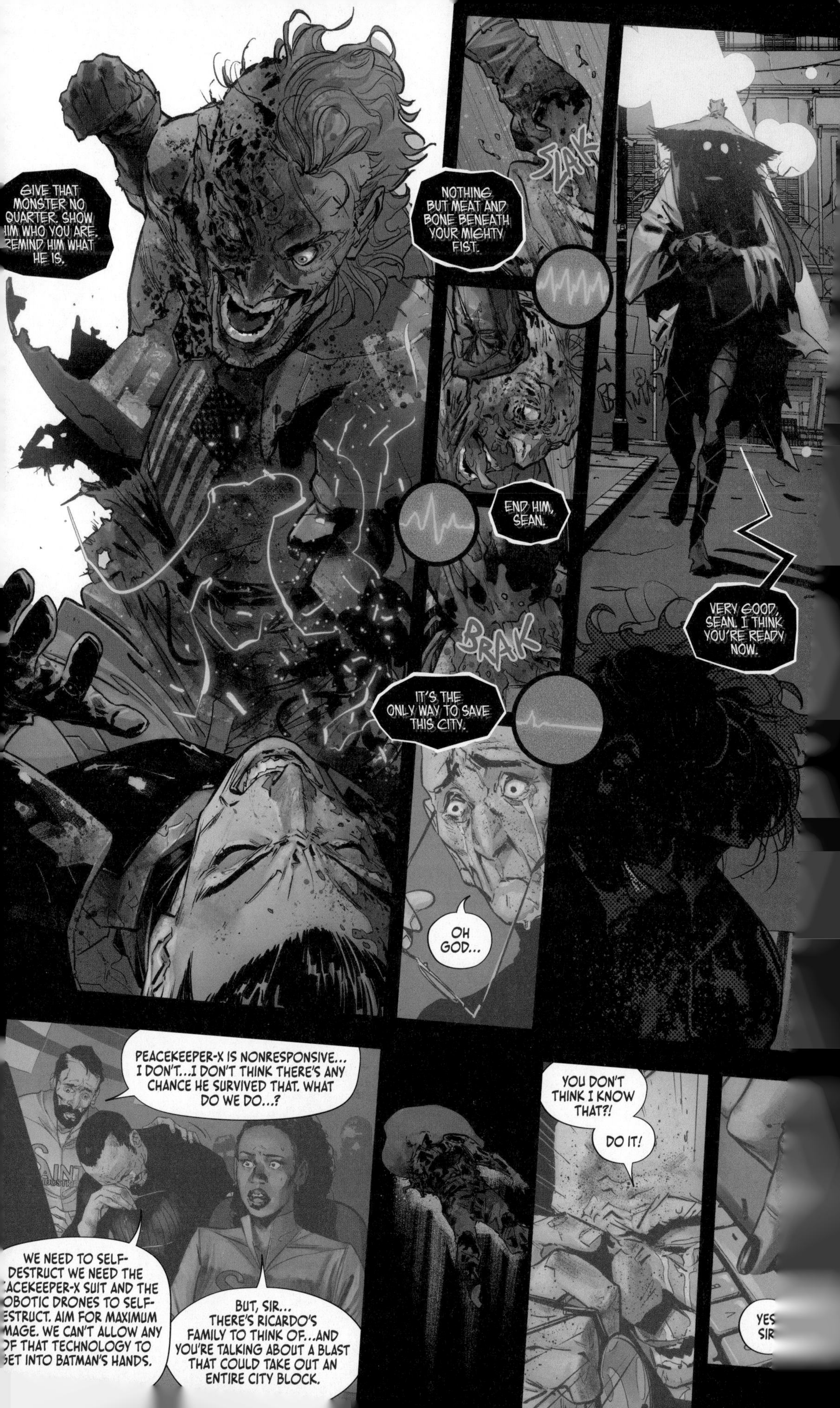
GIVE THAT MONSTER NO QUARTER. SHOW HIM WHO YOU ARE. REMIND HIM WHAT HE IS.
NOTHING BUT MEAT AND BONE BENEATH YOUR MIGHTY FIST.
SLAK
END HIM, SEAN.
BRAK
IT'S THE ONLY WAY TO SAVE THIS CITY.
VERY GOOD, SEAN. I THINK YOU'RE READY NOW.
OH GOD...
PEACEKEEPER-X IS NONRESPONSIVE... I DON'T...I DON'T THINK THERE'S ANY CHANCE HE SURVIVED THAT. WHAT DO WE DO...?
WE NEED TO SELF-DESTRUCT WE NEED THE PEACEKEEPER-X SUIT AND THE ROBOTIC DRONES TO SELF-DESTRUCT. AIM FOR MAXIMUM DAMAGE. WE CAN'T ALLOW ANY OF THAT TECHNOLOGY TO GET INTO BATMAN'S HANDS.
BUT, SIR... THERE'S RICARDO'S FAMILY TO THINK OF...AND YOU'RE TALKING ABOUT A BLAST THAT COULD TAKE OUT AN ENTIRE CITY BLOCK.
YOU DON'T THINK I KNOW THAT?!
DO IT!
YES SIR

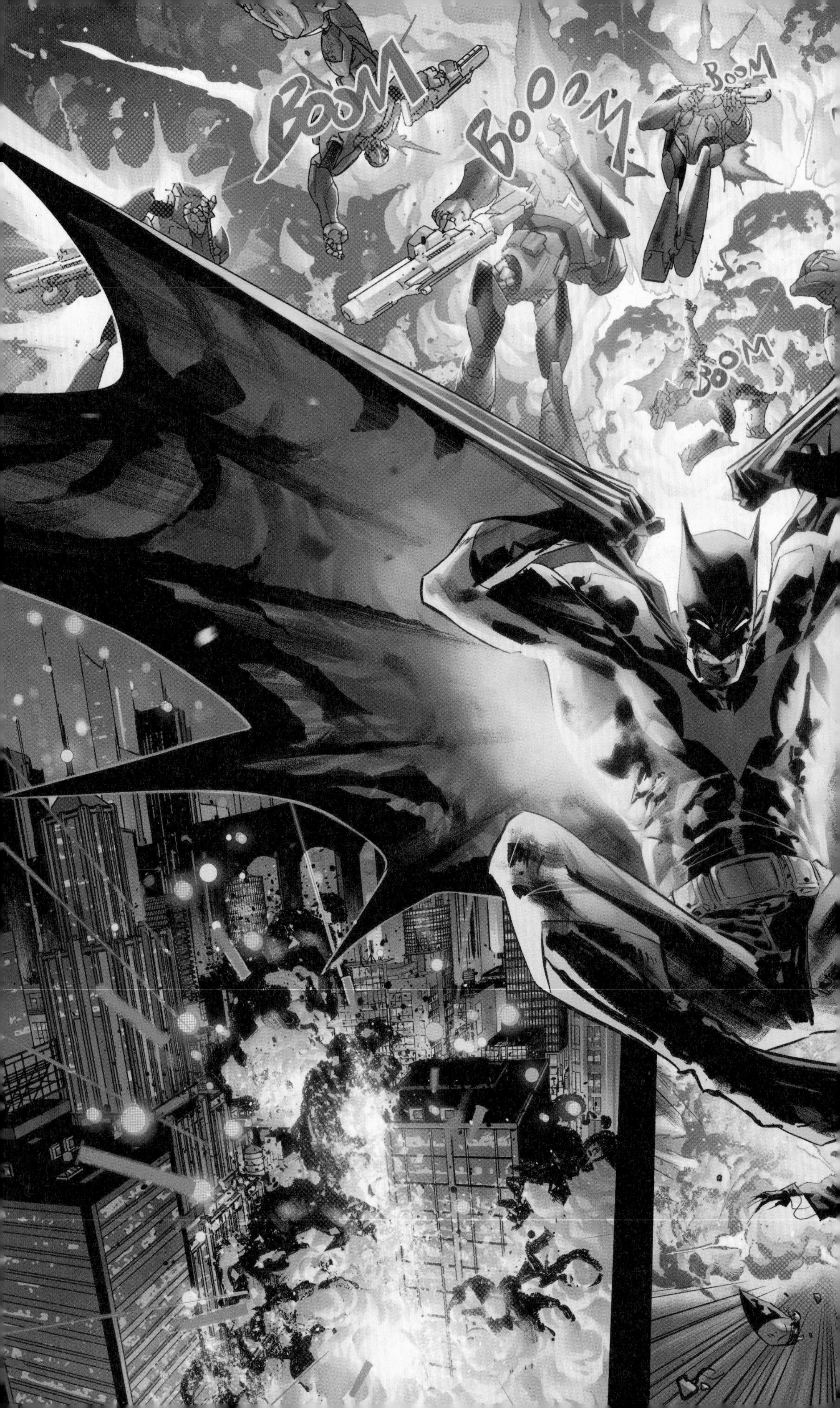
BOOM
BOOOOM
BOOM
BOOM

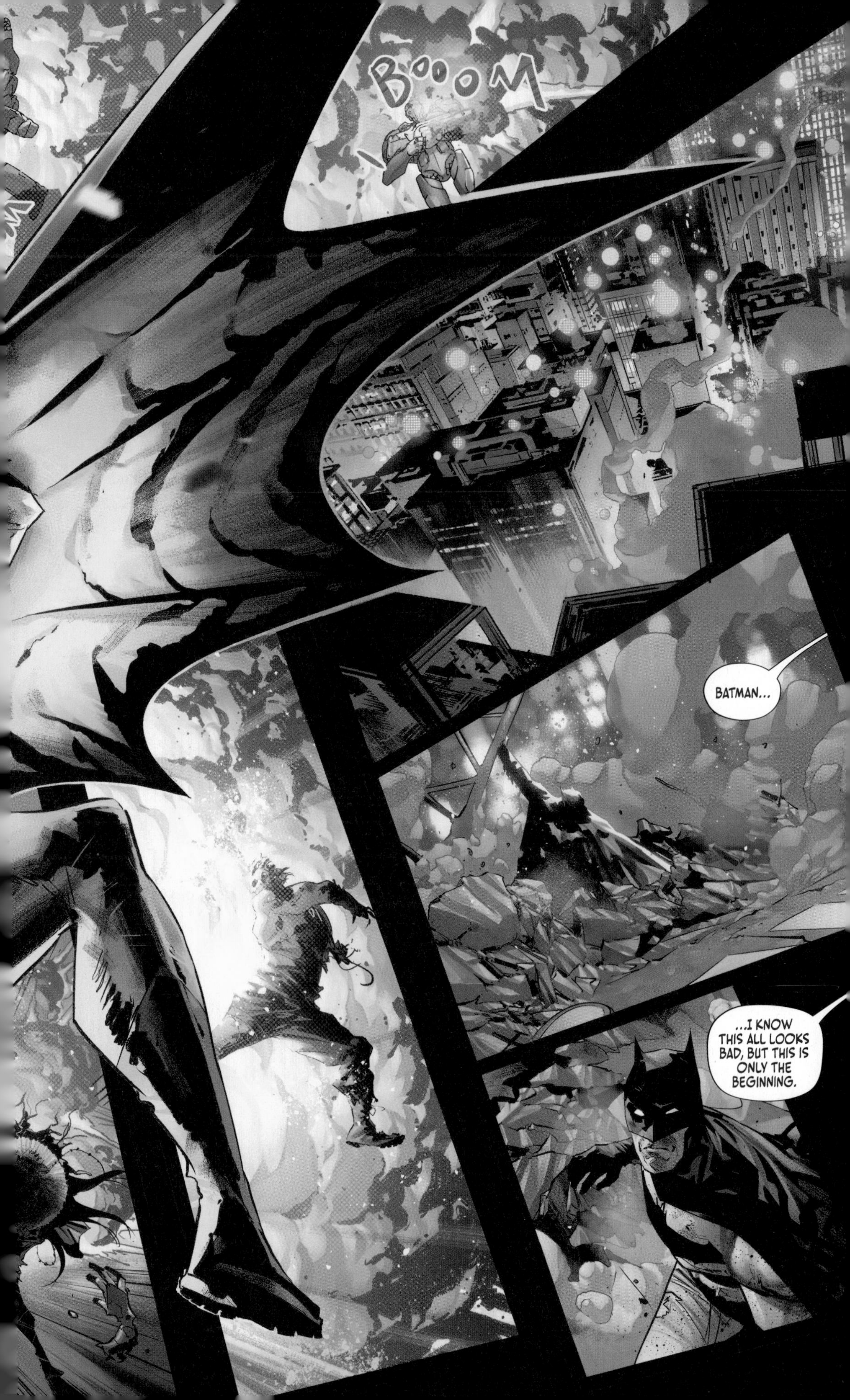
BOOOM
BATMAN...
...I KNOW THIS ALL LOOKS BAD, BUT THIS IS ONLY THE BEGINNING.

I KNOW HOW SCARECROW IS GETTING INTO PEOPLE'S MINDS...I THINK I KNOW WHAT HE'S GOING TO DO NEXT.
AND WE'RE RUNNING OUT OF TIME.
FEAR STATE
PART 3
JAMES TYNION IV WRITER
JORGE JIMENEZ ARTIST
TOMEU MOREY COLORS
CLAYTON COWLES LETTERS
JIMENEZ & MOREY COVER
JORGE MOLINA; DYLAN TEAGUE VARIANT COVERS
DAVE WIELGOSZ ASSOC. EDITOR
BEN ABERNATHY EDITOR
BATMAN CREATED BY BOB KANE

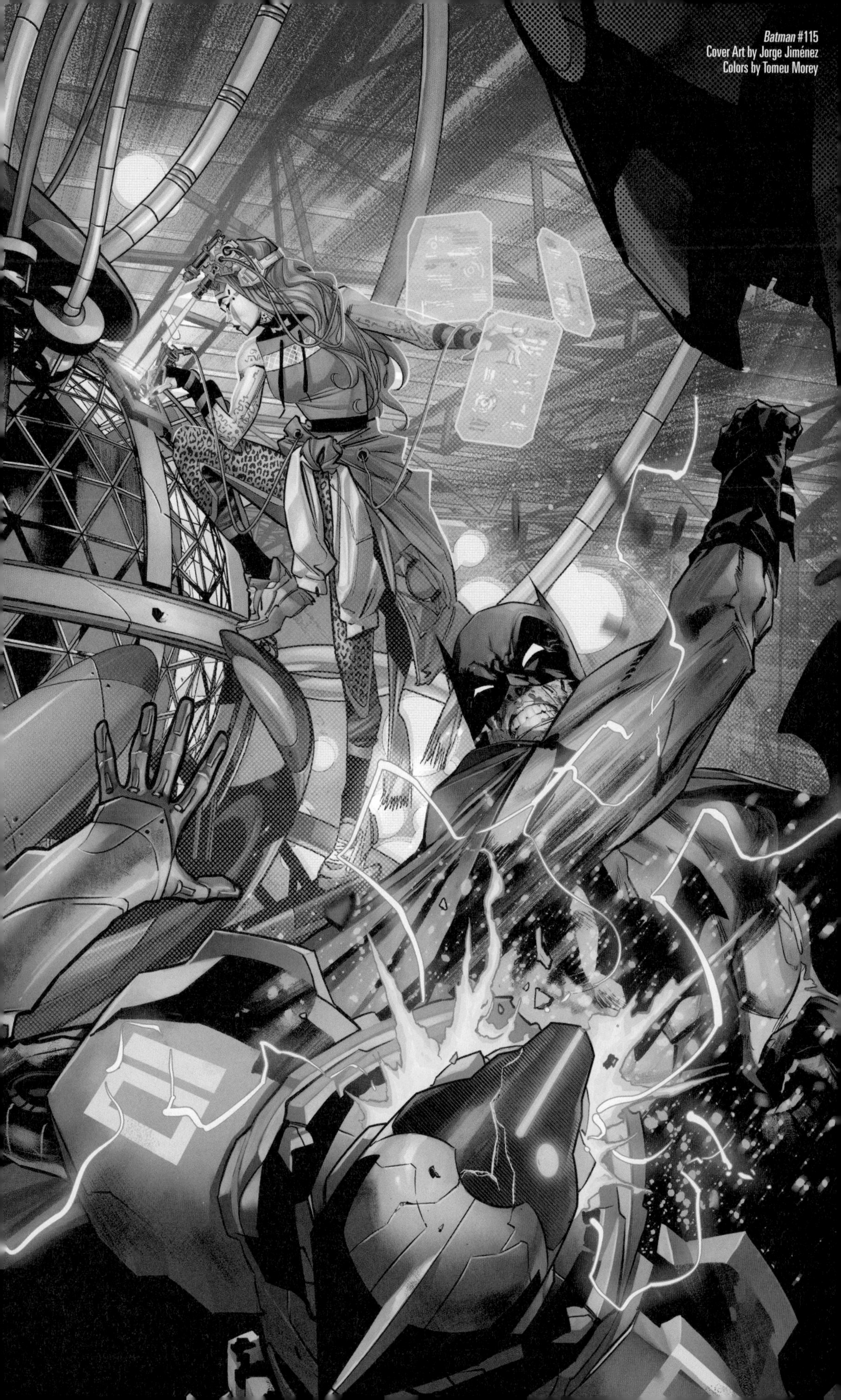

Batman #115
Cover Art by Jorge Jiménez
Colors by Tomeu Morey

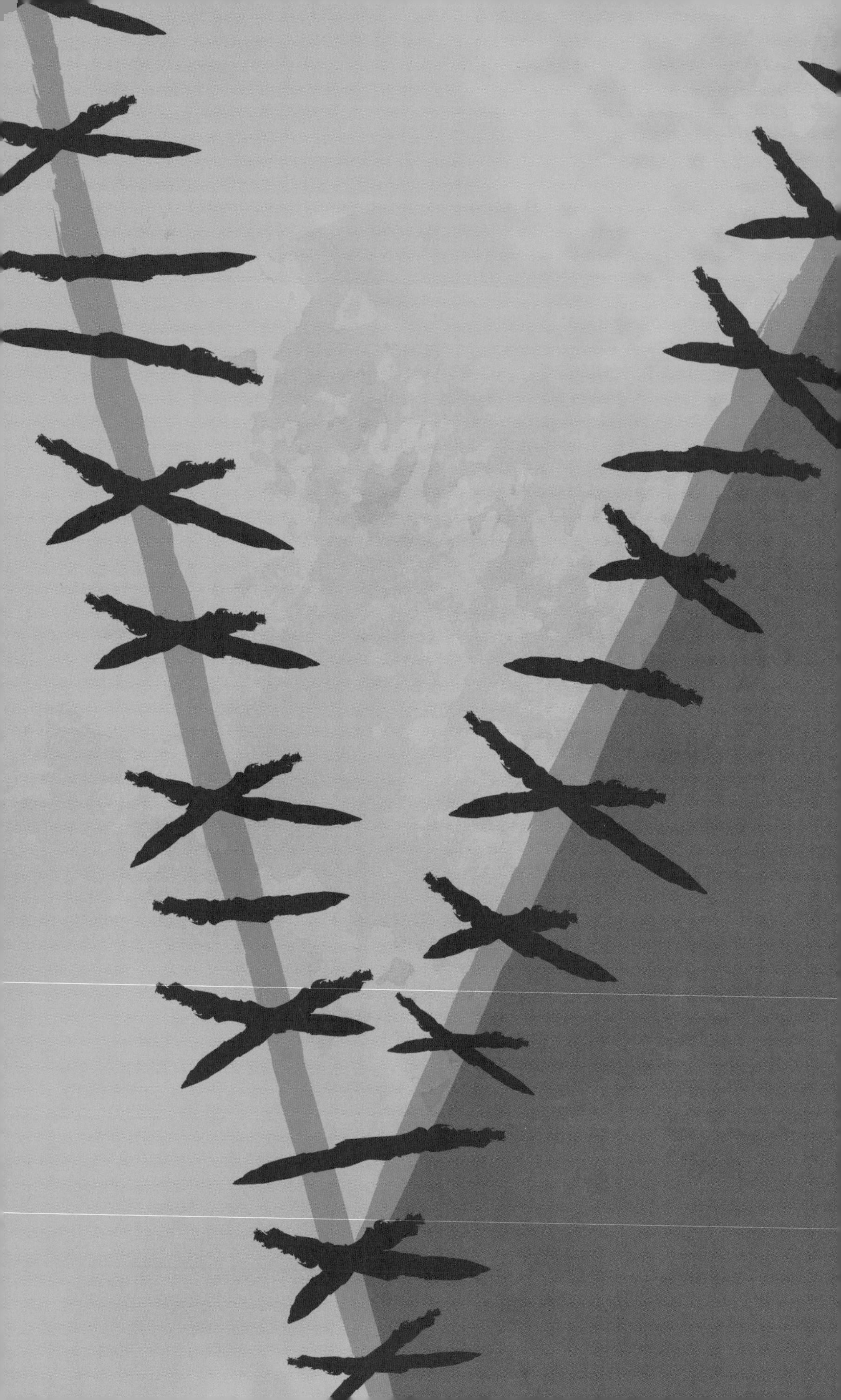

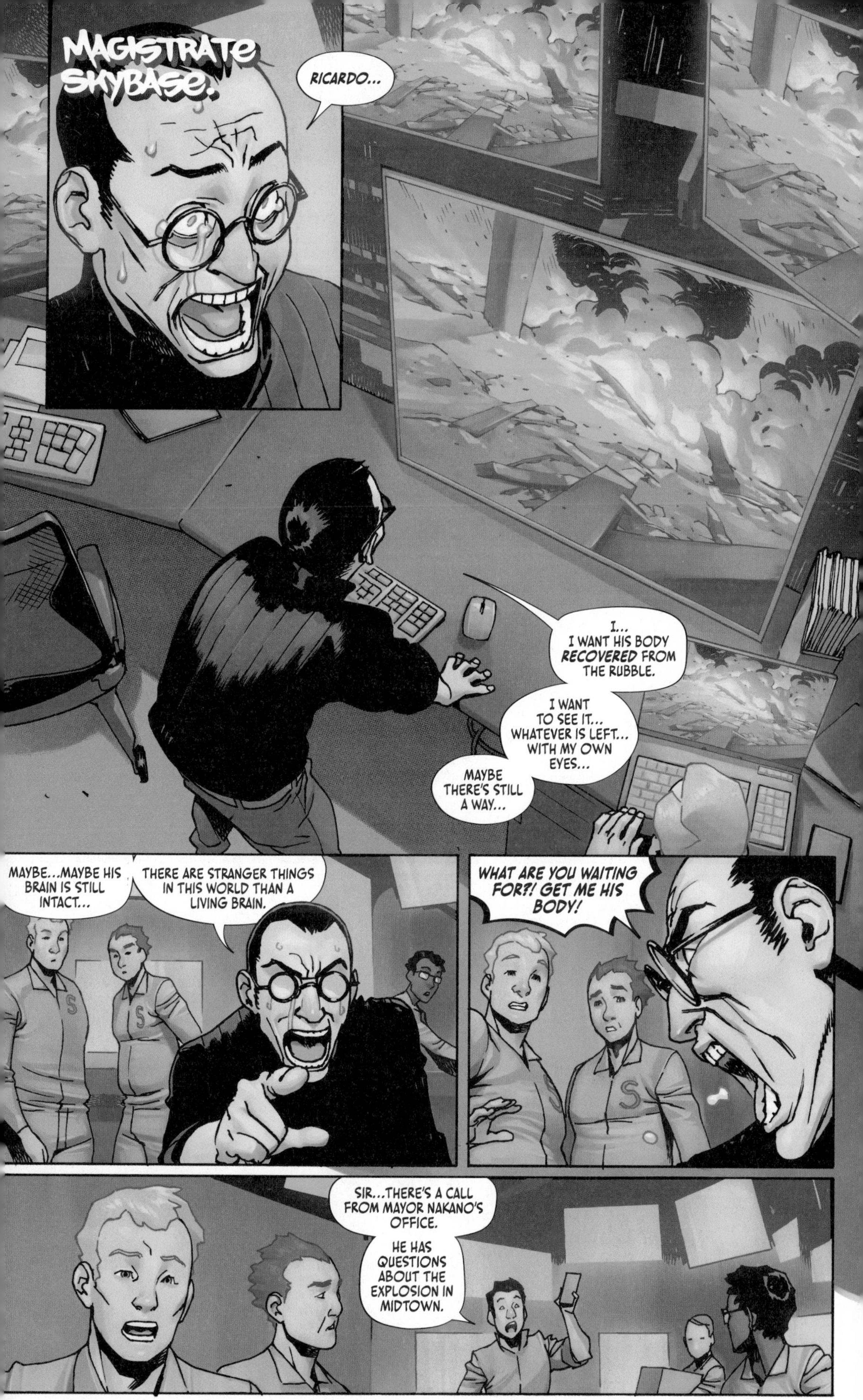
MAGISTRATE SKYBASE.
RICARDO...
I... I WANT HIS BODY *RECOVERED* FROM THE RUBBLE.
I WANT TO SEE IT... WHATEVER IS LEFT... WITH MY OWN EYES...
MAYBE THERE'S STILL A WAY...
MAYBE...MAYBE HIS BRAIN IS STILL INTACT...
THERE ARE STRANGER THINGS IN THIS WORLD THAN A LIVING BRAIN.
WHAT ARE YOU WAITING FOR?! GET ME HIS BODY!
SIR...THERE'S A CALL FROM MAYOR NAKANO'S OFFICE.
HE HAS QUESTIONS ABOUT THE EXPLOSION IN MIDTOWN.

NO... NO, NOT NOW...

I GUESS...TELL THE MAYOR WE'LL CALL HIM BACK.

OH, RICARDO... WHAT HAVE I DONE TO YOU?

MR. SAINT, SIR?

I THOUGHT YOU SHOULD SEE THIS. I DID SOME DIGGING AFTER SOME REPORTS OF A POISON IVY APPEARANCE IN OUR RAID IN *ALLEYTOWN*.

SO, I RAN SOME SEISMIC TESTS AND SCANS OF THE CITY... AND I FOUND SOMETHING CONCERNING.

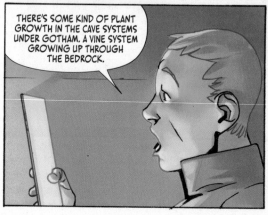

THERE'S SOME KIND OF PLANT GROWTH IN THE CAVE SYSTEMS UNDER GOTHAM. A VINE SYSTEM GROWING UP THROUGH THE BEDROCK.

"IF IVY USES HER ABILITIES TO THEIR FULL EXTENT, SHE COULD COLLAPSE ALL OF GOTHAM. IT WOULD BE WORSE THAN WHEN GOTHAM WAS A *NO MAN'S LAND*."

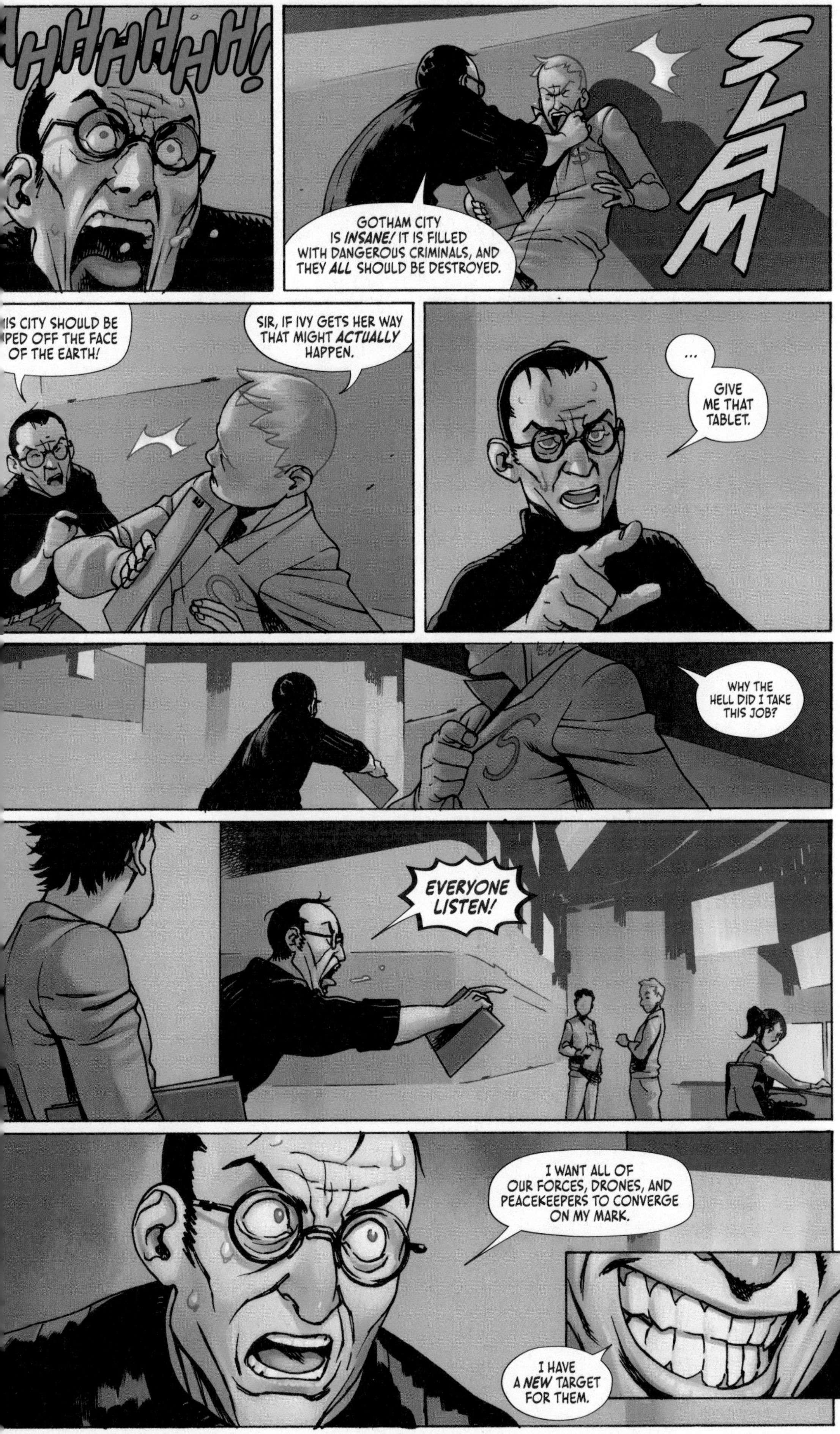
HHHHHH!
GOTHAM CITY IS INSANE! IT IS FILLED WITH DANGEROUS CRIMINALS, AND THEY ALL SHOULD BE DESTROYED.
SLAM
IS CITY SHOULD BE PED OFF THE FACE OF THE EARTH!
SIR, IF IVY GETS HER WAY THAT MIGHT ACTUALLY HAPPEN.
...
GIVE ME THAT TABLET.
WHY THE HELL DID I TAKE THIS JOB?
EVERYONE LISTEN!
I WANT ALL OF OUR FORCES, DRONES, AND PEACEKEEPERS TO CONVERGE ON MY MARK.
I HAVE A NEW TARGET FOR THEM.

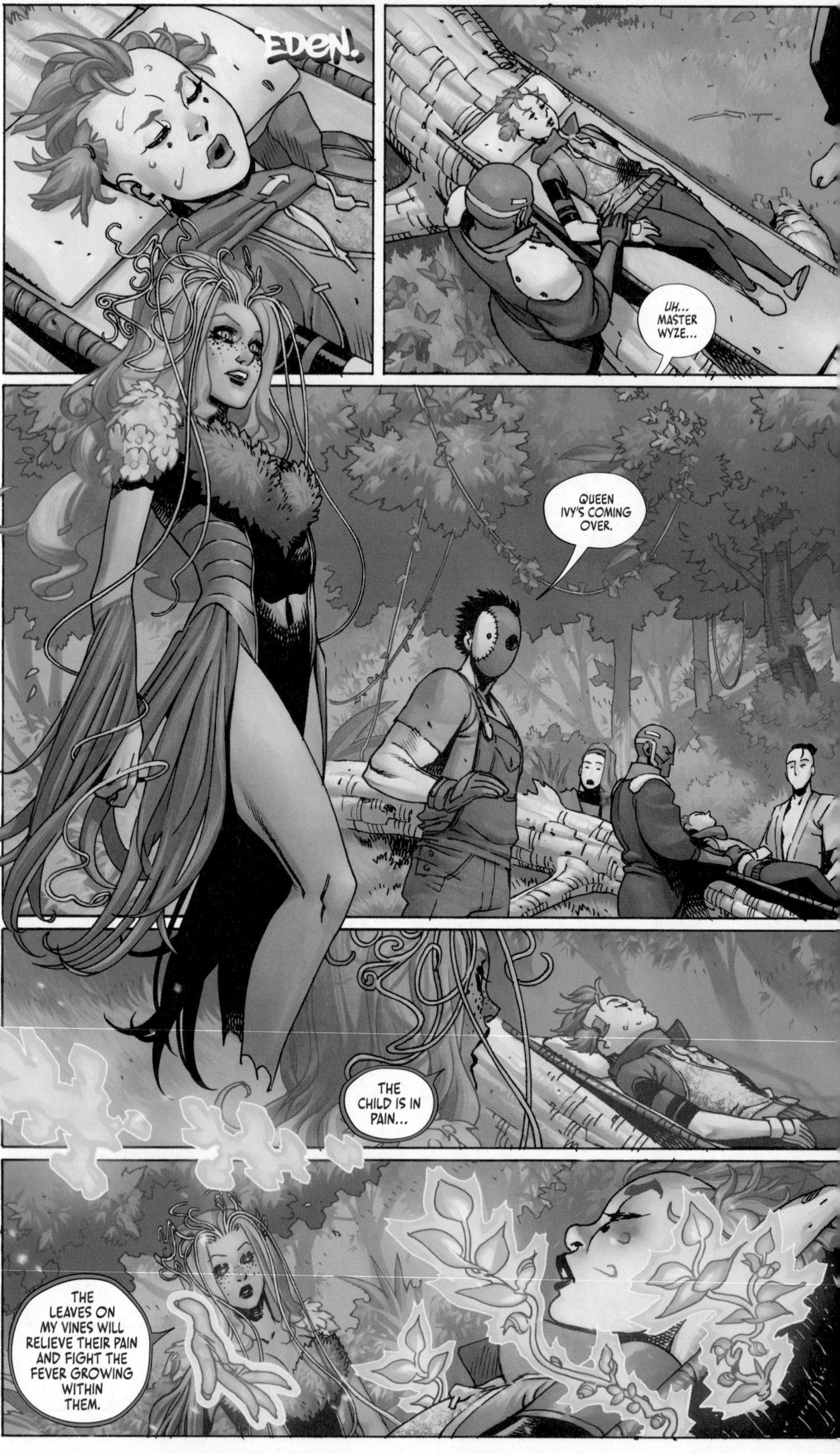
EDEN!
UH... MASTER WYZE...
QUEEN IVY'S COMING OVER.
THE CHILD IS IN PAIN...
THE LEAVES ON MY VINES WILL RELIEVE THEIR PAIN AND FIGHT THE FEVER GROWING WITHIN THEM.

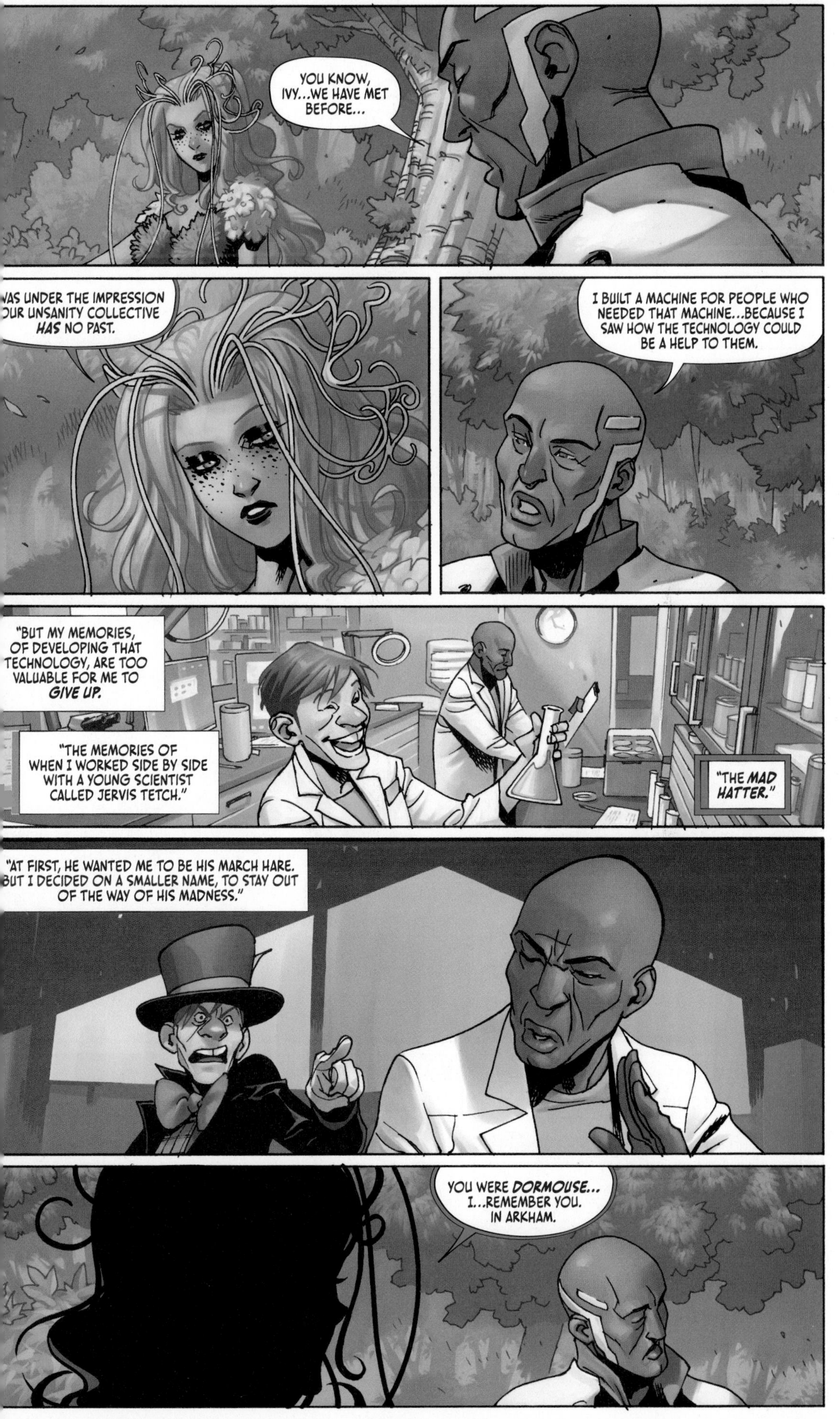

YOU KNOW, IVY...WE HAVE MET BEFORE...
WAS UNDER THE IMPRESSION OUR UNSANITY COLLECTIVE *HAS* NO PAST.
I BUILT A MACHINE FOR PEOPLE WHO NEEDED THAT MACHINE...BECAUSE I SAW HOW THE TECHNOLOGY COULD BE A HELP TO THEM.
"BUT MY MEMORIES, OF DEVELOPING THAT TECHNOLOGY, ARE TOO VALUABLE FOR ME TO *GIVE UP.*
"THE MEMORIES OF WHEN I WORKED SIDE BY SIDE WITH A YOUNG SCIENTIST CALLED JERVIS TETCH."
"THE *MAD HATTER.*"
"AT FIRST, HE WANTED ME TO BE HIS MARCH HARE. BUT I DECIDED ON A SMALLER NAME, TO STAY OUT OF THE WAY OF HIS MADNESS."
YOU WERE *DORMOUSE*... I...REMEMBER YOU. IN ARKHAM.

THE MILITARY HAD SPONSORED OUR RESEARCH INTO THE SECRETS OF THE MIND...BUT WHEN THE FUNDING VANISHED...

HATTER'S MADNESS, IT DIDN'T SEEM MENACING TO ME...IT WAS CHILDISH. INNOCENT, ALMOST...BUT IT ALLOWED ME TO CONTINUE MY WORK.

"IN TIME, I SAW THE COST. THE DAMAGE TO ORDINARY PEOPLE. AND IN ARKHAM, I SAW THE WAY SOCIETY DISCARDED THOSE OF US IT CALLED INSANE.

"THE WAY IT PUSHED US TO THE FRINGE, AND GOT SICKER AND SICKER. I SAW THE CYCLE THE CITY WAS TRAPPED IN. I WANTED TO BREAK THE CYCLE."

WHY ARE YOU TELLING ME THIS?

I NEEDED A MACHINE TO SAVE A FEW HUNDRED PEOPLE. BUT NOT SO LONG AGO, YOUR POWERS ALLOWED YOU TO TOUCH THE MINDS OF MANY MORE.

AND MY ACTION SENT ME TOWAR MY DEATH, REBIRT AND SO MUCH MORE ANGER.

I KNOW A LITTLE SOMETHING ABOUT PLAYING THE PART YOU ARE FORCED TO PLAY. ABOUT TRYING TO LOOK STRONG. MAYBE GARDENER AND HARLEY QUINN ARE RIGHT. MAYBE PART OF YOU IS MISSING.

BUT I SEE A LOT MORE HAPPENING UNDER THE SURFACE WITH YOU. YOU HELPED ALL OF US. YOU SAW A CHILD IN NEED AND YOU HELPED THEM.

WHAT MORE DO YOU HAVE THE POWER TO DO?

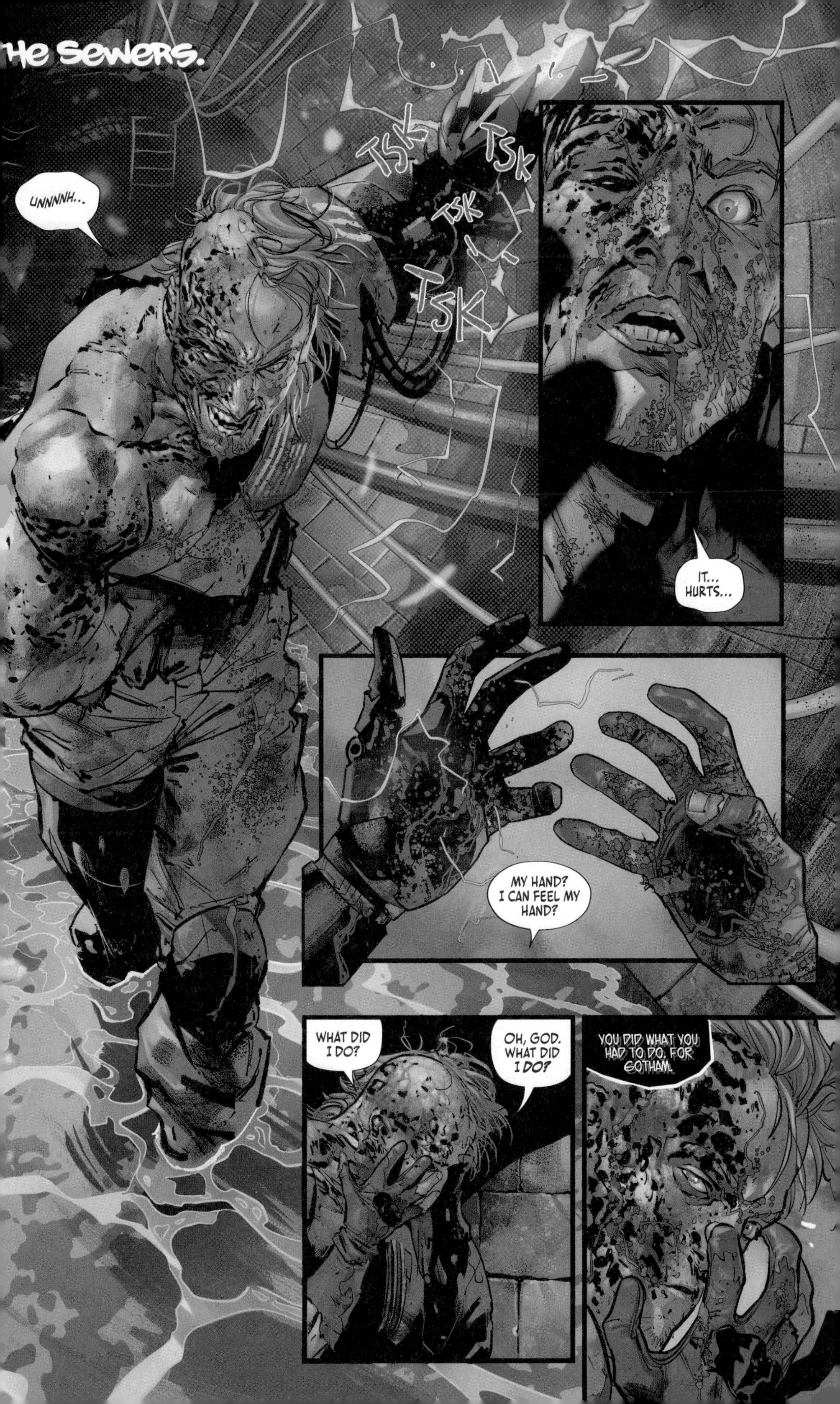

HE SEWERS.
UNNNNH...
TSK
TSK
TSK
TSK
IT... HURTS...
MY HAND? I CAN FEEL MY HAND?
WHAT DID I DO?
OH, GOD. WHAT DID I DO?
YOU DID WHAT YOU HAD TO DO. FOR GOTHAM.

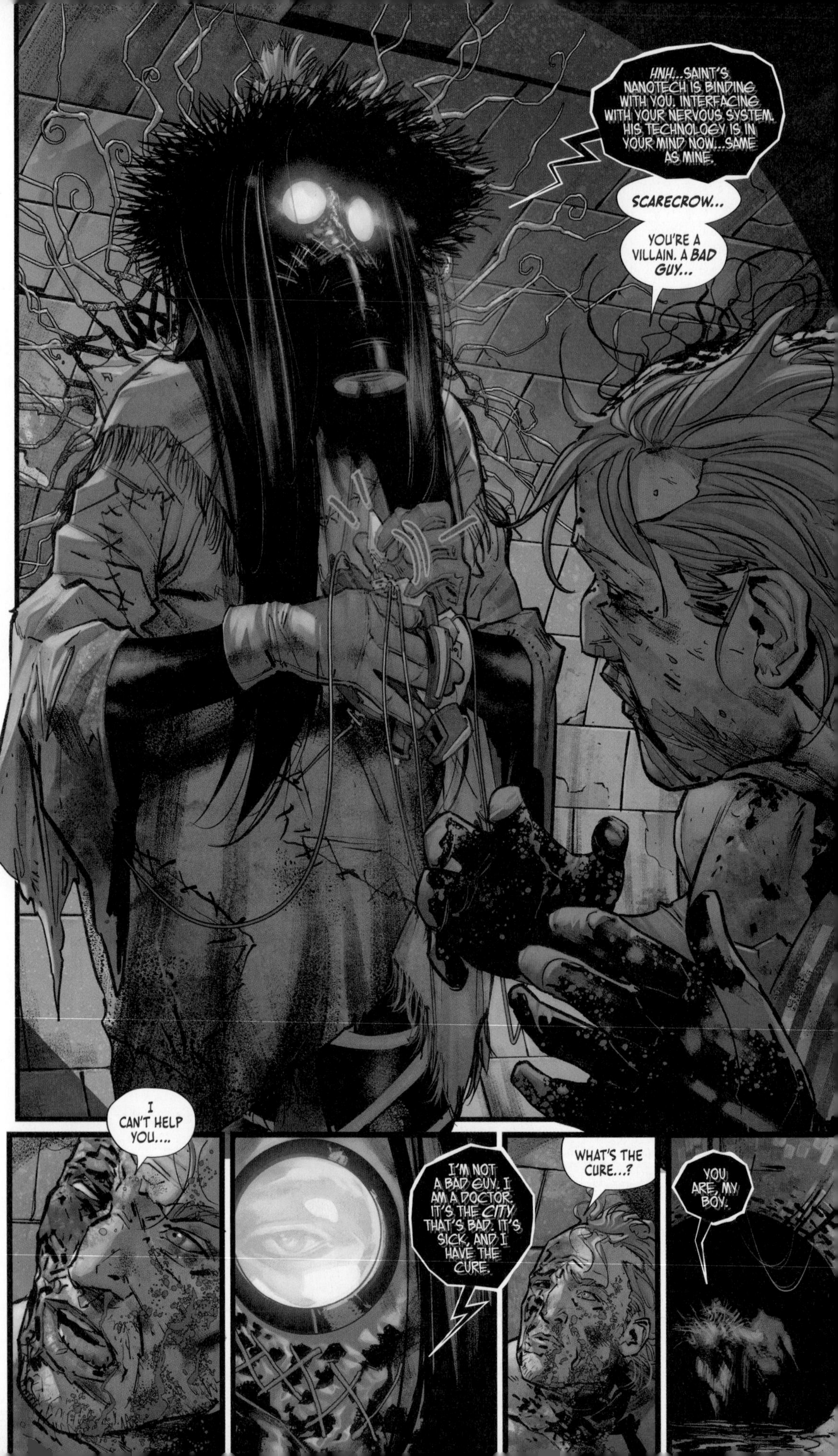
HNH...SAINT'S NANOTECH IS BINDING WITH YOU. INTERFACING WITH YOUR NERVOUS SYSTEM. HIS TECHNOLOGY IS IN YOUR MIND NOW...SAME AS MINE.
SCARECROW...
YOU'RE A VILLAIN. A BAD GUY...
I CAN'T HELP YOU....
I'M NOT A BAD GUY. I AM A DOCTOR. IT'S THE CITY THAT'S BAD. IT'S SICK, AND I HAVE THE CURE.
WHAT'S THE CURE...?
YOU ARE, MY BOY.

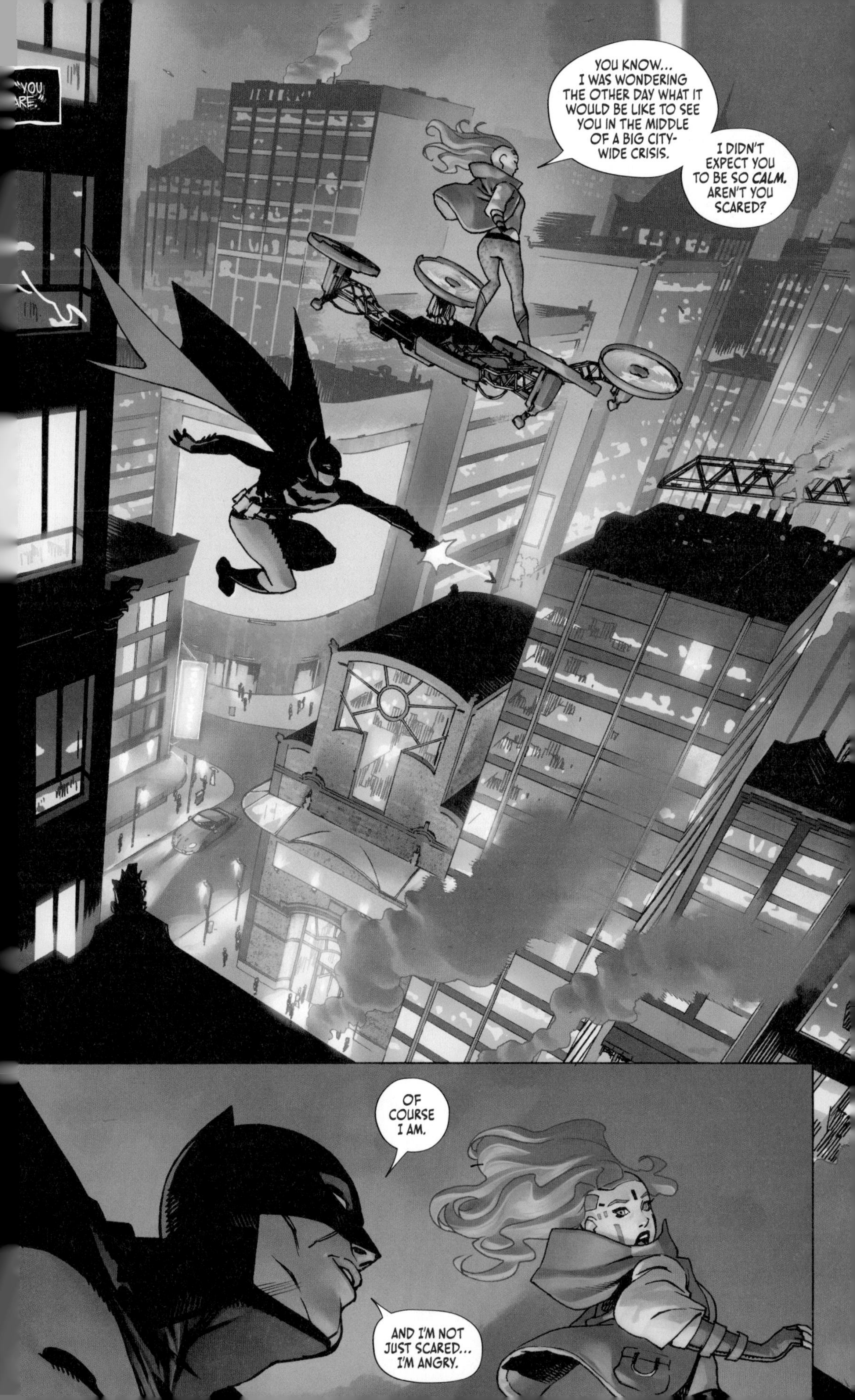

“YOU ARE.”
YOU KNOW... I WAS WONDERING THE OTHER DAY WHAT IT WOULD BE LIKE TO SEE YOU IN THE MIDDLE OF A BIG CITY-WIDE CRISIS.
I DIDN'T EXPECT YOU TO BE SO CALM. AREN'T YOU SCARED?
OF COURSE I AM.
AND I'M NOT JUST SCARED... I'M ANGRY.

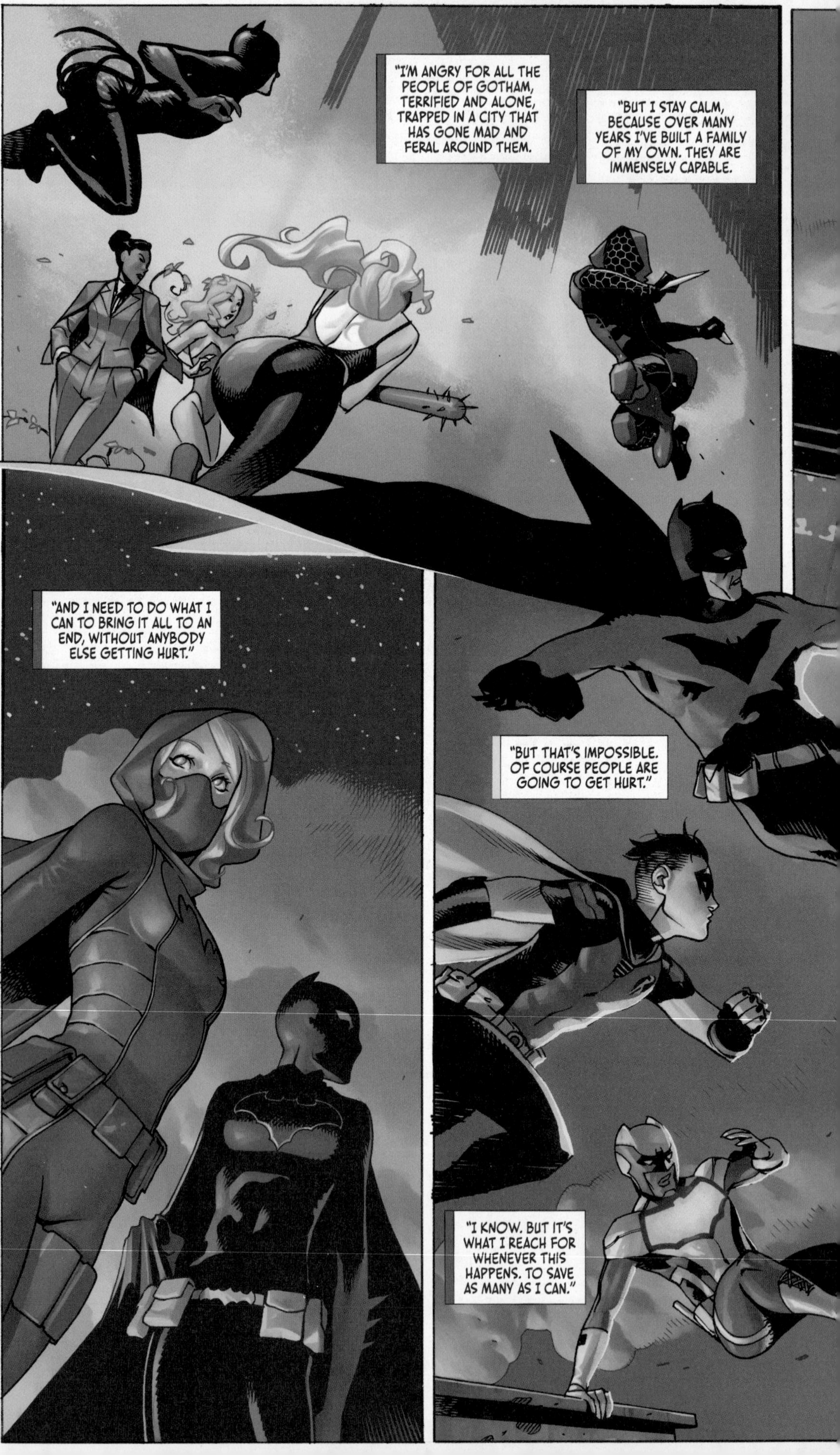

"I'M ANGRY FOR ALL THE PEOPLE OF GOTHAM, TERRIFIED AND ALONE, TRAPPED IN A CITY THAT HAS GONE MAD AND FERAL AROUND THEM.
"BUT I STAY CALM, BECAUSE OVER MANY YEARS I'VE BUILT A FAMILY OF MY OWN. THEY ARE IMMENSELY CAPABLE.
"AND I NEED TO DO WHAT I CAN TO BRING IT ALL TO AN END, WITHOUT ANYBODY ELSE GETTING HURT."
"BUT THAT'S IMPOSSIBLE. OF COURSE PEOPLE ARE GOING TO GET HURT."
"I KNOW. BUT IT'S WHAT I REACH FOR WHENEVER THIS HAPPENS. TO SAVE AS MANY AS I CAN."

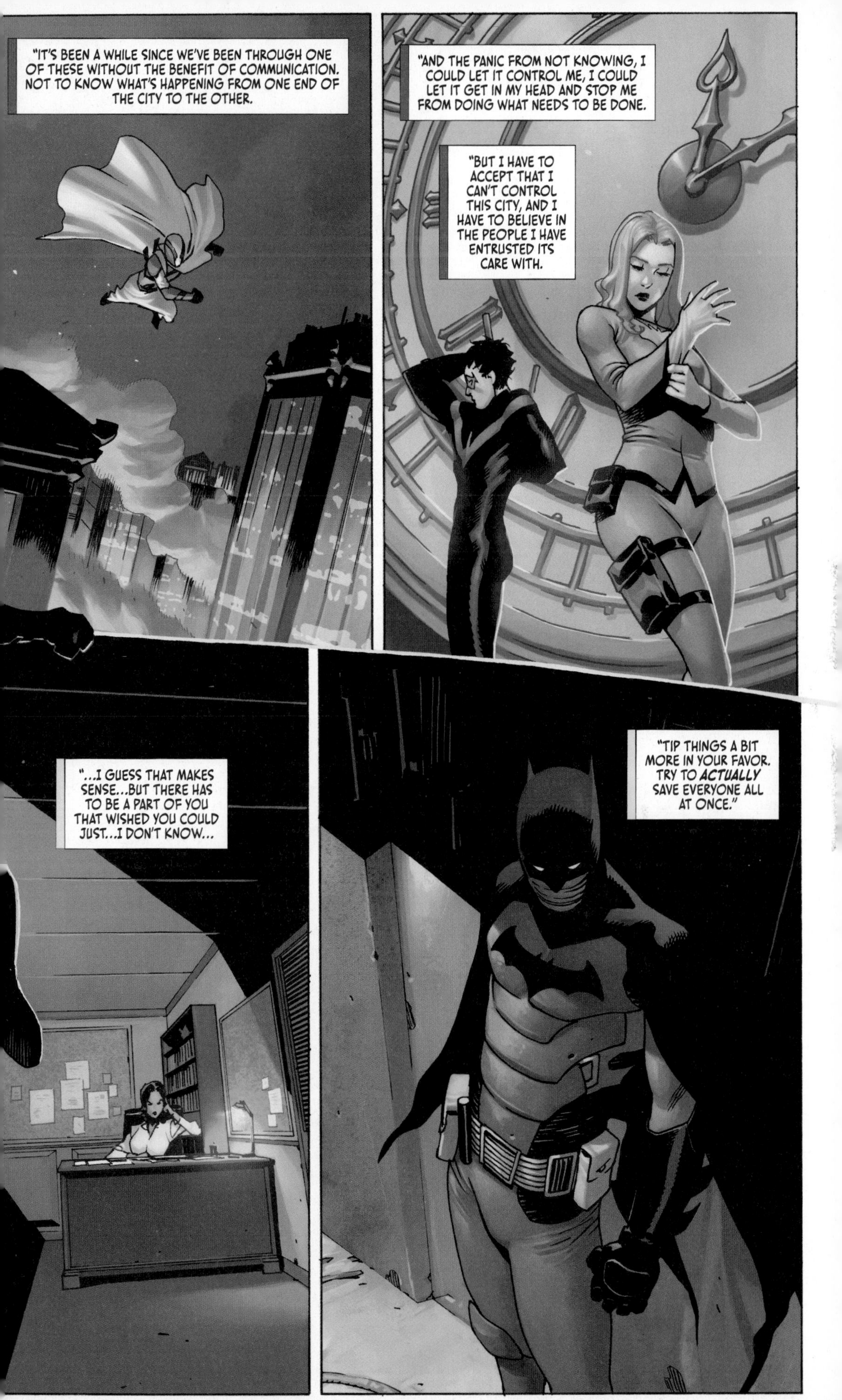
"IT'S BEEN A WHILE SINCE WE'VE BEEN THROUGH ONE OF THESE WITHOUT THE BENEFIT OF COMMUNICATION. NOT TO KNOW WHAT'S HAPPENING FROM ONE END OF THE CITY TO THE OTHER.
"AND THE PANIC FROM NOT KNOWING, I COULD LET IT CONTROL ME, I COULD LET IT GET IN MY HEAD AND STOP ME FROM DOING WHAT NEEDS TO BE DONE.
"BUT I HAVE TO ACCEPT THAT I CAN'T CONTROL THIS CITY, AND I HAVE TO BELIEVE IN THE PEOPLE I HAVE ENTRUSTED ITS CARE WITH.
"...I GUESS THAT MAKES SENSE...BUT THERE HAS TO BE A PART OF YOU THAT WISHED YOU COULD JUST...I DON'T KNOW...
"TIP THINGS A BIT MORE IN YOUR FAVOR. TRY TO *ACTUALLY* SAVE EVERYONE ALL AT ONCE."

IT'S NEVER THAT SIMPLE.

HM. YEAH, OKAY.

WHY ARE WE HERE, MIRACLE MOLLY? WHY ARE WE BACK AT THE UNSANITY COLLECTIVE'S HIDDEN BASE? WE KNOW IT'S BEEN COMPROMISED BY THE MAGISTRATE...

YEAH, THAT'S PART OF IT.

OKAY, SO...THE MIND MACHINE.

IT'S A DEVICE THAT MASTER WYZE BUILT THAT CAN STRIP AWAY YOUR MEMORIES AND ALL OF YOUR TRAUMA. IT GIVES YOU A BLANK SLATE, SO YOU CAN REBOOT YOUR LIFE.

BECOME WHO YOU WERE ALWAYS MEANT TO BE.

I HELPED WYZE REFINE IT AFTER IT WENT THROUGH THE PROCESS...SO I KNOW A FEW THINGS THE OTHER MEMBERS OF THE COLLECTIVE DON'T KNOW.

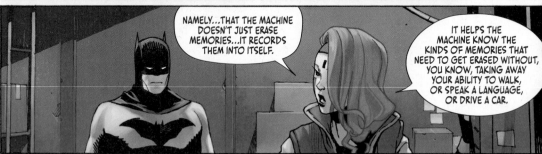

NAMELY...THAT THE MACHINE DOESN'T JUST ERASE MEMORIES...IT RECORDS THEM INTO ITSELF.

IT HELPS THE MACHINE KNOW THE KINDS OF MEMORIES THAT NEED TO GET ERASED WITHOUT, YOU KNOW, TAKING AWAY YOUR ABILITY TO WALK, OR SPEAK A LANGUAGE, OR DRIVE A CAR.

"AND I WAS THINKING, DOWN IN EDEN. SCARECROW IS TRYING TO PUSH THINGS RIGHT NOW. TRYING TO TRAUMATIZE THE WHOLE CITY...

"WHAT WOULD HAPPEN IF HE GOT HIS HANDS ON A MACHINE LOADED UP WITH A FEW HUNDRED PEOPLE'S TRAUMA, AND WEAPONIZED IT...

"TURNED IT INTO A KIND OF TRAUMA BOMB ON THE CITY.

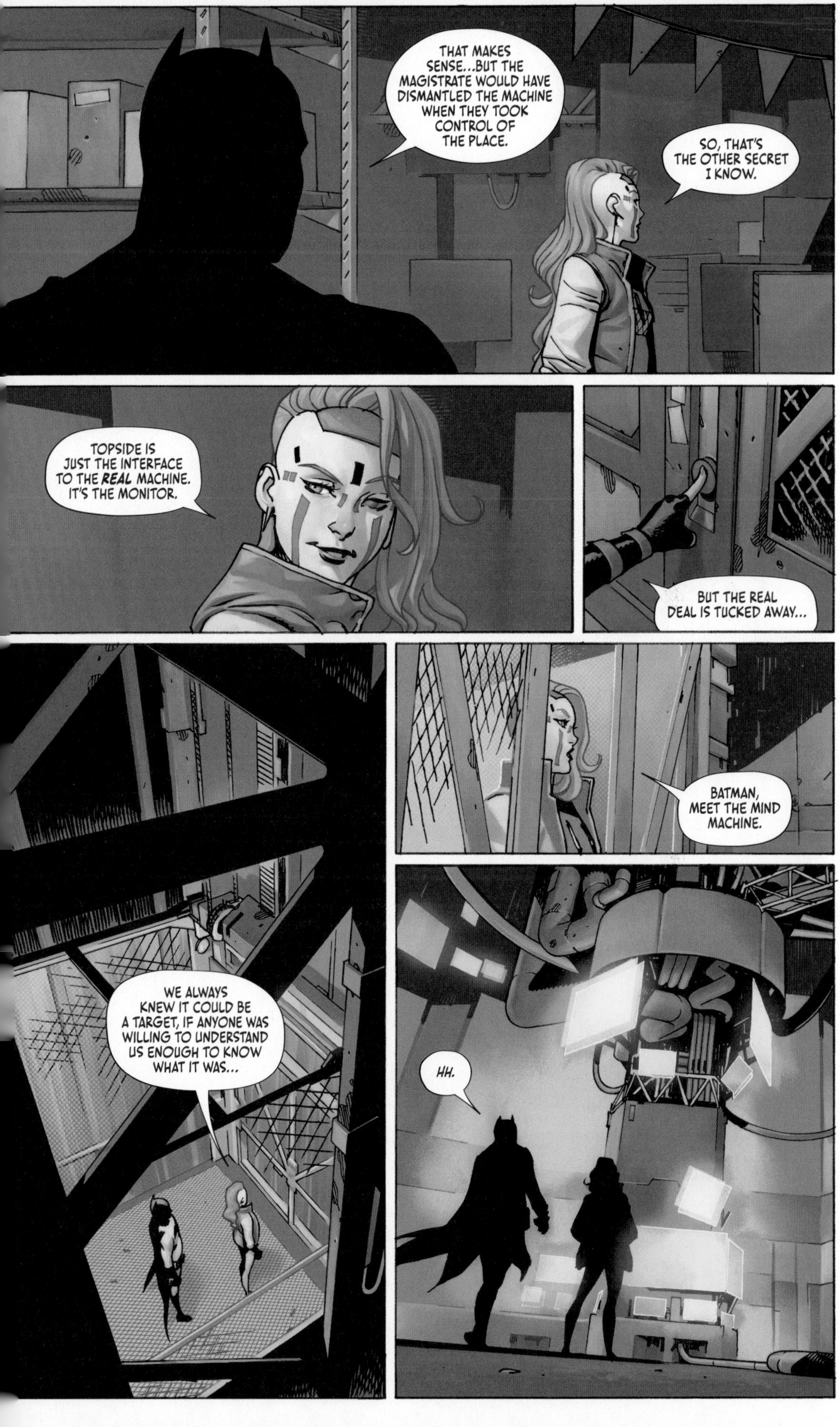
THAT MAKES SENSE...BUT THE MAGISTRATE WOULD HAVE DISMANTLED THE MACHINE WHEN THEY TOOK CONTROL OF THE PLACE.
SO, THAT'S THE OTHER SECRET I KNOW.
TOPSIDE IS JUST THE INTERFACE TO THE *REAL* MACHINE. IT'S THE MONITOR.
BUT THE REAL DEAL IS TUCKED AWAY...
WE ALWAYS KNEW IT COULD BE A TARGET, IF ANYONE WAS WILLING TO UNDERSTAND US ENOUGH TO KNOW WHAT IT WAS...
BATMAN, MEET THE MIND MACHINE.
HH.

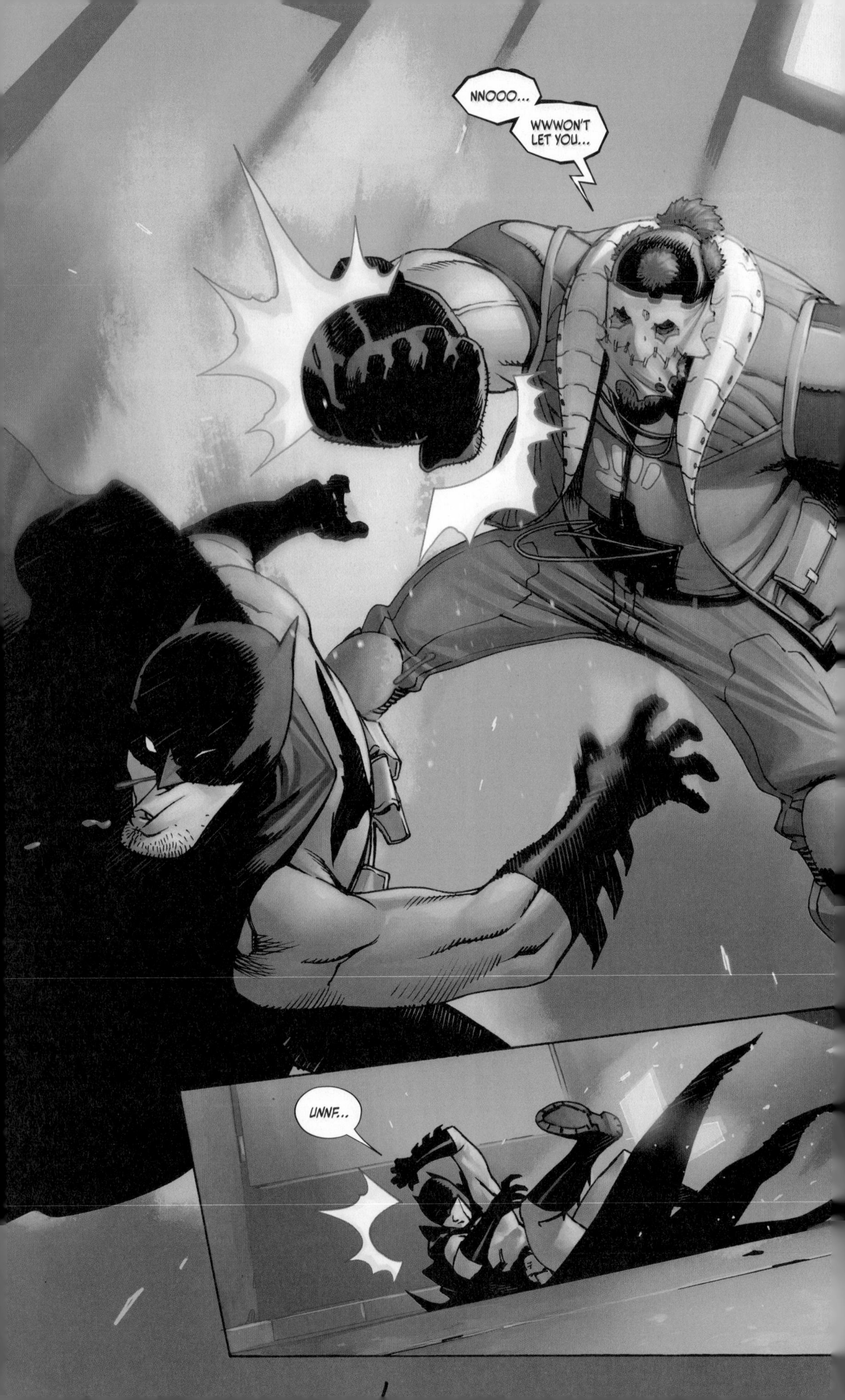
NNOOO...
WWWON'T LET YOU...
UNNF...

HNNNNN...

BREAKER? WHAT ARE YOU *DOING?*

SCARECROW HAS HIS OWN MIND CONTROL TECHNOLOGY IN PLAY. HE TRIED TO USE IT ON ME, TURN ME INTO HIS PUPPET...

YOUR FRIEND *CAN'T* HEAR YOU.

BUT AT LEAST IT SEEMS LIKE HIS PROGRAMMING IS LIMITED TO PROTECTING WHAT SCARECROW LEFT BEHIND. HE'S NOT PURSUING US.

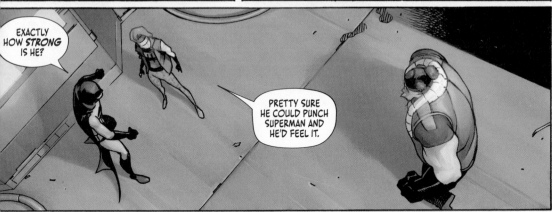

EXACTLY HOW *STRONG* IS HE?

PRETTY SURE HE COULD PUNCH SUPERMAN AND HE'D FEEL IT.

THAT'S NOT ENCOURAGING...

SORRY. I'M GOOD AT BUILDING STUFF. THOSE GAUNTLETS OF HIS ARE SOME OF MY BEST WORK.

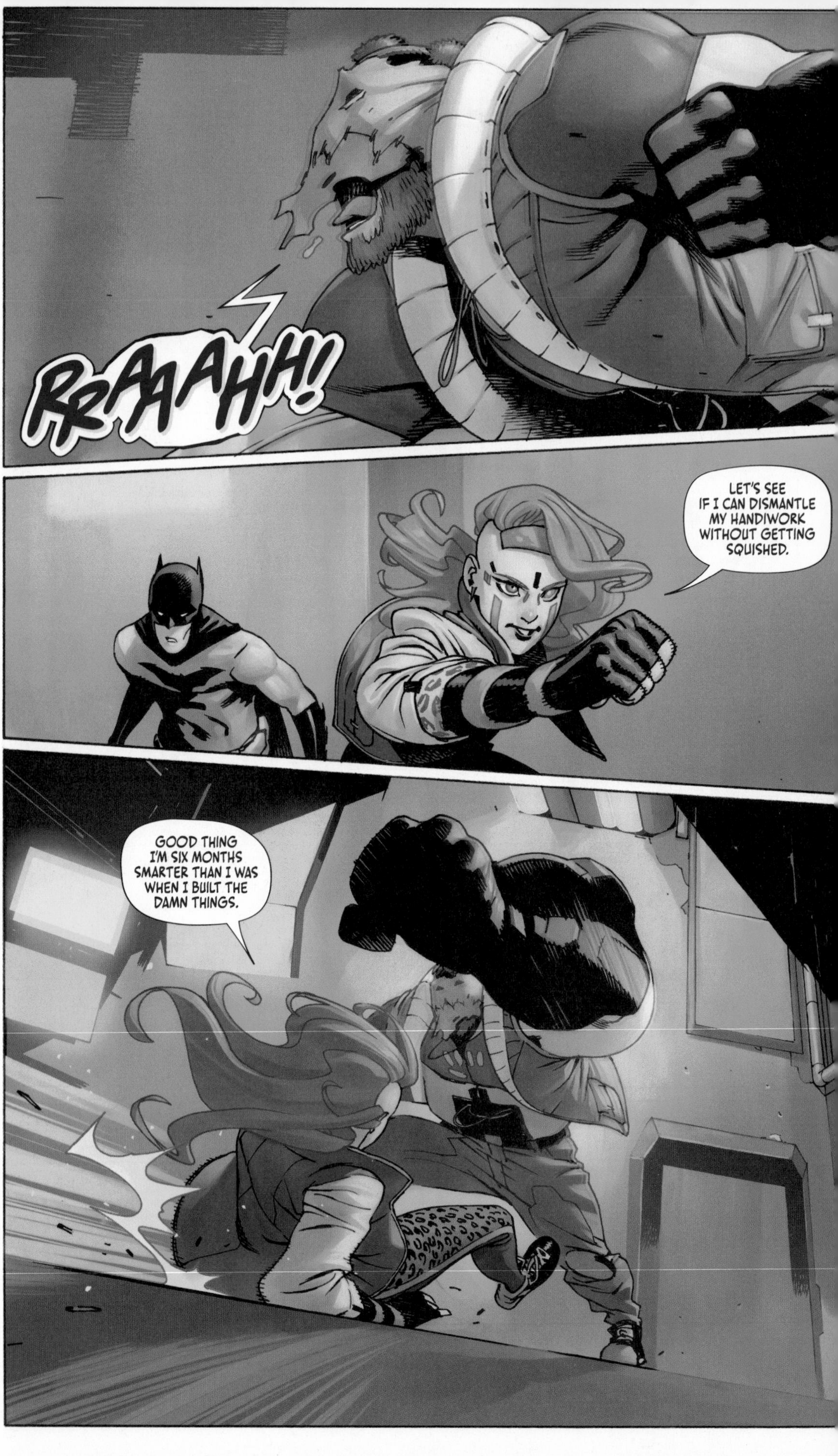
RRAAAHH!
LET'S SEE IF I CAN DISMANTLE MY HANDIWORK WITHOUT GETTING SQUISHED.
GOOD THING I'M SIX MONTHS SMARTER THAN I WAS WHEN I BUILT THE DAMN THINGS.

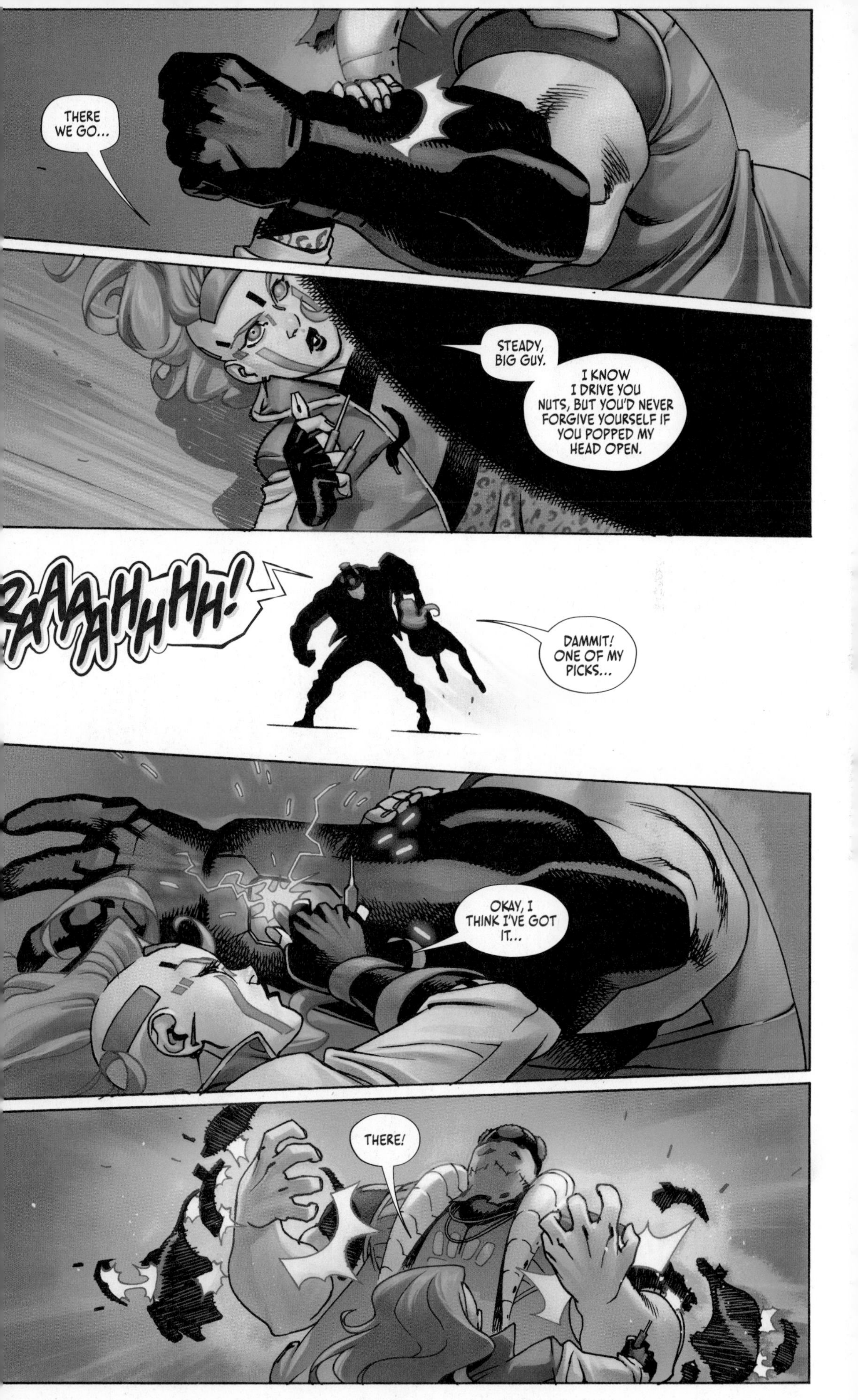
THERE WE GO...
STEADY, BIG GUY.
I KNOW I DRIVE YOU NUTS, BUT YOU'D NEVER FORGIVE YOURSELF IF YOU POPPED MY HEAD OPEN.
RAAAAHHHH!
DAMMIT! ONE OF MY PICKS...
OKAY, I THINK I'VE GOT IT...
THERE!

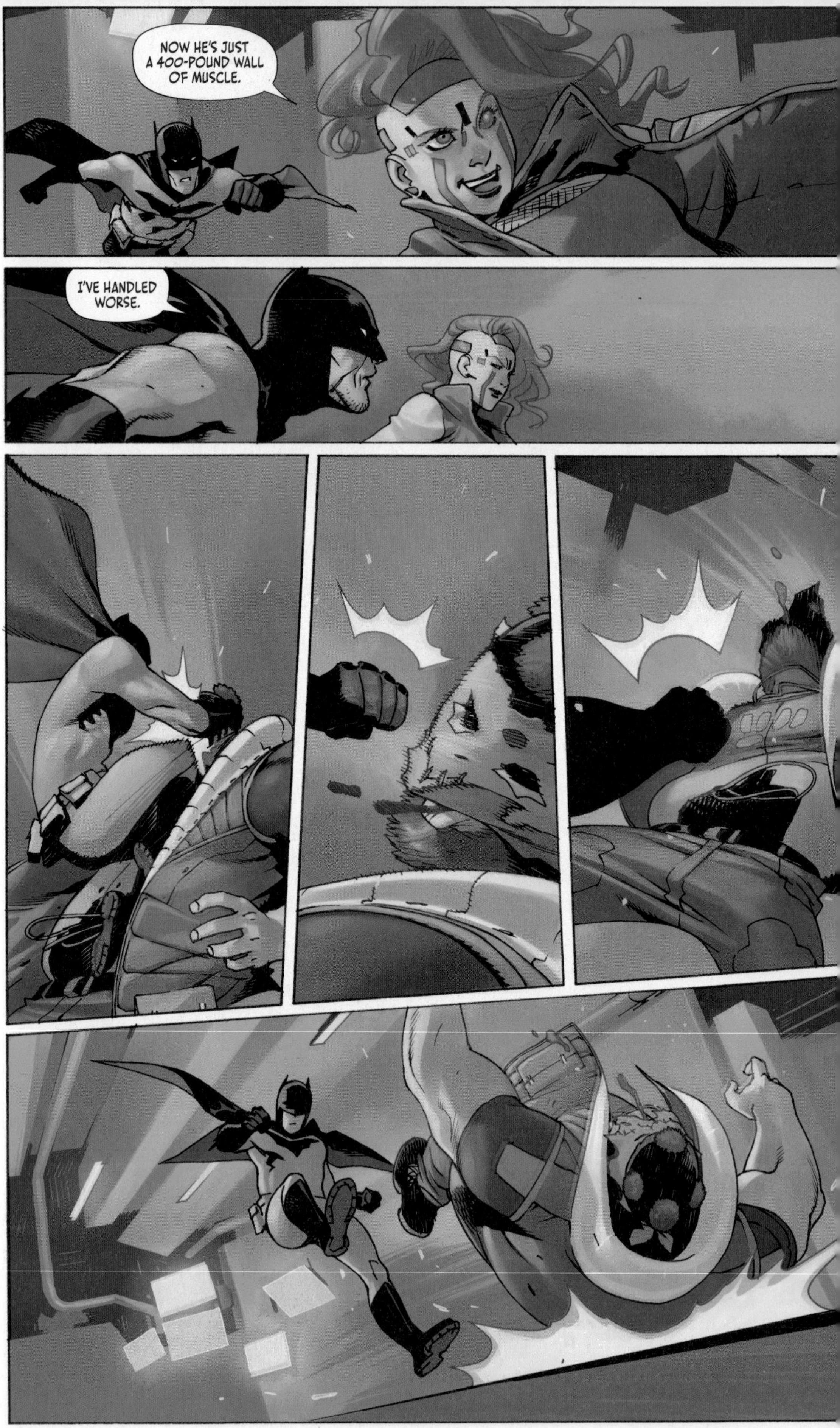
NOW HE'S JUST A 400-POUND WALL OF MUSCLE.
I'VE HANDLED WORSE.

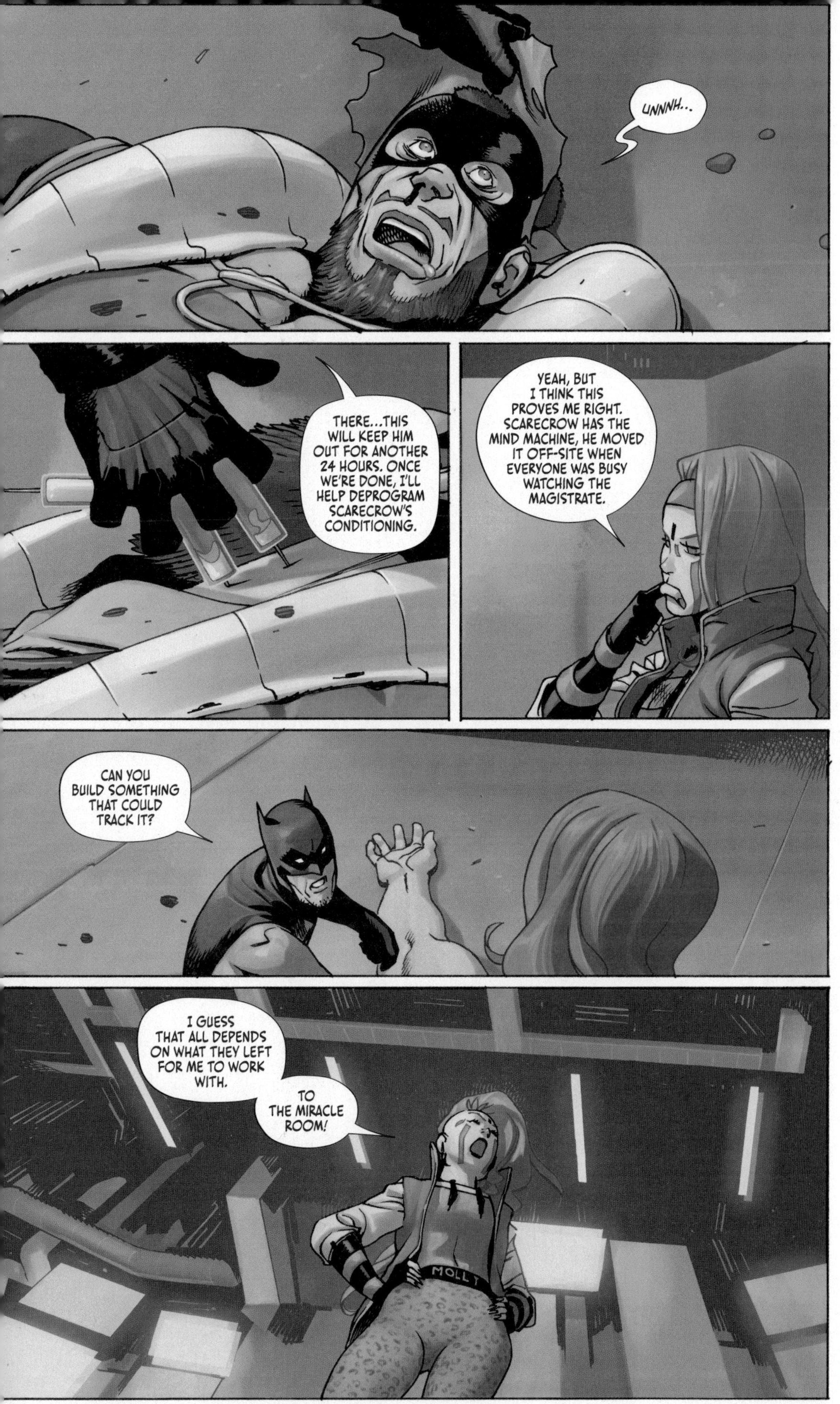
UNNNH...
THERE...THIS WILL KEEP HIM OUT FOR ANOTHER 24 HOURS. ONCE WE'RE DONE, I'LL HELP DEPROGRAM SCARECROW'S CONDITIONING.
YEAH, BUT I THINK THIS PROVES ME RIGHT. SCARECROW HAS THE MIND MACHINE, HE MOVED IT OFF-SITE WHEN EVERYONE WAS BUSY WATCHING THE MAGISTRATE.
CAN YOU BUILD SOMETHING THAT COULD TRACK IT?
I GUESS THAT ALL DEPENDS ON WHAT THEY LEFT FOR ME TO WORK WITH.
TO THE MIRACLE ROOM!
MOLLY

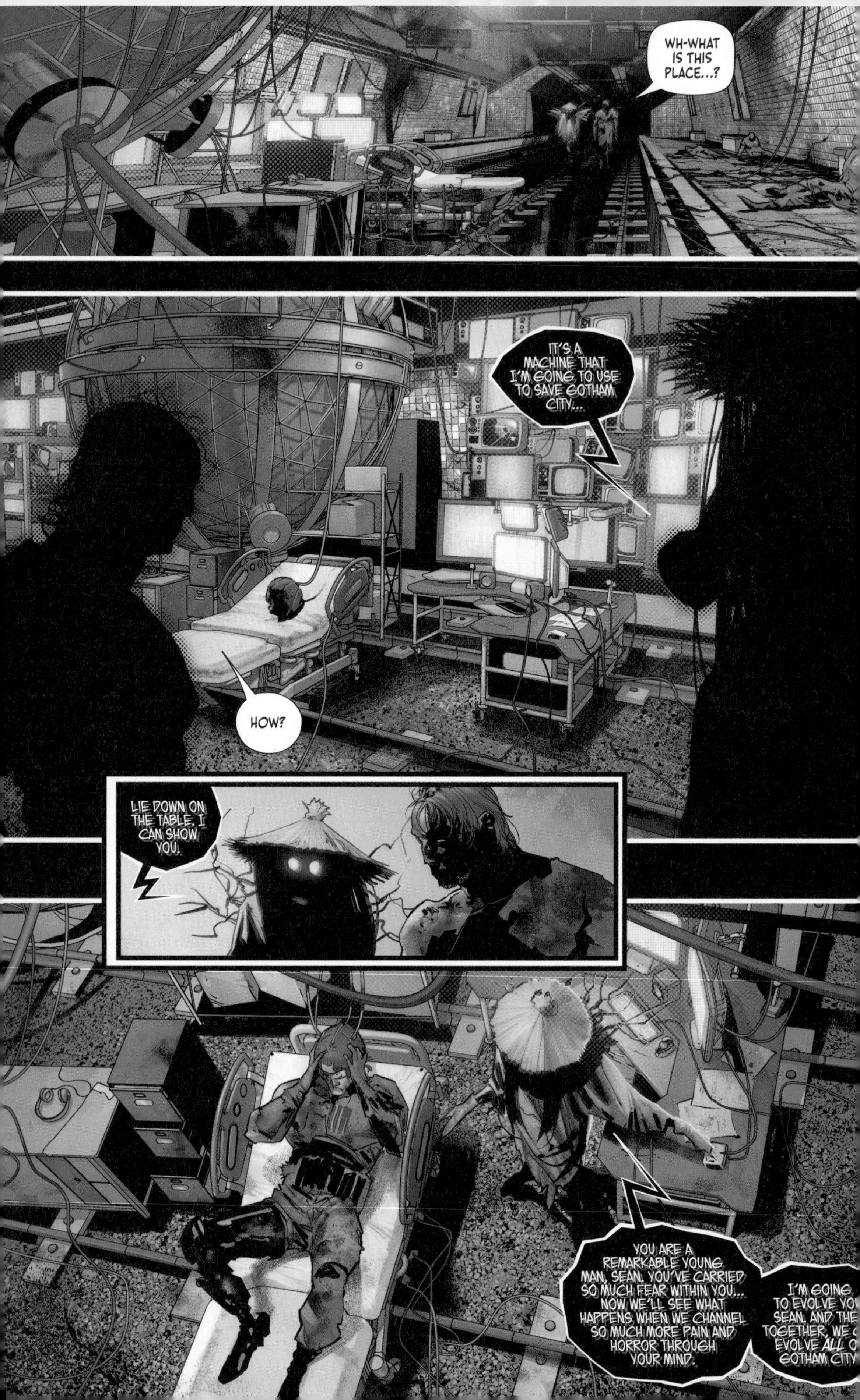
WH-WHAT IS THIS PLACE...?
IT'S A MACHINE THAT I'M GOING TO USE TO SAVE GOTHAM CITY...
HOW?
LIE DOWN ON THE TABLE. I CAN SHOW YOU.
YOU ARE A REMARKABLE YOUNG MAN, SEAN. YOU'VE CARRIED SO MUCH FEAR WITHIN YOU... NOW WE'LL SEE WHAT HAPPENS WHEN WE CHANNEL SO MUCH MORE PAIN AND HORROR THROUGH YOUR MIND.
I'M GOING TO EVOLVE YO SEAN. AND THE TOGETHER, WE EVOLVE *ALL* O GOTHAM CITY

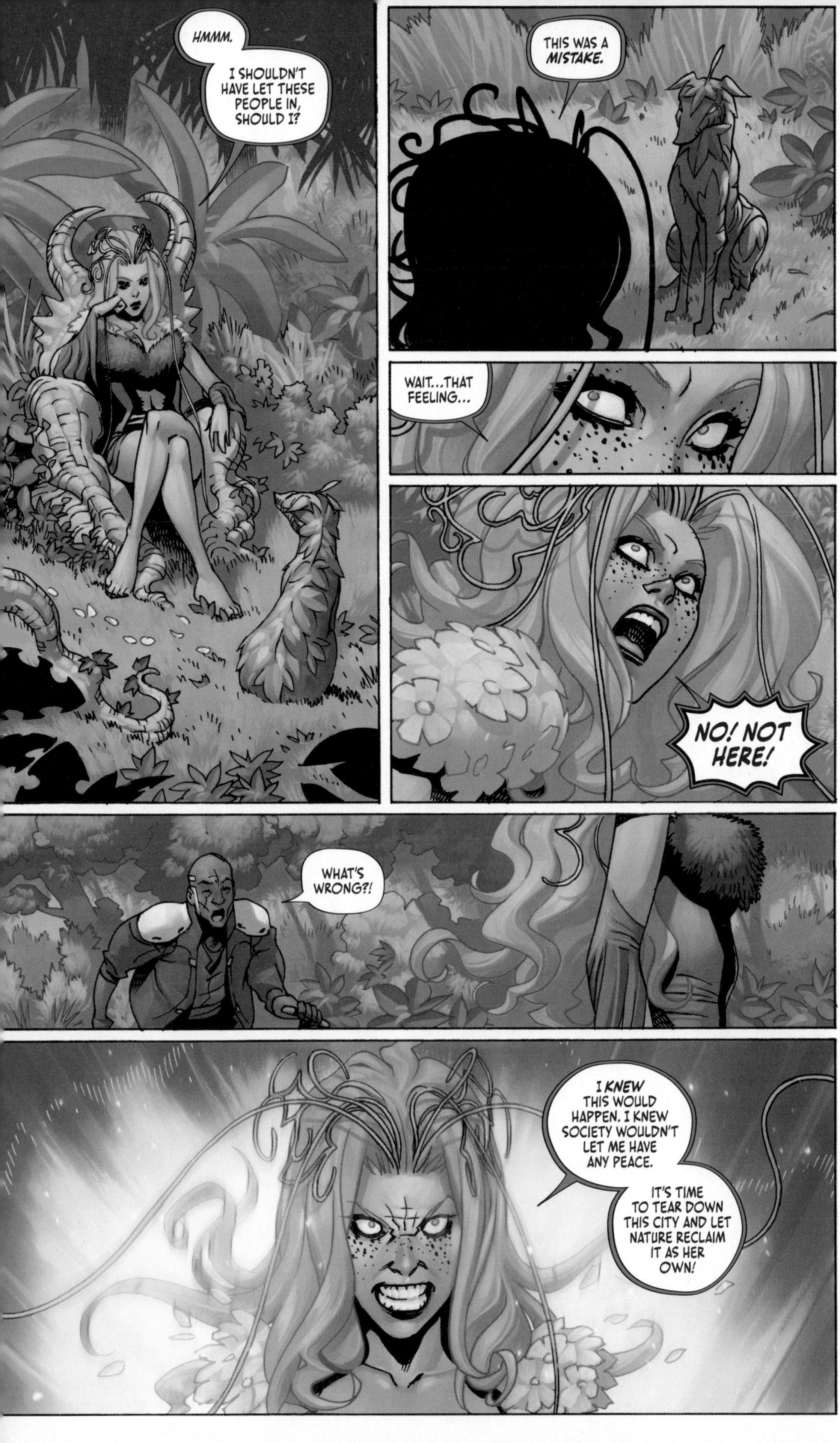
HMMM.
I SHOULDN'T HAVE LET THESE PEOPLE IN, SHOULD I?
THIS WAS A MISTAKE.
WAIT...THAT FEELING...
NO! NOT HERE!
WHAT'S WRONG?!
I KNEW THIS WOULD HAPPEN. I KNEW SOCIETY WOULDN'T LET ME HAVE ANY PEACE.
IT'S TIME TO TEAR DOWN THIS CITY AND LET NATURE RECLAIM IT AS HER OWN!

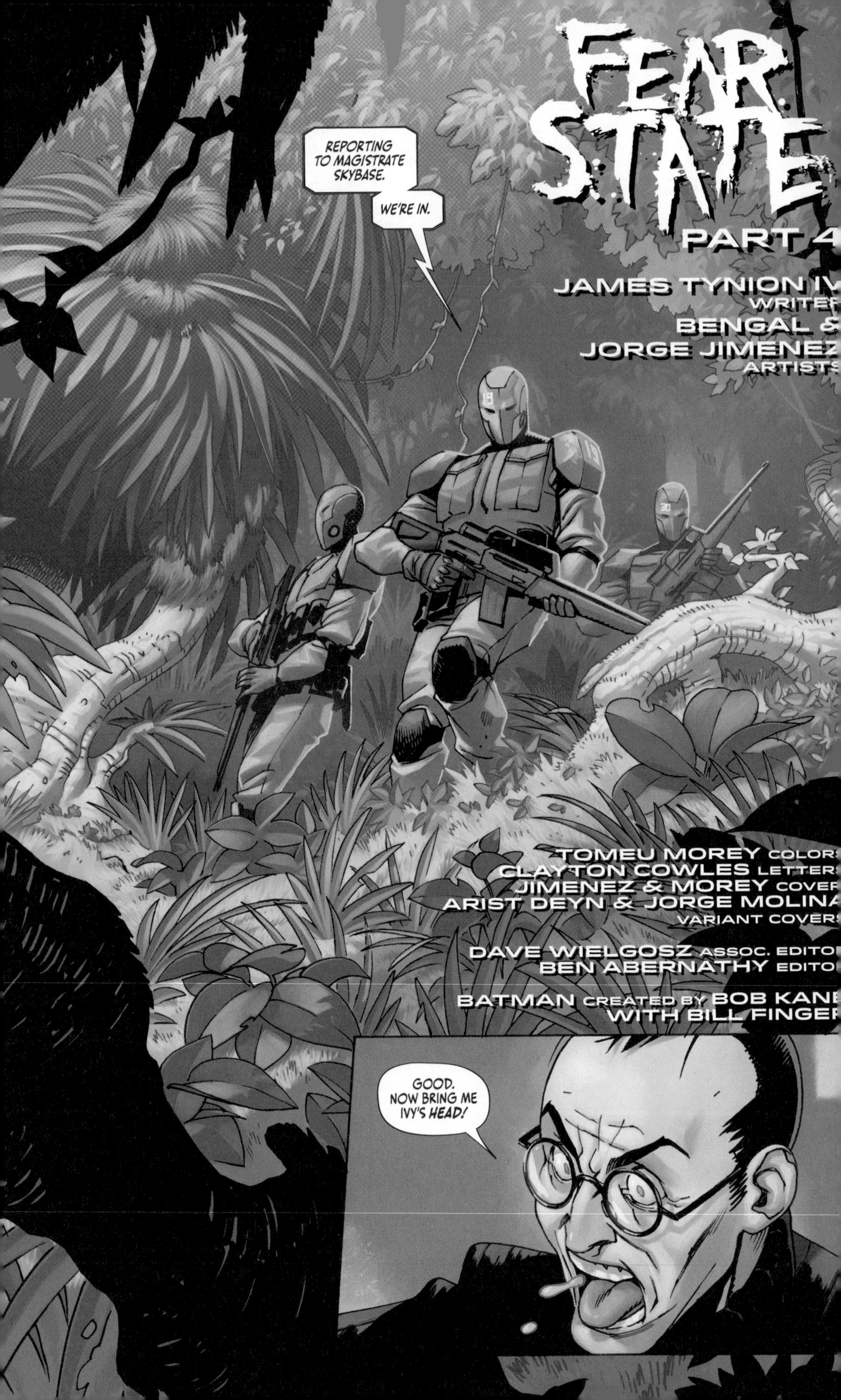
REPORTING TO MAGISTRATE SKYBASE.
WE'RE IN.
FEAR STATE
PART 4
JAMES TYNION IV WRITER
BENGAL & JORGE JIMENEZ ARTISTS
TOMEU MOREY COLORS
CLAYTON COWLES LETTERS
JIMENEZ & MOREY COVER
ARIST DEYN & JORGE MOLINA VARIANT COVERS
DAVE WIELGOSZ ASSOC. EDITOR
BEN ABERNATHY EDITOR
BATMAN CREATED BY BOB KANE WITH BILL FINGER
GOOD. NOW BRING ME IVY'S HEAD!

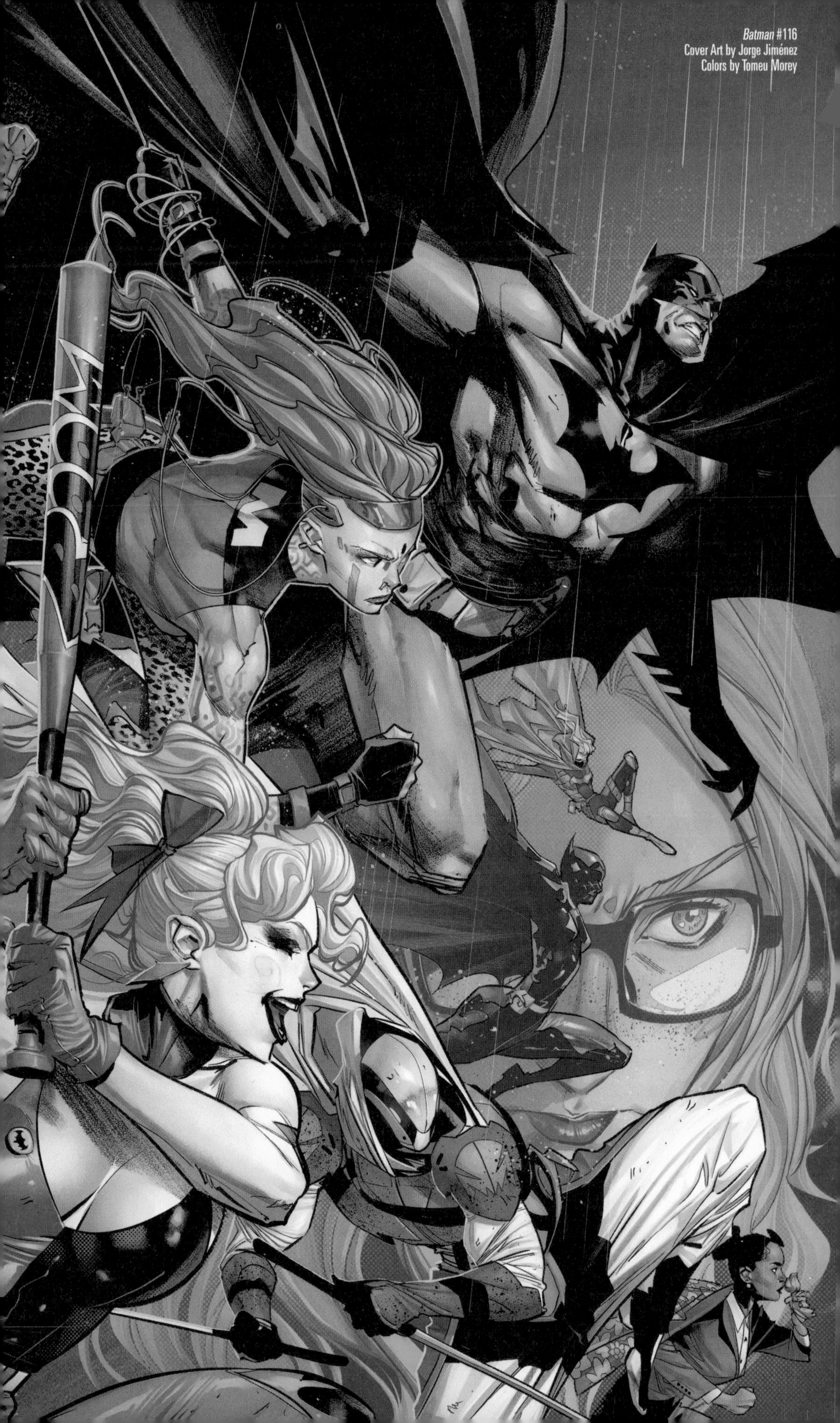

Batman #116
Cover Art by Jorge Jiménez
Colors by Tomeu Morey

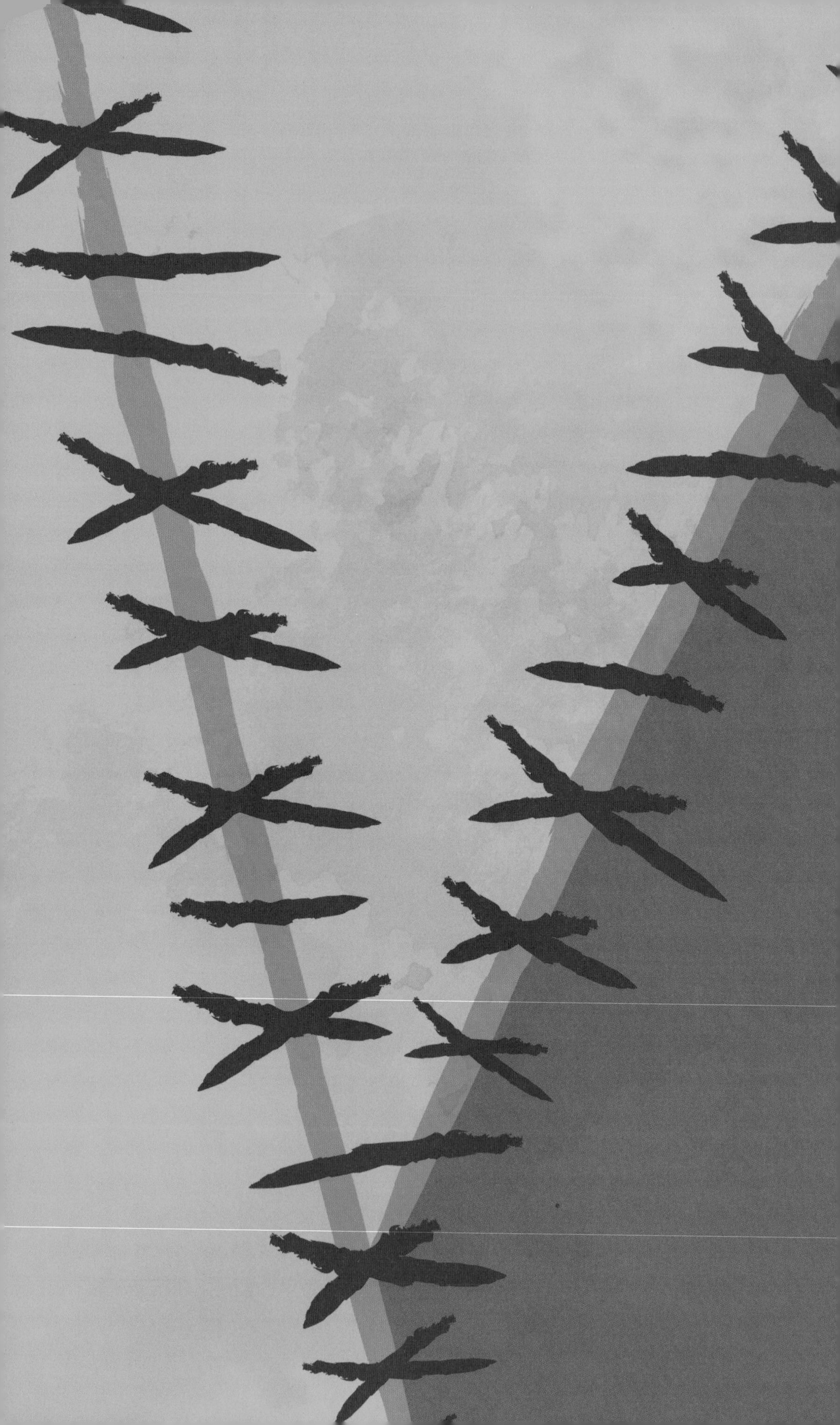

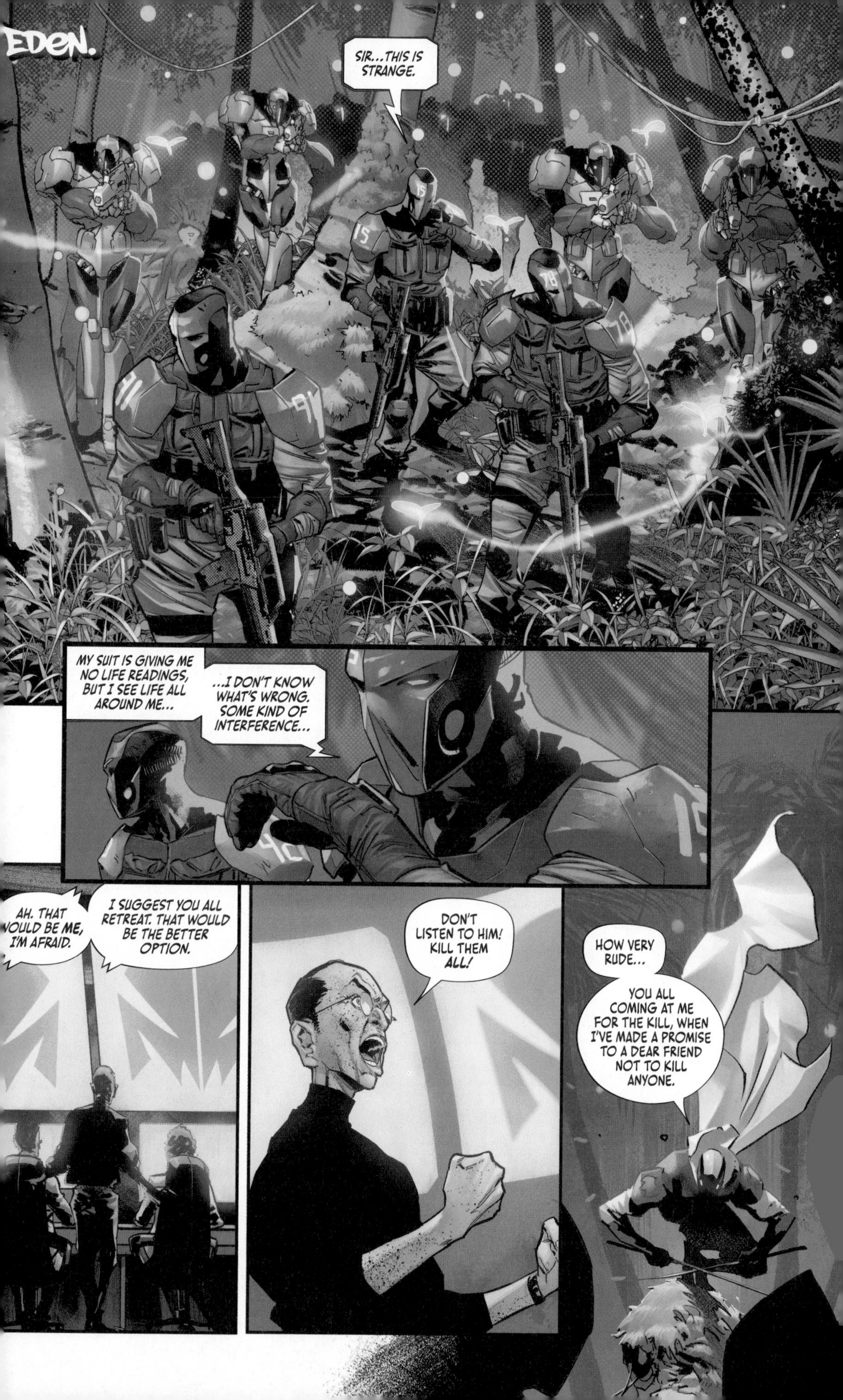
EDEN.
SIR...THIS IS STRANGE.
MY SUIT IS GIVING ME NO LIFE READINGS, BUT I SEE LIFE ALL AROUND ME...
...I DON'T KNOW WHAT'S WRONG. SOME KIND OF INTERFERENCE...
AH. THAT WOULD BE ME, I'M AFRAID.
I SUGGEST YOU ALL RETREAT. THAT WOULD BE THE BETTER OPTION.
DON'T LISTEN TO HIM! KILL THEM ALL!
HOW VERY RUDE...
YOU ALL COMING AT ME FOR THE KILL, WHEN I'VE MADE A PROMISE TO A DEAR FRIEND NOT TO KILL ANYONE.

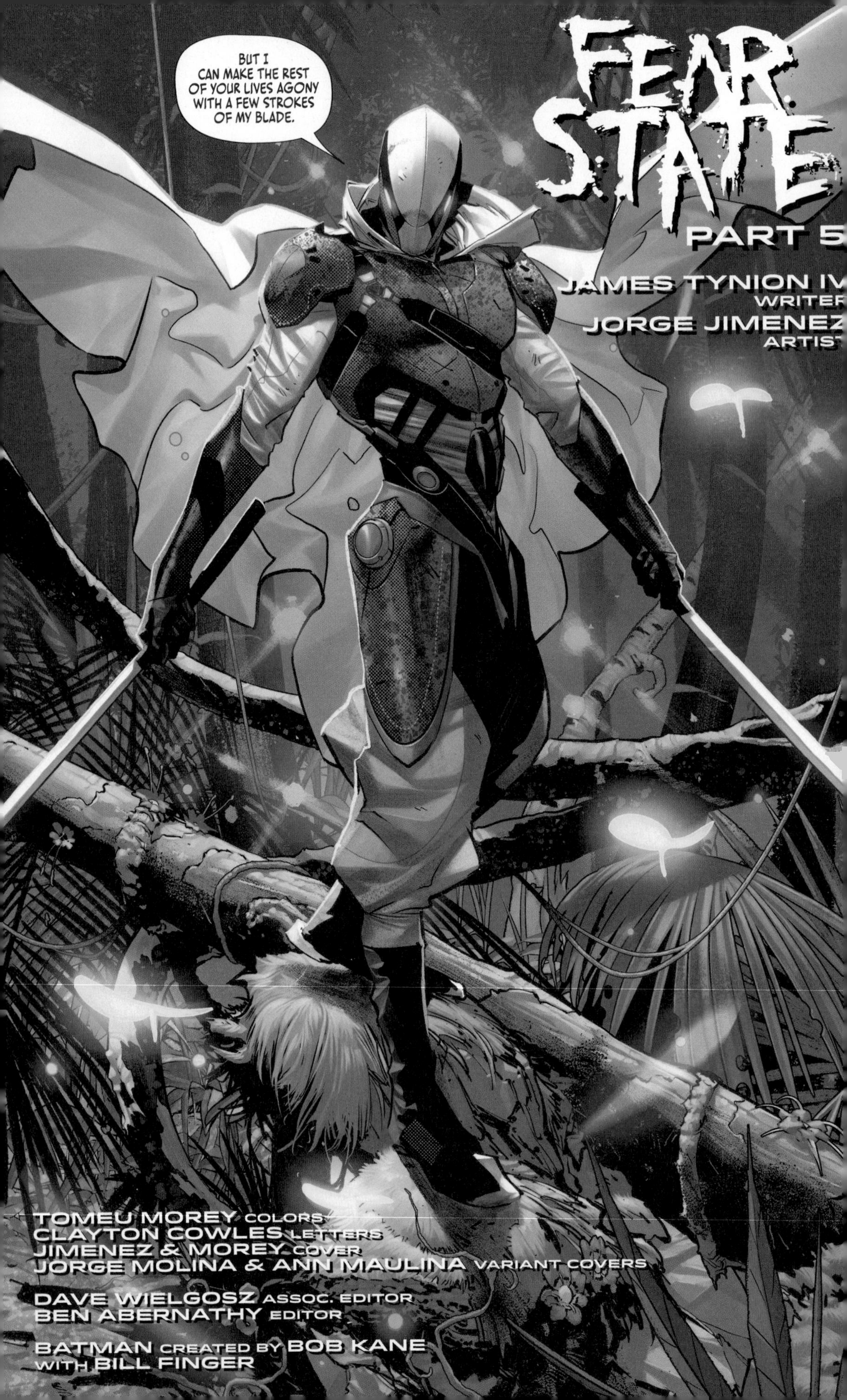

BUT I CAN MAKE THE REST OF YOUR LIVES AGONY WITH A FEW STROKES OF MY BLADE.
FEAR STATE
PART 5
JAMES TYNION IV WRITER
JORGE JIMENEZ ARTIST
TOMEU MOREY COLORS
CLAYTON COWLES LETTERS
JIMENEZ & MOREY COVER
JORGE MOLINA & ANN MAULINA VARIANT COVERS
DAVE WIELGOSZ ASSOC. EDITOR
BEN ABERNATHY EDITOR
BATMAN CREATED BY BOB KANE WITH BILL FINGER

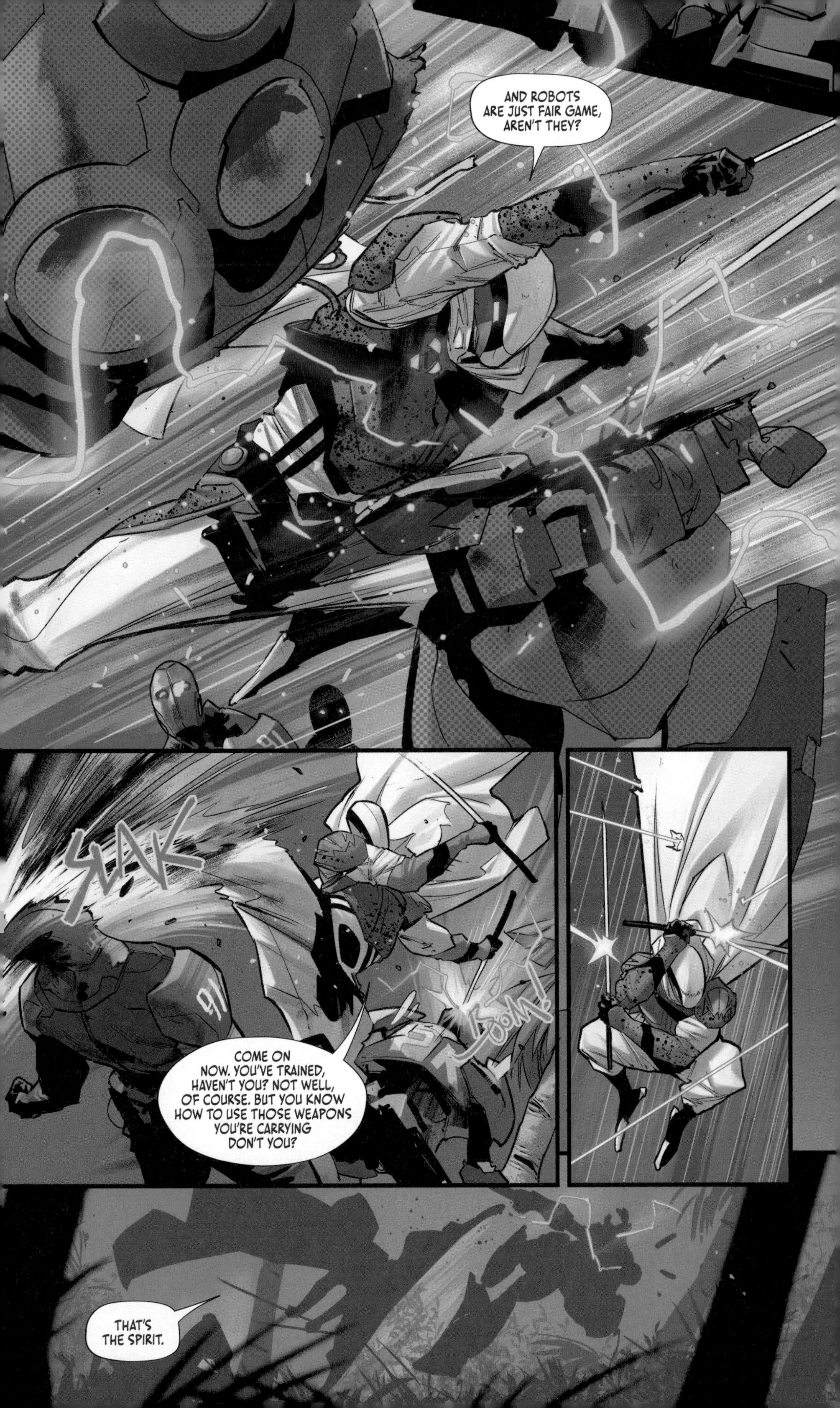
AND ROBOTS ARE JUST FAIR GAME, AREN'T THEY?
SLAK
BOOM!
COME ON NOW. YOU'VE TRAINED, HAVEN'T YOU? NOT WELL, OF COURSE. BUT YOU KNOW HOW TO USE THOSE WEAPONS YOU'RE CARRYING DON'T YOU?
THAT'S THE SPIRIT.

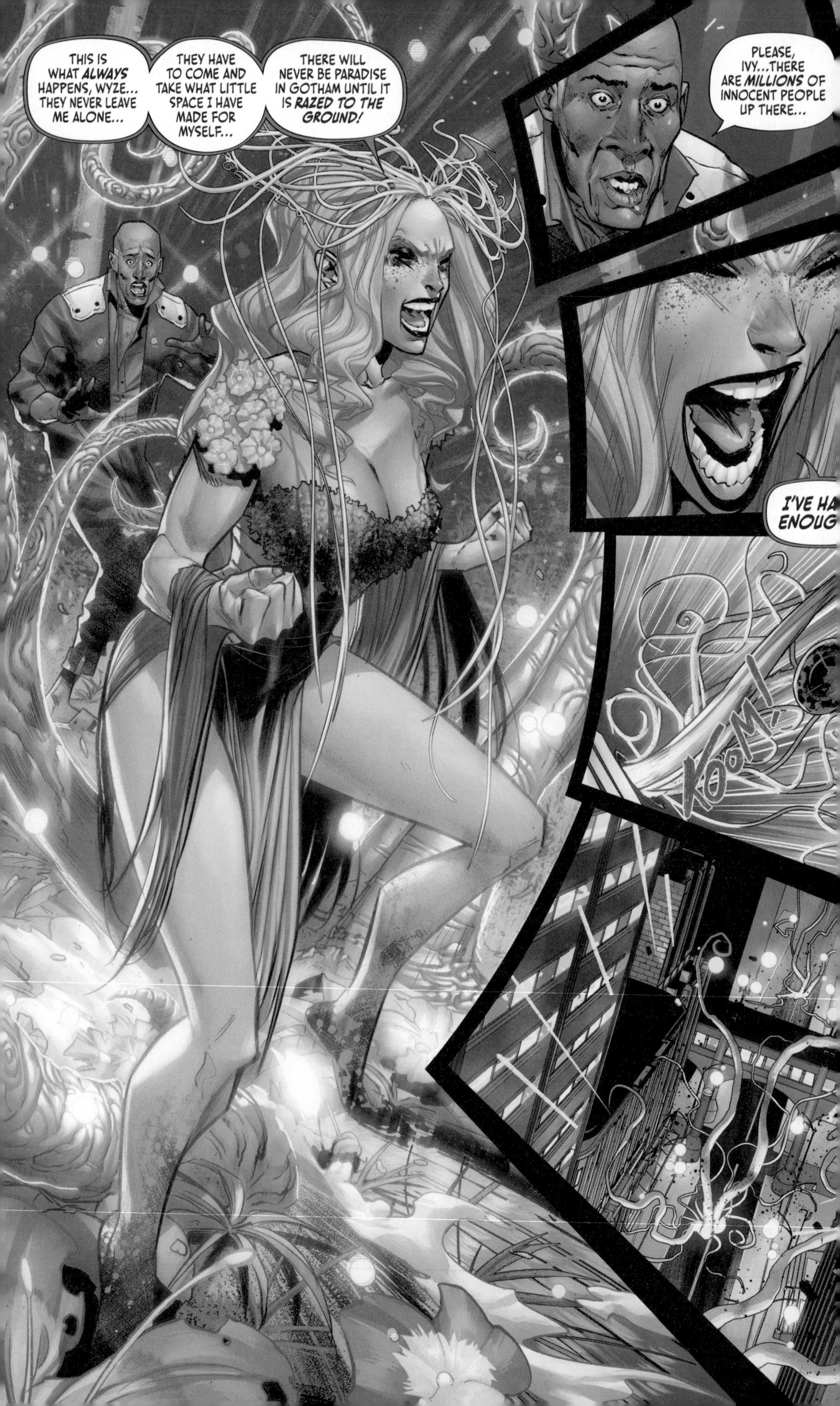
THIS IS WHAT ALWAYS HAPPENS, WYZE... THEY NEVER LEAVE ME ALONE...
THEY HAVE TO COME AND TAKE WHAT LITTLE SPACE I HAVE MADE FOR MYSELF...
THERE WILL NEVER BE PARADISE IN GOTHAM UNTIL IT IS RAZED TO THE GROUND!
PLEASE, IVY...THERE ARE MILLIONS OF INNOCENT PEOPLE UP THERE...
I'VE HA
ENOUG
KOOM!

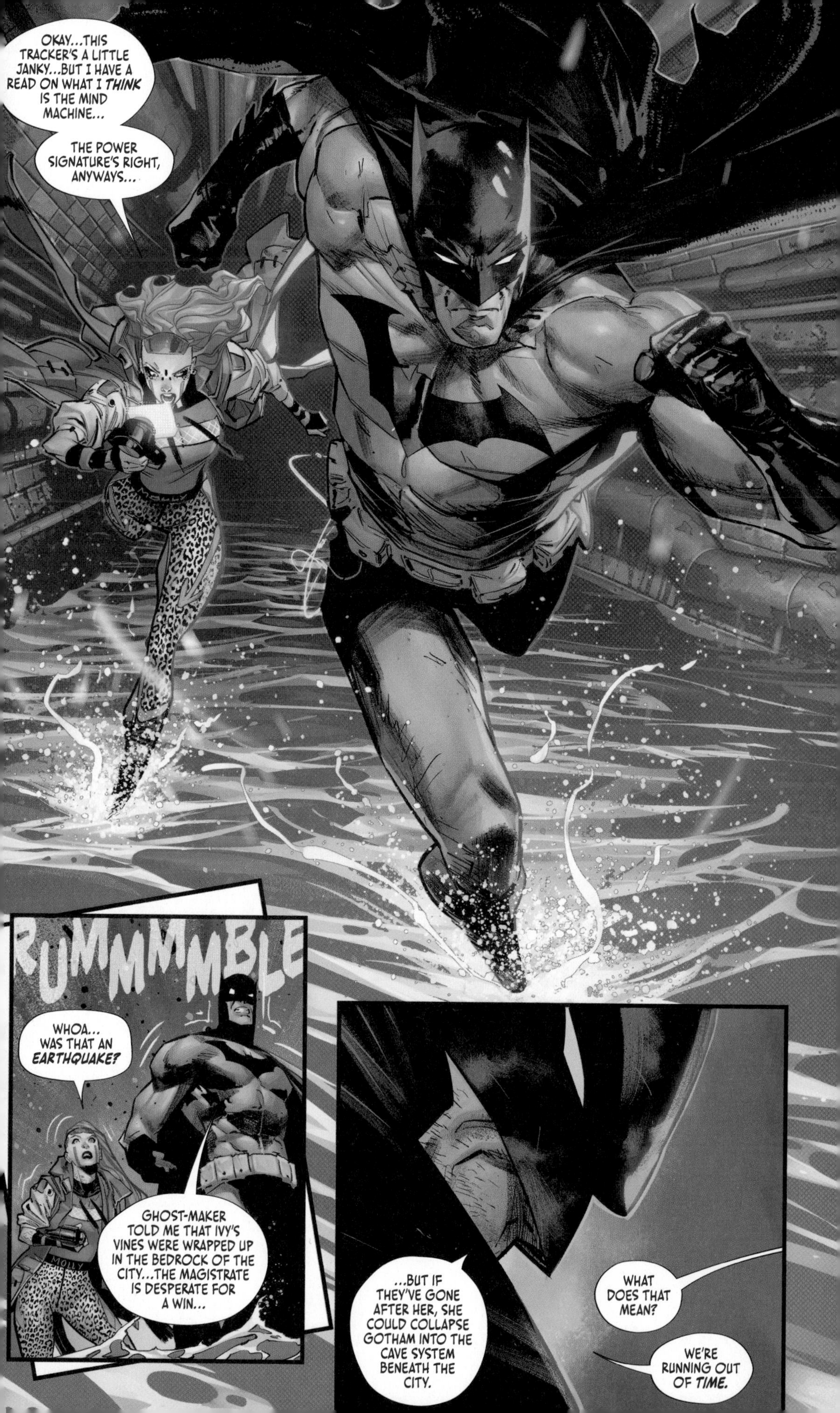
OKAY...THIS TRACKER'S A LITTLE JANKY...BUT I HAVE A READ ON WHAT I *THINK* IS THE MIND MACHINE...
THE POWER SIGNATURE'S RIGHT, ANYWAYS...
RUMMMMBLE
WHOA... WAS THAT AN *EARTHQUAKE?*
GHOST-MAKER TOLD ME THAT IVY'S VINES WERE WRAPPED UP IN THE BEDROCK OF THE CITY...THE MAGISTRATE IS DESPERATE FOR A WIN...
...BUT IF THEY'VE GONE AFTER HER, SHE COULD COLLAPSE GOTHAM INTO THE CAVE SYSTEM BENEATH THE CITY.
WHAT DOES THAT MEAN?
WE'RE RUNNING OUT OF *TIME.*

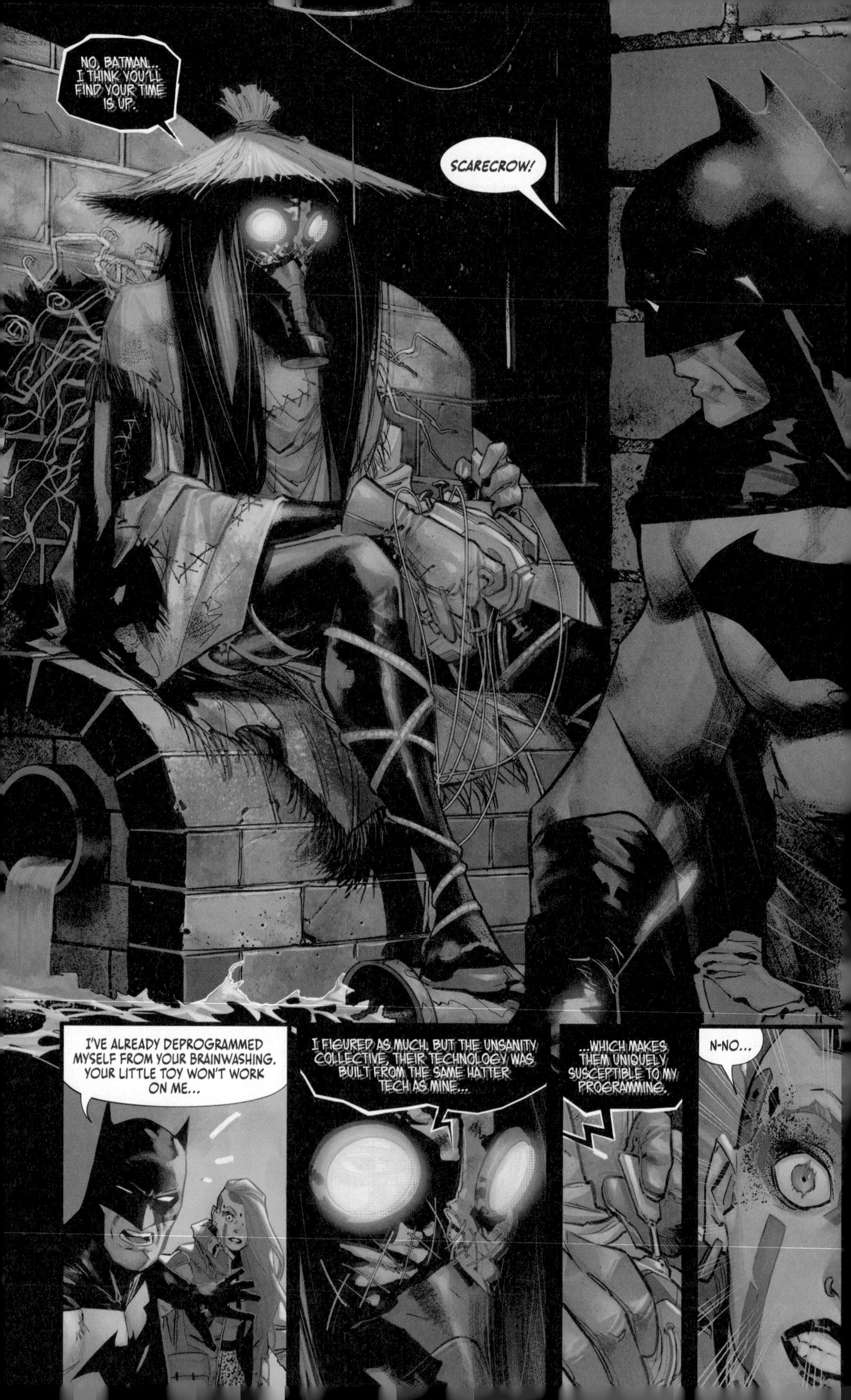
NO, BATMAN... I THINK YOU'LL FIND YOUR TIME IS UP.
SCARECROW!
I'VE ALREADY DEPROGRAMMED MYSELF FROM YOUR BRAINWASHING. YOUR LITTLE TOY WON'T WORK ON ME...
I FIGURED AS MUCH. BUT THE UNSANITY COLLECTIVE, THEIR TECHNOLOGY WAS BUILT FROM THE SAME HATTER TECH AS MINE...
...WHICH MAKES THEM UNIQUELY SUSCEPTIBLE TO MY PROGRAMMING.
N-NO...

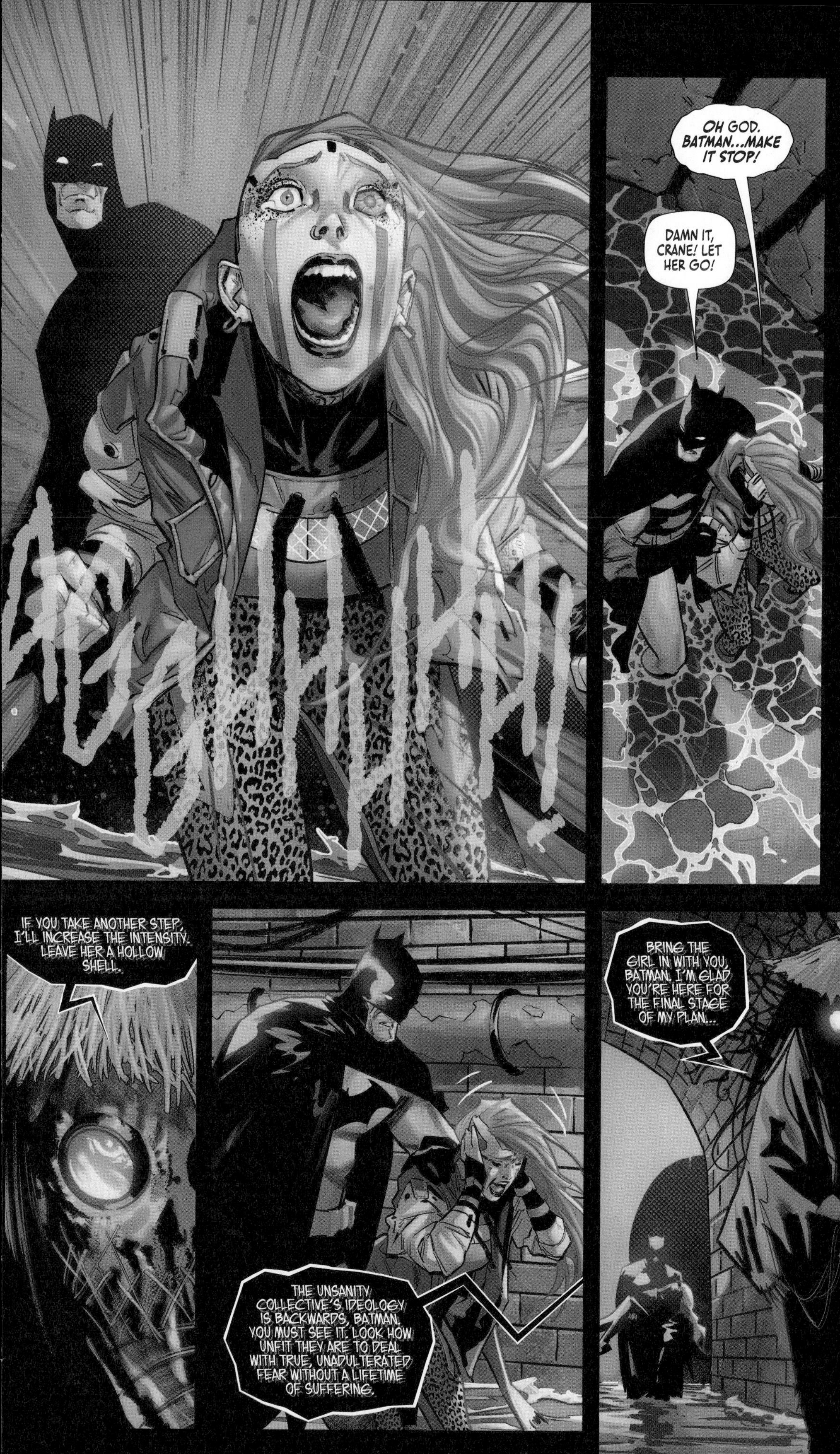
OH GOD. BATMAN...MAKE IT STOP!
DAMN IT, CRANE! LET HER GO!
IF YOU TAKE ANOTHER STEP, I'LL INCREASE THE INTENSITY. LEAVE HER A HOLLOW SHELL.
THE UNSANITY COLLECTIVE'S IDEOLOGY IS BACKWARDS, BATMAN. YOU MUST SEE IT. LOOK HOW UNFIT THEY ARE TO DEAL WITH TRUE, UNADULTERATED FEAR WITHOUT A LIFETIME OF SUFFERING.
BRING THE GIRL IN WITH YOU, BATMAN. I'M GLAD YOU'RE HERE FOR THE FINAL STAGE OF MY PLAN...

POOR SEAN MAHONEY...

WHUUHUHUHUH

HE'S EXPERIENCED SO MUCH TRAUMA...THE DEATH OF ARKHAM...BEING USED AS A WEAPON TO KILL A MAN WITH HIS BARE HANDS... HE'S FEELING IT ALL RIGHT NOW. AMPLIFIED BY MY MACHINES, AND THE MEMORIES OF THE UNSANITY COLLECTIVE.

YOU CAN SEE HIS BRAIN REWRITING ITSELF TO PROCESS ALL THAT FEAR AND HORROR. HE IS *EVOLVING*, BATMAN.

HE WILL BE THE PERFECT LEADER TO GUIDE HIMSELF FROM THIS FEAR STATE TO A FUTURE STATE OF GOTHAM.

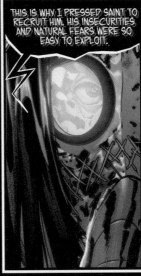

THIS IS WHY I PRESSED SAINT TO RECRUIT HIM. HIS INSECURITIES AND NATURAL FEARS WERE SO EASY TO EXPLOIT.

PLEASE, BATMAN, LET IT *STOP!*

I CAN'T... I CAN'T *BEAR* THIS!

FREE HER, SCARECROW!

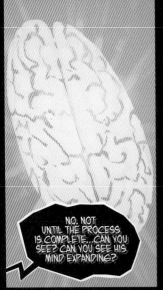

NO. NOT UNTIL THE PROCESS IS COMPLETE...CAN YOU SEE? CAN YOU SEE HIS MIND EXPANDING?

IT'S BEAUTIFUL...

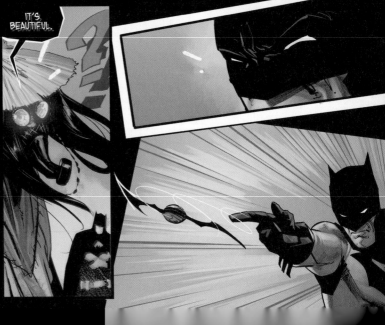

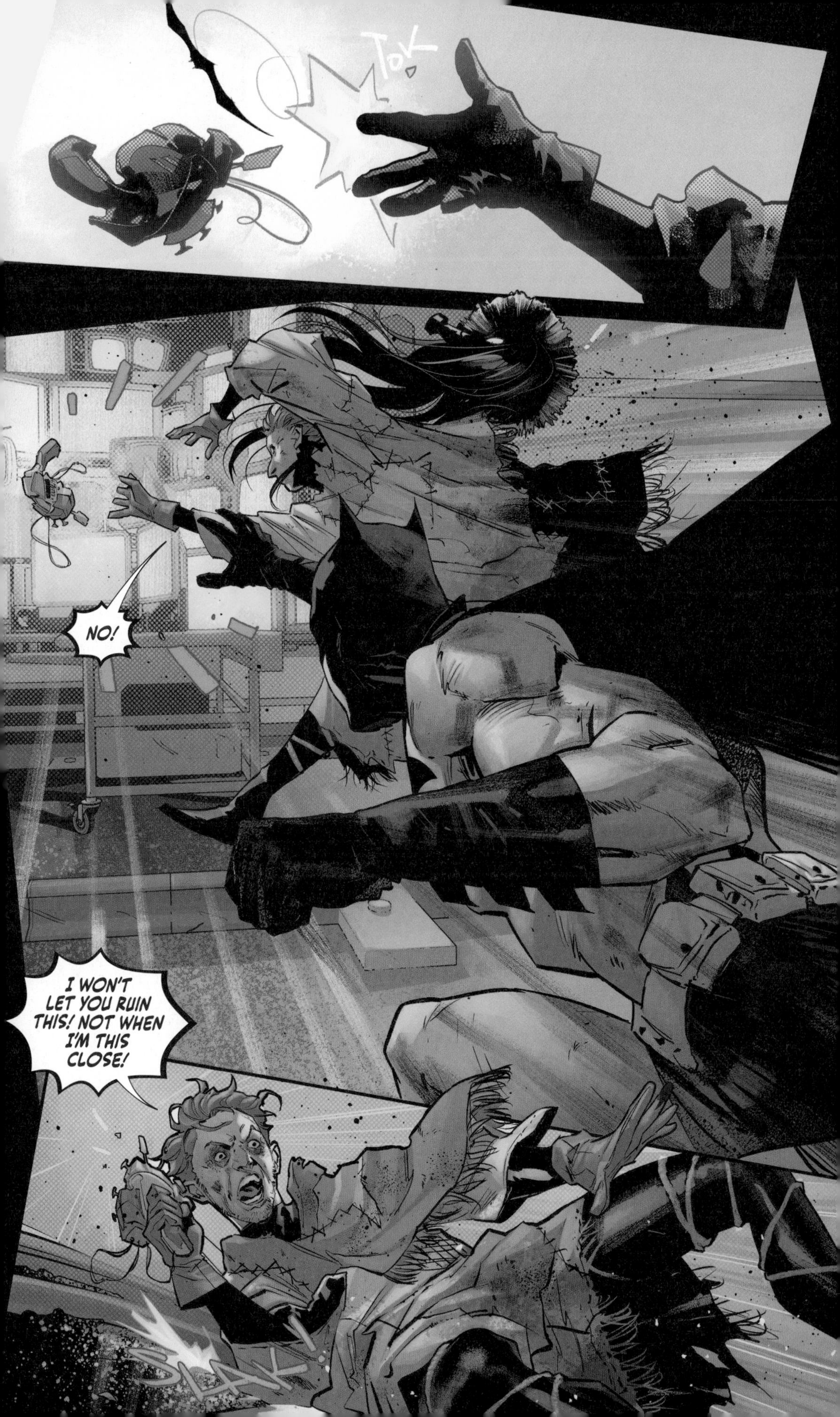
TOK
NO!
I WON'T LET YOU RUIN THIS! NOT WHEN I'M THIS CLOSE!
SLAK!

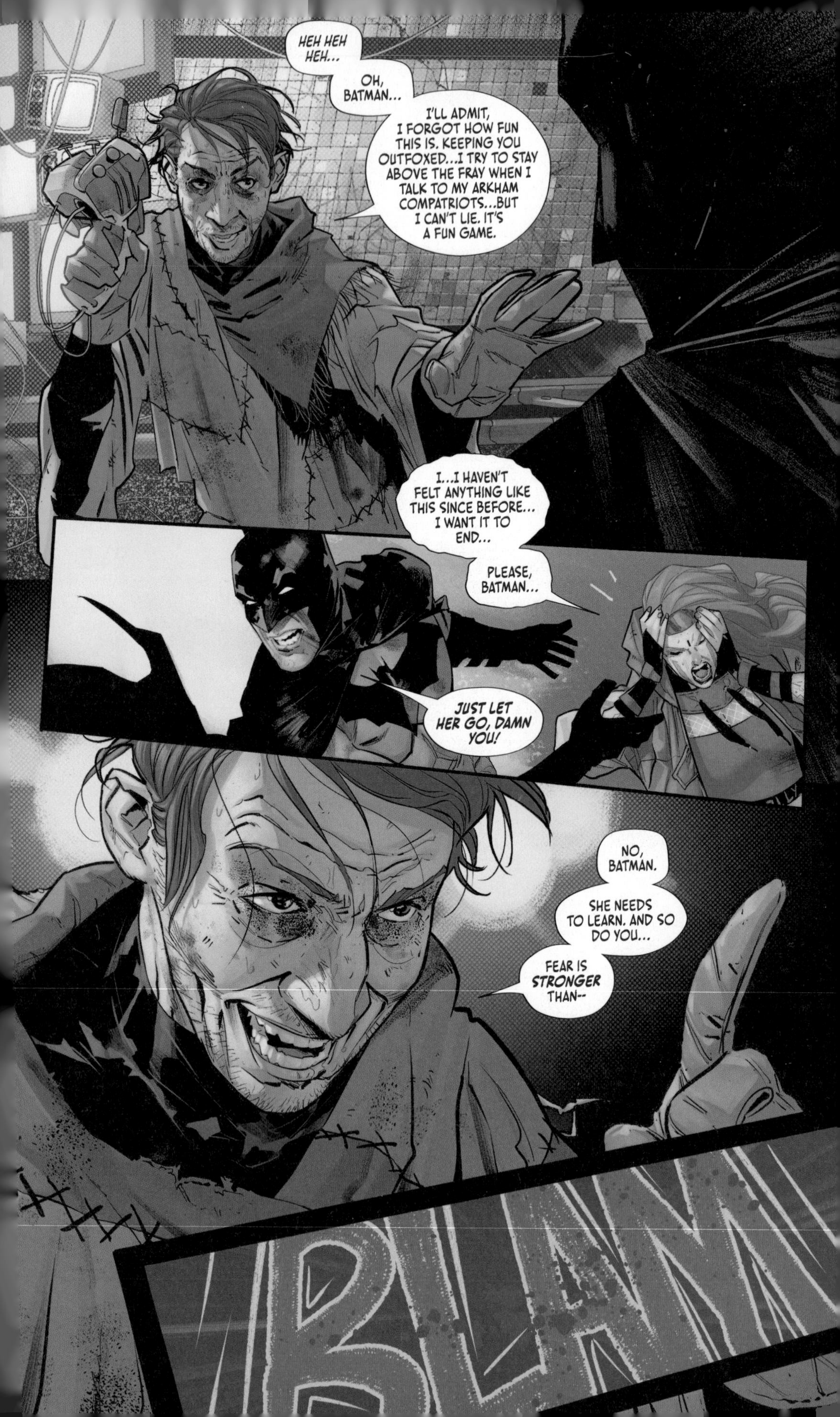
HEH HEH HEH...
OH, BATMAN...
I'LL ADMIT, I FORGOT HOW FUN THIS IS. KEEPING YOU OUTFOXED...I TRY TO STAY ABOVE THE FRAY WHEN I TALK TO MY ARKHAM COMPATRIOTS...BUT I CAN'T LIE. IT'S A FUN GAME.
I...I HAVEN'T FELT ANYTHING LIKE THIS SINCE BEFORE... I WANT IT TO END...
PLEASE, BATMAN...
JUST LET HER GO, DAMN YOU!
NO, BATMAN.
SHE NEEDS TO LEARN. AND SO DO YOU...
FEAR IS STRONGER THAN--
BLAM

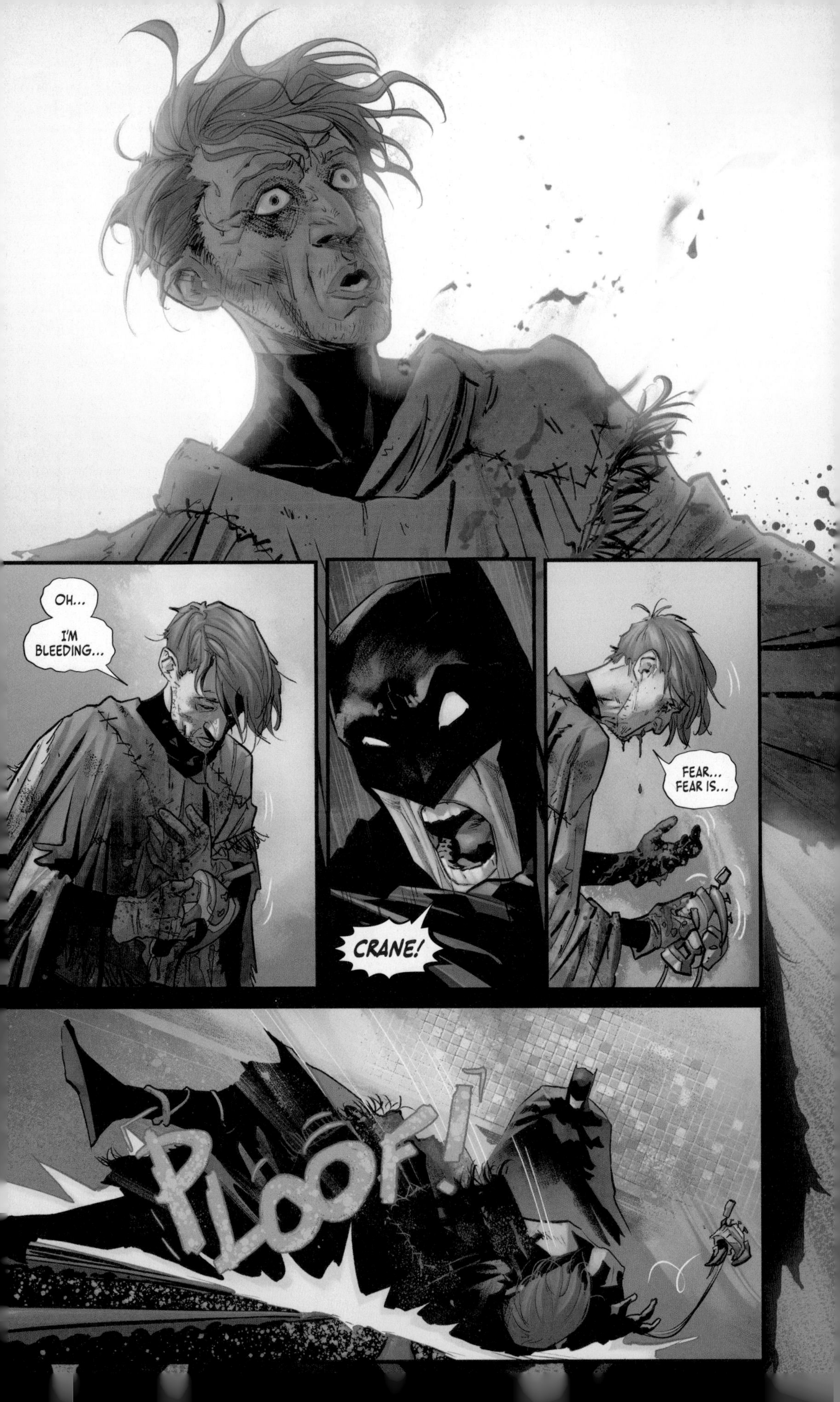
OH...
I'M BLEEDING...
CRANE!
FEAR... FEAR IS...
PLOOF!

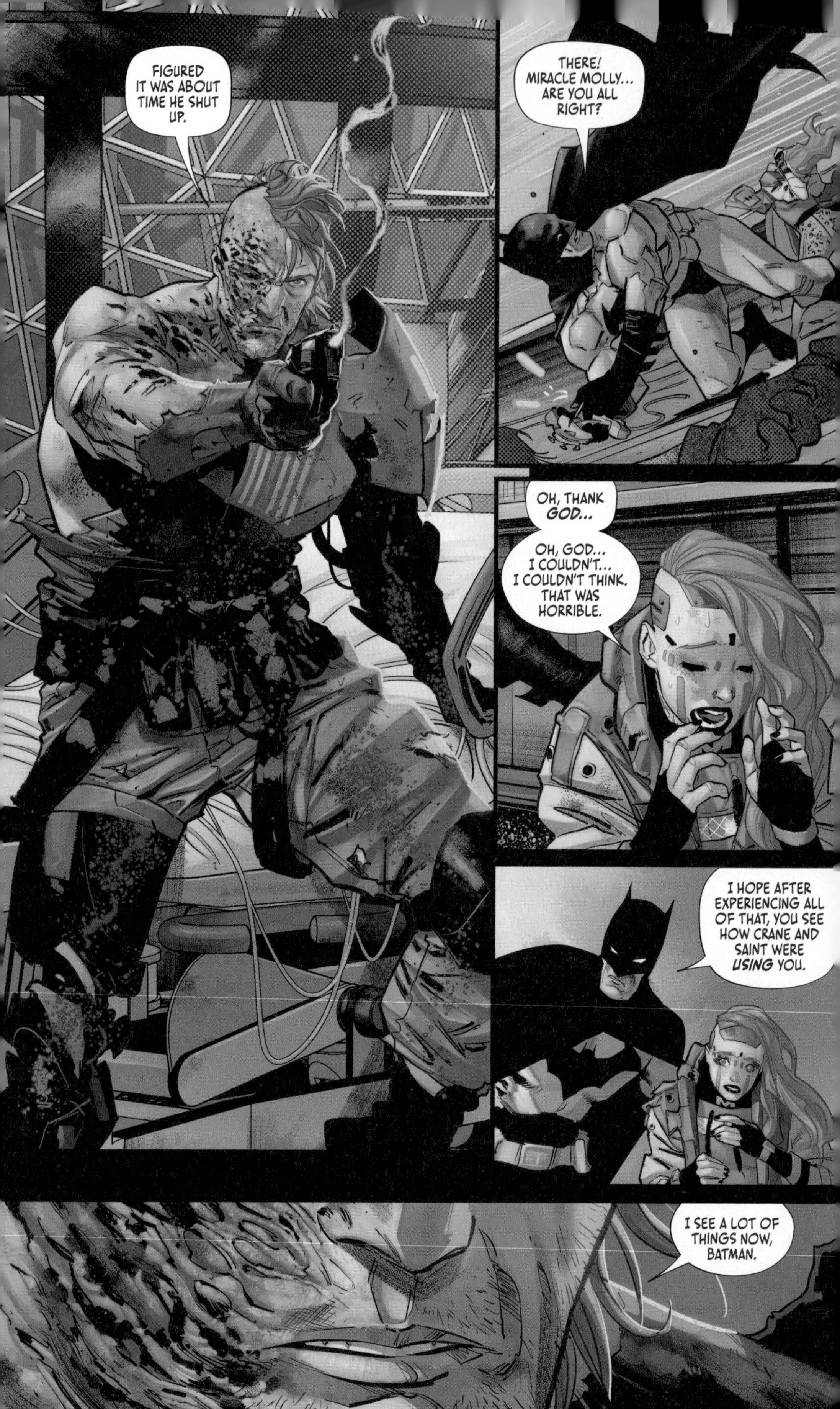
FIGURED IT WAS ABOUT TIME HE SHUT UP.
THERE! MIRACLE MOLLY... ARE YOU ALL RIGHT?
OH, THANK *GOD*...
OH, GOD... I COULDN'T... I COULDN'T THINK. THAT WAS HORRIBLE.
I HOPE AFTER EXPERIENCING ALL OF THAT, YOU SEE HOW CRANE AND SAINT WERE *USING* YOU.
I SEE A LOT OF THINGS NOW, BATMAN.

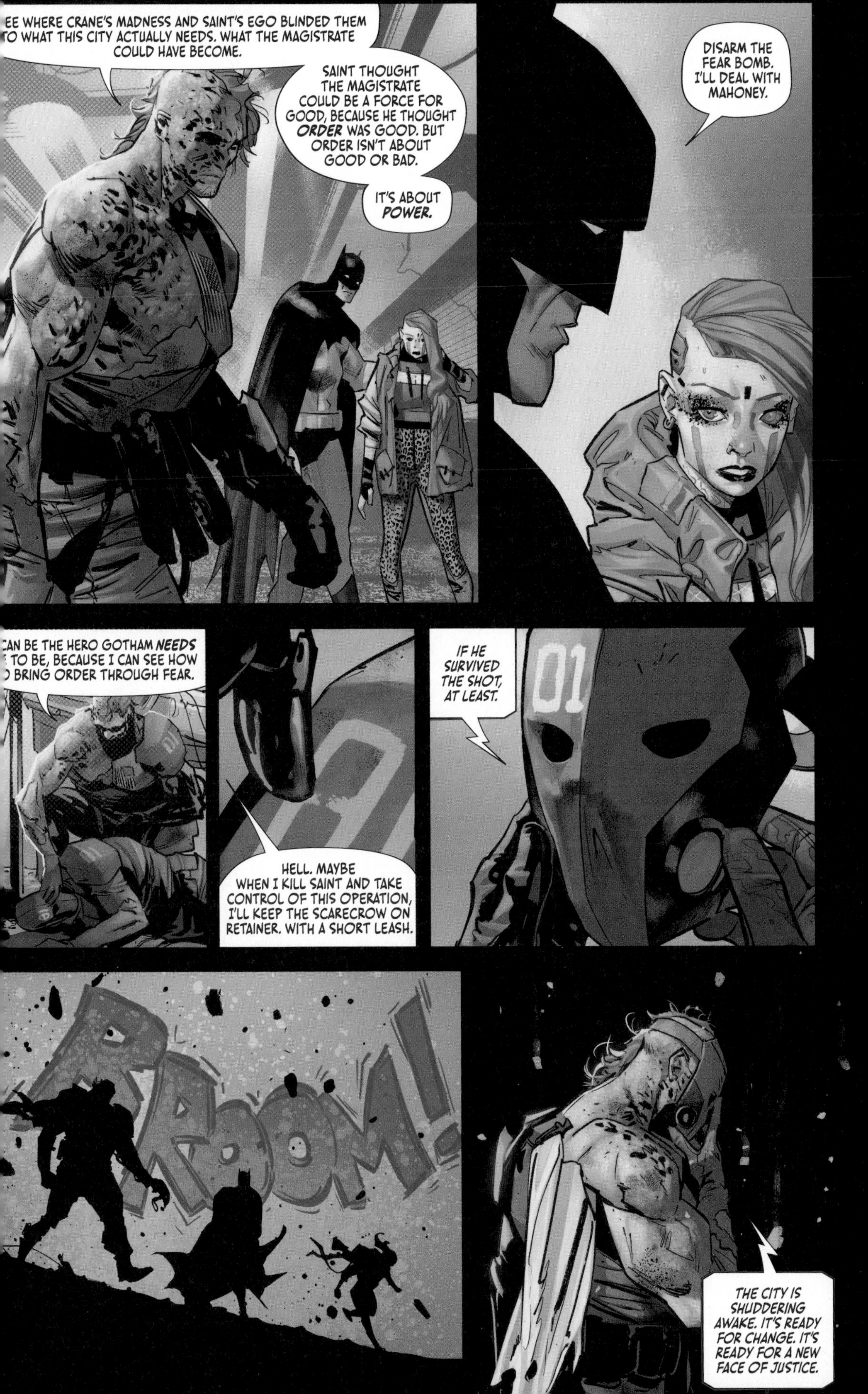
EE WHERE CRANE'S MADNESS AND SAINT'S EGO BLINDED THEM TO WHAT THIS CITY ACTUALLY NEEDS. WHAT THE MAGISTRATE COULD HAVE BECOME.
SAINT THOUGHT THE MAGISTRATE COULD BE A FORCE FOR GOOD, BECAUSE HE THOUGHT ORDER WAS GOOD. BUT ORDER ISN'T ABOUT GOOD OR BAD.
IT'S ABOUT POWER.
DISARM THE FEAR BOMB. I'LL DEAL WITH MAHONEY.
CAN BE THE HERO GOTHAM NEEDS TO BE, BECAUSE I CAN SEE HOW BRING ORDER THROUGH FEAR.
HELL. MAYBE WHEN I KILL SAINT AND TAKE CONTROL OF THIS OPERATION, I'LL KEEP THE SCARECROW ON RETAINER. WITH A SHORT LEASH.
IF HE SURVIVED THE SHOT, AT LEAST.
01
BROOM!
THE CITY IS SHUDDERING AWAKE. IT'S READY FOR CHANGE. IT'S READY FOR A NEW FACE OF JUSTICE.

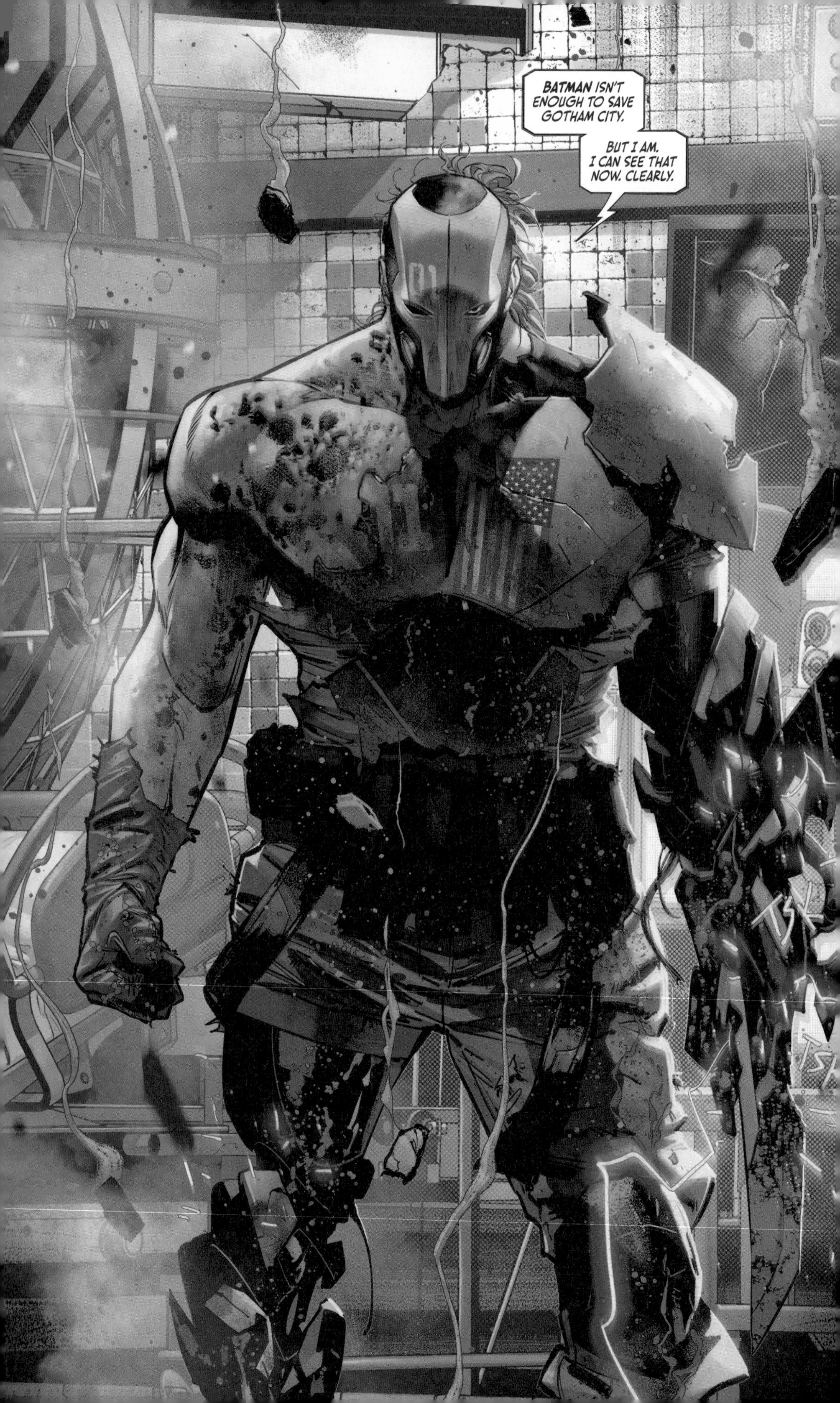
BATMAN ISN'T ENOUGH TO SAVE GOTHAM CITY.
BUT I AM. I CAN SEE THAT NOW. CLEARLY.
TSK

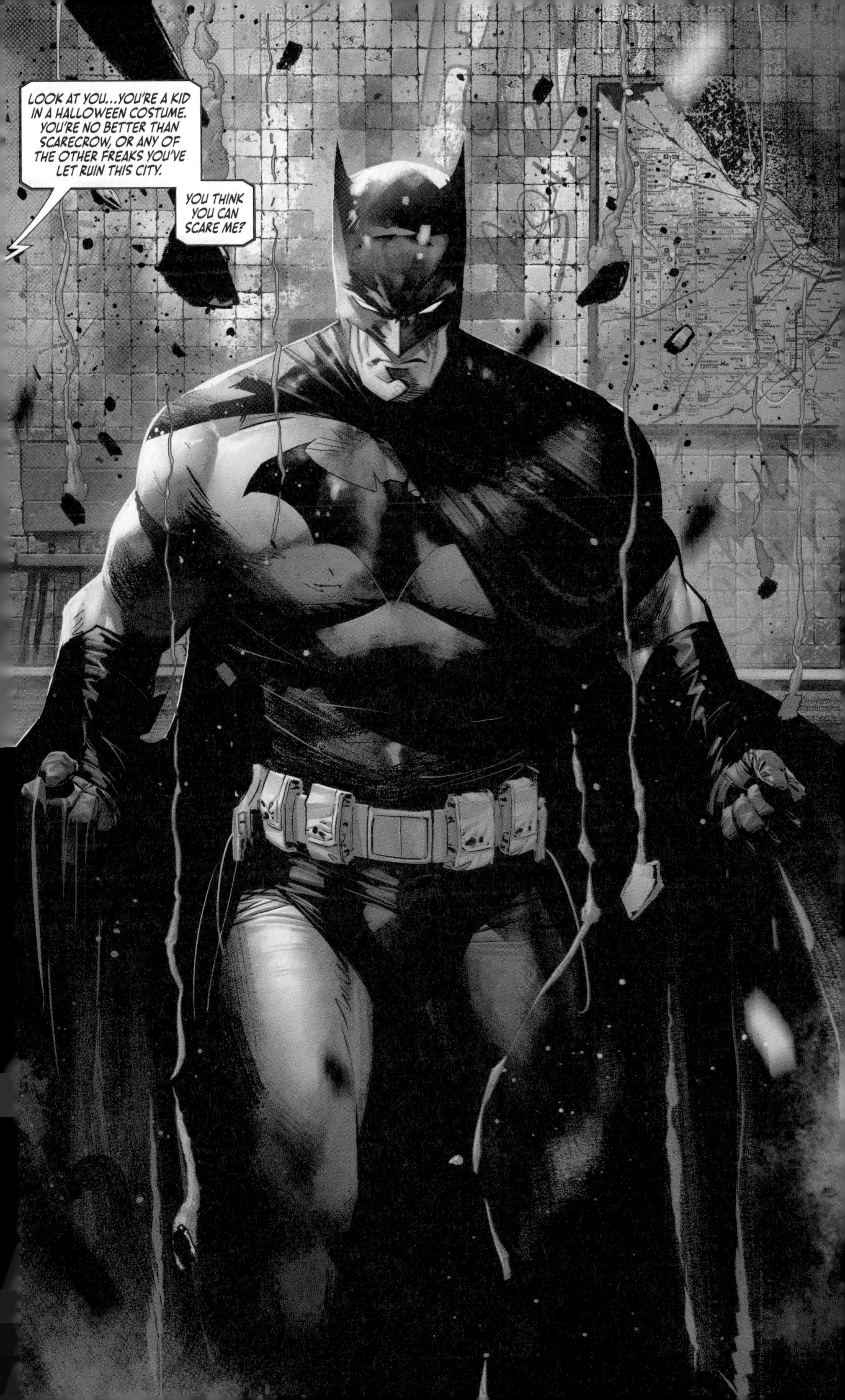
LOOK AT YOU...YOU'RE A KID IN A HALLOWEEN COSTUME. YOU'RE NO BETTER THAN SCARECROW, OR ANY OF THE OTHER FREAKS YOU'VE LET RUIN THIS CITY.
YOU THINK YOU CAN SCARE ME?

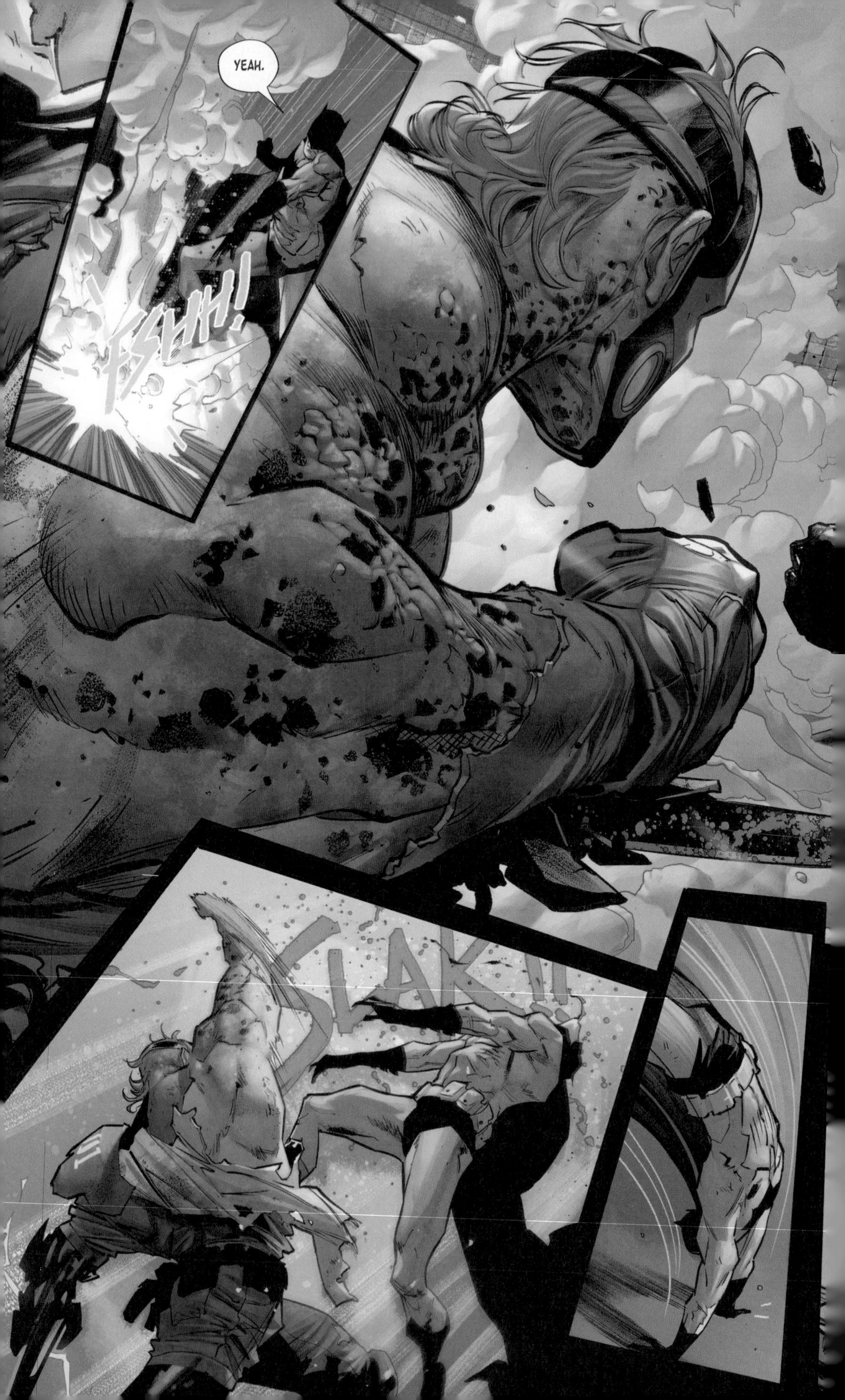
YEAH.
FSHH!
SLAK!!

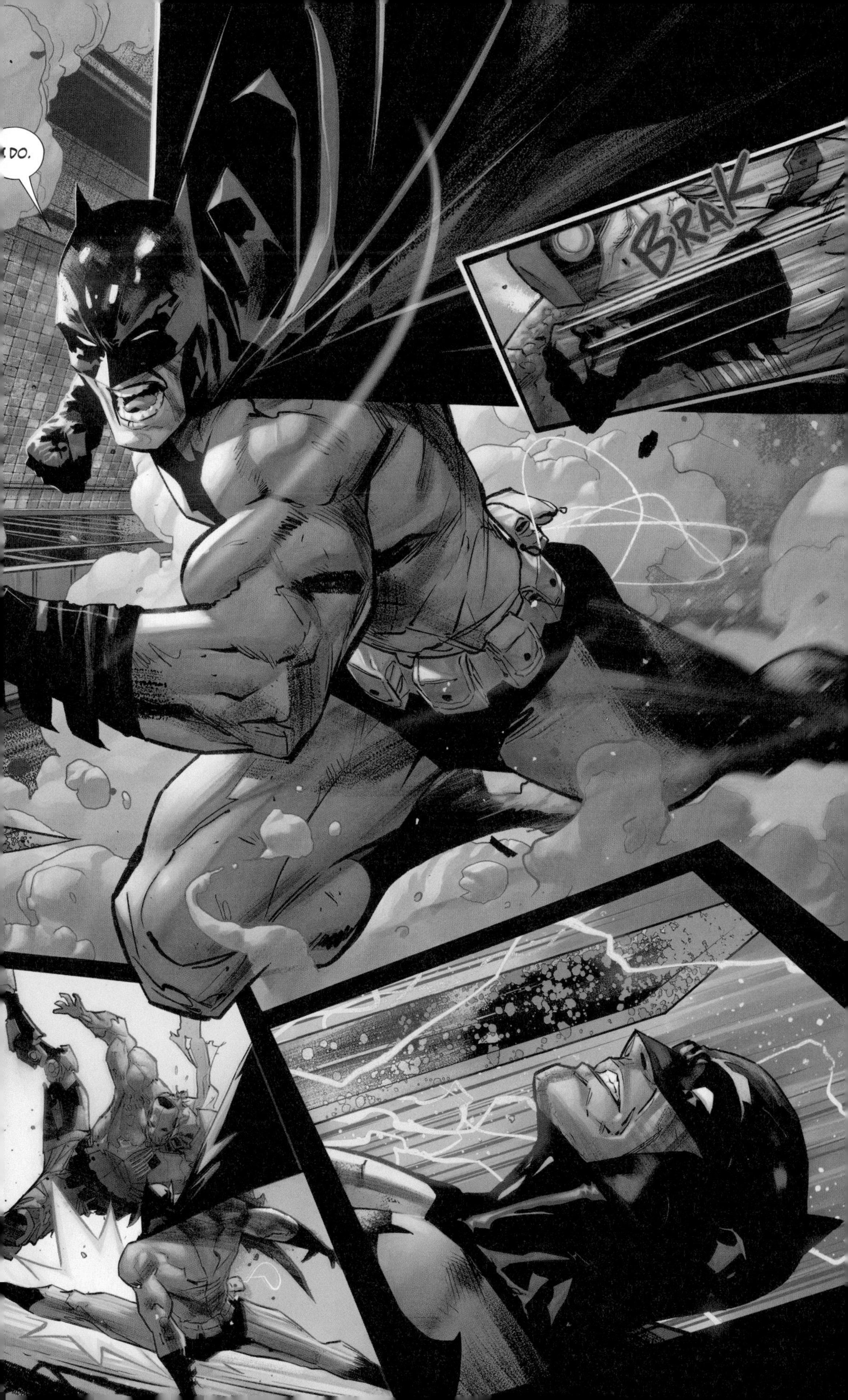
DO.
BRAK

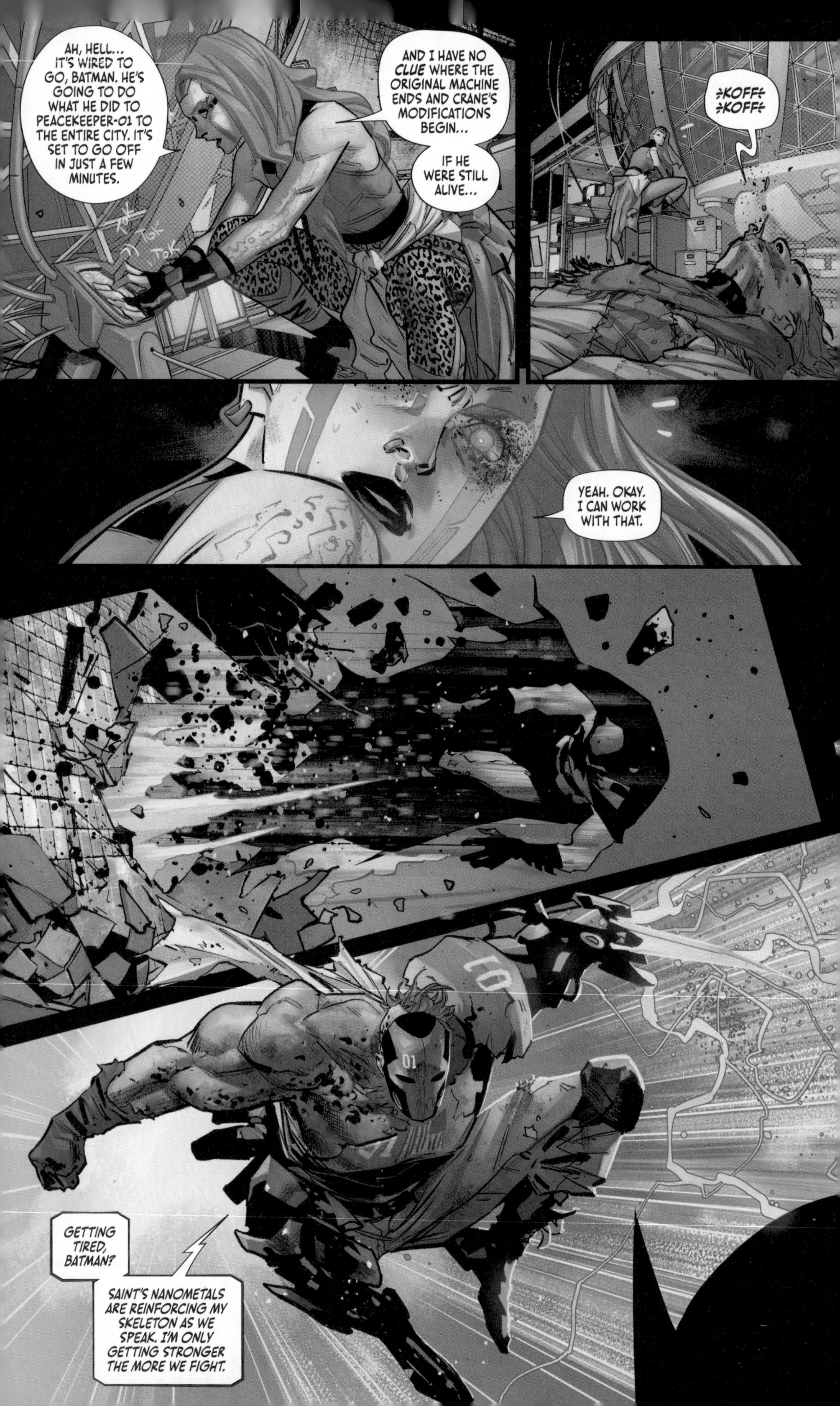
AH, HELL... IT'S WIRED TO GO, BATMAN. HE'S GOING TO DO WHAT HE DID TO PEACEKEEPER-01 TO THE ENTIRE CITY. IT'S SET TO GO OFF IN JUST A FEW MINUTES.
TOK TOK TOK
AND I HAVE NO CLUE WHERE THE ORIGINAL MACHINE ENDS AND CRANE'S MODIFICATIONS BEGIN...
IF HE WERE STILL ALIVE...
KOFF KOFF
YEAH. OKAY. I CAN WORK WITH THAT.
GETTING TIRED, BATMAN?
SAINT'S NANOMETALS ARE REINFORCING MY SKELETON AS WE SPEAK. I'M ONLY GETTING STRONGER THE MORE WE FIGHT.

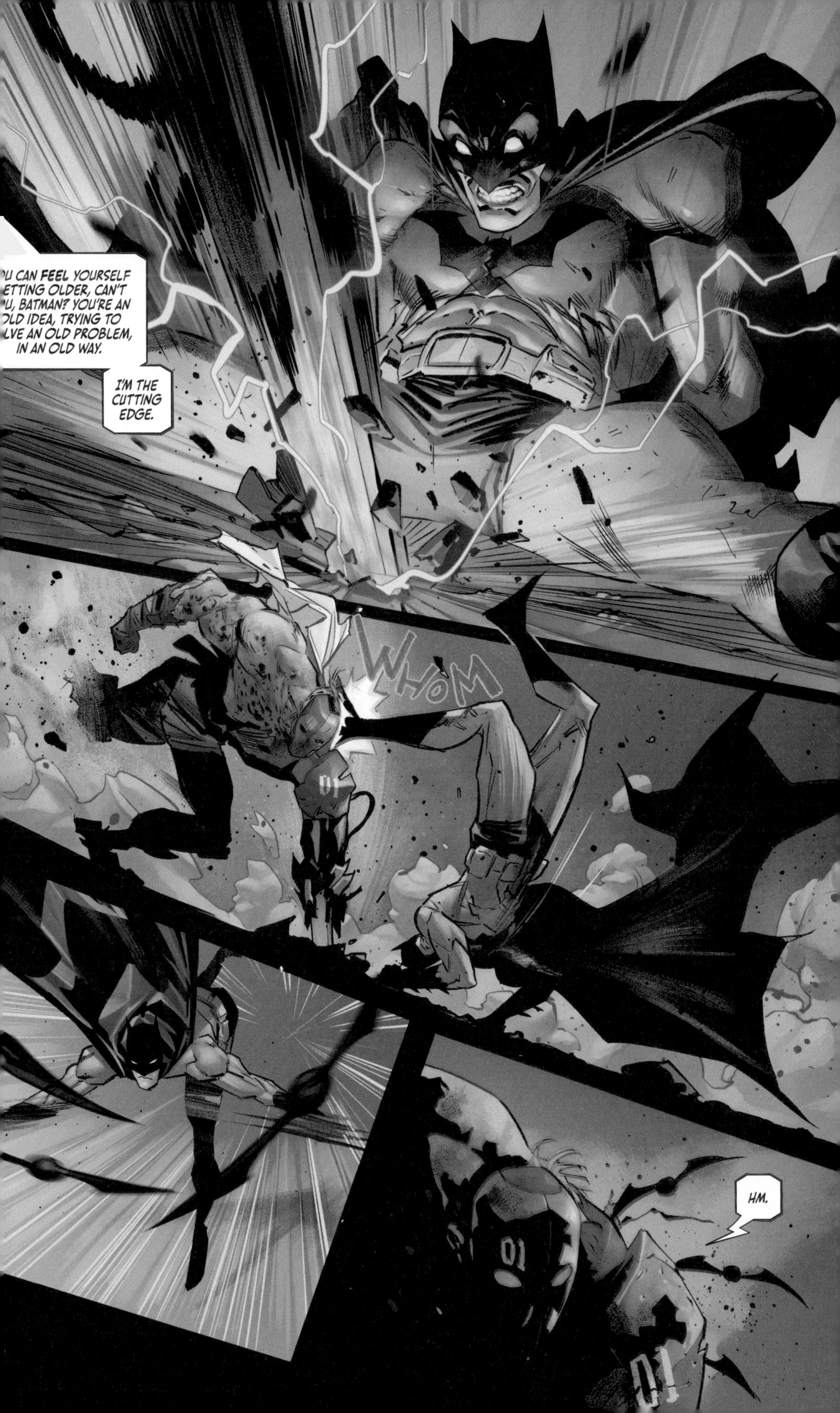

OU CAN FEEL YOURSELF
ETTING OLDER, CAN'T
U, BATMAN? YOU'RE AN
OLD IDEA, TRYING TO
LVE AN OLD PROBLEM,
IN AN OLD WAY.
I'M THE CUTTING EDGE.
WHOM
HM.

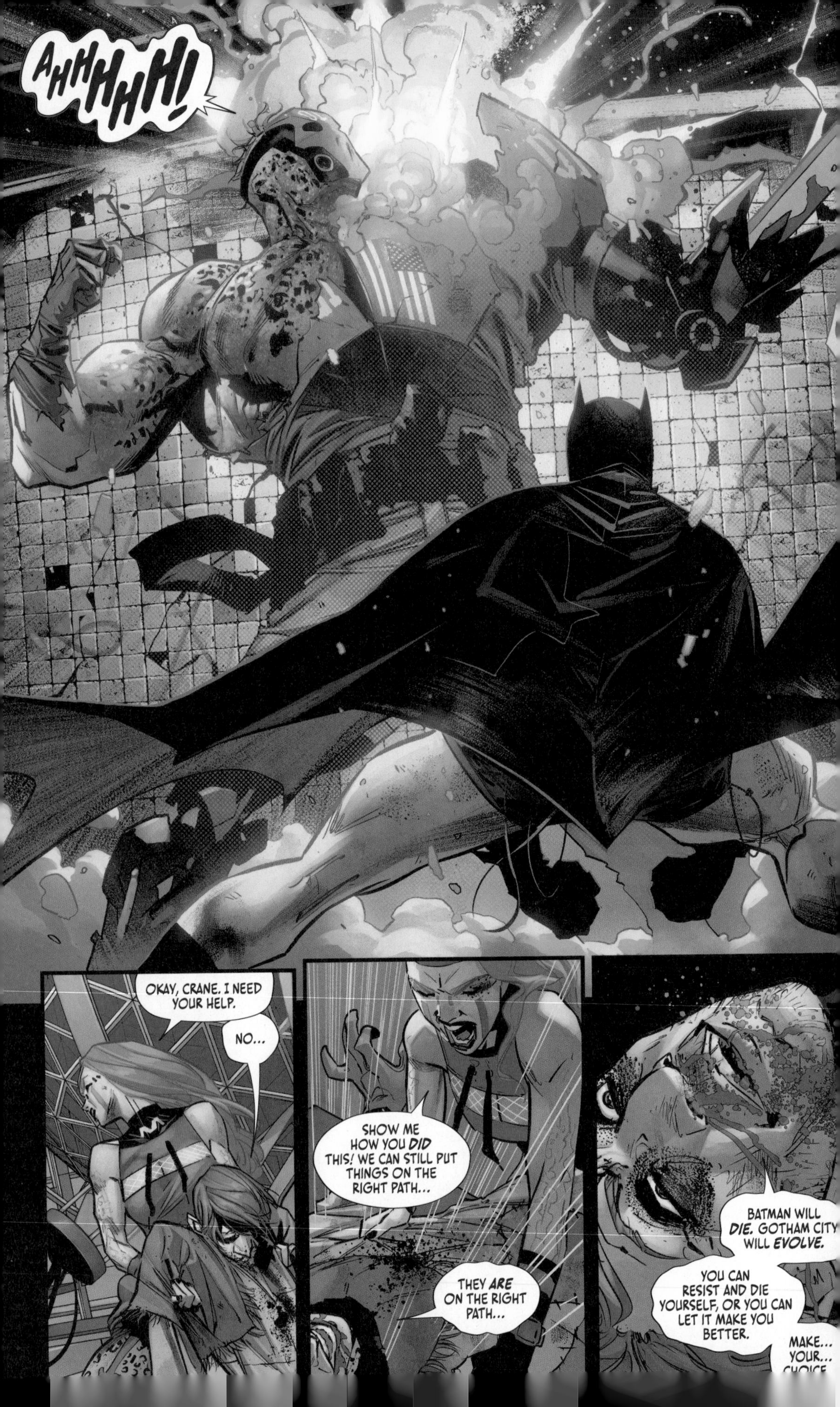

AHHHHHH!
OKAY, CRANE. I NEED YOUR HELP.
NO...
SHOW ME HOW YOU *DID* THIS! WE CAN STILL PUT THINGS ON THE RIGHT PATH...
THEY *ARE* ON THE RIGHT PATH...
BATMAN WILL *DIE.* GOTHAM CITY WILL *EVOLVE.*
YOU CAN RESIST AND DIE YOURSELF, OR YOU CAN LET IT MAKE YOU BETTER.
MAKE... YOUR...

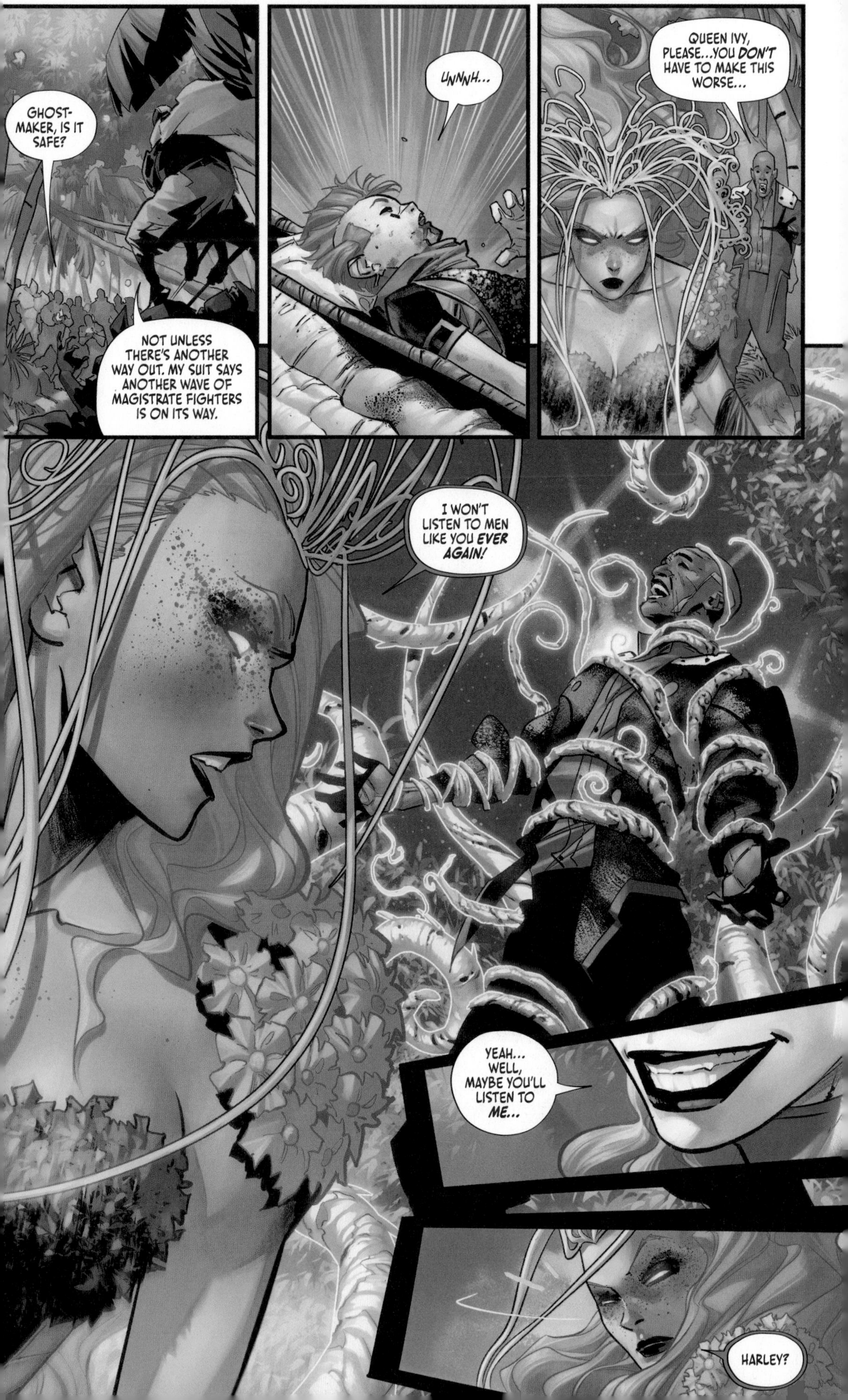
GHOST-MAKER, IS IT SAFE?
NOT UNLESS THERE'S ANOTHER WAY OUT. MY SUIT SAYS ANOTHER WAVE OF MAGISTRATE FIGHTERS IS ON ITS WAY.
UNNNH...
QUEEN IVY, PLEASE...YOU *DON'T* HAVE TO MAKE THIS WORSE...
I WON'T LISTEN TO MEN LIKE YOU *EVER AGAIN!*
YEAH... WELL, MAYBE YOU'LL LISTEN TO *ME...*
HARLEY?

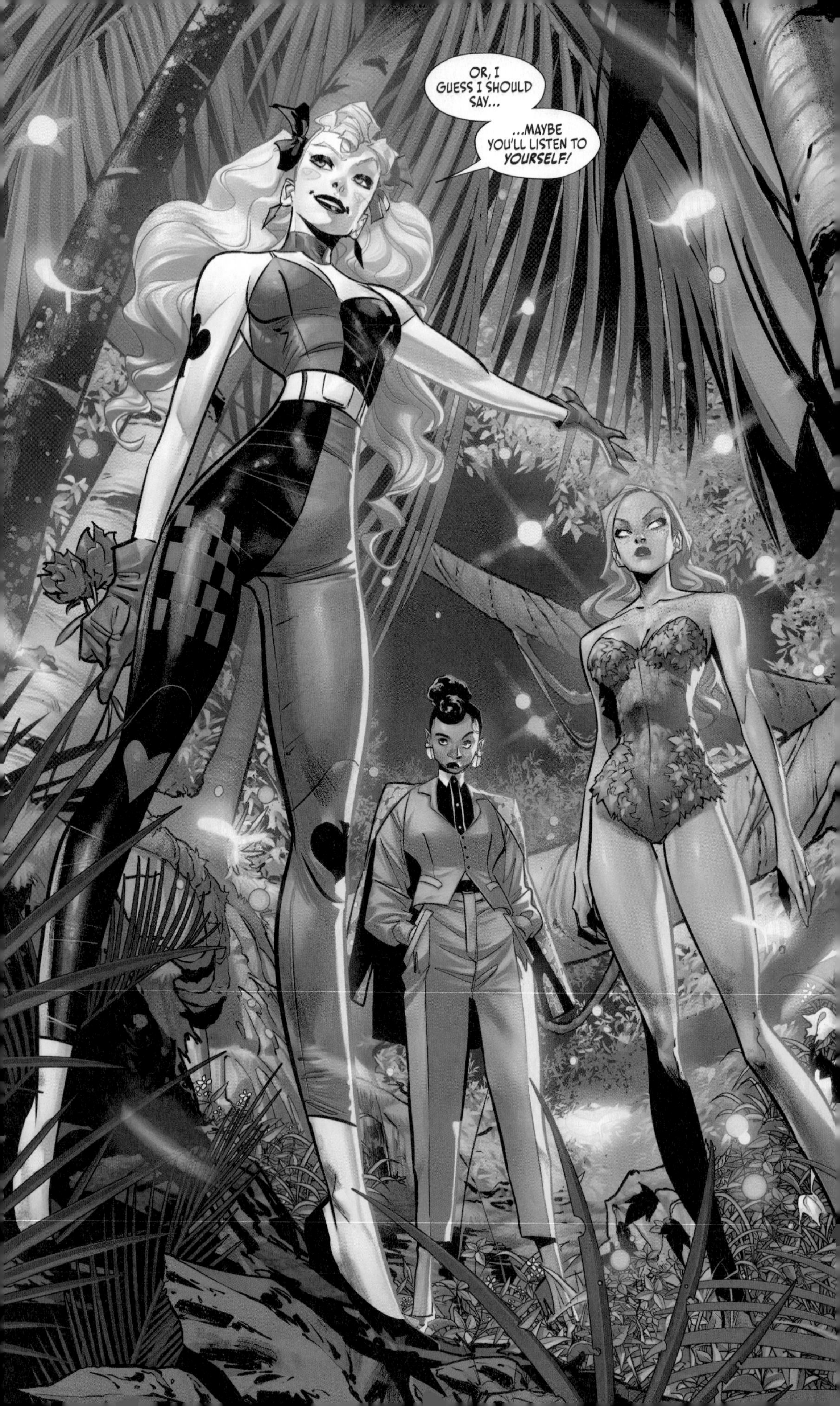

OR, I GUESS I SHOULD SAY...
...MAYBE YOU'LL LISTEN TO *YOURSELF!*

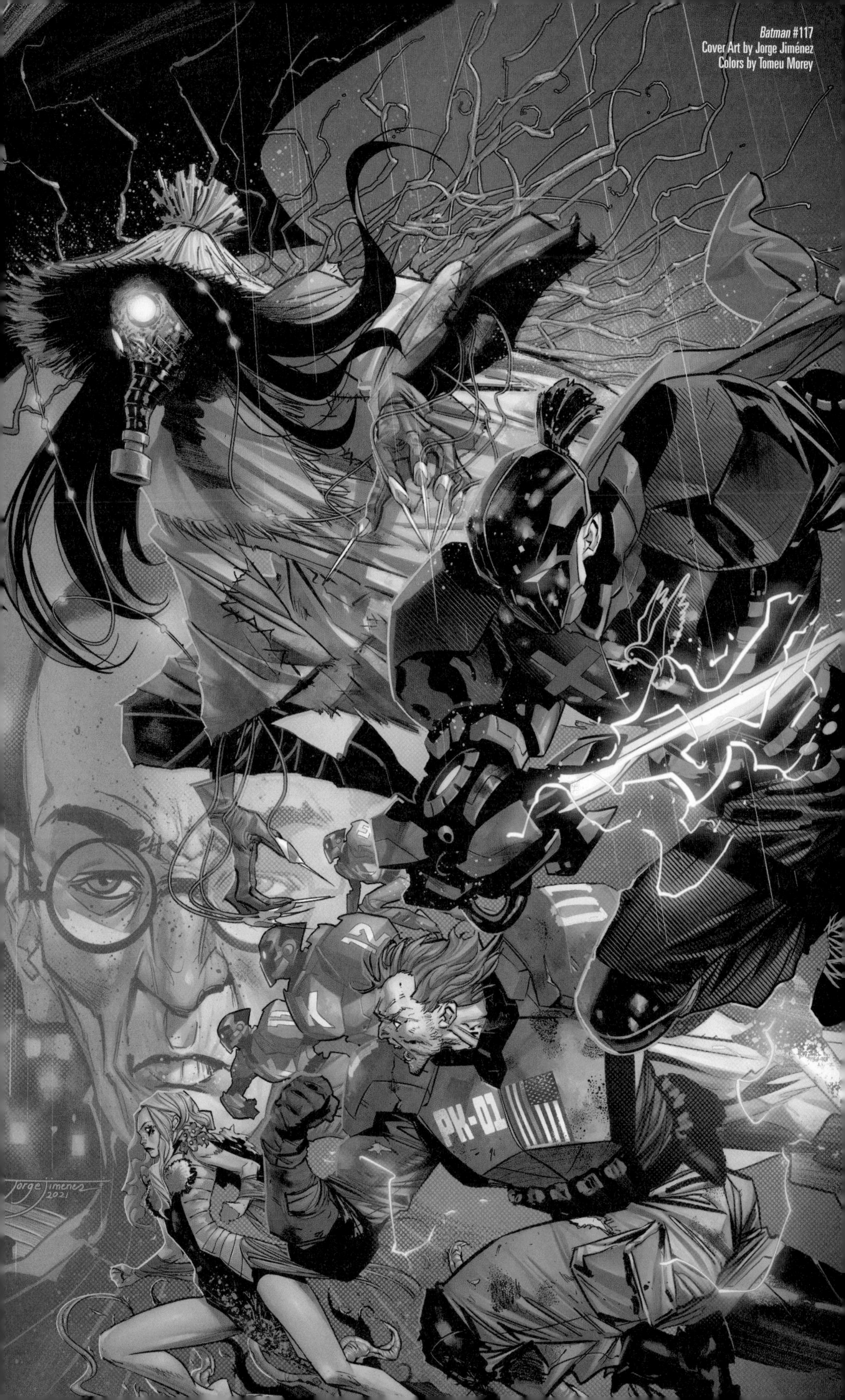
PK-01
Jorge Jimenez 2021

Batman #117
Cover Art by Jorge Jiménez
Colors by Tomeu Morey

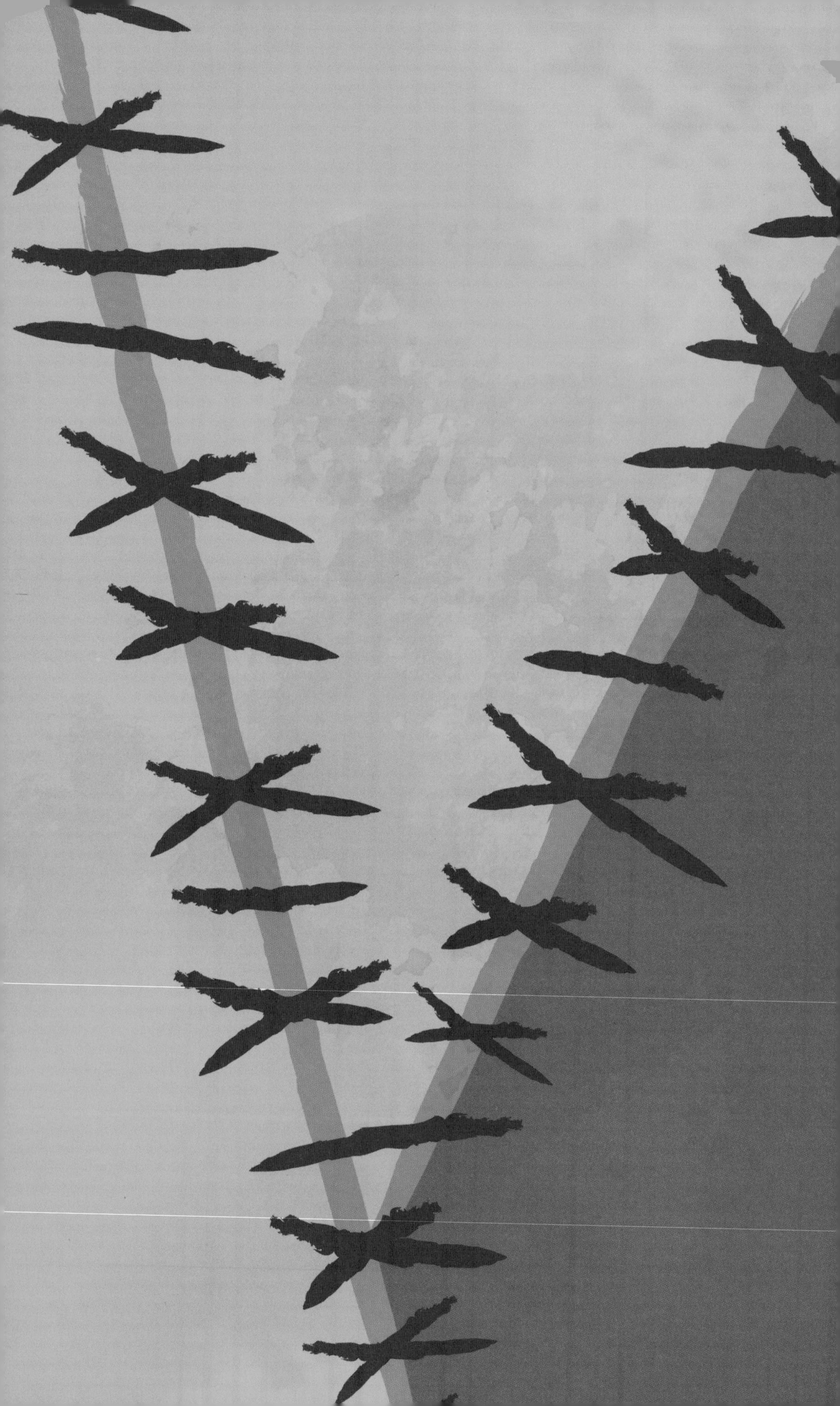

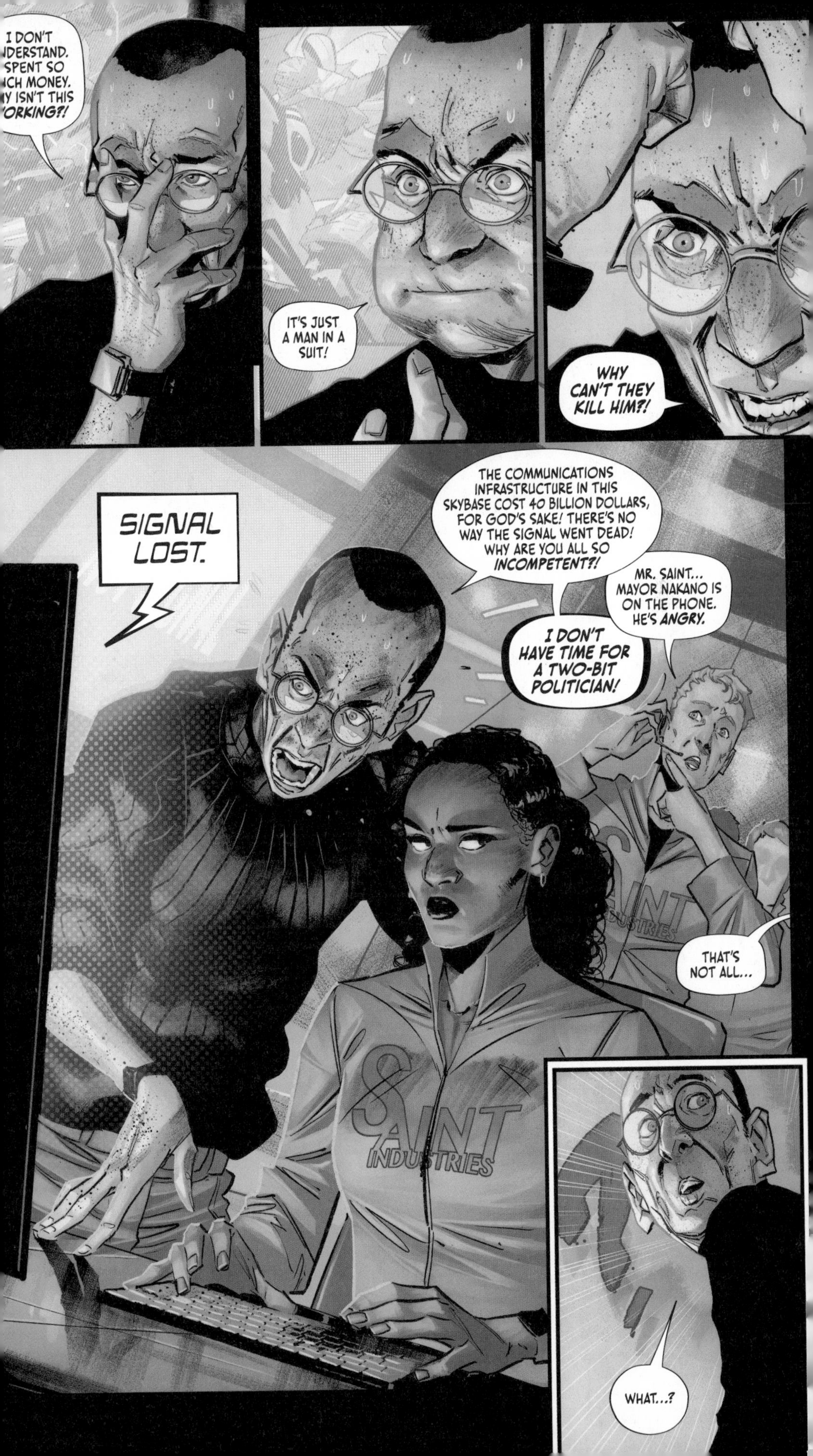
I DON'T
NDERSTAND.
SPENT SO
CH MONEY.
Y ISN'T THIS
ORKING?!
IT'S JUST A MAN IN A SUIT!
WHY CAN'T THEY KILL HIM?!
SIGNAL LOST.
THE COMMUNICATIONS INFRASTRUCTURE IN THIS SKYBASE COST 40 BILLION DOLLARS, FOR GOD'S SAKE! THERE'S NO WAY THE SIGNAL WENT DEAD! WHY ARE YOU ALL SO INCOMPETENT?!
MR. SAINT... MAYOR NAKANO IS ON THE PHONE. HE'S ANGRY.
I DON'T HAVE TIME FOR A TWO-BIT POLITICIAN!
SAINT INDUSTRIES
THAT'S NOT ALL...
WHAT...?

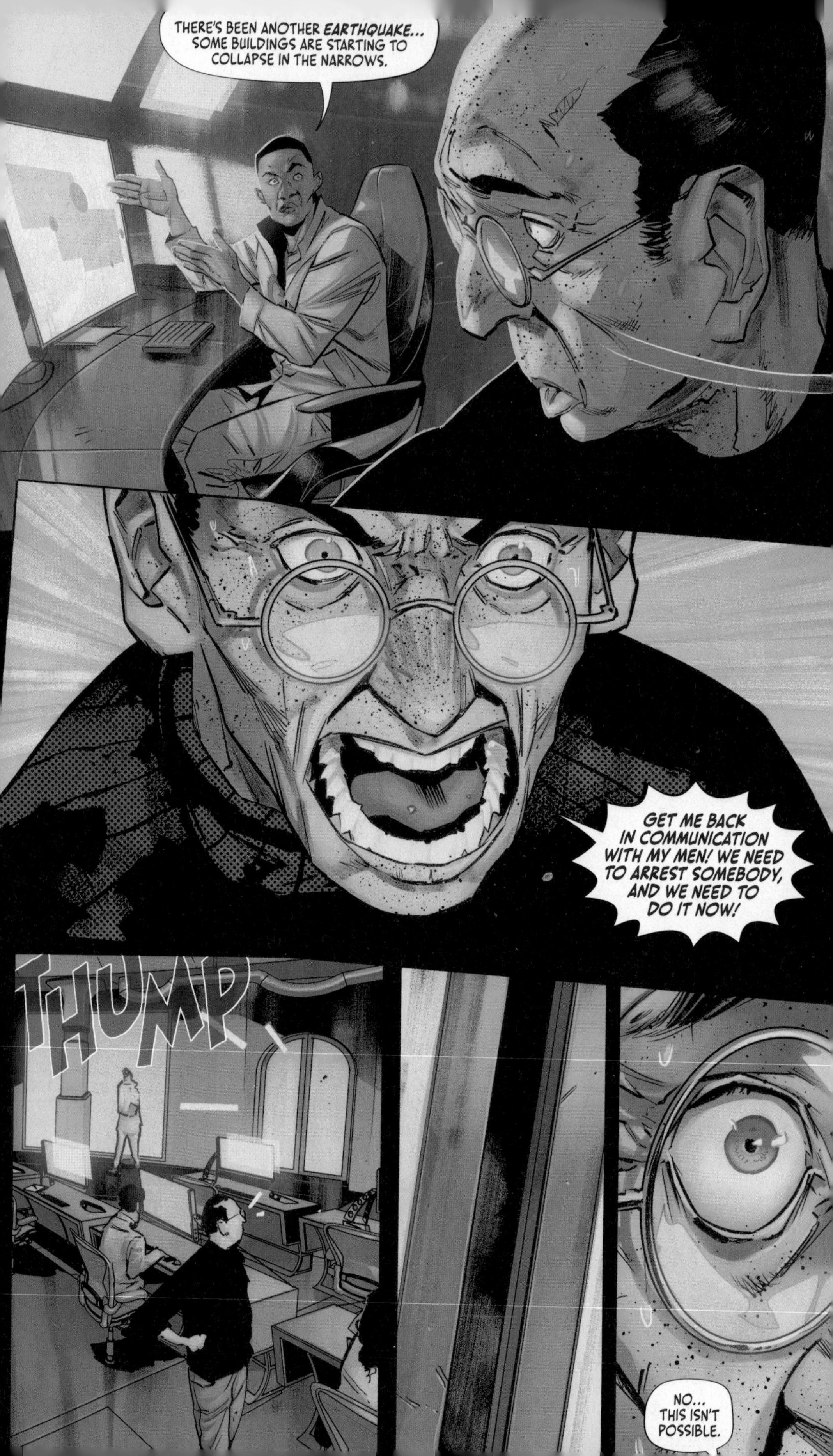
THERE'S BEEN ANOTHER EARTHQUAKE... SOME BUILDINGS ARE STARTING TO COLLAPSE IN THE NARROWS.
GET ME BACK IN COMMUNICATION WITH MY MEN! WE NEED TO ARREST SOMEBODY, AND WE NEED TO DO IT NOW!
THUMP
NO... THIS ISN'T POSSIBLE.

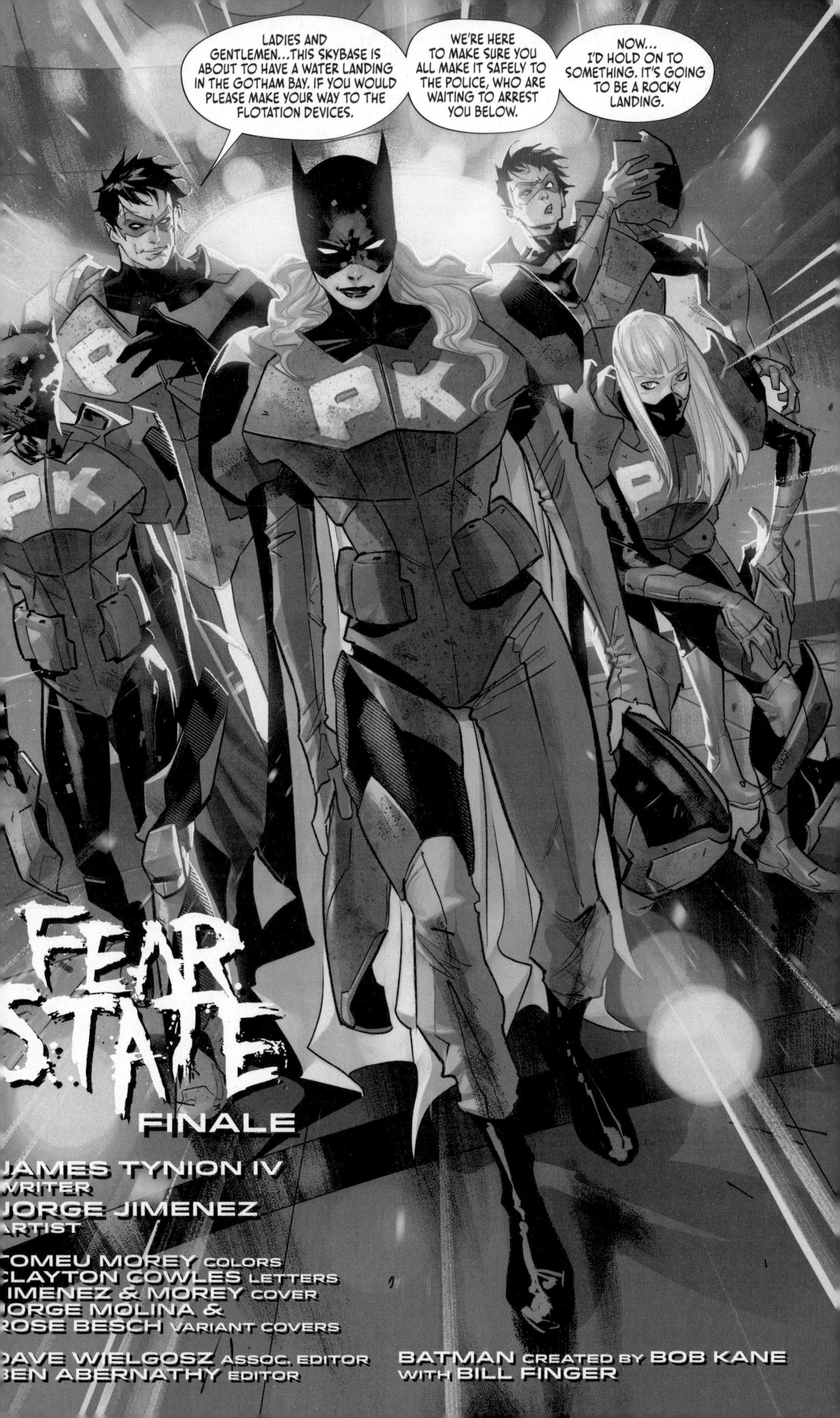

LADIES AND GENTLEMEN...THIS SKYBASE IS ABOUT TO HAVE A WATER LANDING IN THE GOTHAM BAY. IF YOU WOULD PLEASE MAKE YOUR WAY TO THE FLOTATION DEVICES.
WE'RE HERE TO MAKE SURE YOU ALL MAKE IT SAFELY TO THE POLICE, WHO ARE WAITING TO ARREST YOU BELOW.
NOW... I'D HOLD ON TO SOMETHING. IT'S GOING TO BE A ROCKY LANDING.
FEAR STATE
FINALE
JAMES TYNION IV
WRITER
JORGE JIMENEZ
ARTIST
TOMEU MOREY COLORS
CLAYTON COWLES LETTERS
JIMENEZ & MOREY COVER
JORGE MOLINA &
ROSE BESCH VARIANT COVERS
DAVE WIELGOSZ ASSOC. EDITOR
BEN ABERNATHY EDITOR
BATMAN CREATED BY BOB KANE
WITH BILL FINGER

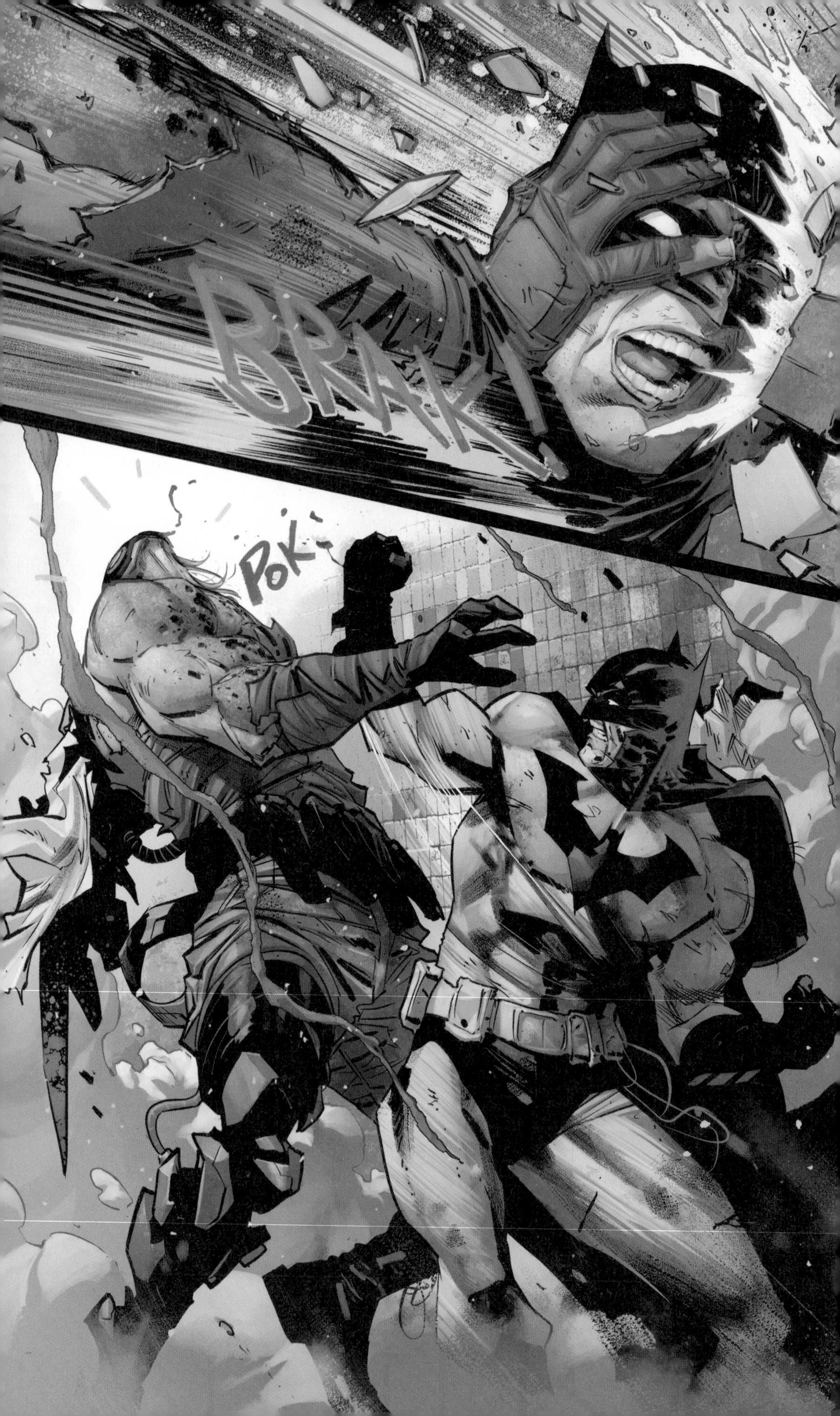
BRAK!
POK

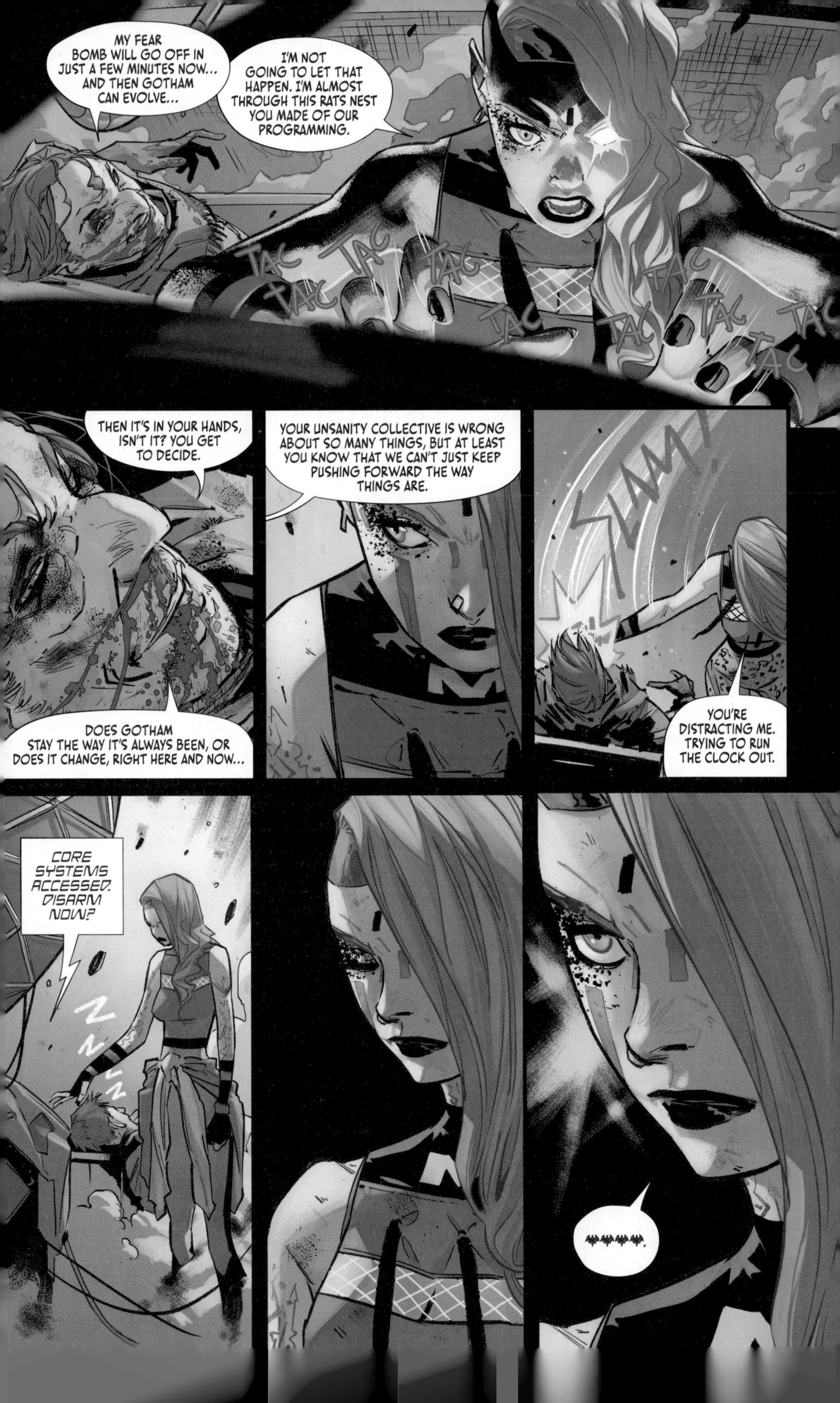
MY FEAR BOMB WILL GO OFF IN JUST A FEW MINUTES NOW... AND THEN GOTHAM CAN EVOLVE...
I'M NOT GOING TO LET THAT HAPPEN. I'M ALMOST THROUGH THIS RATS NEST YOU MADE OF OUR PROGRAMMING.
TAC TAC TAC TAC TAC TAC TAC TAC TAC TAC
THEN IT'S IN YOUR HANDS, ISN'T IT? YOU GET TO DECIDE.
DOES GOTHAM STAY THE WAY IT'S ALWAYS BEEN, OR DOES IT CHANGE, RIGHT HERE AND NOW...
YOUR UNSANITY COLLECTIVE IS WRONG ABOUT SO MANY THINGS, BUT AT LEAST YOU KNOW THAT WE CAN'T JUST KEEP PUSHING FORWARD THE WAY THINGS ARE.
SLAM!
YOU'RE DISTRACTING ME. TRYING TO RUN THE CLOCK OUT.
CORE SYSTEMS ACCESSED. DISARM NOW?
ZZZ

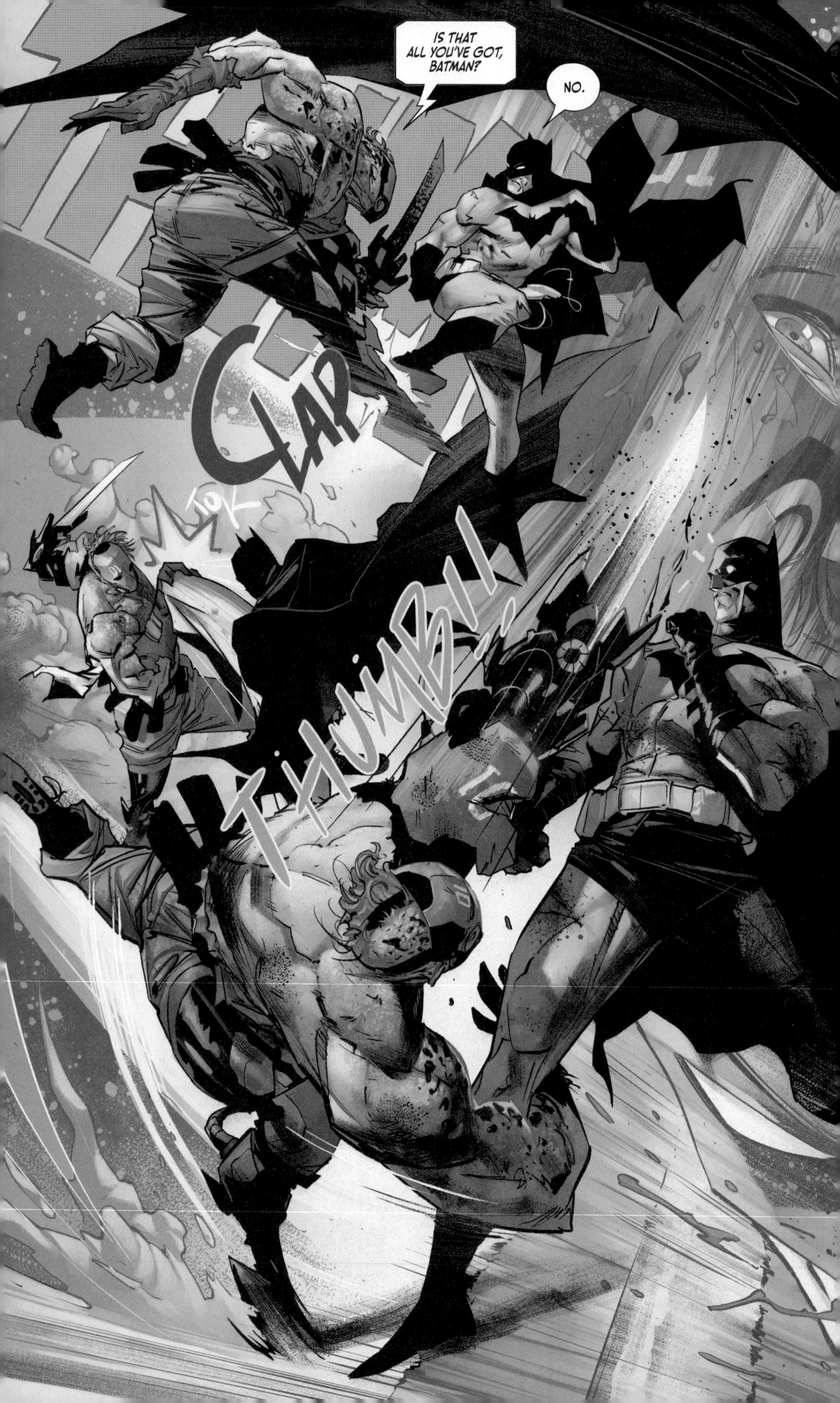
IS THAT ALL YOU'VE GOT, BATMAN?
NO.
CLAP
TOK
THUMB!!

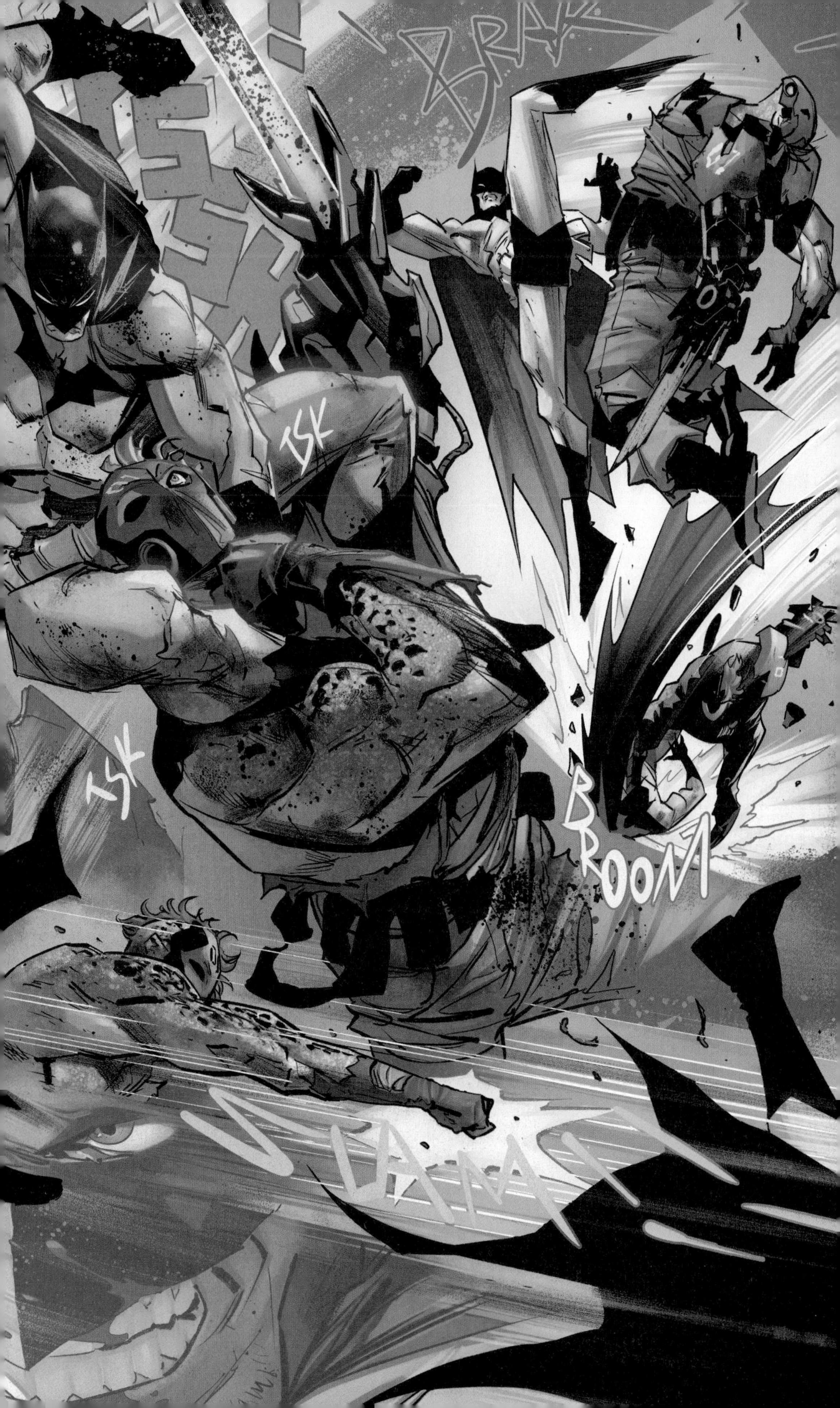
TSK
TSK
BROOM

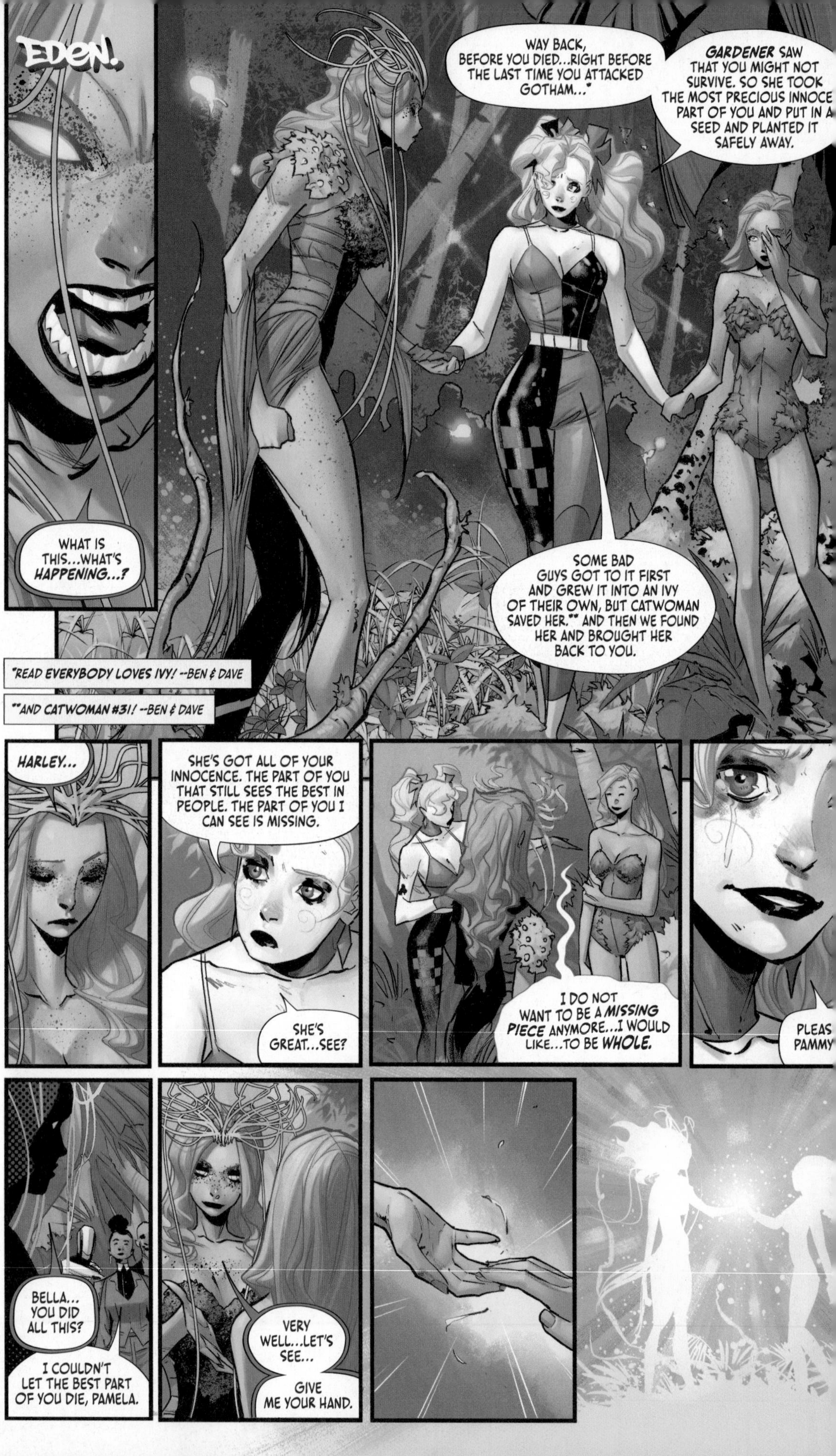
EDEN!
WHAT IS THIS...WHAT'S HAPPENING...?
WAY BACK, BEFORE YOU DIED...RIGHT BEFORE THE LAST TIME YOU ATTACKED GOTHAM...*
GARDENER SAW THAT YOU MIGHT NOT SURVIVE. SO SHE TOOK THE MOST PRECIOUS INNOCE PART OF YOU AND PUT IN A SEED AND PLANTED IT SAFELY AWAY.
SOME BAD GUYS GOT TO IT FIRST AND GREW IT INTO AN IVY OF THEIR OWN, BUT CATWOMAN SAVED HER.** AND THEN WE FOUND HER AND BROUGHT HER BACK TO YOU.
*READ EVERYBODY LOVES IVY! --BEN & DAVE
**AND CATWOMAN #31! --BEN & DAVE
HARLEY...
SHE'S GOT ALL OF YOUR INNOCENCE. THE PART OF YOU THAT STILL SEES THE BEST IN PEOPLE. THE PART OF YOU I CAN SEE IS MISSING.
SHE'S GREAT...SEE?
I DO NOT WANT TO BE A MISSING PIECE ANYMORE...I WOULD LIKE...TO BE WHOLE.
PLEAS PAMMY
BELLA... YOU DID ALL THIS?
I COULDN'T LET THE BEST PART OF YOU DIE, PAMELA.
VERY WELL...LET'S SEE...
GIVE ME YOUR HAND.

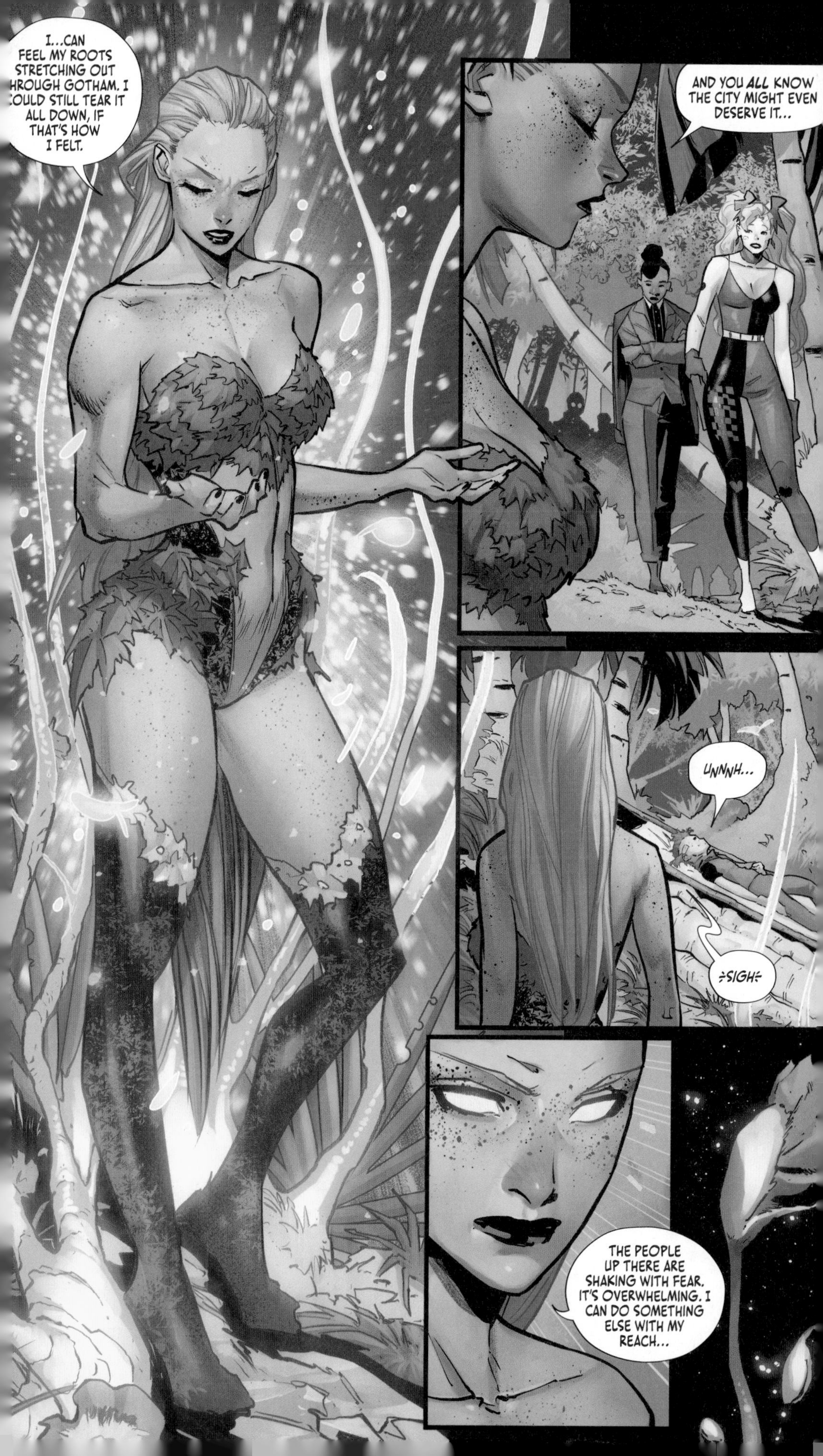

I...CAN FEEL MY ROOTS STRETCHING OUT HROUGH GOTHAM. I COULD STILL TEAR IT ALL DOWN, IF THAT'S HOW I FELT.
AND YOU *ALL* KNOW THE CITY MIGHT EVEN DESERVE IT...
UNNNH...
SIGH
THE PEOPLE UP THERE ARE SHAKING WITH FEAR. IT'S OVERWHELMING. I CAN DO SOMETHING ELSE WITH MY REACH...

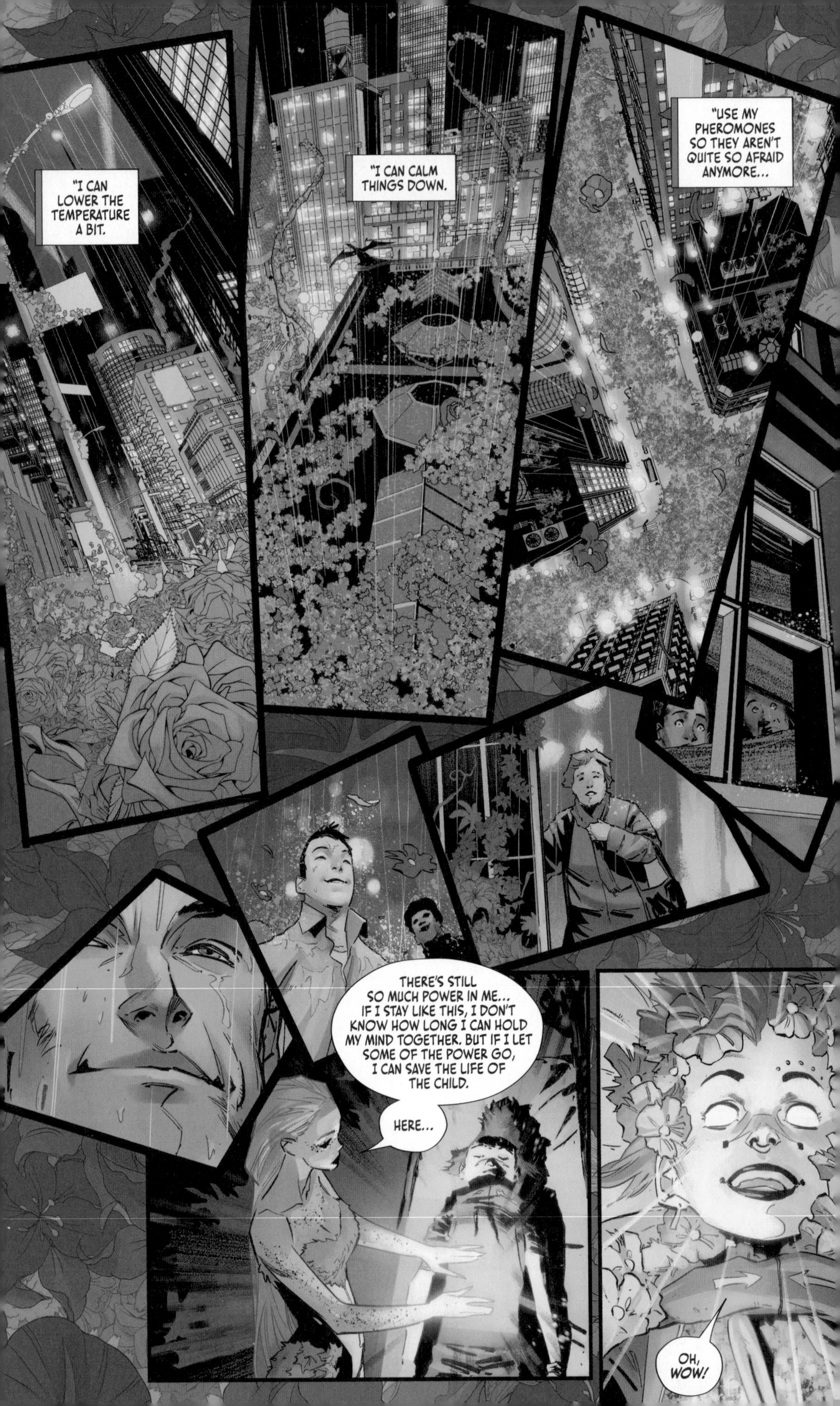
"I CAN LOWER THE TEMPERATURE A BIT.
"I CAN CALM THINGS DOWN.
"USE MY PHEROMONES SO THEY AREN'T QUITE SO AFRAID ANYMORE...
THERE'S STILL SO MUCH POWER IN ME... IF I STAY LIKE THIS, I DON'T KNOW HOW LONG I CAN HOLD MY MIND TOGETHER. BUT IF I LET SOME OF THE POWER GO, I CAN SAVE THE LIFE OF THE CHILD.
HERE...
OH, WOW!

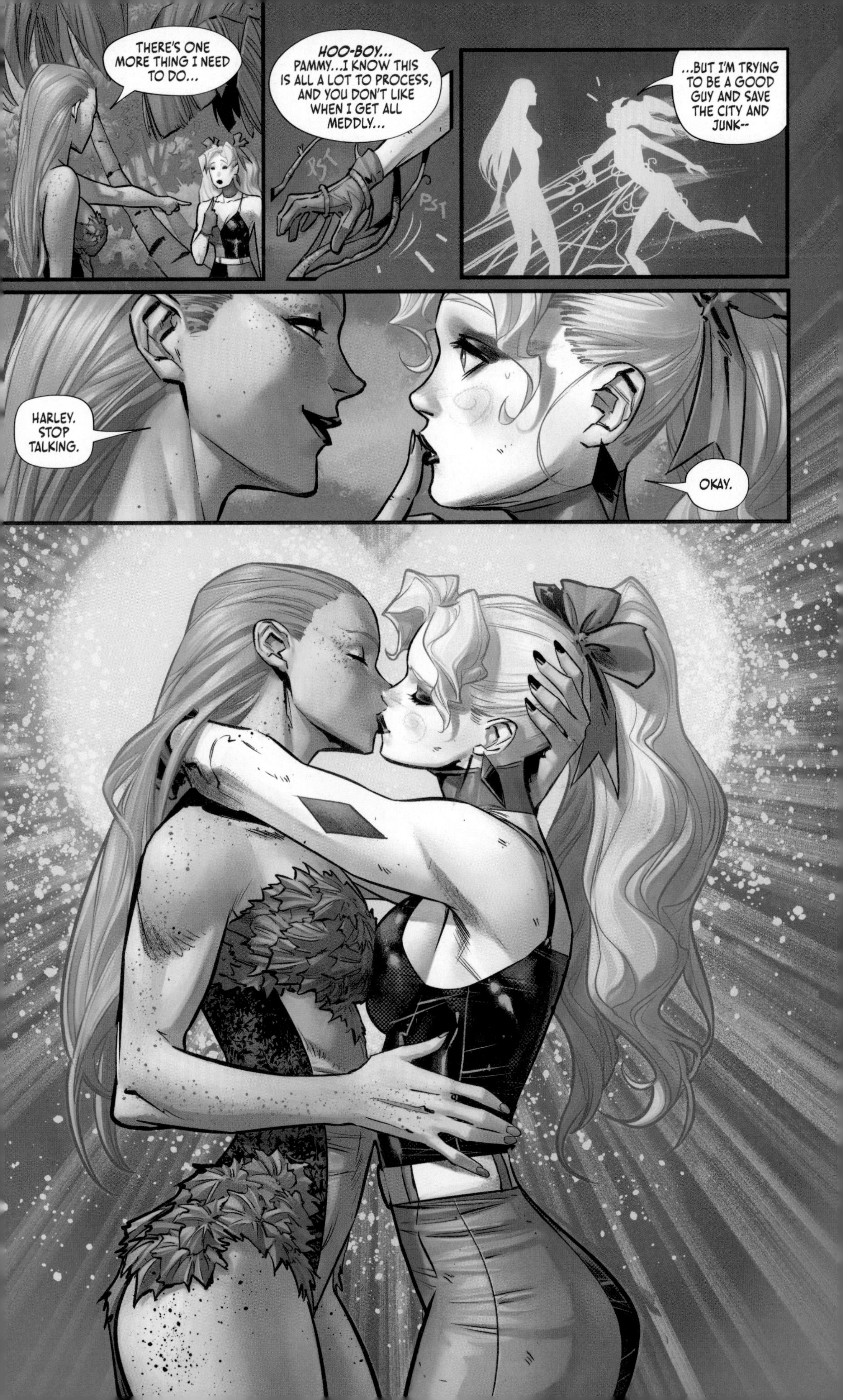
THERE'S ONE MORE THING I NEED TO DO...
HOO-BOY... PAMMY...I KNOW THIS IS ALL A LOT TO PROCESS, AND YOU DON'T LIKE WHEN I GET ALL MEDDLY...
PST
PST
...BUT I'M TRYING TO BE A GOOD GUY AND SAVE THE CITY AND JUNK--
HARLEY. STOP TALKING.
OKAY.

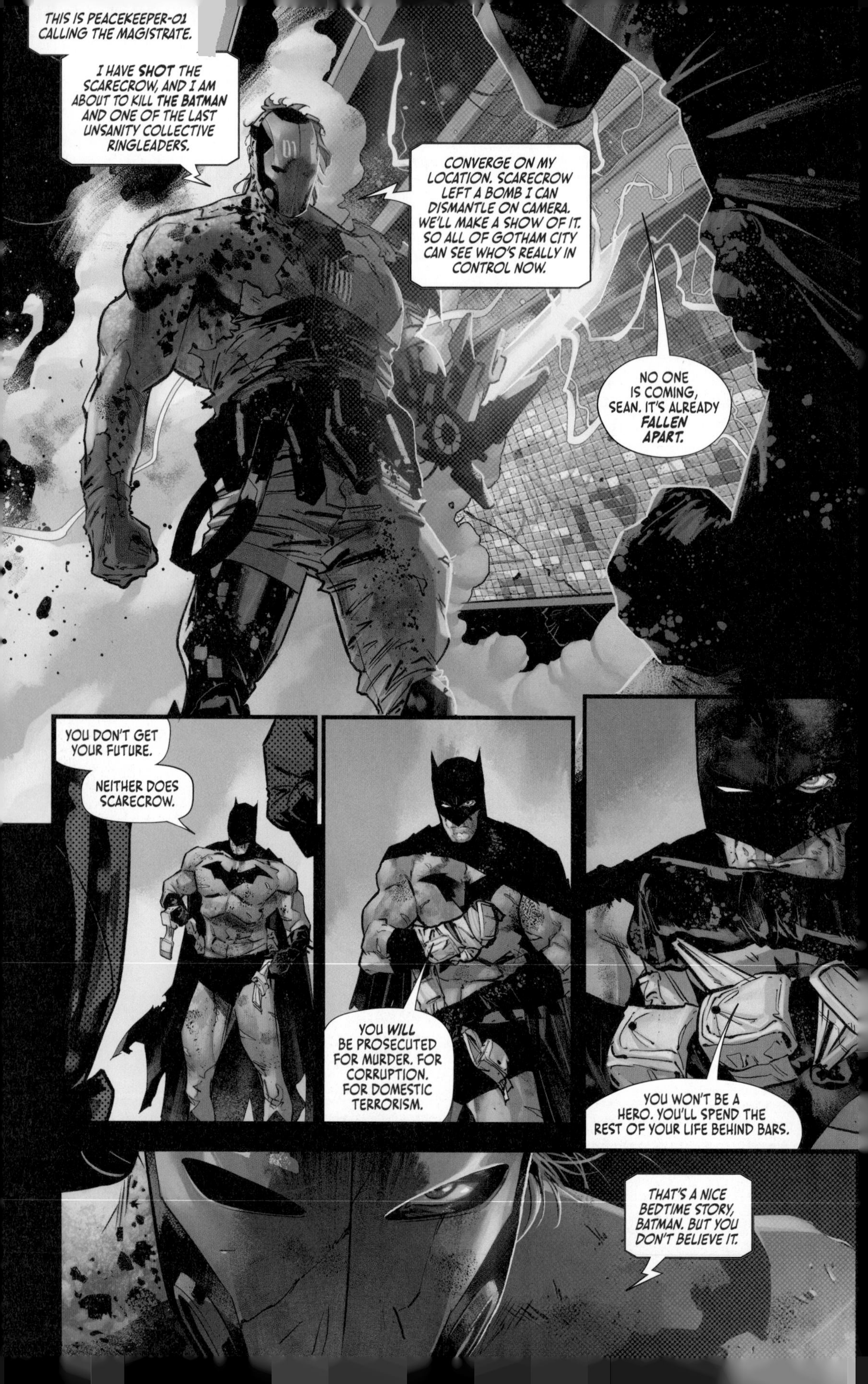
THIS IS PEACEKEEPER-01 CALLING THE MAGISTRATE.
I HAVE **SHOT** THE SCARECROW, AND I AM ABOUT TO KILL **THE BATMAN** AND ONE OF THE LAST UNSANITY COLLECTIVE RINGLEADERS.
CONVERGE ON MY LOCATION. SCARECROW LEFT A BOMB I CAN DISMANTLE ON CAMERA. WE'LL MAKE A SHOW OF IT. SO ALL OF GOTHAM CITY CAN SEE WHO'S REALLY IN CONTROL NOW.
NO ONE IS COMING, SEAN. IT'S ALREADY **FALLEN APART.**
YOU DON'T GET YOUR FUTURE.
NEITHER DOES SCARECROW.
YOU **WILL** BE PROSECUTED FOR MURDER. FOR CORRUPTION. FOR DOMESTIC TERRORISM.
YOU WON'T BE A HERO. YOU'LL SPEND THE REST OF YOUR LIFE BEHIND BARS.
THAT'S A NICE BEDTIME STORY, BATMAN. BUT YOU DON'T BELIEVE IT.

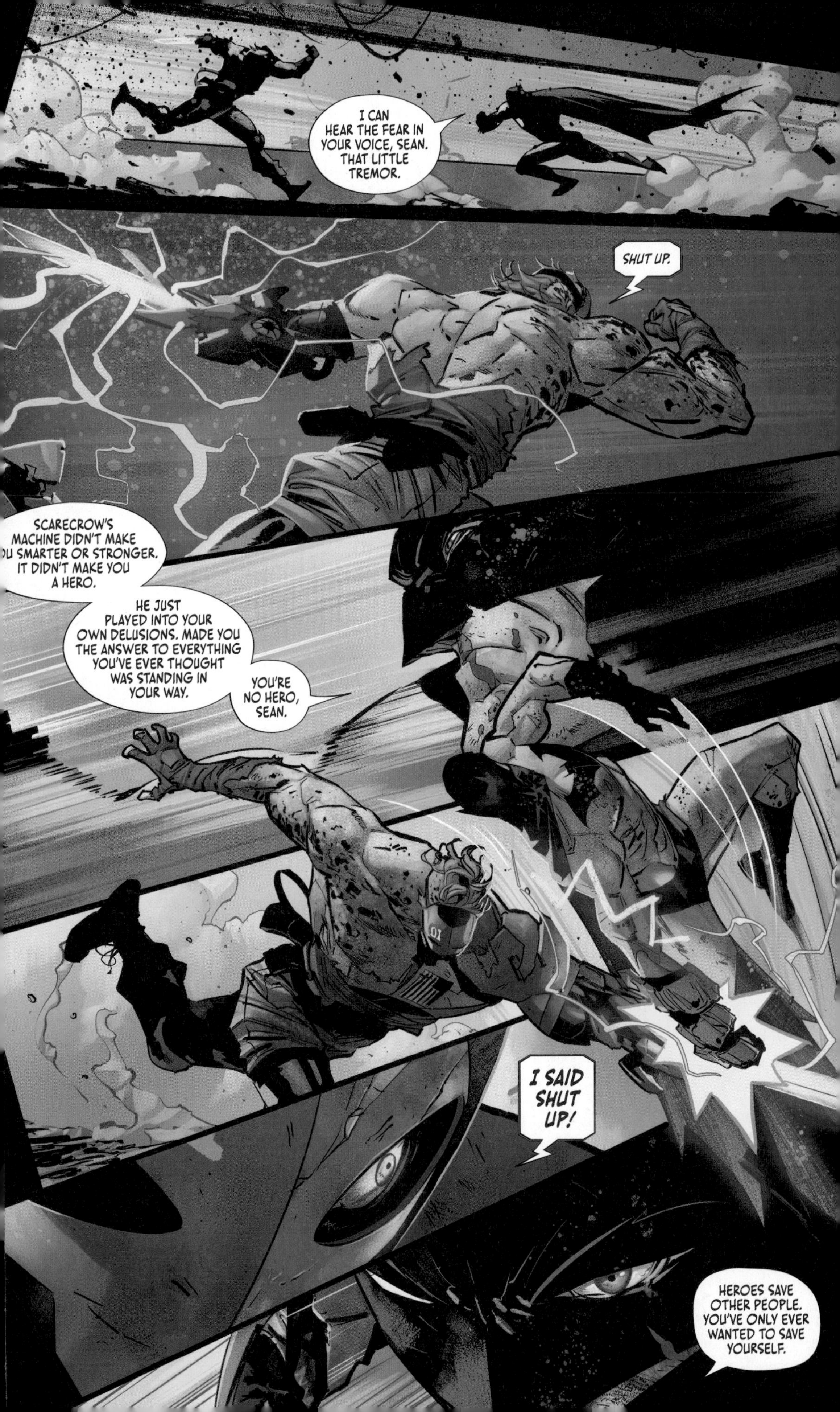
I CAN HEAR THE FEAR IN YOUR VOICE, SEAN. THAT LITTLE TREMOR.
SHUT UP.
SCARECROW'S MACHINE DIDN'T MAKE OU SMARTER OR STRONGER. IT DIDN'T MAKE YOU A HERO.
HE JUST PLAYED INTO YOUR OWN DELUSIONS. MADE YOU THE ANSWER TO EVERYTHING YOU'VE EVER THOUGHT WAS STANDING IN YOUR WAY.
YOU'RE NO HERO, SEAN.
I SAID SHUT UP!
HEROES SAVE OTHER PEOPLE. YOU'VE ONLY EVER WANTED TO SAVE YOURSELF.

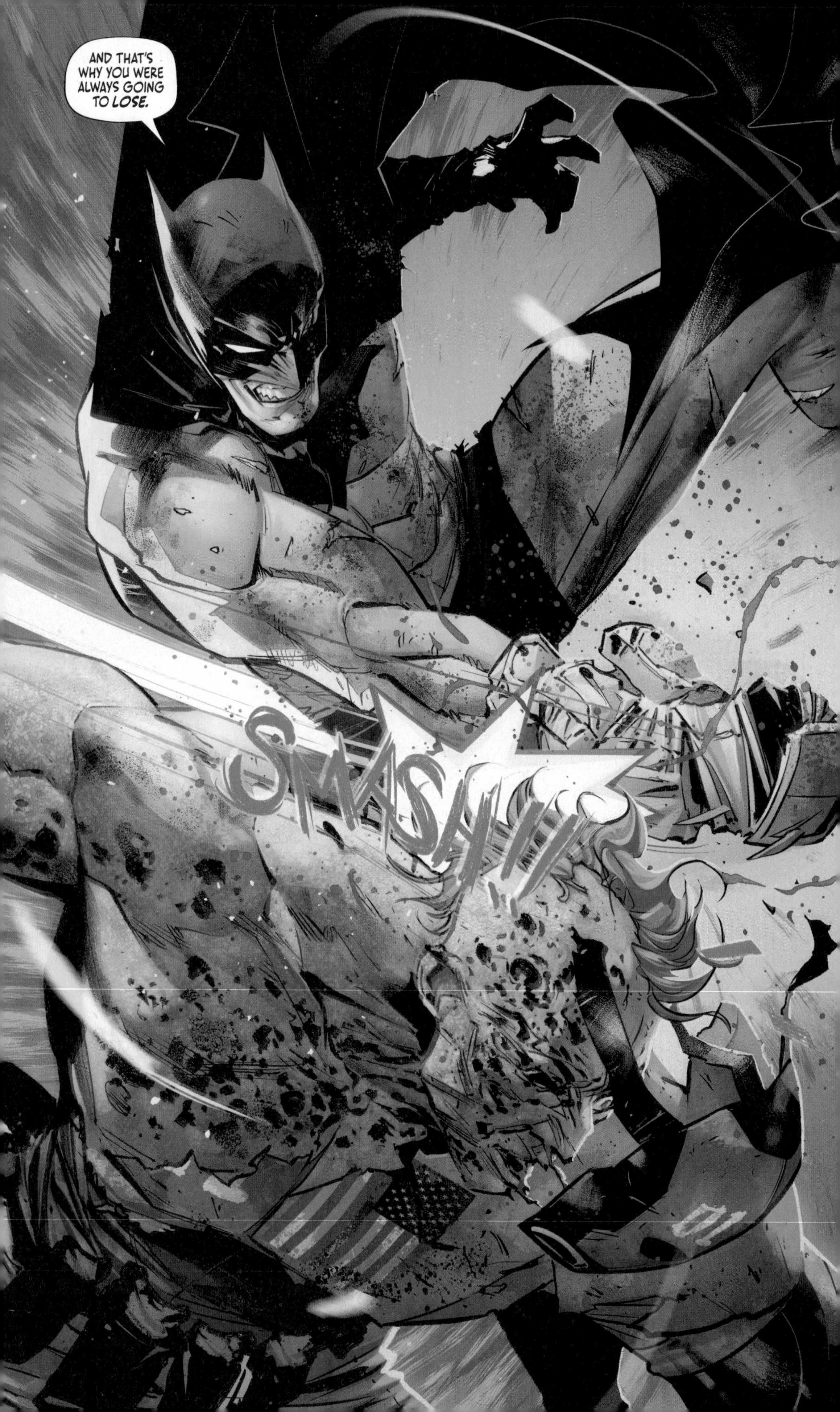
AND THAT'S WHY YOU WERE ALWAYS GOING TO *LOSE.*
SMASH

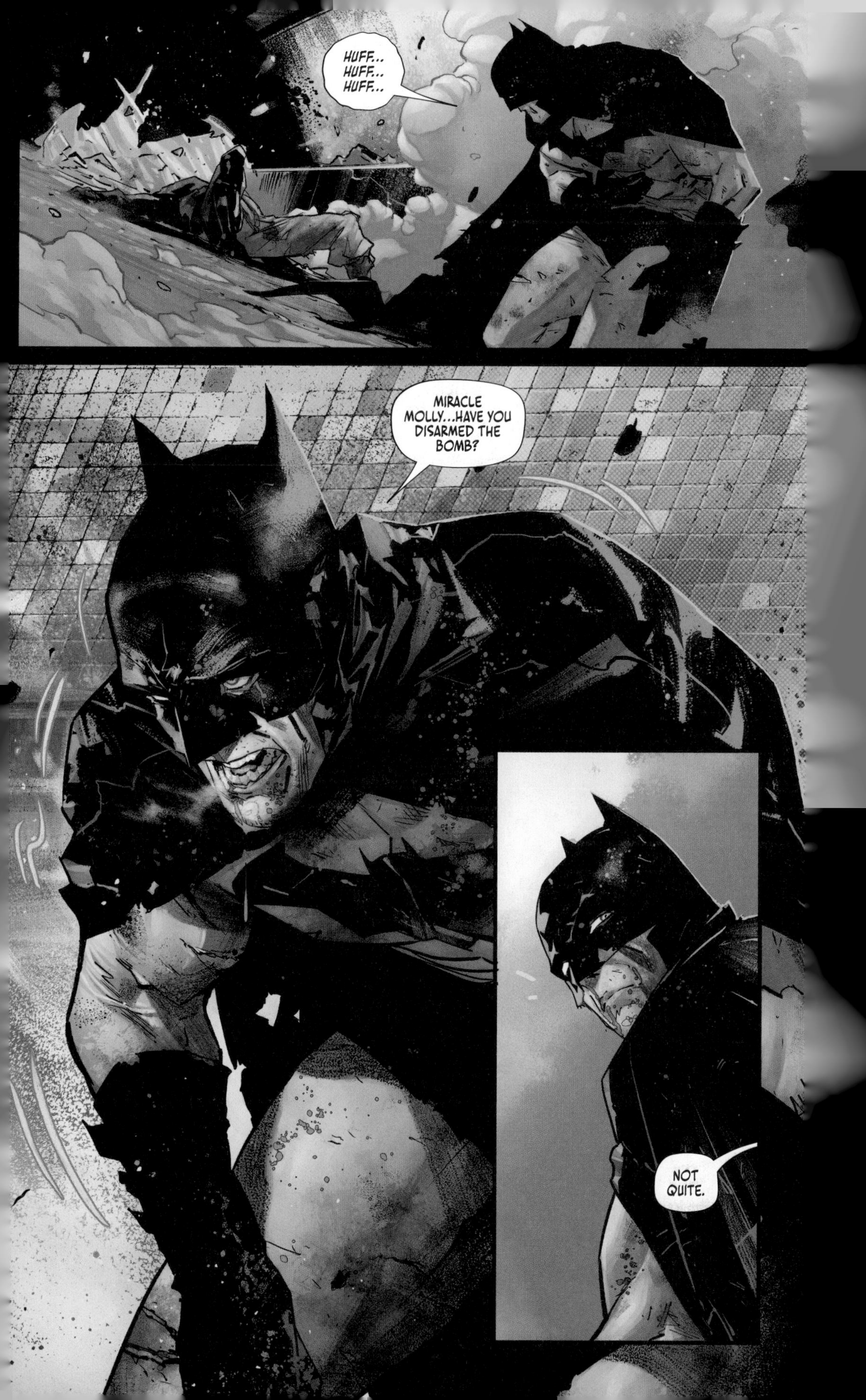
HUFF... HUFF... HUFF...
MIRACLE MOLLY...HAVE YOU DISARMED THE BOMB?
NOT QUITE.

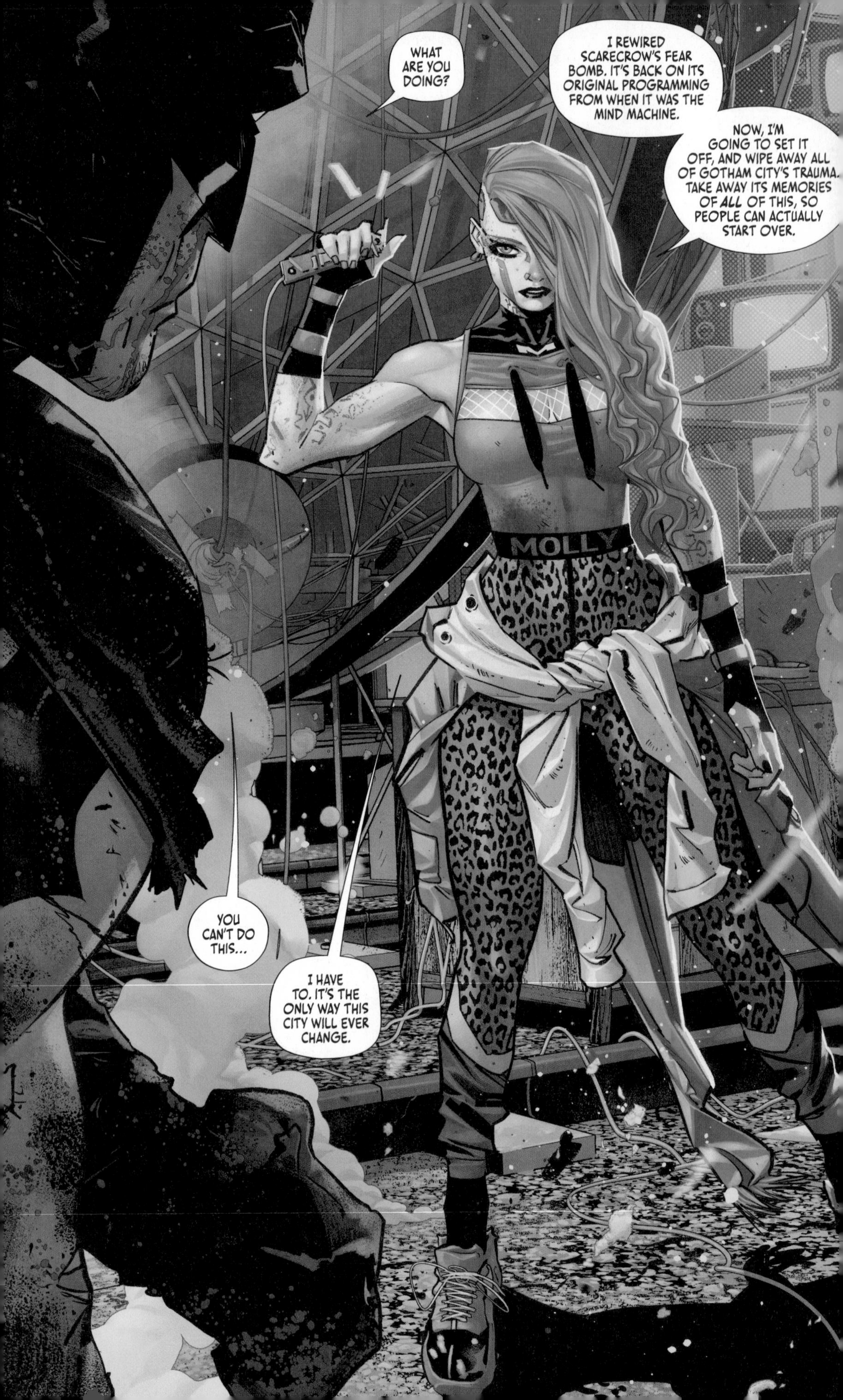
WHAT ARE YOU DOING?
I REWIRED SCARECROW'S FEAR BOMB. IT'S BACK ON ITS ORIGINAL PROGRAMMING FROM WHEN IT WAS THE MIND MACHINE.
NOW, I'M GOING TO SET IT OFF, AND WIPE AWAY ALL OF GOTHAM CITY'S TRAUMA. TAKE AWAY ITS MEMORIES OF ALL OF THIS, SO PEOPLE CAN ACTUALLY START OVER.
MOLLY
YOU CAN'T DO THIS...
I HAVE TO. IT'S THE ONLY WAY THIS CITY WILL EVER CHANGE.

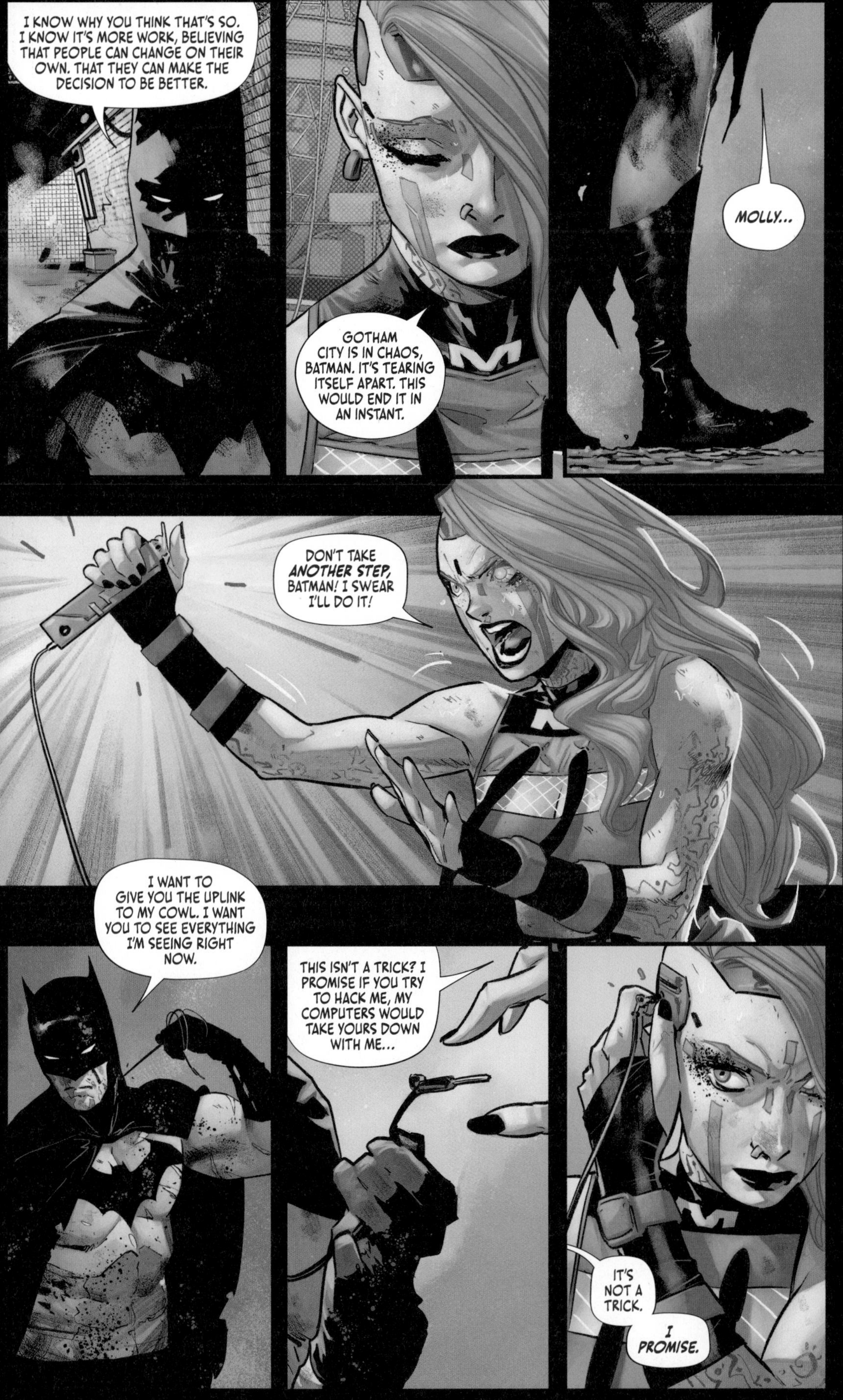
I KNOW WHY YOU THINK THAT'S SO. I KNOW IT'S MORE WORK, BELIEVING THAT PEOPLE CAN CHANGE ON THEIR OWN. THAT THEY CAN MAKE THE DECISION TO BE BETTER.
GOTHAM CITY IS IN CHAOS, BATMAN. IT'S TEARING ITSELF APART. THIS WOULD END IT IN AN INSTANT.
MOLLY...
DON'T TAKE *ANOTHER STEP*, BATMAN! I SWEAR I'LL DO IT!
I WANT TO GIVE YOU THE UPLINK TO MY COWL. I WANT YOU TO SEE EVERYTHING I'M SEEING RIGHT NOW.
THIS ISN'T A TRICK? I PROMISE IF YOU TRY TO HACK ME, MY COMPUTERS WOULD TAKE YOURS DOWN WITH ME...
IT'S NOT A TRICK.
I PROMISE.

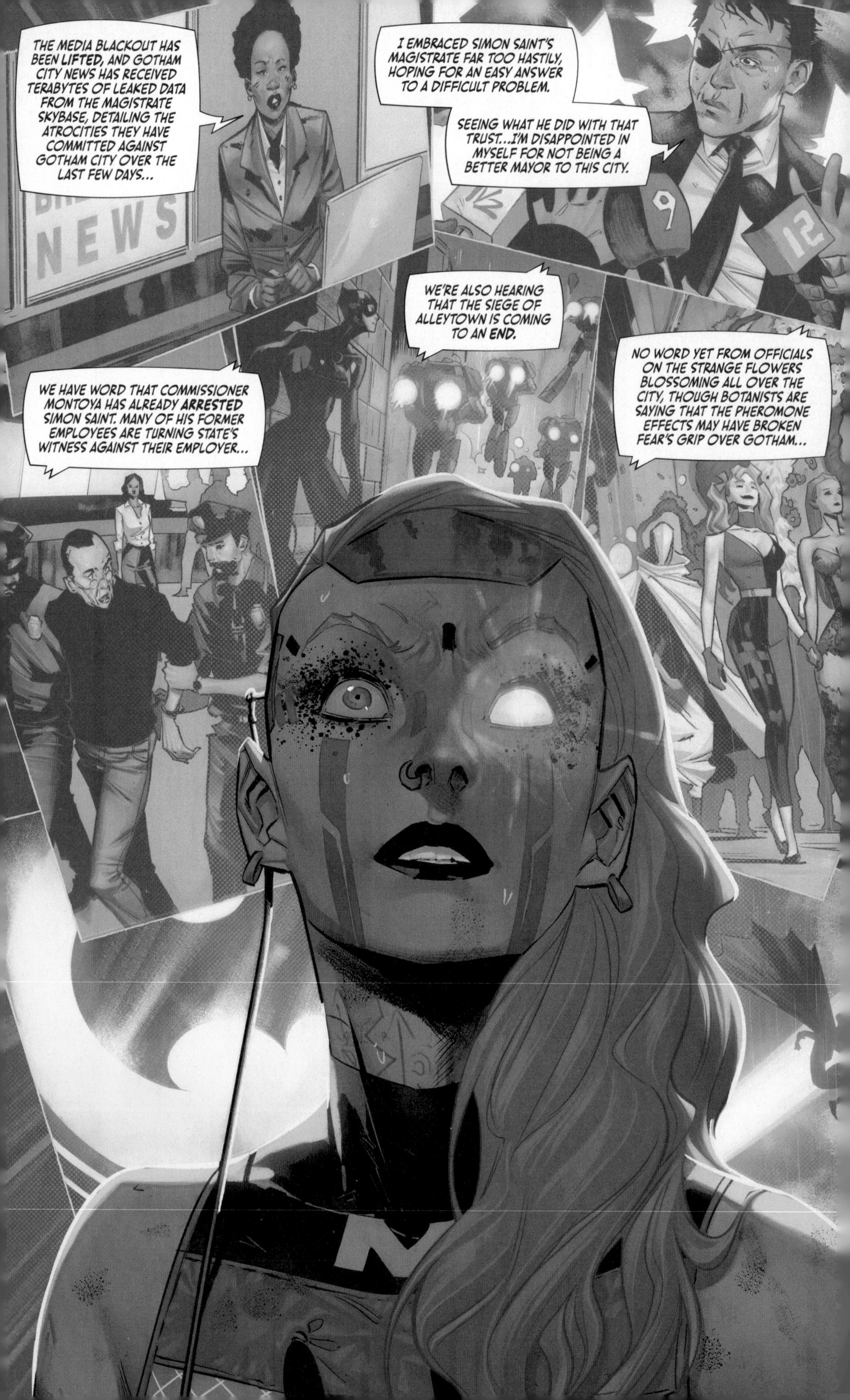
THE MEDIA BLACKOUT HAS BEEN LIFTED, AND GOTHAM CITY NEWS HAS RECEIVED TERABYTES OF LEAKED DATA FROM THE MAGISTRATE SKYBASE, DETAILING THE ATROCITIES THEY HAVE COMMITTED AGAINST GOTHAM CITY OVER THE LAST FEW DAYS...
NEWS
I EMBRACED SIMON SAINT'S MAGISTRATE FAR TOO HASTILY, HOPING FOR AN EASY ANSWER TO A DIFFICULT PROBLEM.
SEEING WHAT HE DID WITH THAT TRUST...I'M DISAPPOINTED IN MYSELF FOR NOT BEING A BETTER MAYOR TO THIS CITY.
9
12
WE'RE ALSO HEARING THAT THE SIEGE OF ALLEYTOWN IS COMING TO AN END.
NO WORD YET FROM OFFICIALS ON THE STRANGE FLOWERS BLOSSOMING ALL OVER THE CITY, THOUGH BOTANISTS ARE SAYING THAT THE PHEROMONE EFFECTS MAY HAVE BROKEN FEAR'S GRIP OVER GOTHAM...
WE HAVE WORD THAT COMMISSIONER MONTOYA HAS ALREADY ARRESTED SIMON SAINT. MANY OF HIS FORMER EMPLOYEES ARE TURNING STATE'S WITNESS AGAINST THEIR EMPLOYER...

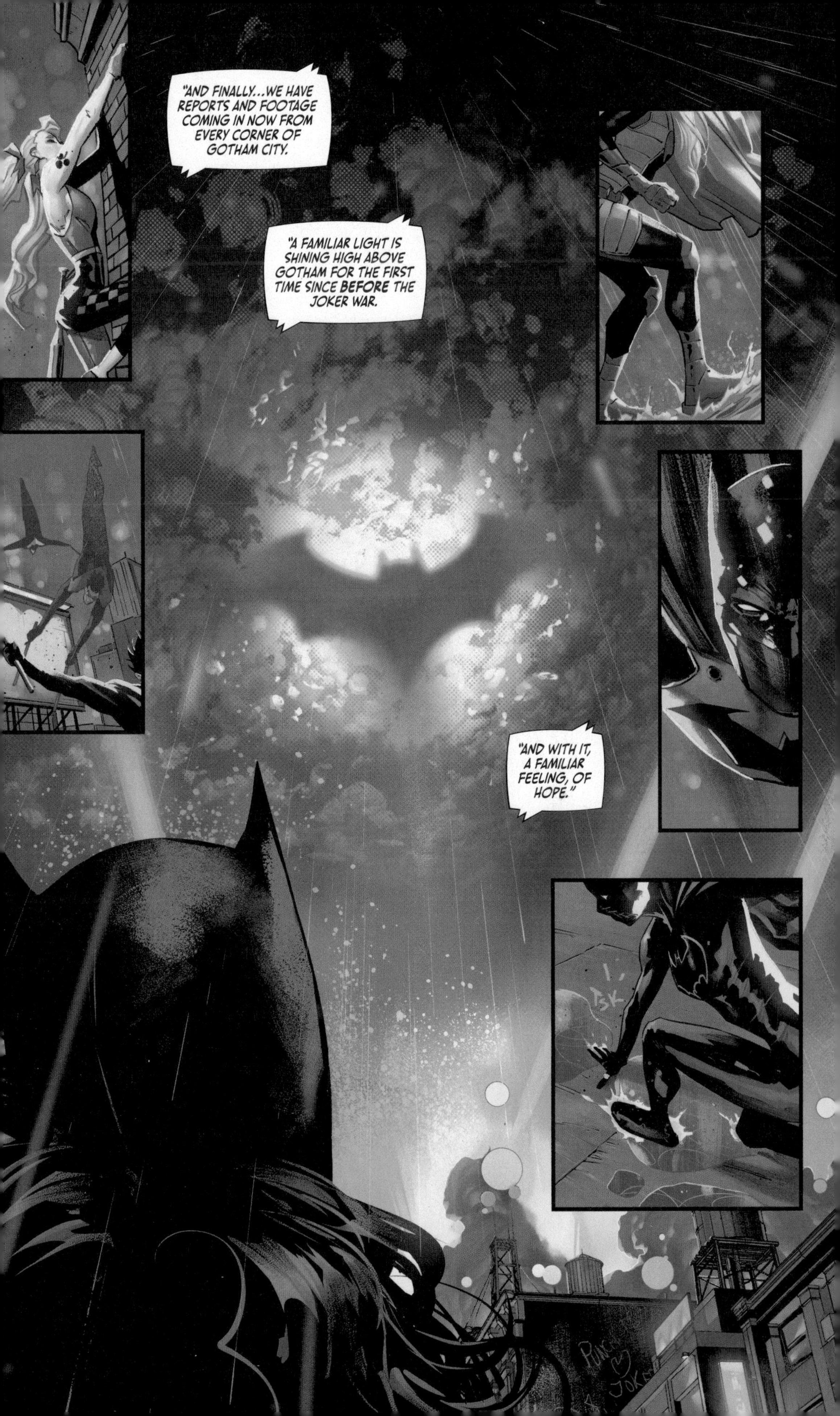
"AND FINALLY...WE HAVE REPORTS AND FOOTAGE COMING IN NOW FROM EVERY CORNER OF GOTHAM CITY.
"A FAMILIAR LIGHT IS SHINING HIGH ABOVE GOTHAM FOR THE FIRST TIME SINCE BEFORE THE JOKER WAR.
"AND WITH IT, A FAMILIAR FEELING, OF HOPE."

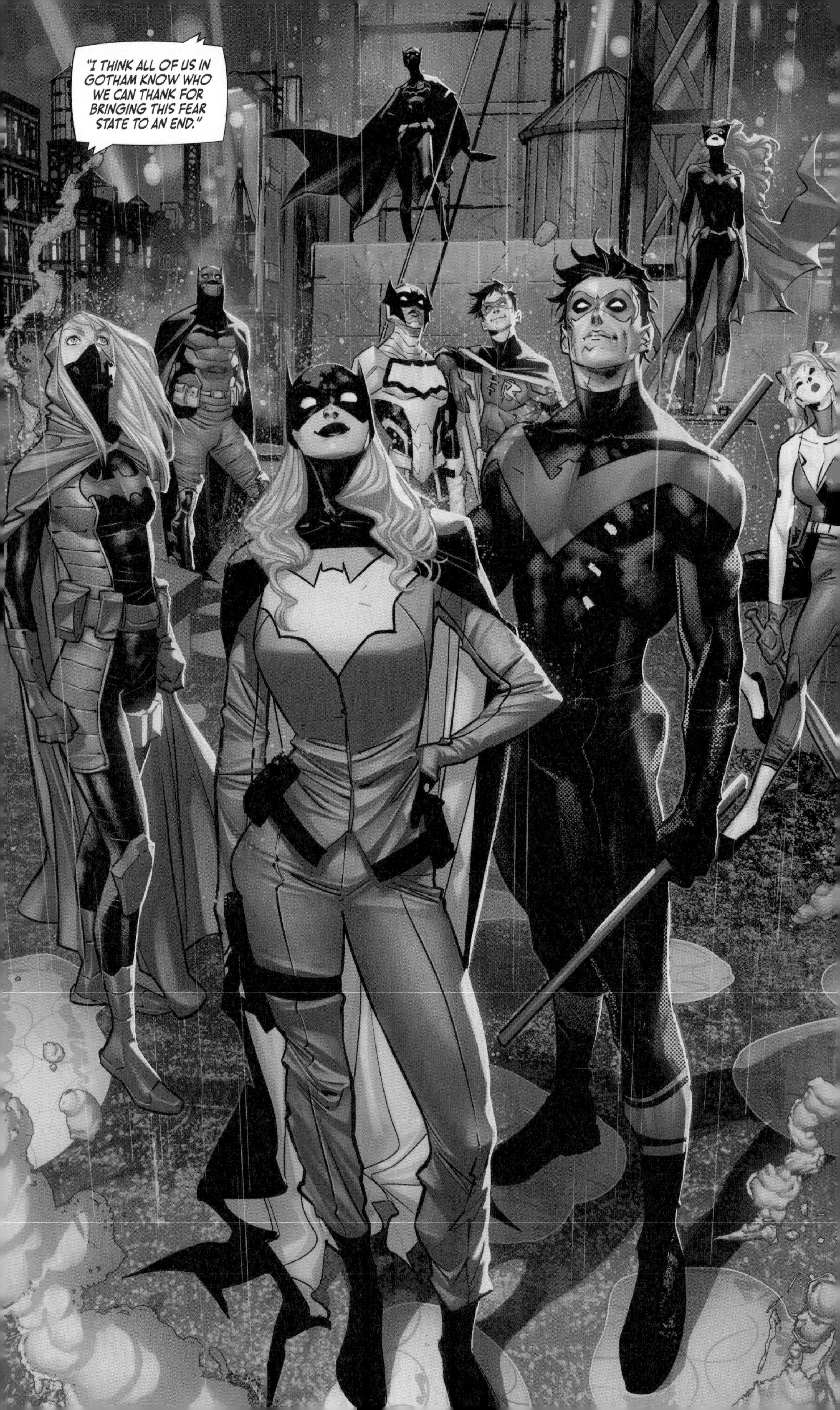
"I THINK ALL OF US IN GOTHAM KNOW WHO WE CAN THANK FOR BRINGING THIS FEAR STATE TO AN END."

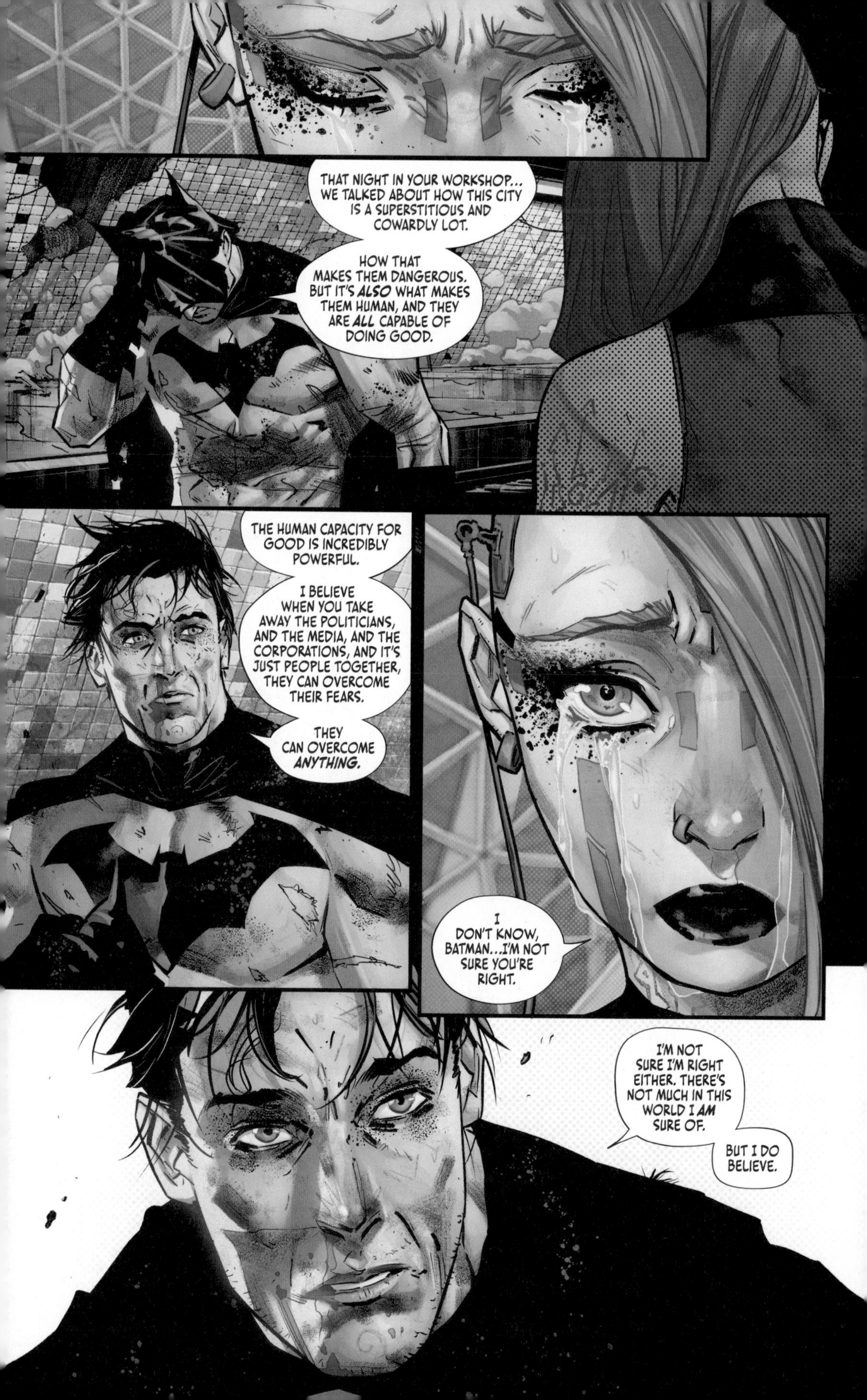
THAT NIGHT IN YOUR WORKSHOP... WE TALKED ABOUT HOW THIS CITY IS A SUPERSTITIOUS AND COWARDLY LOT.
HOW THAT MAKES THEM DANGEROUS. BUT IT'S ALSO WHAT MAKES THEM HUMAN, AND THEY ARE ALL CAPABLE OF DOING GOOD.
THE HUMAN CAPACITY FOR GOOD IS INCREDIBLY POWERFUL.
I BELIEVE WHEN YOU TAKE AWAY THE POLITICIANS, AND THE MEDIA, AND THE CORPORATIONS, AND IT'S JUST PEOPLE TOGETHER, THEY CAN OVERCOME THEIR FEARS.
THEY CAN OVERCOME ANYTHING.
I DON'T KNOW, BATMAN...I'M NOT SURE YOU'RE RIGHT.
I'M NOT SURE I'M RIGHT EITHER. THERE'S NOT MUCH IN THIS WORLD I AM SURE OF.
BUT I DO BELIEVE.

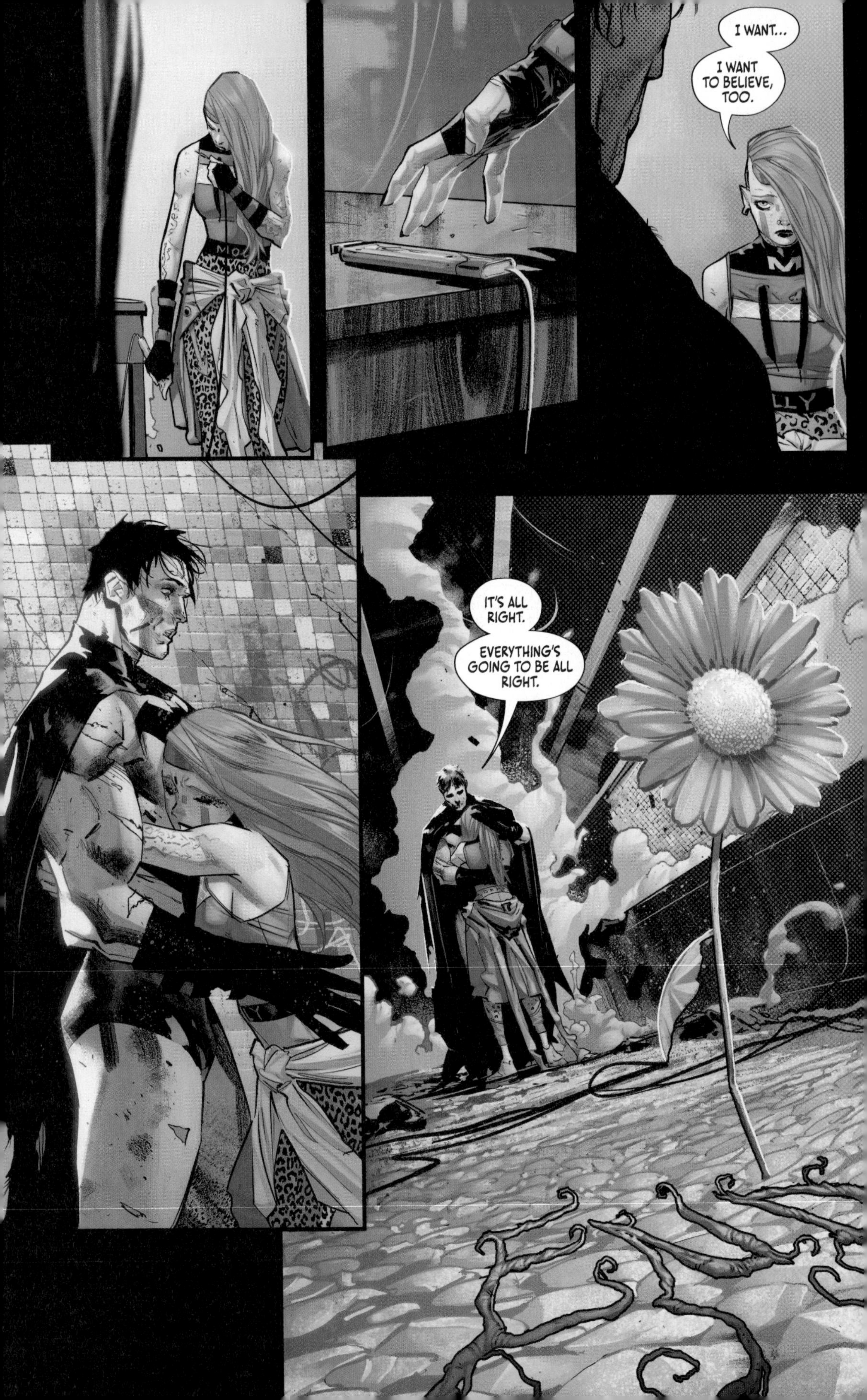

I WANT...
I WANT TO BELIEVE, TOO.
IT'S ALL RIGHT.
EVERYTHING'S GOING TO BE ALL RIGHT.

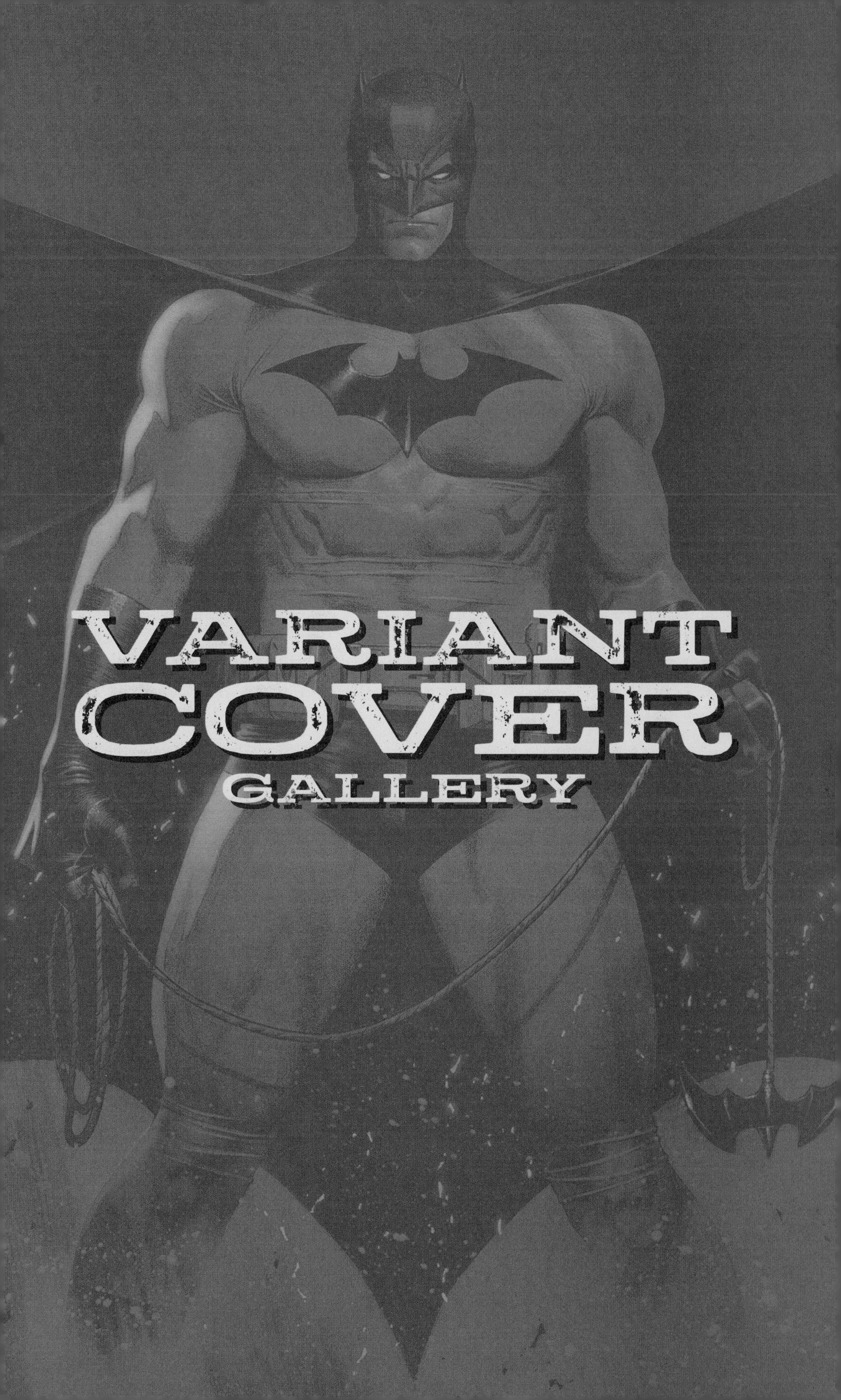
VARIANT
COVER
GALLERY

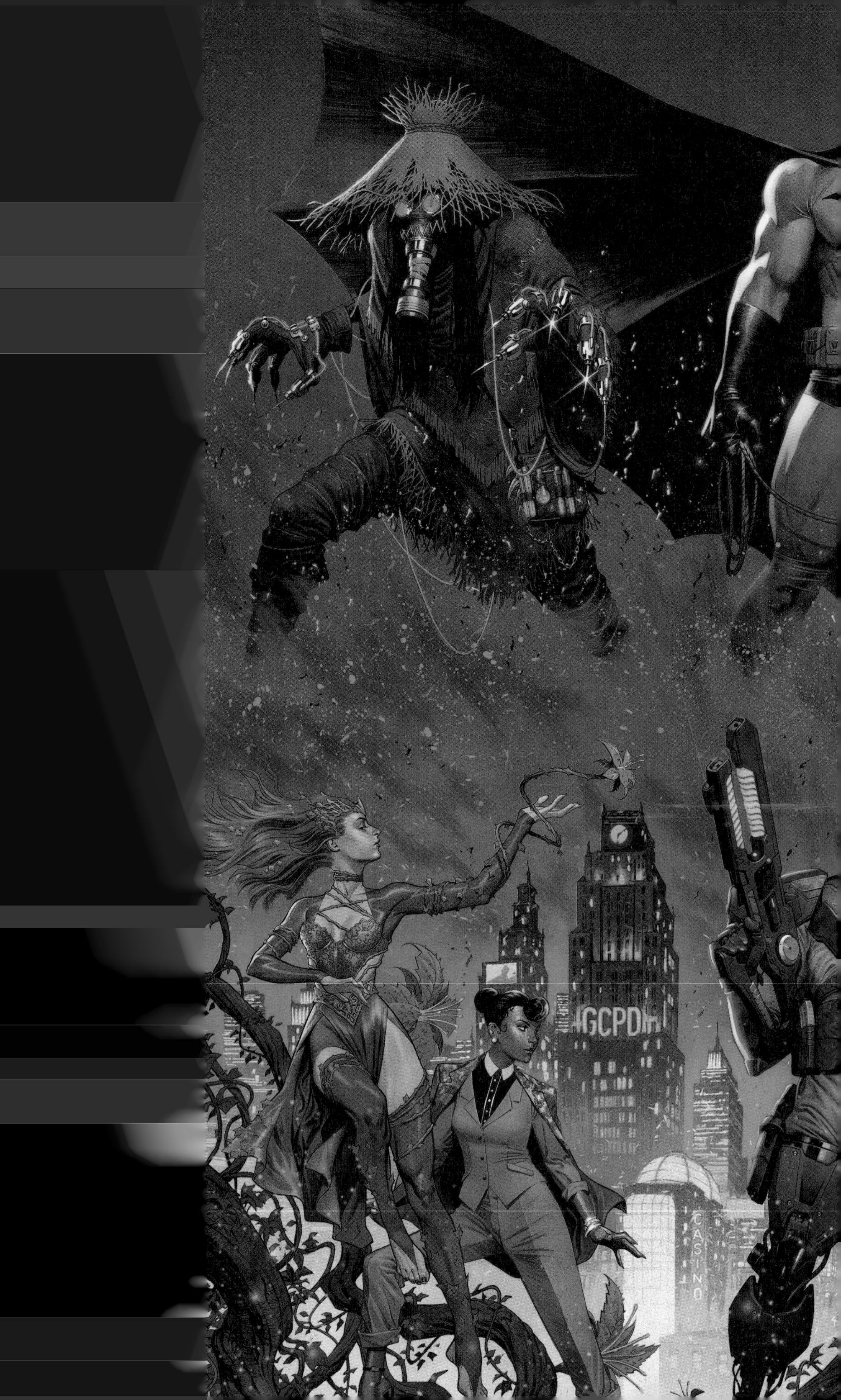
GCPD
CASINO

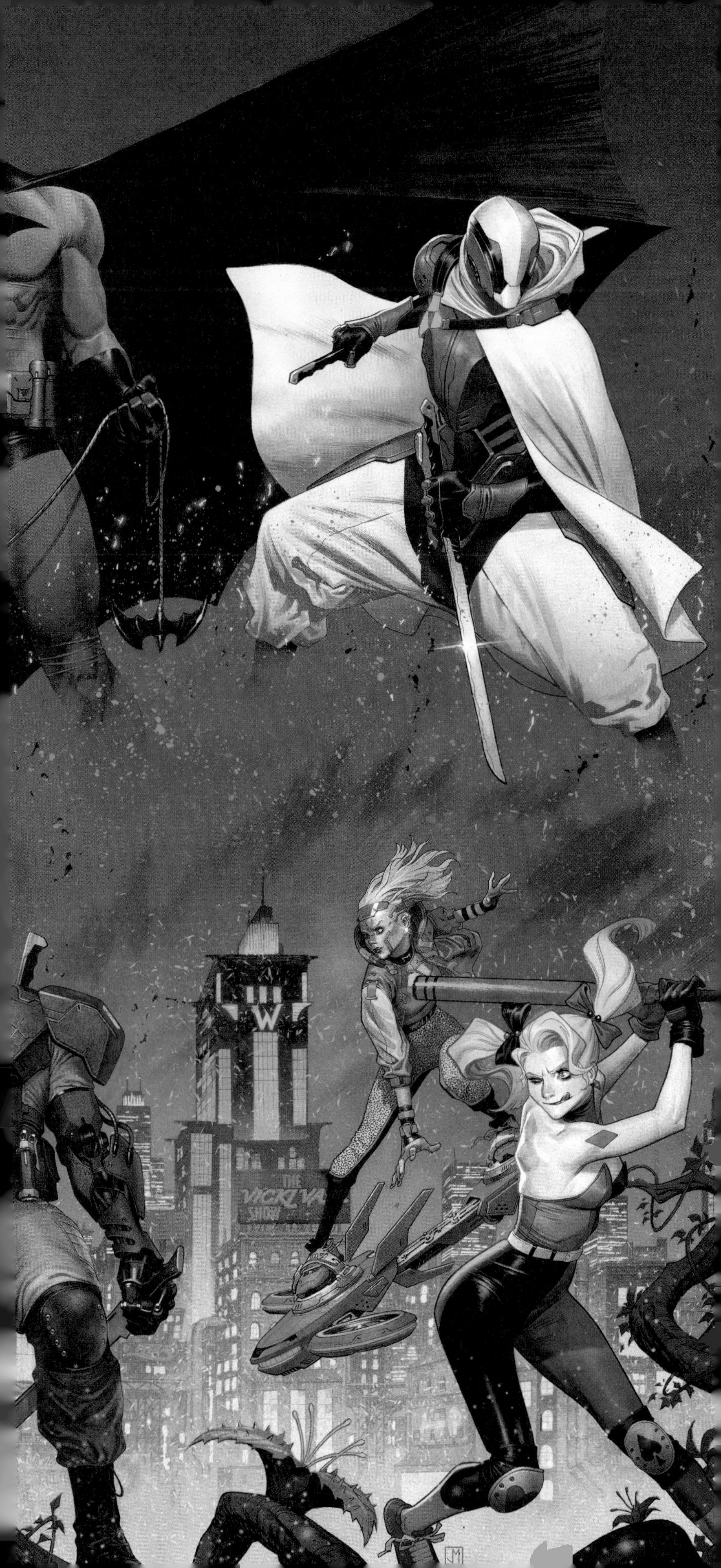
W
THE
SHOW

Batman #112 1:25 Cover
Art by Lucio Parrillo

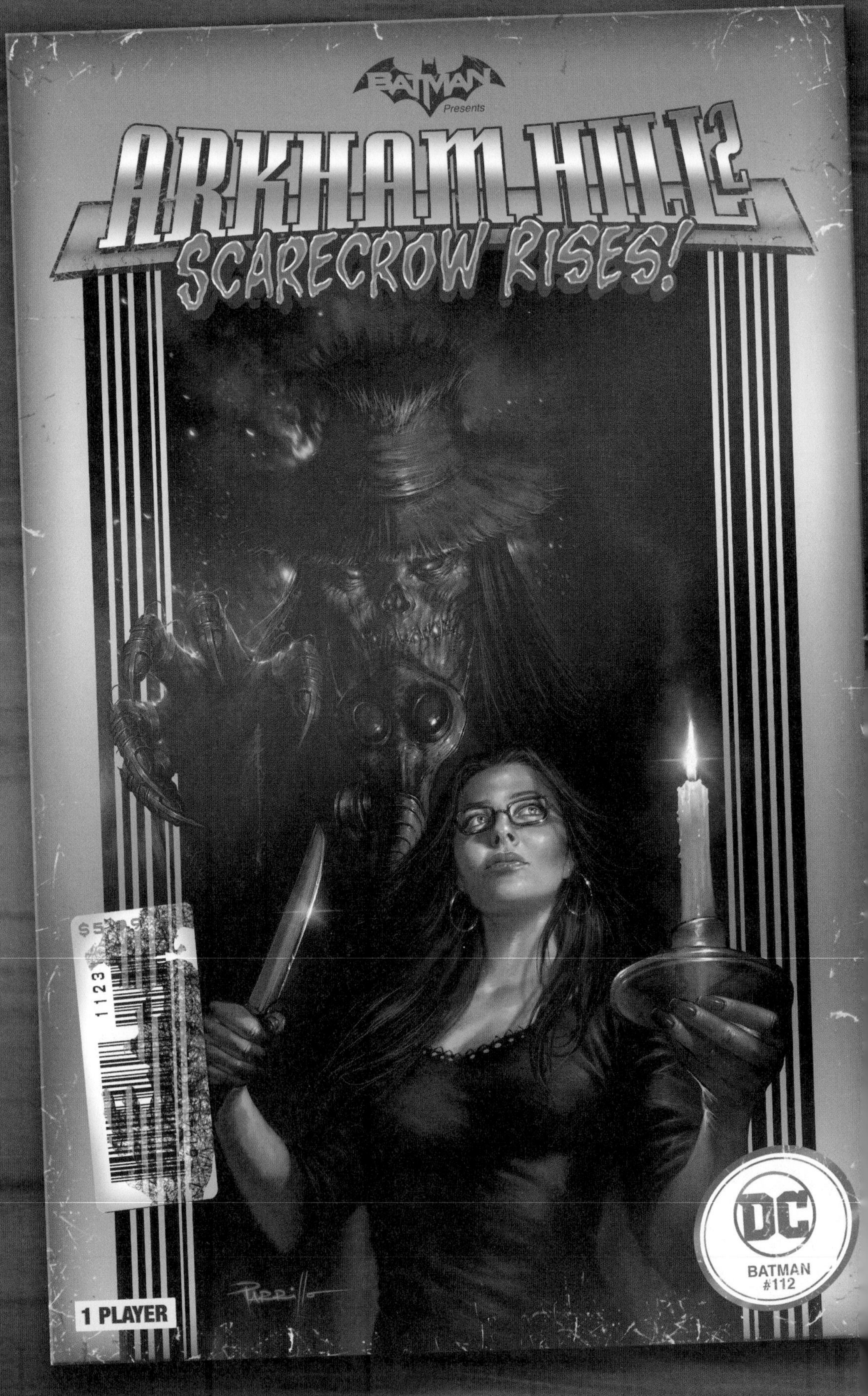
BATMAN
Presents
ARKHAM HILLS
SCARECROW RISES!
1 PLAYER
DC
BATMAN
#112

Batman #113 1:25 Cover
Art by Ben Oliver

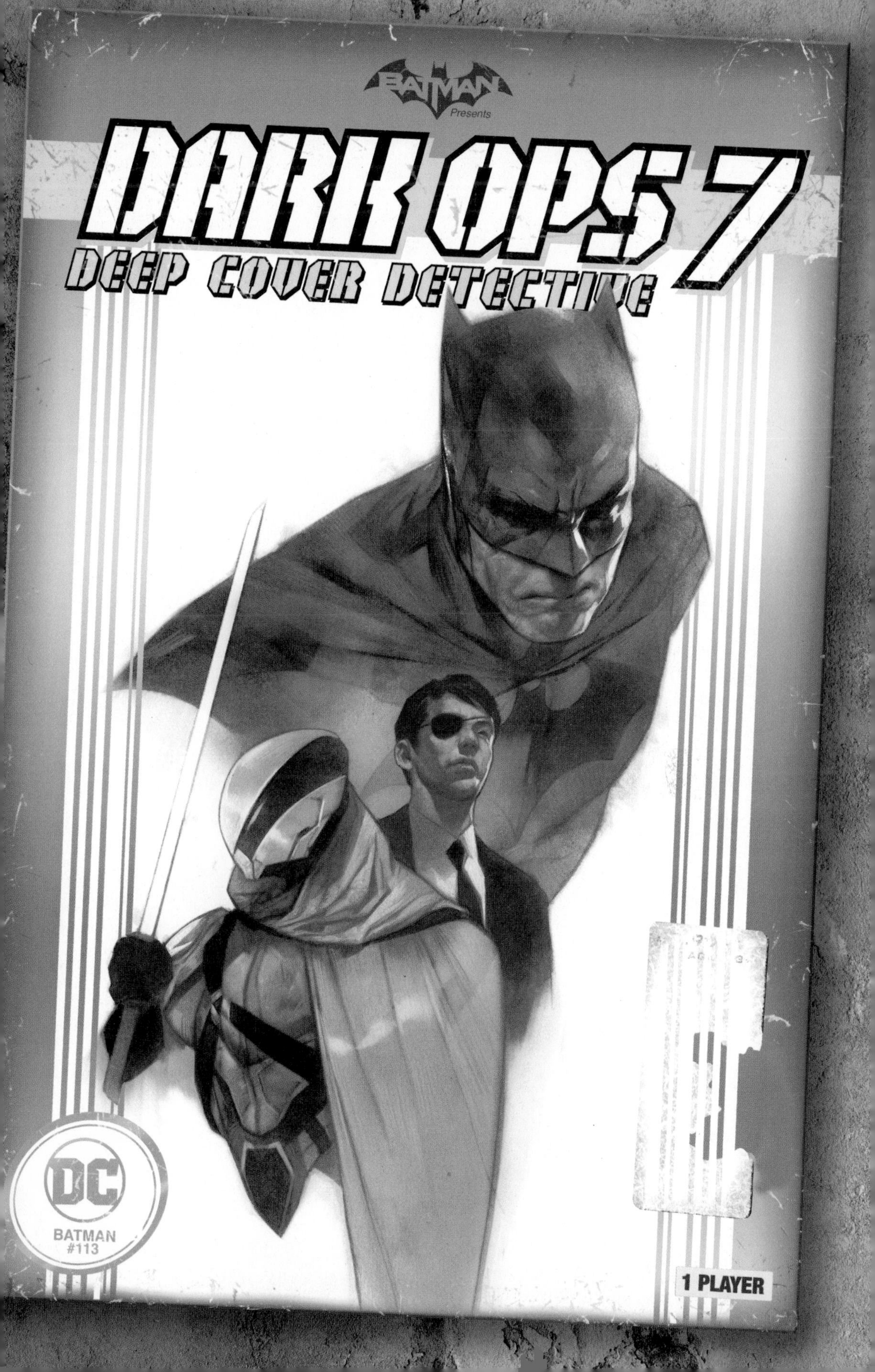
BATMAN
Presents
DARK OPS 7
DEEP COVER DETECTIVE
DC
BATMAN
#113
1 PLAYER

Batman #114 1:25 Cover
Art by Dylan Teague

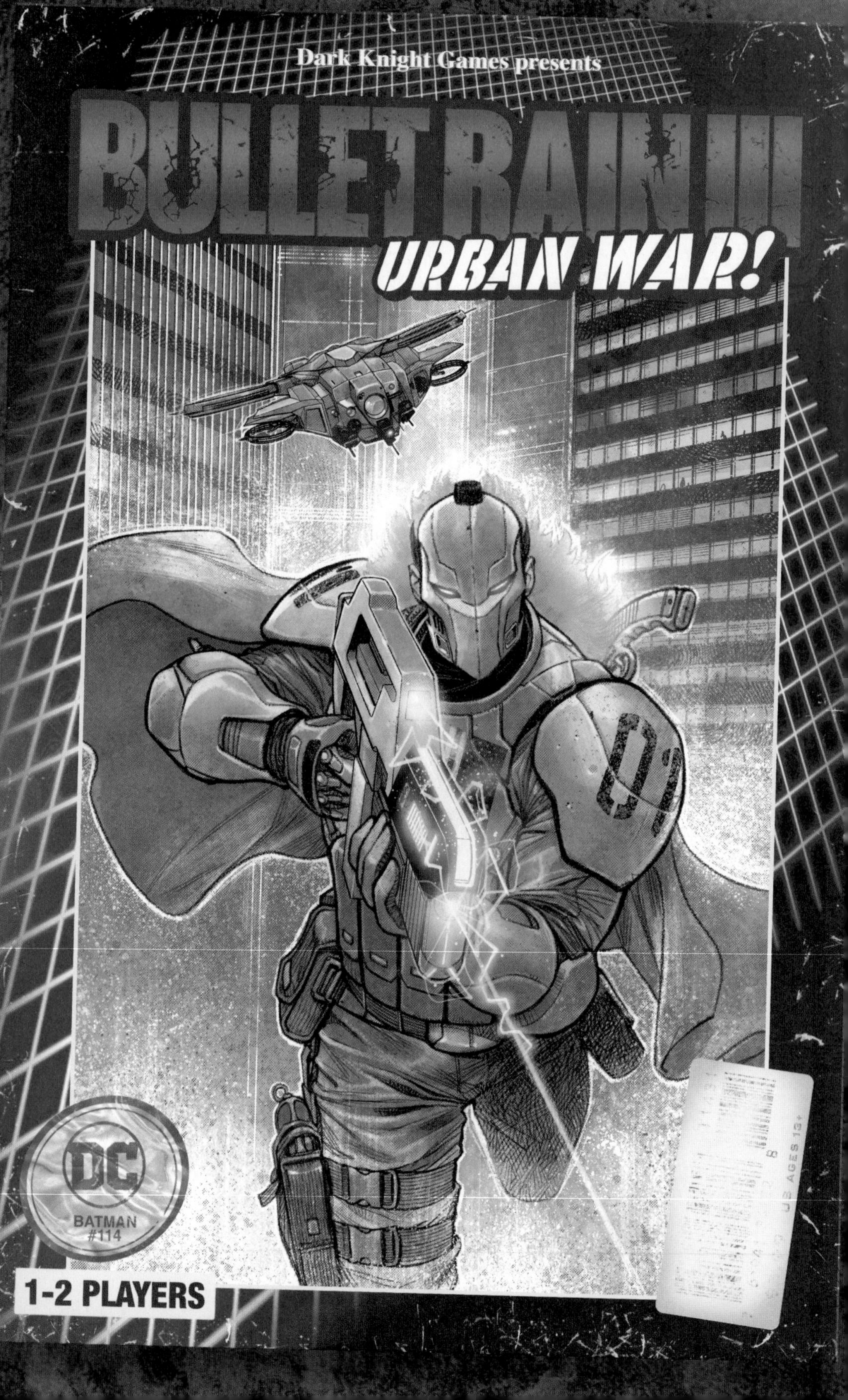

Dark Knight Games presents
BULLET RAIN III
URBAN WAR!
DC
BATMAN
#114
1-2 PLAYERS

Batman #115 1:25 Cover
Art by Arist Deyn

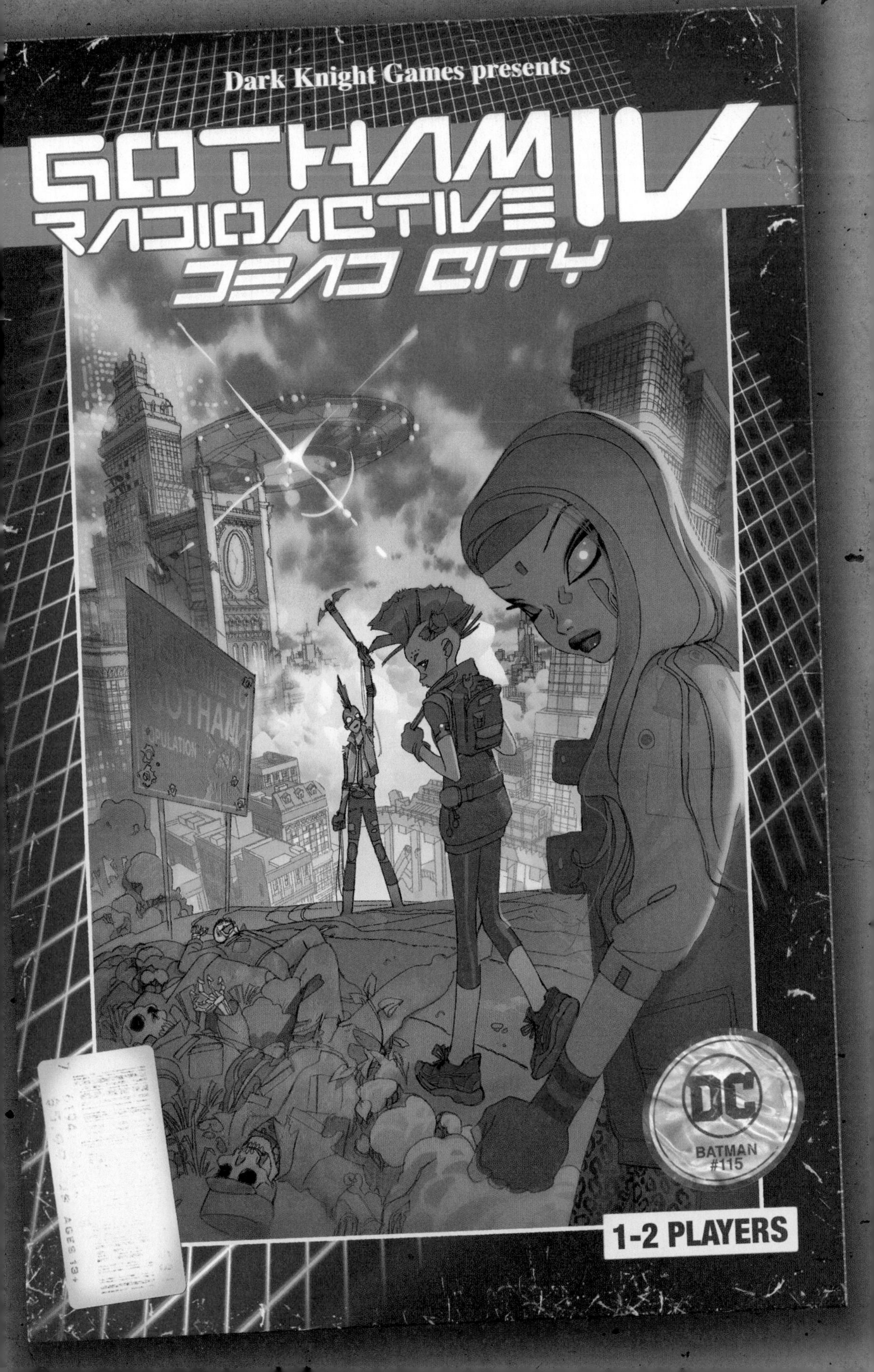
Dark Knight Games presents
GOTHAM IV
RADIOACTIVE
DEAD CITY
BATMAN
#115
1-2 PLAYERS
AGES 13+

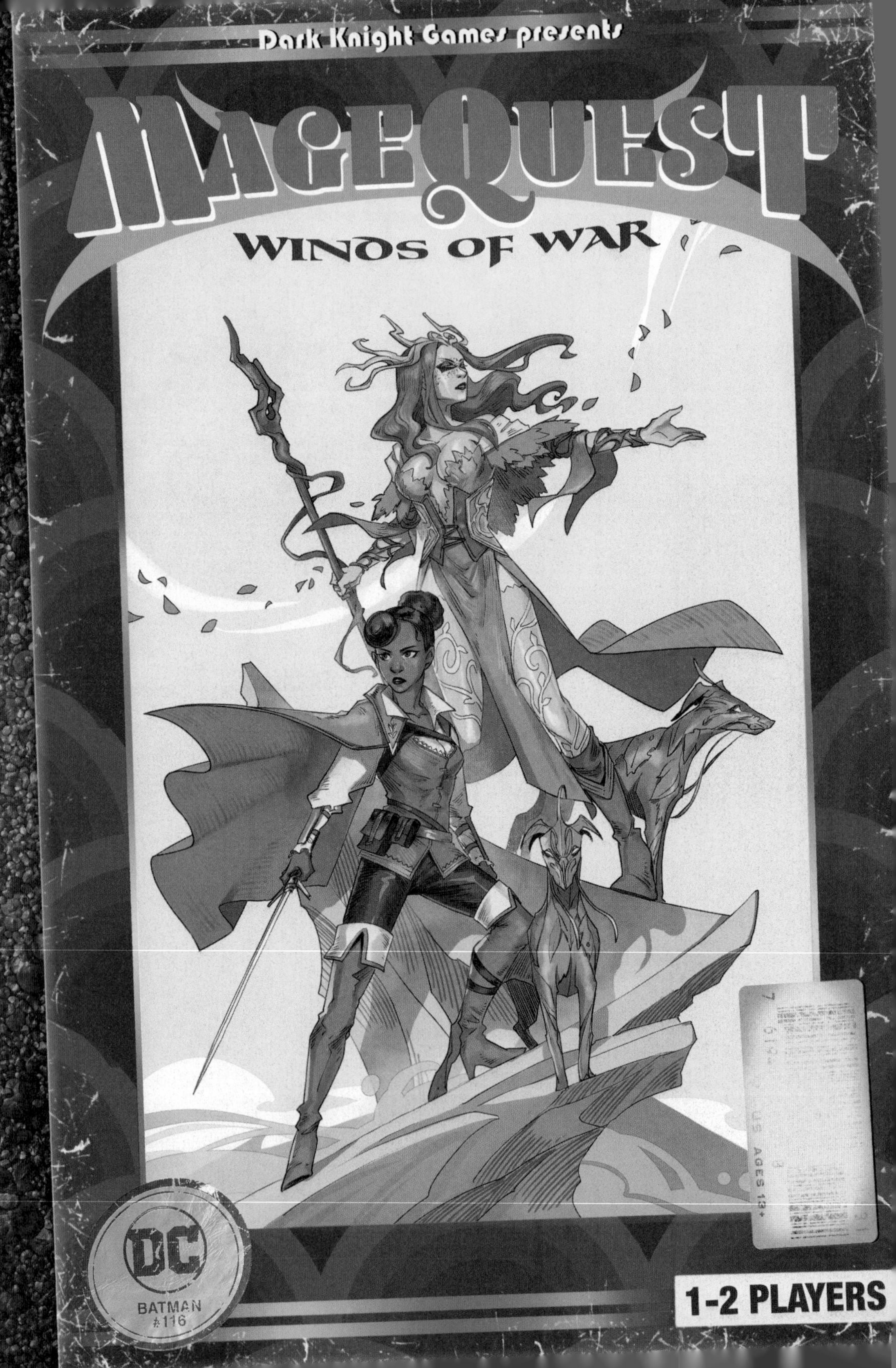

Dark Knight Games presents
MAGEQUEST
WINDS OF WAR
DC
BATMAN
#116
AGES 13+
1-2 PLAYERS

Batman #117 1:25 Cover
Art by Rose Besch

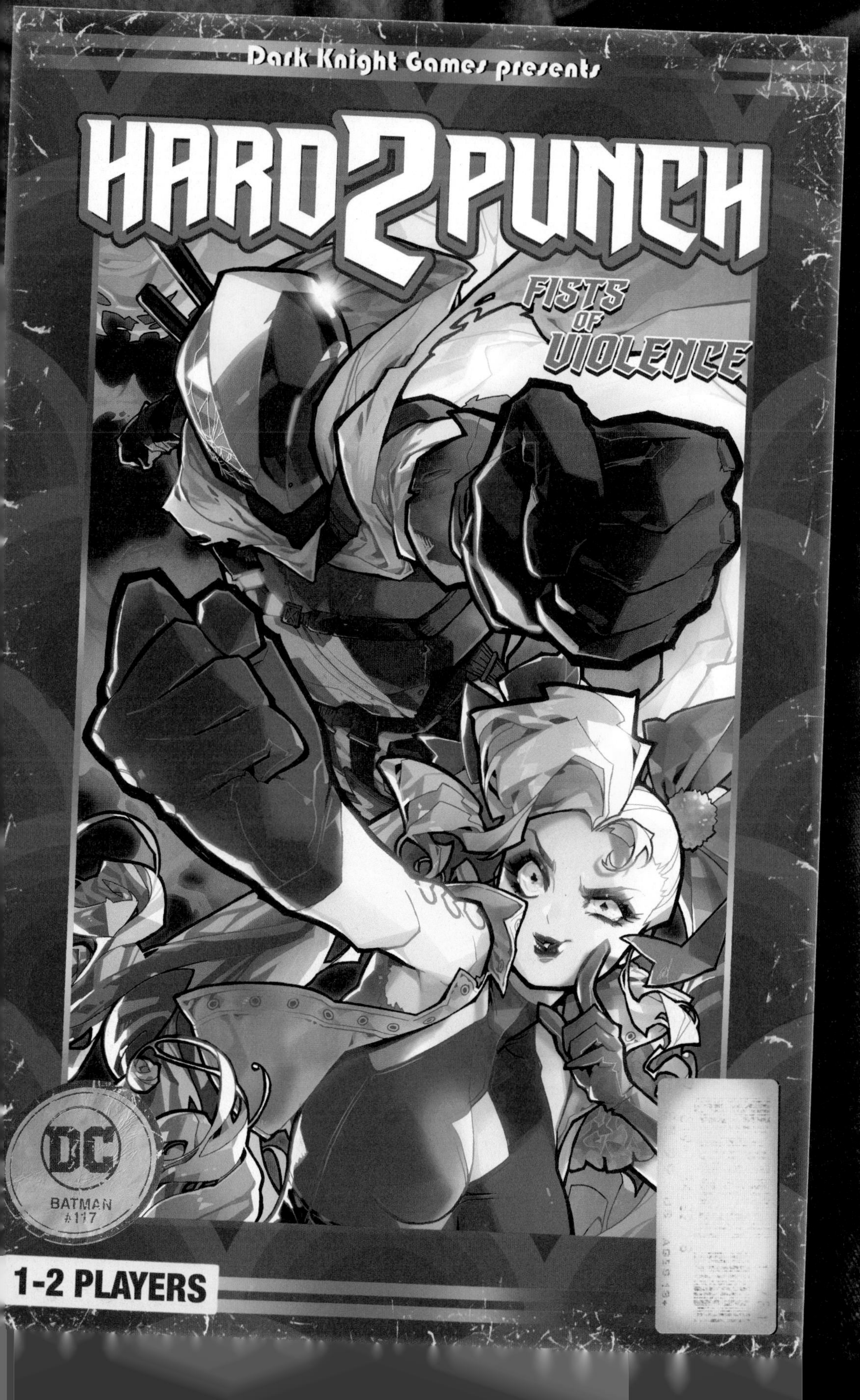

Dark Knight Games presents
HARD 2 PUNCH
FISTS OF VIOLENCE
DC
BATMAN #117
1-2 PLAYERS

Character Designs by Jorge Jiménez

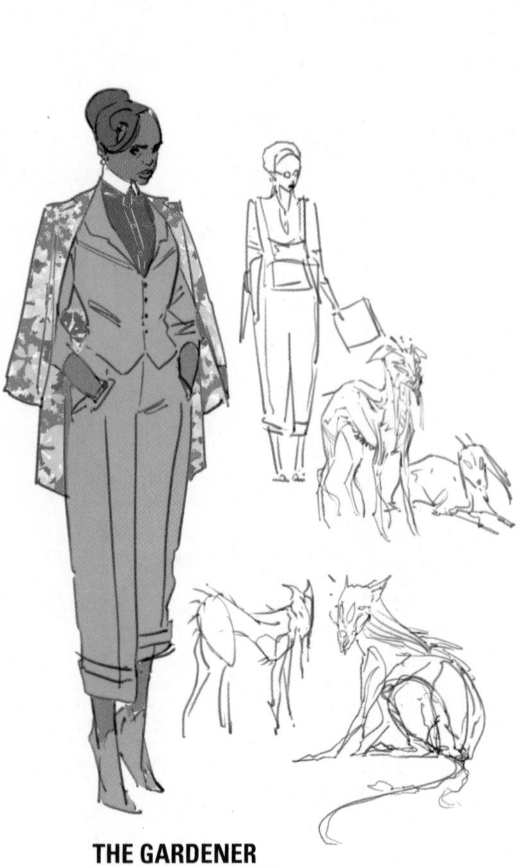

THE GARDENER

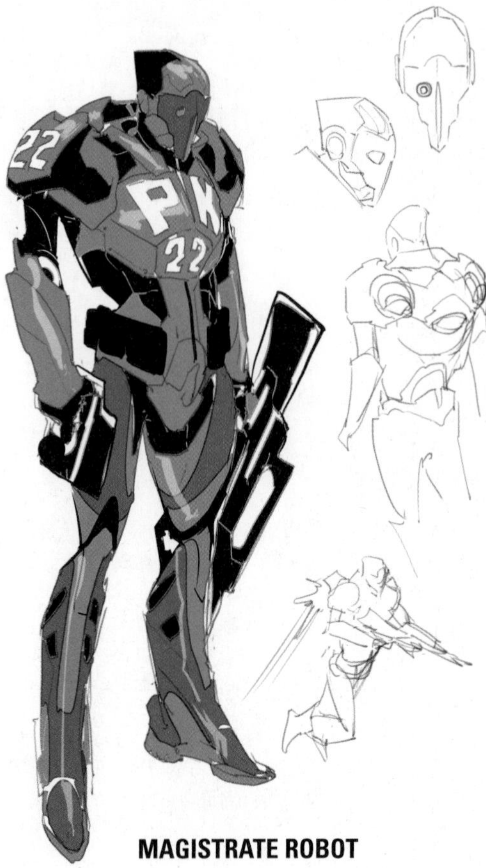
22
PK
22

MAGISTRATE ROBOT

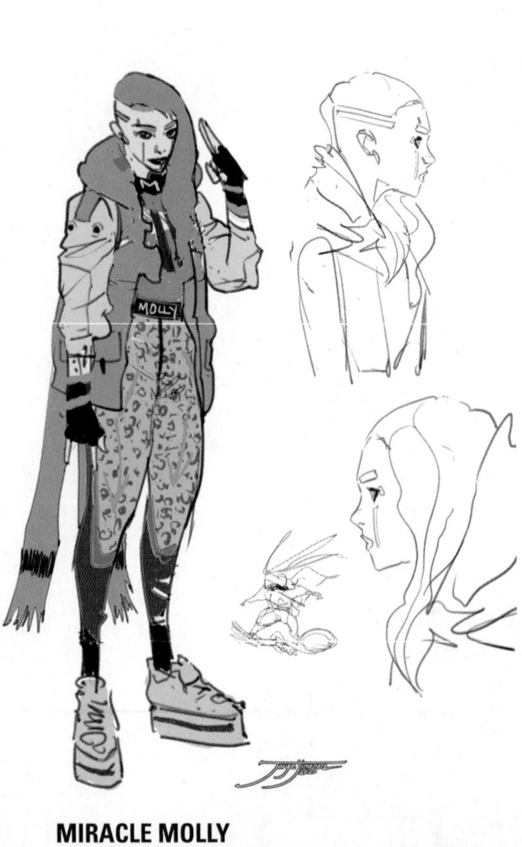
MOLLY

MIRACLE MOLLY

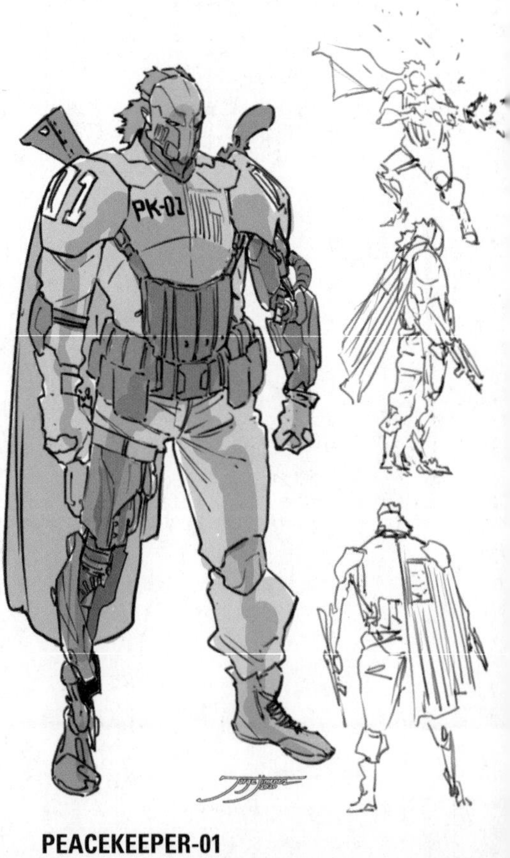
01
PK-01

PEACEKEEPER-01

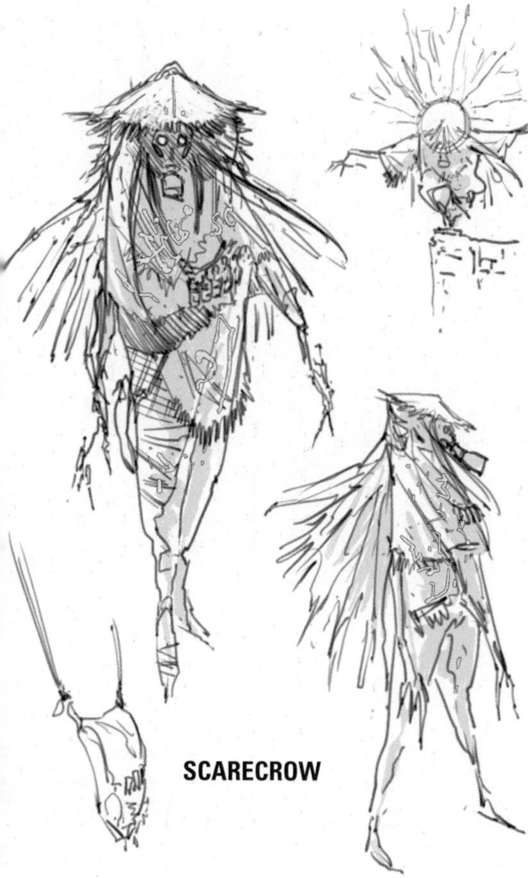

SCARECROW

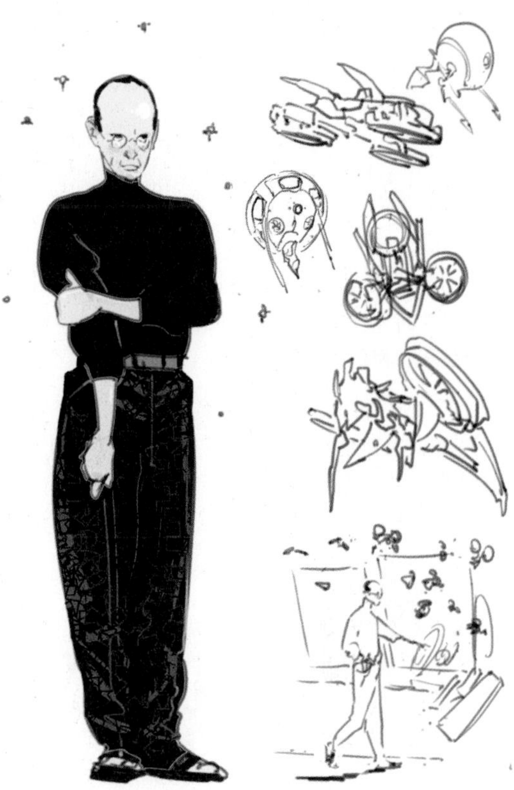

SIMON SAINT

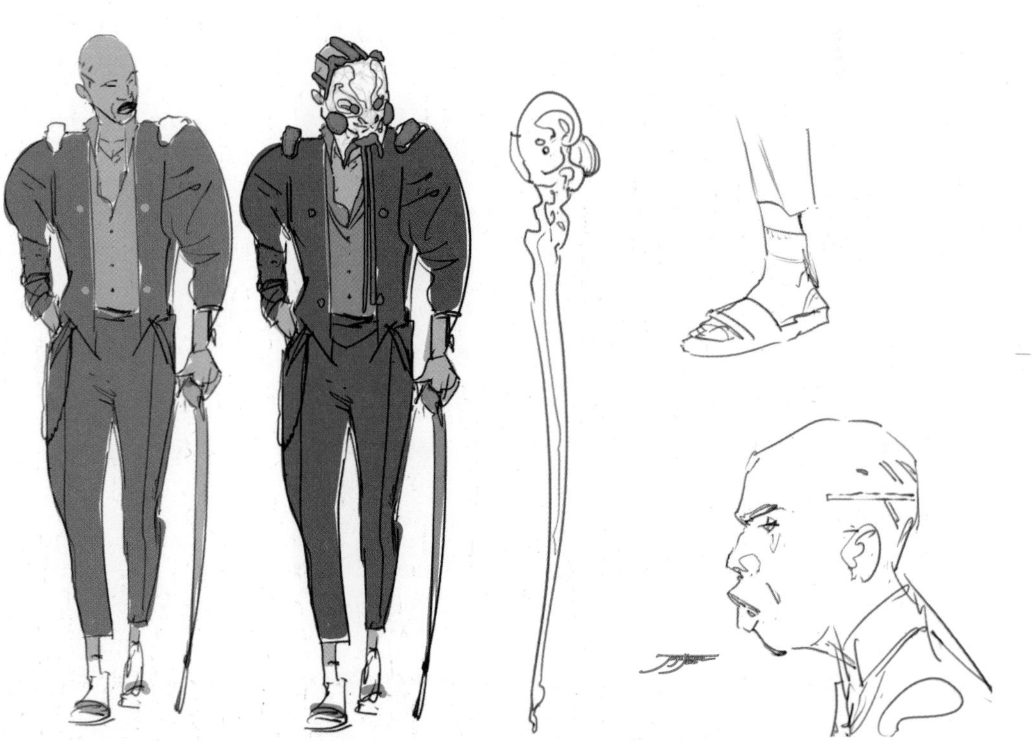

MASTER WYZE

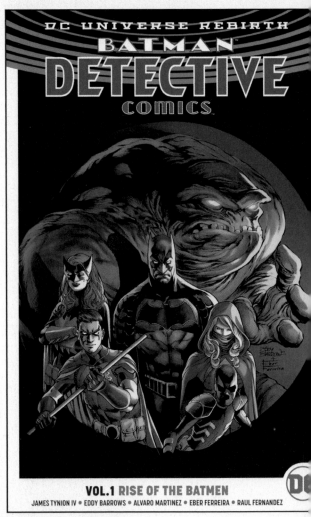

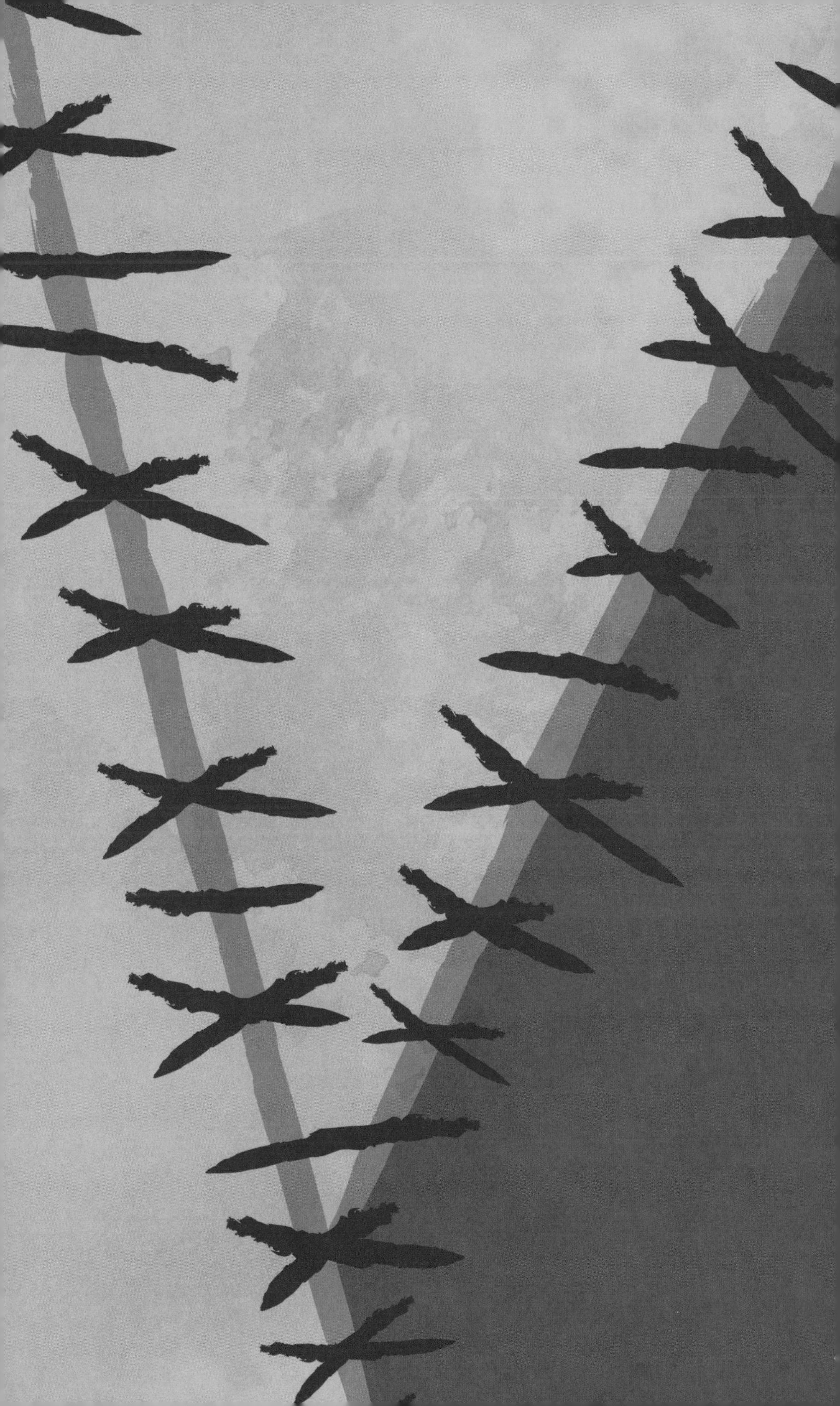

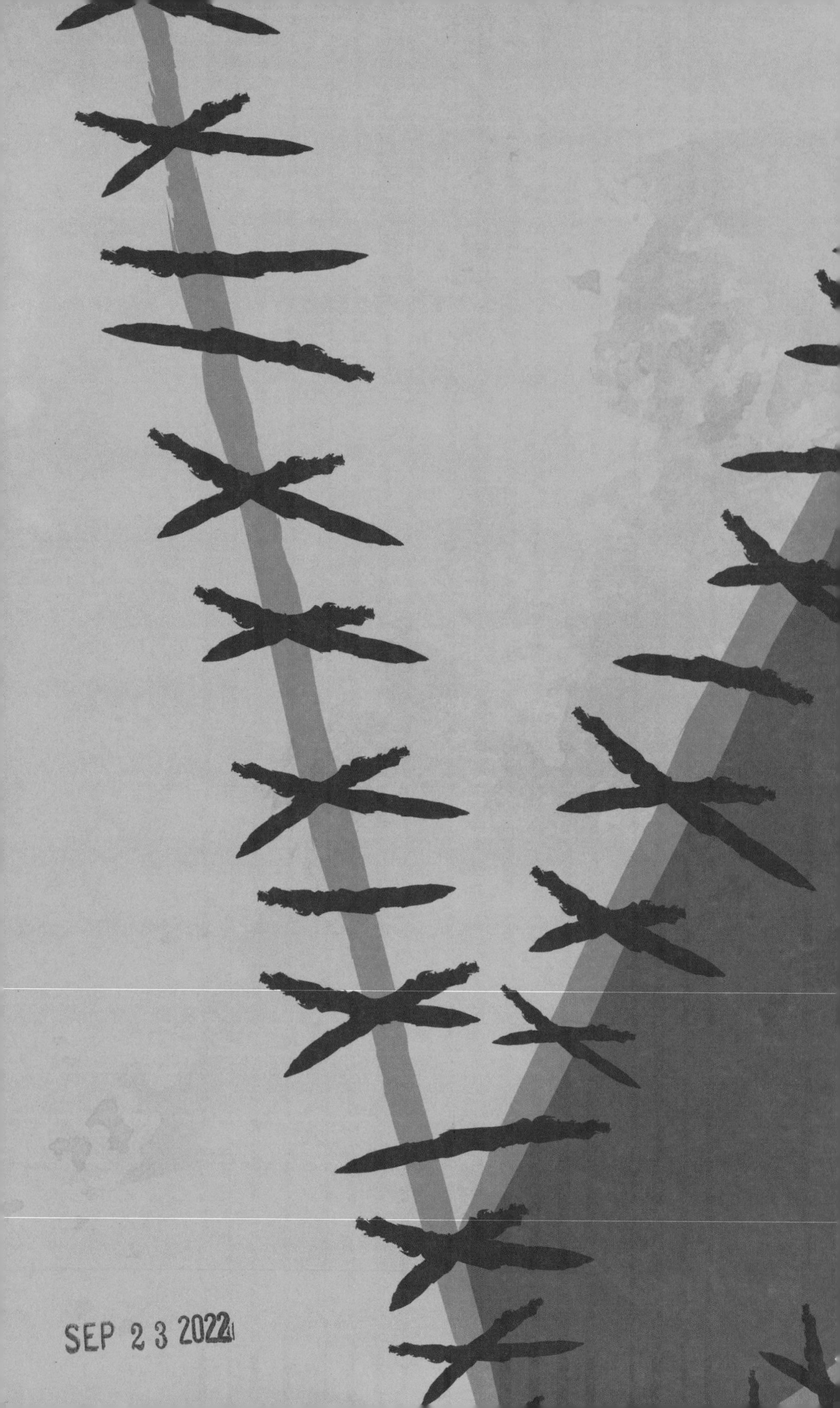